DATE DUE			

The Catholic Tradition:
The Church, Vol. 2

The Catholic Tradition

REV. CHARLES J. DOLLEN
DR. JAMES K. McGOWAN
DR. JAMES J. MEGIVERN
EDITORS

The Catholic Tradition

The Church

Volume 2

A Consortium Book

Library of Congress Card Catalog Number: 79-1977
ISBN: 0-8434-0727-1
ISBN: 0-8434-0725-5 series

The publisher gratefully acknowledges permission to quote from the
following copyrighted sources. In cases where those properties contain
scholarly apparatus such as footnotes, such footnotes have been omitted
in the interest of the general reader.

ANDREWS AND McMEEL, INC.
American Catholic Dilemma: An Inquiry into the Intellectual Life by
Thomas F. O'Dea, © 1958, Sheed and Ward, Inc.; The Church by Hans
Küng, © 1967, Sheed and Ward, Inc.; The Splendour of the Church by
Henri de Lubac, S.J., translated by Michael Mason, © 1967, Sheed and
Ward, Inc. Reprinted by permission of Andrews and McMeel, Inc.

DOUBLEDAY & COMPANY, INC.
Models of the Church by Avery Dulles, S.J. Copyright © 1974 by Avery
Dulles. Used by permission of Doubleday & Company, Inc.

HARPER & ROW, PUBLISHERS, INC.
The Remaking of the Church, pages 71–136, by Richard P. McBrien.
Copyright © 1973 by Richard P. McBrien. Reprinted by permission of
Harper & Row, Publishers, Inc.

B. HERDER BOOK CO.
The Theology of the Mystical Body by Émile Mersch, S.J., translated
by Cyril Vollert, S.J., S.T.D., copyright 1951.

MACMILLAN PUBLISHING CO., INC.
Selections from The Spirit of Catholicism by Karl Adam, translated by
Justin McCann, O.S.B., 1930.

THE MISSIONARY SOCIETY OF ST. PAUL THE APOSTLE IN THE
STATE OF NEW YORK
Lay People in the Church by Yves Congar. Copyright © 1957, 1965 by
Geoffrey Chapman Ltd. Reprinted by permission of Paulist Press.

Table of Contents

THE CATHOLIC TRADITION: The Church

Karl Adam
1876-1966

Karl Adam was born in Bavaria and studied philosophy and theology in Regensburg, then theology and history in Munich, where he was ordained a priest in 1900. In 1917 the University of Strasbourg invited him, a dogmatic theologian, to teach moral theology. He only stayed until 1919 when the University of Tübingen offered him the chair of dogmatic theology. There he remained until just after World War II as scholar, teacher, minister of souls. He loved the town and its tradition, turning down an invitation to go to the University of Bonn in 1925. Tübingen had established itself as a place where theology was, as Adam put it, "a theology of life," which tried to throw into relief "the surging inner life of theological truths as they have grown in their organic interaction and in their oneness with the highest ultimate forces of revelation." At the same time, that theology "has not failed to come to grips with recent philosophy and the radical findings of historical theology."

Adam's early studies led him into the Fathers, especially St. Augustine whose thought had a lasting impact on him. He felt that Augustine more than any other early Christian thinker had brought out the essential core of Christianity: the mystery of the Incarnation. "Christianity is Christ. This is the message that gives foundation and content not only to the moral impera- tives and ethical standards, but also to the dogmas, the truths of faith." *This in turn led to his understanding of the Church. "The Church is the body permeated through and through by the redemptive might of Jesus.*"

In the summer of 1923 Karl Adam delivered a series of lectures to a mixed audience at the University of Tübingen. They were published the following year as The Essence of Catholicism, *but when the 1930 English translation was made it was called* The Spirit of Catholicism. *This was Adam's masterpiece and was translated into eleven languages. It was prompted in part by a work of the same title by the non-Catholic Marburg historian of religion, Friedrich Heiler.*

Heiler had sounded something of an alarm to the Protestant world. "The Roman Church," *he wrote,* "is exercising today a very strong attraction on the non-Catholic world... A vigorous Catholic propaganda is promoting and intensifying the existing trend toward Catholicism . . . Catholic voices are already proclaiming with assurance of victory the imminent collapse of Protestantism.*" Adam was disturbed with several aspects of Heiler's analysis and saw the need to set the record straight, as far as what was actually happening in Catholicism and why.*

Karl Adam has been called "the most successful theologian of our age," *in the sense that he shaped the view of Christ and the Church held by a generation of Catholics in the Western world. Few men have left such a mark as he.*

THE SPIRIT OF CATHOLICISM

CHAPTER III

THE CHURCH THE BODY OF CHRIST

The Church is his body, the fullness of him that filleth all in all (Eph. i, 23).

When we define the Church as essentially the Kingdom of God and the Body of Christ, it follows as her first particular attribute that she is supernatural and heavenly. The Church is ordinated towards the invisible, spiritual and eternal. Of this we have spoken already. But the Church is not only invisible. Because she is the Kingdom of God, she is no haphazard collection of individuals, but an ordered system of regularly subordinated parts. And because the Church is the Body of Christ, she is essentially an organism, with its members purposively interrelated, and a visible organism. That is her second particular attribute. The advocates of a purely spiritual religion, both in ancient and modern Christianity, have maintained that the divine is in the Church as a sort of freely suspended force, as a saving power that invisibly penetrates into this or that person. But that is not so. On the contrary the divine is objectivised, is incarnated in the community, and precisely and only in so far as it is a community.

That is to say that the supernatural redemptive might of Jesus, as it operates in the Church, is not tied to a single person, so far as he is a person, and is not manifested in a single person, but essentially only in the totality, in the community of individuals. The Spirit of Jesus is objectivised and introduced into our earthly life, not through the medium of specially gifted personalities, but exclusively in and through the community, in and through the union of the many in one. So the Church possesses the Spirit of Christ, not as a many of single individuals, nor as a sum of spiritual personalities, but as the compact unity of the faithful, as a community that transcends the individual personalities. This union, this community, is a fundamental datum of Christianity, not a thing created by the voluntary or forced association of the faithful, not a mere secondary and derivative thing depending on the good pleasure of Christians, but a thing which is antecedent to any Christian personality, a supra-personal thing, which does not presuppose Christian personalities, but itself creates and produces them. The Christian community is not created by the faithful; on the contrary the community creates them. The Christian community, the Church as a fellowship, comes first, and the Christian personality, the Church as a sum of such personalities, is second. The Church did not spring into being when Peter and Paul, James and John, grasped the mystery of Jesus, His God-man being, and on the basis of their common faith formed a fellowship which was called after Him. No, the Church was already in existence-fundamentally, germinally, virtually—before Peter and John became believers. The Church as a whole, as a community, as an organic unity is a divine creation. In the last resort she is nothing else than the unity of fallen humanity accomplished by the Sacred Humanity of Jesus, the Kosmos of men, mankind as a whole, the many as one.

This is a thought which does not lie on the surface, but we must grasp it if we would understand the visible nature of the Church, her external manifestation. If Christ is what the Church confesses Him to be, the Incarnate God and Saviour of men—as indeed He is—then it must be His mission to reunite to God mankind as a unity, as a whole, and not this or that individual man. The wretchedness of fallen humanity, the essence of the original sin, consisted in this, that the supernatural union with God, in which man was originally created, and through which alone he could attain his perfection, his wholeness, his completion, was by Adam's fall broken and dissolved. When Adam fell away from God, all humanity in him and through him fell away likewise. That is a basic conviction of Christianity, which was adumbrated in certain post-canonical Jewish writings, and received formulation as a Christian doctrine especially at the hands of St. Paul. At the basis of this Christian dogma of an original and inherited sin, and of our redemption through the new man Christ, lies the

4

great and striking thought that mankind must not be regarded as a mass of homogeneous beings successively emerging and passing away, nor merely as a sum of men bound together by unity of generation, as being descendants of one original parent, but as one single man. So closely are men assimilated to one another in their natural being, in body and in mind, so profoundly are they interlocked in thinking, willing, feeling, and acting, so solidary is their life, their virtue and their sin, that they are considered in the divine plan of redemption only as a whole, only as a unity, only as one man. This one man is not the individual man, but the whole man, the totality of the innumerable expressions of that humanity which is reproduced in countless individuals. This one man includes all men who were thousands of years ago and all who shall be thousands of years hence. Such is the one man, the whole man. And the guilt and destiny of every single man are not merely his own guilt and his own destiny; they concern the whole of humanity in proportion to the importance which Providence has assigned him in the organism of humanity.

These are thoughts that may seem strange to the modern man, or which at least would have seemed so a short time ago. The individualism of the Renaissance, the dismemberment of man and his relations in the age of Enlightenment, and finally the subjective idealism of Kant, whereby our minds were taught to relinquish the objective thing, the trans-subjective reality, and to indulge in boundless subjectivism: these influences tore us from the moorings of our being, and especially from our true and essential basis, that humanity which produces, supports and enfolds us. We became imprisoned within the walls of our own selves, unable any more to attain to humanity, to the full, whole man. The category "humanity" became foreign to our thought, and we thought and lived only in the category of self. Humanity as wholeness and as fulness had to be rediscovered.

But there is now beginning, under the influence of early Christian ideas, of socialism and of the great war—quite apart from purely philosophical, epistemological reactions—a gradual revolution of our whole mental attitude. We are beginning to feel uncomfortable in the narrow hermitage of our own selves and are seeking a way out. And we are discovering that we are not alone, but that by us, with us, round us, in us, is all humanity. We are realising with astonishment that we belong profoundly to this humanity, that a community of being and destiny, and a joint liability bind us to it. We are learning that we come to our whole self only by its means, that our individual being broadens out into the whole man only in it and through it. With this new mental attitude we are able to appreciate the fundamental Christian conceptions of the first man and the new man, of Adam and Christ, in their profound significance. Adam, the first man, called to share by grace in the divine life, represented in God's eyes the whole of mankind. Adam's fall was the fall of mankind. Detached from its original supernatural goal, mankind then, like some planet detached from its sun, revolved only in crazy gyration round itself. Its own self became the centre of its striving and yearning. Man came to feel God, the very source of his spiritual life, as a burden. The first "autonomous" man in the ethico-religious sense was Adam, when he took the fruit of the tree of life. And so man no longer had any source whence he might renew his strength, except his own small self. He had abandoned the eternal source of living water, and dug himself a poor cistern in his own self. And the waters of this cistern were soon exhausted. Man fell sick and died. His self was his sickness and his self was his death. And all mankind died with him. Then, according to the eternal decision of God's love, the New Man came, the man of the new, permanent and indissoluble union with God, Christ the Lord. In Him erring mankind, man radically cut off from the divine source of his life, was finally reunited to God, to the Life of all lives, to the Fount of all power, truth and love. Mankind—not merely this man and that, not you and I only, but the whole of mankind, the unity of all men—was brought home again from its terrible diaspora, from its dispersion, back to the living God. The whole man came once more into being, permanently united with God, and so effectively united that he could never more, as the unity of mankind, be for any fault cut off from the divine source of his life. Therefore Christ, as the God-man, is the new humanity, the new beginning, the whole man in the full meaning of the phrase.

Whence it follows clearly that the Church was already, in the mystery of the Incarnation, established as an organic community. The "many," the sum total of all who need redemption, are in their inner relationship to one another, in their inter-relation and correlation, in their organic communion, objectively and finally the Body of Christ, never more separable from Him for all eternity.

It is clear therefore, in the light of the redemption, that the Church did not come into being only when Peter and John and Paul became believers. It became objectively existent when the divine Word united humanity, the unity of all men who needed redemption, with Himself in His divine and human being. The Incarnation is for Christians the foundation and planting of that new communion which we call the Church. The Body of Christ and the Kingdom of God came into being as objective reality at the moment when the Word was made flesh.

We must take these fundamental dogmatic thoughts to heart if we would appreciate the Catholic conception of the Church in all its profundity. Only so shall we understand why the idea of community is its dominant idea, and why the community cannot be the product of the faithful, a creation of these or those persons, but must be a supra-personal unity, a unity which permeates and embraces the whole of redeemed humanity. As such a unity the Church is nothing vague or un-defined, but the actual inner unity of redeemed humanity united with Christ. In the Catholic conception of the Church the decisive element is not this or that person, but all mankind.

Two important consequences follow from this. One of these has already been developed, the fact, namely, that the organ of the redeeming spirit of our divine Saviour, its incarnation and manifestation, is not the individual personality, but the community as community. The purpose of Christ is realised in the community. Therefore the visibility of the Church does not consist merely in the visibility of its individual members, but in the visibility of its compact unity, of its community. But while there is a community, a comprehensive unity, there is distribution and co-ordination of functions. That is the second consequence that follows from the mystery of the Incarnation. The Christian untiy is no mere mechanical unity, but a unity with inner differentiation, an organic unity. The Body of Christ, if it be a true body, must have members and organs with their special tasks and functions, which each in its measure serves the development of the essential form of the body and which therefore serve one another. When St. Paul, the first apostle to formulate the expression "Body of Christ," develops this conception in the twelth chapter of his First Epistle to the Corinthians, he already stresses this point and speaks of the organic functioning of this body: "Now there are diversities of graces, but the same Spirit. Now there are diversities of ministries, but the same Lord. And there are diversities of operations, but the same God, who worketh all in all. . . . For as the body is one and hath many members; and all the members of the body, whereas they are many, yet are one body: so also is Christ. . . . God indeed hath set some in the Church, first apostles, secondly prophets, thirdly doctors; after that miracle-workers, then the graces of healings, governments, kinds of tongues, interpretations of speeches." It is therefore the view of the apostle that the community is of its nature differentiated, that the body works as a unity through a diversity of organic functions, that the unity of the whole attests the unity of the spirit of Jesus. It is true that St. Paul does not distinguish the various functions of the one organism with theological precision. Such precision came with later developments and with the speculation that sprang from them. Time made it clear that some of the gifts, such as those of the apostolate, of teaching, and of government belong to the nature of the Church and could not be discarded; whereas others, such as the gifts of prophecy, miracles and tongues, were the manifestation of a superabundant Christian life, and to be regarded not as structurally necessary to that life, but rather as signs and expressions of it.

But the fundamental thought, that the Body of Christ is and must be an organic body, that it works by its very nature in a manifold of functions, and that this manifold is bound together by the one Spirit of Christ into an inner unity: this thought is native to St. Paul, and it is the heritage and fundamental principle of the whole Christian Gospel.

Let us now consider more nearly the organisation of the Body of Christ, its unity in fulness, and fulness in unity. The first point to be insisted on is this, that since the community and not the individual is the bearer of the Spirit of Jesus, and since its visibility consists especially in the manifestation of this essential unity, therefore the visible organism of the Church postulates for its visibility a real principle of unity in which the supra-personal unity of all the faithful obtains perceptible expression and which supports, maintains and protects this unity. The pope is the visible expression and the abiding guarantee of this unity. So, if we regard the matter thus, it becomes plain that the original nature of the Church, her fundamental determination as a unitary organism, achieves its purest expression in the papacy. Were the Gospels silent regarding Peter's call to be the rock, and the key-bearer, and the pastor of the Church, the very nature of the Church itself, with that necessity and force whereby every essential form implanted is an organism presses to its full realisation, would have produced the papacy out of its own bosom. In the papacy the community strives after and achieves the consciousness of its essential and necessary unity. In the papacy it grasps and realises itself as the one Kingdom of God, as the one Body of Christ on the earth. And so the Catholic never regards the pope as separated from this unity, as an independent factor, as a charismatical personality, as a personality possessed of supernatural powers like a Moses or an Elias. The pope is to him the visible embodiment of the unity of the Church, that real principle whereby redemption-needing mankind achieves its form as complete and perfect unity. In the pope, his unity with his brethren becomes visible to the Catholic. His view broadens and his eye passes beyond all the limitations of personalities, beyond all bounds of nations and civilisations, beyond all seas and deserts. And the whole massive Christendom, with all the organic interrelation of its parts, its great and sacred communion of love, becomes manifest for him in the pope, and stands out before him as a sublime and glorious reality. Therefore no misuse of papal authority and no human failings in the wearers of the tiara can rob him of his veneration and his love for the papacy. When he kisses the pope's hand, he kisses all his brethren, who are joined together into one in the person of the pope. His heart broadens out into the heart of all Christendom, of the unity in fulness.

Moreover the pope himself teaches, acts, strives, suffers only from out of this unity. It is true, that, inasmuch as he is by the wise disposition of Providence at the same time bishop of Rome, he can make regulations and give decisions which are valid only for his immediate Roman flock and which therefore possess only a local significance. But when he speaks as pope, as successor of St. Peter, then he speaks as the visible basis and pledge of unity, out of the compact fulness of the Body of Christ, as that principle in which the supra-personal unity of the Body of Christ has achieved visible reality for the world of space and time. Therefore he does not speak as a despot in his own right, as some absolute monarch, but as the head of the Church, in intimate vital relationship to the complete organism of the Church. So he cannot, like a Delphic Oracle, give dogmatic decisions purely at his own discretion and according to his own subjective notions. On the contrary, he is bound, as the Vatican Council emphatically declares, bound strongly in conscience, to proclaim and interpret that revelation which is contained in the written and unwritten mind of the Church, in the twin sources of our faith, sacred Scripture and Tradition.

On the other hand, it is of the nature of the Church as a supra-personal unity, and thereby also of the nature of the papacy, that the pope should not be regarded as a mere representative of the Church, as a sort of mouthpiece of the general mind. For the very reason that the community is not exhaustively represented by the members of the Church nor owes its original existence to them, but is a supra-personal unity established in the Incarnate God, a principle of organisation which is effective in and of itself, a power in its own right: for that reason the pope, in whom this community by Christ's will obtains visible form, rules absolutely *ex sese*, that is to say that in his activity he is in no respect dependent on any member of the Body of Christ, neither on the whole episcopate, nor on individual bishops, nor on the rest of the faithful. He is not merely one "pastor" alongside others; he is the pastor to whom alone the sheep of the Divine Pastor are committed (cf. Jn. xxi, 15 ff.). And he is not merely one stone in the holy building, nor only the first stone, but the rock (cf. Mt. xvi, 18), to whom all other stones have no other relation than that they are supported by it, and are in their whole being and activity dependent upon it. The new Code of Canon Law (canon 218 § I, 2) formulates with truly monumental power this papal plenipotency (*suprema et plena potestas jurisdictionis in universam ecclesiam*), which is "independent of every human authority" and immediately embraces not only all and single "churches," but also all and single "pastors and faithful."

What the pope is for the whole Church, that in an analogous sense the bishop is for the particular community, for the diocese. He is the representative and objective form of its inner unity, he is the mutual love of its members made visible, the organic interrelation of the faithful made perceptible (Möhler). That explains why the Catholic knows no more venerable names on earth than those of pope and bishop, and why in the centuries when the western world was impregnated with the Catholic consciousness, no honour was too great, no ornament too precious to be bestowed upon pope and bishop. This did not, and does not, hold good of the person of pope or bishop—no one makes so sharp a distinction between the person and his office as does the Catholic—but it did and does hold good exclusively of their sublime function, that namely of representing and assuring the unity of the Body of Christ in the world. When a man is present at a pontifical High Mass, and sees with amazement the vast circumstance of pomp and splendour, the rich ceremonial with which the person and the actions of the pontifex are surrounded, if he sees in all this nothing but a consequence and survival of the court ceremonial of Rome and Constantinople, he has grasped only half the truth. The motive force, the dominant idea of this magnificence, is the joy of the Catholic in his Church, in her overpowering unity, in that affirmation of the communion of the brethren, of the one Body of Christ, which is so to say personified in the bishop. One God, one faith, one love, one single man: that is the stirring thought which inspires all the Church's pageantry and gives it artistic form. It is a seeking and finding of love, of love for Christ and for the brethren who in Him are bound together into one.

This fundamental conception of papacy and episcopacy of itself answers the objections raised against the primitiveness of Church authority on the ground that Christ preached humility and brotherly love. This criticism sees in our Lord's words, when He settled the dispute among His disciples, "the strictest internal argument" against the hypothesis that He instituted the papacy. The disciples were irritated by the request of the sons of Zebedee, that they should sit the one on the right and the other on the left of the Lord in His Kindgom. Jesus called them to Him and said: "You know that they who seem to rule over the Gentiles lord it over them: and their princes have power over them. But it is not so among you. But whosoever will be greater, shall be your ministers. And whosoever will be first among you shall be the servant of all. For the Son of man also is not come to be ministered unto, but to minister, and to give his life a redemption for many" (Mk. x, 42-45).

In these words Jesus discards for His disciples that absolute power, that domination, which was exercised by contemporary rulers, especially by the Hellenistic princes. The mark of the disciple of Jesus is to be service, and not brutal domination. In God's Kingdom there is to be no "lording it over them" and no "letting them feel one's power," but loving ministry and ministering love. The words themselves make it plain enough that the Master is not excluding all authority and all power from His society, but only that power which is essentially brutal and domineering. This meaning of our Lord's words is brought out still more clearly by the evangelist Luke (xxii, 24 ff.) who gives Mark's logion in the form: "He that is the greater among you, let him become as the younger: he that is the leader as he that serveth." By those words Jesus makes it perfectly clear that there shall be those who are "leaders." So that his recommendation of brotherly humility and love is not directed against the principle of authority in itself, but against the egotistical misuse of this principle. How else could Jesus have set Himself up as a pattern of service and brotherly love, and yet in the same breath call Himself the "Son of Man," that is the Lord of the future and of the judgment, the holder of authority? Just as His brotherly service does not exclude His supreme dignity as Son of Man, so his recommendation of humility and love cannot be intended in an anti-hierarchical sense. Therefore it is a misinterpretation of the plain intention of Jesus to argue that the idea of a primacy is irreconcilably opposed to His teaching concerning humility and brotherly love. The contrary is true. The teaching of Jesus obtains its luminous fulfilment exactly in papacy and episcopacy, if they be correctly conceived. For the papacy, regarded in the light of the supernatural essence of the Church, is nought else but a personification of love, the manifestation of the unity of the Body of Christ on earth. It is therefore in its essential nature the exact opposite of domination; it is born not of brutality, but of love. Papacy and episcopacy are divine power put to the service of love. Certainly the pope has sometimes to speak out in sharp and peremptory admonition. It is as when Paul cried: "Shall I come to you with a rod?" (1 Cor. iv, 21). And sometimes his anathema rings through the world "in the same tones and with the same language" (Heiler) as St. Paul used when he excluded the incestuous Corinthian from the Christian community. Nevertheless, even this angry and corrective love remains love, love for the community of brethren. The pope has in so far the primacy of love. Nor is there any hierarchy in the Church that may express itself otherwise than in ministering love. Woe to the pontiff who misuses his primacy of love for personal ends, to gratify his lust of power, his avarice, or other passions! He sins against the Body of Christ, he offers violence to Jesus. He has to render an account beyond that required of any other member of the Body of Christ. How terribly at the Judgment may the words sound in his ears, when the risen Lord shall ask him: "Peter, lovest thou me, lovest thou me more than these?" That is the great and sacred privilege of his office, to love Christ and His Body more than all other men, to realise that honourable title which Gregory the Great assumed: "Servant of the servants of God" (Servus servorum Dei). Pope Pius XI, in his first Encyclical, laid it down that those who preside are nothing but "servants of the general weal, servants of the servants of God, especially of the weak and needy, after the pattern of the Lord."

The pope's office is essentially service of the community, love and devotion. And when we prescind from the office, when we consider only the personality of pope or bishop, then there is no distinction of rank in the Church, then the saying of Jesus is true: "Ye are all brethren" (Mt. xxiii, 8). In the same Encyclical Pope Pius lays stress on the point that "only in this kingdom is there a true equality of right, wherein all are endowed with the same greatness and the same nobility, being ennobled by the same precious Blood of Christ." In the Kingdom of Christ there is only one kind of nobility, namely nobility of soul. The wearer of the tiara is the rock of the Church and has the charism of that office not for himself, but for his brethren. For himself he has no greater Christian rights and no lesser Christian duties than the poorest beggar in the streets. Indeed he is in especial need of the mercy of God and requires the intercessions of his brethren. And if his conscience be burdened with sin, then he also must kneel at the feet of his confessor, who may be the homeliest Capuchin friar. And were he to appeal to Jesus with the request of the Sons of Zebedee: "Lord, grant that I may sit at Thy right hand or Thy left in Thy glory," then would his director give him the same answer: "You know not what you ask. Can you drink the chalice which Jesus drank?"

Church history demonstrates, to every unbiassed student, how earnestly and austerely most wearers of the tiara have taken their personal obligations, and how their lofty office has not impaired their humility, love and devotion, but transformed and deepened them. It is true that there have been popes, especially in the tenth century and at the Renaissance, who have given sad evidence of the frailty of human nature. But their number fades into insignificance before the dazzling company of saints and martyrs which the See of Rome has already given to the world. The words of the Protestant theologian Walter Köhler about Pope Pius X are true *mutatis mutandis* of the overwhelming majority of the popes of Rome: "He recked nothing of the political power of the modern state. He was a priest, and his endeavour was to hold the Host aloft, to look neither to right nor left, and to bear his Saviour through the world." Such is the idea of the papacy and such its essential nature: to bear the Saviour through the world, to devote self to Christ in the service of the community.

So all egotism, all domination, all special privilege is fundamentally foreign to the Church. And therefore and in that measure the Church fulfils the noblest dreams of democratic equality. Unity and brotherly love have here built themselves a house, a house in which, as St. Cyprian says and St. Augustine repeats (*De bapt. c. Don.* vii, 49), only those dwell who are of one heart and one mind. The spirit of the Master pervades that dwelling, the spirit which enriched us with the luminous words: "One only is your Master, ye all are brethren."

CHAPTER IX

THE CATHOLICITY OF THE CHURCH

I became all things to all men, that I might save all (I Cor. ix, 22).

The Church is the Kingdom of God thoroughly leavening all mankind in slow but irresistible process, the Body of Christ embracing the whole of fallen humanity in a supra-personal unity. Therefore of her nature she rests upon faith in the divine Redeemer, in Christ. As the supra-personal unity of mankind reunited to God she obtains in Peter's office the perfect expression of this unity and its guarantee, while her inward life, with the loving commerce which characterises it, is realised in the Communion of Saints. Such is the sequence of thought developed in the previous chapters.

The "notes," or characteristic marks of the Church, follow directly from her essential nature. Let us investigate first her most outstanding and most obvious attribute, that which is meant when one speaks of the "Catholic" Church: her catholicity. Ignatius of Antioch is the first witness for this title of "catholic" (Smyrn. viii, 2) and he indicates at the same time the reason why the church must be catholic, that is to say, must have an essential aptitude for propagating itself over the whole earth ($\chi\alpha\vartheta$' $\delta'\lambda o\nu$) and embracing all humanity. "Where Christ is," he says, "there also is the Catholic Church." Since Christ came to redeem all mankind, therefore His Body is essentially related to all mankind. The whole of redemption-needing mankind is potentially present in it. And so the Church is not complete until she has in progressive process embraced all mankind. This trend towards the wole of mankind is native to her.

The Church's attractive power, her appeal to all men, has its source in the missionary injunction of the risen Christ: "Go ye and teach all nations, baptizing them in the name of the Father and of the Son and of the Holy Ghost" (Matt. xxviii, 19). This command represents in the broadest outline the fundamental motives of our Lord's Gospel of the Kingdom. His Kingdom of God had in it "from the start the tendency to become a universal religion" (Holtzmann). For it is a great spiritual creation that stands above all national interests or other worldly considerations, and that is of a purely moral and religious character. Its gifts are forgiveness of sin and grace, and its requirements are those moral imperatives which apply to all men and are set forth in the Sermon on the Mount. The citizens of this Kingdom are the children of God, and they pray in the *Our Father* to the common Father of all men. The preachers of this Kingdom have their mission not only to the Jews, but also to the whole world, for they are the salt of the earth and the light of the world. Jesus Himself, in His messianic consciousness, takes His stand above all merely national aspirations. He is not merely the Son of David, but the Son of Man. He belongs to all men and not to the Jews alone. Even if He had not after His Resurrection expressly given His apostles this great missionary injunction, yet in view of the supra-national and fundamentally universal aim of His Gospel of the Kingdom, we should have to say at the very least that He displayed a potential universalism. But if we turn from His Gospel to the living Jesus Himself, if we remind ourselves of the open repugnance and strong distaste with which He criticised and rejected all the caste prejudice, narrowness, pettiness and pride of the Pharisees, if we think of the boundless generosity with which He welcomed every trace of nobility, purity and goodness which He encountered, though it were in publicans and sinners, and if finally we observe that in His parables of the prodigal son, of the Pharisee and publican, and of the marriage feast to which beggars and the lame and blind are invited, the radiance of His redeeming love penetrates to the most wretched and forsaken corners of our humanity: then we realise that it is a psychological monstrosity to say with Harnack that "the Gentile mission cannot have lain within the horizon of Jesus." It is an incontrovertible fact that the mission of the Gentiles not only lay within the horizon of contemporary Judaism, where it degenerated into a dreary proselytism (cf. Matt. xxiii, 15), but that it also gave a special colour to the promises of the prophets. Jesus lived and moved in the world of the prophets. Therefore their hopes—even if we ignore His messianic consciousness—could not have been unknown to Him, and their spirit must have had its effect upon His large-hearted and liberal attitude. And in fact He never avoided pagans when they came

16

to Him. He healed the sick daughter of the Syrophenician woman (Mk. vii, 24) and the sick servant of the pagan centurion (Matt. viii, 5 ff.; Luke vii, 1 ff.). On both occasions He does what He does with a hearty goodwill and undisguisedly expresses His appreciation of their dispositions: "O woman, great is thy faith." "Amen I say to you, I have not found so great faith in Israel. And I say to you that man shall come from the east and the west and shall sit down with Abraham and Isaac and Jacob in the kingdom of heaven" (Matt. viii, 10-11). Our Lord here expressly confirms the promises of the prophets in their full scope. The parable of the Good Samaritan, which contains a severe rebuke to the Jews, teaches that practical charity was to be found rather among the heretical Samaritans than among the orthodox priests and levites. And we know also that Jesus frequently (Matt. viii, 28; xv, 21) entered heathen territory, and that therefore He did not shun the heathen, but rather sought contact with them. Yet if, despite this fundamental friendliness towards the Gentiles, He deliberately confined His own and His disciples' preaching to the people of Israel, there were sound practical reasons for that course. It was important that the forces at hand for the preaching of the Gospel should not be dissipated, and the preachers had to take account of natural and religious facts. Of natural facts, in so far as their own people, with their special history and with their ethico-religious monotheism, provided the strongest natural foundation on which to build the Kingdom of God. Of religious facts, in so far as Jesus, like the prophets before Him and like Paul after Him, regarded Israel as the chosen people who because of their covenant with Jehovah seemed to be especially called to deepen the faith which they had carried though the centuries into faith in the Triune God. No doubt we may here trace in our Lord's attitude a strain of nationalism. But it is far from being an exclusive nationalism. It did not exclude, but included, the conversion of the Gentiles. Israel—as the prophets conceived the matter—was to be the foundation and nucleus of the new Kingdom of God, a Kingdom which was to embrace all peoples and nations, and therefore also the Gentiles. So long as the Jewish people had not forfeited this claim, they had an historical and religious right that the Kingdom, germinally contained in the whole of their age-long development, should be fulfilled and completed in them.

Therefore while Jesus lived on the earth He belonged to His own people. From among them He called the twelve apostles, in order to fashion the new Israel. And when He had by His Resurrection proved Himself the "Son of God in power" (Rom. i, 4) and as such had bidden His disciples evangelise the whole world, it was from this Jewish sapling that the mighty tree grew, in whose branches dwell the birds of the air. The catholicity of the new society, which was to embrace all languages and all men, was manifested at the very beginning in the pentecostal miracle of tongues. The life of the young plant, in its early days needed a protective sheath of Jewish custom; but this sheath was not able to hinder or restrict further development, and it was decisively set aside by St. Peter and St. Paul. St. Peter was the first to admit a pagan, the centurion Cornelius, into the Christian community; and St. Paul, by his vigorous reasoning as much as by his strong action, finally demolished the barriers of Jewish legalism and gave Christianity free course into the world. The universal character, which is implicit in our Lord's preaching, was made explicit by St. Peter and St. Paul. It has been maintained recently that by making Christianity co-terminous with the Church, St. Paul was unfaithful to our Lord's fundamental thought. But that is to overlook the fact that St. Paul conceives the Church, not as one particular sect, but as a society embracing the whole of redeemed humanity. The Church is not an institution to be established within humanity, which for that reason introduces new lines of division and produces a sectional organisation and a sort of new synagogue. On the contrary, it is so world wide in its nature that it breaks down all barriers and all divisions. It is as big and as wide as humanity itself.

This world-wide spirit, rooted in the preaching of our Lord, has been taken over in its full breadth and depth by the Catholic Church, and by her alone. The Church is not one society or one church alongside many others, nor is she just a church among men; she is the church of men, the church of mankind. It is this claim that gives her action its persevering determination and its grandeur. The interests of the Church have never been subordinated to purely national interests, nor has the Church ever put herself for long in bondage to any state. Her members belong to this or that nation, and national interests are bound to exert some influence on the Church's action. There have even been times when the Church seemed to be no more than a handmaid of the German Emperor or the French king. But those were only episodes, only brief and passing checks in her world-wide mission. She had to fight hard for it again and again, in bitter struggles, but she won for herself, in virtue of her mission to all mankind, her spiritual freedom from princes and peoples, and so secured the sovereignty of the Kingdom of God and the independence of Christian faith and morals. As such a supra-national power which assembles all men and all peoples in one Kingdom of God, she is able, far more than any national organi-sation, such as the Anglican, Swedish, or Russian churches, to evoke the best that lies dormant in the individual peoples and to make it serviceable for the propagation of the Kingdom of God. All peoples, each with their special aptitudes, are her children and all bring their gifts into the sanctuary. The elasticity, fresh-ness of mind and sense of form of the Roman combine with the penetration, profundity and inwardness of the German, and with the sobriety, discretion and good sense of the Anglo-Saxon. The piety and modesty of the Chinaman unite with the subtlety and depth of the Indian, and with the practicality and initiative of the American. It is unity in fulness, fulness in unity. The individ-ual life of men and peoples—the most precious thing in the world and unique in character—flows with its rich and sparkling waters in all the innumerable courses and channels dug by missionaries in far lands; and those countless tributaries flow into the Church, and purified in the Holy Spirit by its infallible teaching, merge into a single mighty stream, into one great flood which flows through all humanity, fertilising and purifying as it goes. That is the true conception of the Catholic Church. It is a great, supra-national tidal wave of faith in God and love of Christ, nourished and supported by the special powers of every individual nation and of every individual man, purified and inspired by the divine spirit of truth and love.

How is this catholicity of the Chruch realised? The internal catholicity of the Church, its essential aptitude for the whole of mankind, is of fundamental importance for its world-conquering power, its external catholicity. This internal catholicity of the Church is based upon two particular qualities, and first on a resolute affirmation of the whole of revelation in all its living fulness. Unlike all non-catholic communions, the Church affirms, completely and entirely, the whole of holy Scripture, both the Old Testament and the New. She affirms therefore not only the theology of St. Paul, but also the mysticism of St. John, not only St. Matthew's teaching concerning the Church and doctrinal authority, but also the faith and works of St. James and St. Peter. There is no thought in holy Scripture which is for her antiquated or unseasonable. Nor does she allow one truth to be obscured or garbled for the benefit of another. And by the side of holy Scripture stand extra-scriptural Tradition. The Gospel itself is based upon oral teaching, upon the preaching of Christ, of His disciples and of that apostolic succession of teachers which began with the first pupils of the apostles. Therefore the formation in the Christian communities of a living stream of tradition was natural and inevitable. The New Testament is certainly an important expression, but it is by no means an exhaustive expression, of this apostolic tradition which filled and permeated the whole consciousness of the Church. Oral tradition, the apostolic teaching alive and active in the Christian communities, that is prior to and more fundamental than the Bible. Nay, it is even the basis which sustains the Bible, both in its inspiration and in its canon. It is more comprehensive than the Bible, for it attests a mass of ritual and religious usage, of customs and rules, which is only slightly indicated in the Bible. And it possesses a quality which the Bible as a written document has not and cannot have, and which constitutes its pre-eminent merit, namely, that living spirit of revelation, that vitality of revealed thought, that "instinct of the faith" which stands behind every written and unwritten word, and which we call the "mind of the Church". This spirit of revelation lives in the living hearts of the faithful, and is quickened and promoted by the apostolic teaching authority under the guidance of the Holy Ghost. It is the most genuine, primary and precious heritage from the preaching of Jesus and His apostles. It is by means of this spirit that revelation acquires its inward unity, its inter-connexion and its ultimate meaning. Now, because the Church accepts as revelation the whole of holy Scripture and the whole of that extra-scriptural Tradition which has come down from the teaching of Christ and His apostles,

without restricting herself to particular revealed thoughts, such
as the notion of the Fatherhood of God or of the certainty of
forgiveness, and because the Church accepts and affirms that
full Christian life and experience which originated in Christ was
by the apostles conveyed to mankind, therefore she is able out
of her abundance to be something for all men and to give something to all men. She is become "all things to all men." Like St.
Paul at Corinth, she gives the "little ones in Christ" milk and
not meat, for they "are not yet able" for meat. To those who
are not yet delicate enough of hearing and perception to appreciate the profound spirituality and delicate inward power of the
Christian message, and to understand the "liberty of the children
of God," those who are not ready for St. Augustine's rule, "Love
and do what you will," the Church in her sermons and instructions indicates the stern commandments of the Decalogue,
insists upon the obligations of Christian morality and holds up
the aweful majesty of that Judge who condemns to everlasting
fire all those who fail in mercy and in love. If love of God cannot
achieve it, at least fear of His justice will deliver them from their
earthliness and self-seeking and give them a spiritual life based on
a fear of God which for all its imperfection is yet supernatural.
And when souls are alive to her voice and can understand her
doctrine of inwardness and love, then she allures them by the
sweetest methods, by the Mystery of the Tabernacle, by devotion
to the Sacred Heart, by the Stations of the Cross and by her
Rosary. Thus she leads the simplest and rudest of souls to a
height of spiritual life wherein the cry "Abba, Father!" is experienced in its full meaning, to the heights where St. Paul and St.
John abide. And it may happen that a man is so penetrated with
love of Christ and zeal for His Kingdom that his soul is stirred
to its depths by those words of the Gospel: "If thou wilt be
perfect, go see what thou hast and give to the poor; and come,
follow me" (Matt. xix, 21). Then deserts and great cities alike
are peopled with hermits and monks. There is no state of religious development which the comprehensive influence of the
Church cannot grip and mould. It is impossible to describe the
infinite variety of forms in which the religious and moral life of
Catholics is expressed. In this region individualism is the rule
and an unrestricted freedom of religious self-expression the
dominant law.

Yet, however various these expressions may be, they have all sprung in their fundamental forms from the living tradition, from that abundance and variety of life which is our inheritance in Scripture and Tradition, yes in Scripture alone and even in St. John and St. Paul alone, we have not merely the spiritual, but the sensible also, though it be the sensible transfigured into the spiritual. We have not only certainty of forgiveness, but also the severe imperative, the commandments and the doctrine of merit. We have not only personal spiritual experience, but also service of the community and official authority. And above all we have mysticism; for wherever there is genuine religion, there you must have mysticism. The fundamental forms of Catholicism may be determined without difficulty or dialectic from the Scriptures and even from St. Paul alone. For revelation does not consist merely in this or that inspiring idea. On the contrary, it is original, comprehensive, mighty life. It is something holy and but half-expressed, "a reality, which is fruitful in resources; a depth, which extends into mystery."

So the fulness of Catholicism wells out of the fulness of the revelation of the Old and New Testaments, out of the fulness of Scripture and Tradition. But it is a fulness in unity, for it is animated by one spirit and by one soul. The life of Catholicism grows, but it does not outgrow itself. The Church has advanced, past all hesitation and reverses, "till the whole truth 'self-balanced on its centre hung' ."

There are indeed, apparent disturbances of this inward equipoise, especially when heresies have arisen and compelled the Church to withdraw a truth which has been abused or to emphasise another which has been denied. But a mere attitude of antagonism to heresy, whether it be to Gnosticism, Arianism, Lutheranism or Modernism, is not the proper attitude of Catholicism.

Such an attitude, on the contrary, is the creature of its time and represents a temporary shifting of the balance in order to meet and discomfit heresy. And Catholicism displays its vitality, its inner unity and truth, most clearly in the fact that it always ultimately regains its balance, after such temporary disturbances, though it may take it centuries to do so. The strong force which gives it back its inner equipoise is the vital spirit of revelation transmitted in its teaching authority, or, more profoundly, the Holy Spirit living in it. The Holy Spirit gives that secret energy which infuses new life into the weakened parts of the organism and repairs all unnatural dislocations in the Body of Christ. It could be shown in detail how Catholicism has sometimes repelled and rejected outright an heretical position with all its implications, reasons and consequences in order to prevent any contamination of revealed truth, and then, when the danger of such contamination was past, has taken over those elements of truth which heresy had grasped but wrongly emphasised, and moulding them into harmony with the whole of revelation, has consciously built them into her teaching and maintained them. The Church alone, says Cardinal Newman, "has succeeded in thus rejecting evil without sacrificing the good, and in holding together in one things which in all other schools are incompatible." It is the spirit of revelation living in the Church, the vitality and consistency of Catholic thought, that "active tradition," as the schoolmen call it, which prevents any injury to the Catholic whole and ever restores its massive unity and inward harmony. It is the same living spirit of revelation, manifested in the teaching authority, which gives the Church its flexibility and power of expansion, and enables it to adapt itself to every age, to every civilisation, and to every mental outlook. It is indeed the propelling and progressive principle in Catholicism. All other Christian bodies, in so far as they have maintained a positive belief, have attached themselves to a fixed and rigid principle. In Lutheranism and Calvinism it is the letter of the Bible; in the schismatical churches of the East it is the Bible and "passive" tradition, that is to say, the tradition of the ancient Fathers and most ancient Councils. Therefore these churches are in danger of treating revelation as so much dead capital, as a store of gold which must be passed on to future generations in a merely external fashion, and of overlooking the vital energies that lie in the revelation and work for the further development of its germinal content. To this danger of petrifaction and ossification the Orthodox Church has succumbed. Or there is the opposite danger, that in an effort to accommodate religion to modern needs and requirements, its inner connexion with revelation is sacrificed, and an entirely novel Christianity, the religion of German idealism, or what you will, is summoned into life. This is the danger that meances Protestantism. But Catholicism is safe from both possibilities. The vitality of the spirit which inspires her teaching authority is manifested constantly in this, that acting as a living power it lays hold of the revelation enshrined in Scripture and passive Tradition, and discloses as it advances the fruitful energies that they contain. In the Catholic Church alone may we discern an organic growth in the consciousness of the faith. There is no petrifaction here; yet there is on the other hand nothing erratic or abrupt, but an organic development. Thus the Church has a message for the men of every age. For the dogmatic development is no fortuitious one, but corresponds to the needs and problems of the contemporary Church. Since they who bear the spirit of the revelation are themselves living men and living members of the body of the faithful, they are in constantly sympathy with the questions and needs of the "learning Church," of the community of the faithful. They are able to bring revealed truth into connexion with those needs and questions, and from its store to provide those answers for which the faithful look. So there is a constant movement in the exposition of the faith, and a continual dispensation of the store of revelation for the benefit of hungry souls. The revelation does not grow old, but remains ever new and full of life. It is timeless, it is immediate present, though century succeed century.

Not to lose the thread of the argument, let us summarise what has been said. We have laid it down that the external catholicity of the Church, her world-conquering power, rests upon her internal catholicity. And we have pointed out that the first element in this internal catholicity is a comprehensive affirmation of the whole of revelation, and a vitalising of this revelation by that living spirit of revelation which resides in the teaching authority of the Church.

The second element in her internal catholicity is her comprehensive affirmation of the whole man, of human nature in its completeness, of the body as well as the soul, of the senses as well as the intellect. The mission of the Church is to the entire man. According to the teaching of the Church—as that was formulated at Trent against the Lutheran conception—original sin by no means destroyed the natural structure of man's being, nor is it synonymous with what St. Paul calls the law of our members, that is with concupiscence. It is true that the understanding is darkened by it and the will weakened; but these effects are not the direct and immediate consequences of original sin. They are the direct results of the loss of our original, supernatural union of life and love with God, whereby we were in our whole being diverted from our original, supernatural end. Consequently the natural structure of our being remains fundamentally unimpaired. Though original sin brought a weakening of nature, it did not bring as well a physical deterioration or corruption of our bodily and mental powers.

So the Church, starting from this basis, is able to enlist man's entire nature, his body and its sensitive life, his reason and his will, in the service of the Kingdom of God. Since man's nature is not essentially damaged in its natural powers, but only by diversion from its supernatural end, that is to say be a false orientation, therefore so soon as this false orientation is mended and man is replaced by baptism in his original, living union with God, that nature can be gripped in all its powers by the Church's preaching. The Church as the Body of Christ lays hold of all that is of God, and therefore of man's body, his senses and his passions, just as much as of his intellect and will. And in redeeming his body and senses and passions by sanctifying grace from their earthliness and selfishness and reclaiming them for God, she not only wins them back for His Kingdom, but also ennobles and deepens them. So the Church destroys man's old earthly structure to its foundations, but she takes over the old stones for the new building and gives them for the first time their true positions, their proper meaning, their full beauty and their glory. Therefore the conception of nature, so far from being destroyed by Catholicism, is enormously deepened. As man came from the hand of God, in the beauty of his body, in the ardour of his sense life, in the storm and stress of his passsions, with keen intellect and mighty will, even so does the Church affirm him and even so would she have him be. She would mould this man of ardent, stormy passions and clear-sighted strength so that he may belong to God, and that he may by union with the original basis of his life bring all the greatness and the glory of his natural gifts into inward harmony and perfection.

Hence two further elements in that catholicity which gives the Church her comprehensive power of attraction. The first of these is that she loves and understands man's nature, his bodily and sensitive structure, as well as his mental powers. In acute and prolonged conflicts with Gnostics, Manicheans, Albigenses, Bogomili, and other similar sects, she has guarded the rights and the dignity of the human body, and in particular the rights and dignity of marriage. She does not regard the body as a "garment of shame," but as a holy and precious creation of God. And she teaches that this gift is so precious and so necessary for man, that the body that is dissolved in death will one day be raised again by God, to be the ministering organ of the immortal soul. Therefore the Church loves this body so related to God, and inspires her artists to represent, in its nobility and beauty, the unspeakable beauty of divinity and holiness. She adorns the humblest village churches with images of our Lord and our Lady and the saints, in order to raise her children by visible things to things invisible, from the beauty of this earth to the beauty of heaven. Art is native to Catholicism, since reverence for the body and for nature is native to it.

This reverence for the body leads the Church further to a careful consideration for man's sensible needs. Since we are not pure spirits, but spirits enmeshed in body, we grasp spiritual things by means of things visible and sensible. Hence the whole sacramental system of Christianity and the Church. Our Lord Himself submitted to baptism. He has granted us communion in His Body and Blood by the visible signs of bread and wine, and in other ways conjoined spiritual blessing with sensible means. He bade His disciples anoint the sick with oil, He never ate bread without first blessing it, He never dismissed a child without laying His hand upon it. Even so, the Church joins her spiritual benefits to sensible signs. Besides the sacraments she employs the sacramentals. In distinction from the sacraments, they rest upon ecclesiastical ordinance and not upon the institution of Christ. Their efficacy is not derived therefore from a positive act of our Lords' will, but from the intercession of the whole Church and from their devout employment. They are supplications for blessing and grace made by the faithful and by the whole Church, and objectively manifested in visible signs. When the Catholic uses Holy Water, or makes the sign of the Cross on the forehead of one he loves, or fixes on his wall blessed palms and blessed flowers, his action signifies a devout communion with the intercessory prayer of the whole Church, that God may help him in all his needs. Each and every element of his mundane life, from marriage ring and bridal bed down to the blessed salt which he gives to a sick beast, is drawn by the blessing of the Church into a supernatural relation with God. By this means the whole activity of the Catholic in all its aspects is directed towards heaven—by visible things to things invisible. It is true that abuses are possible and that the sacramentals may be degraded into magical charms. But wherever there are men there will be abuses, nor should we judge a good thing by its abuse, but contrariwise. In elevating men by these sensible means to appreciate the supra-sensible, the Church obtains religious influence over those whose minds are as yet wholly immersed in the things of sense. She is able to bring a ray of divinity and holiness even into their small and poor lives. So she is not only the Church of the nations, she is the Church of the people.

As the Church affirms man's sensible nature, so does she also affirm and lay hold of his spiritual nature, and especially human reason. She aims deliberately at conquering the world of the mind. Her whole theology, from the apologists and the schools of Alexandria and Antioch, through early and late Scholasticism down to our own day, is dominated by confidence in the illuminating power of reason. Her conception of faith presupposes that human reason can of itself recognise the so-called *praeambula fidei*, i.e. the spirituality of the human soul and the existence of God—realities which transcend sensible experience—and that reason can establish the credibility of revelation on historical and philosophical grounds. The supernatural certitude of faith is the gift of God, but in so far as it is built upon these rational presuppositions, philosophy becomes the handmaid of faith (*ancilla fidei*). The Church does not in this propose to interfere in any way with the independence of the profane sciences in their own proper sphere. Indeed, the Vatican Council expressly renounces any such intention (Sess. III, cap. 4). What she wishes to establish is the fact that human reason, while remaining true to itself, can by its own principles advance to a point where

God becomes visible as the fundamental basis and ultimate meaning of all reality, and where knowledge passes over into faith, philosophy into theology. Whenever men have doubted or denied the capacity of the human mind to transcend the limits of experience, whenever they have attempted to paralyse or kill man's profound yearning for absolute truth, then the Church had come forward in defence of reason, whether against Averroes and Luther, or against Kant. And the more our own age becomes weary of subjective idealism and seeks to rediscover the objective world, the more grateful will it be to Pope Pius X that in his much-abused anti-modernist Encyclical "Pascendi" he denounced all positivism, pragmatism and phenomenalism and defended the power of reason to transcend and surpass experience, thus exorcising those twin bugbears of solipsism and scepticism which menace all knowledge. The catholicity of the Church is manifested not least in this, that she does not allow knowledge and faith to be separated and set in an unhealthy antagonism, but conjoins them in intimate harmony, making knowledge accessible to faith and faith to knowledge. Her greatest minds, Origen, Augustine, Aquinas and Newman, make it their life's task to establish this synthesis of faith and knowledge. Nor do the theologians of our day know of any more important task than that of making modern knowledge fruitful for the faith. Catholicism lays its hand on every branch of knowledge, seeking everywhere the golden grains of truth, that it may adorn its sanctuary with them.

We have described the first consequence which follows from the high value which the Church sets upon our human nature and indicated its relation to her world-wide influence. The second consequence shall be treated very briefly. It is her definitely affirmative attitude towards all that is natural, genuine and incorrupt in the pre-Christian and non-Christian world. So far as paganism is genuine paganism, that is to say, revolt from the living God, self-deification or the deification of nature, it has no more resolute foe than Catholicism. But there is more in paganism than revolt. There break forth even in paganism, from out of the uncorrupted sources of human nature, noble and pure impulses, thoughts and resolves, not only in philosophy and art, but also in religion and morality. The seeds of truth, as the Fathers constantly declare, are to be found everywhere, among Romans as among Greeks, among Indians as among Negroes. What we have to do is to free these seeds from the non-Christian growth that chokes them and to redeem them for the Kingdom of God. The Church is pursuing this task of purification and redemption when she takes the wisdom of the pagan philosophers, of Plato, or Aristotle, or Plotinus, or the Stoics, and makes it minister to the Incarnate Word. She does not hesitate even to take over pagan ritual and pagan symbols, whenever such things can be Christianised and reformed. This is not weakness, or unprincipled accommodation, but practical catholicism. It is a direct consequence of that fundamental Catholic conviction that every genuine value, everything that comes from pure and uncorrupted nature, belongs to God and has citizen rights in His Kingdom. Therefore the Church sets up no barrier against non-Christian culture, and no barrier against antiquity. She sets up her barrier only against sin. It was her loving hand that preserved for us many of the treasures of antiquity when the ancient world collapsed under the assault of the Germanic peoples. And were those same treasures, and the whole spiritual achievement of antiquity to be in danger, in our own time, of being frittered away and squandered by modern vandals in their greed for gold, and were some frigid instinct for the practical and useful, for the idols of our time, to deprive men of sympathetic feeling for the spirit of antiquity and to destroy our humanist institutions, then the Church would stand forth once again, as she did in the Middle Ages, and taking the "gold of the Egyptians" hand it on to her sons and daughters.

Such is Catholicism: an affirmation of values along the whole line, a most comprehensive and noblest accessibility to all good, a union of nature with grace, of art with religion, of knowledge with faith, "so that God may be all in all." Let others be "ever hunting for a fabulous primitive simplicity; we repose in Catholic fulness." Catholicism knows no other watchword than the sentence of St. Paul: "I became all things to all men that I might save all. And I do all things for the gospel's sake" (I Cor. ix, 22-23).

Christopher Henry Dawson

1889-1970

Historian Christopher Dawson was born in Wales of Anglican parents, and educated at Winchester and Trinity College, Oxford. He became a Roman Catholic in 1914. He lectured in University College, Exeter, from 1930 to 1936, and in 1947-1948 he delivered the Gifford lectures at the University of Edinburgh. In 1958 he became the first Chauncey Stillman Professor of Roman Catholic Studies in Harvard University, a chair he occupied until 1962.

Dawson's first book, The Age of the Gods *(1928), set forth a basic thesis that he was to return to often in his career, i.e., that religion forms the foundation of every culture. In affirming this he did not think of himself as either theologian or philosopher, but rather as a "metahistorian," a historian concerned with the large questions and the broad conclusions. In his 1929 work,* Progress and Religion, *he analysed the historical implications of the way in which the idea of progress had fascinated Europeans for the previous century, during which various secular alternatives to Christianity vied for attention and adoption. Some of these served to clarify what were and what were not distinctively Christian values in Western culture.*

Later works, such as Religion and Culture *(1958) and* Understanding Europe *(1952) were widely acclaimed, but for many the book that constituted Dawson's greatest contribution was* The Making of Europe *(1932). It is subtitled "An Introduction to the History of European Unity," and begins with the modest statement: "I do not think that it is necessary to make any apology for writing a book on the period usually known as the Dark Ages. . . .It was the most creative age of all, since it created not this or that manifestation of culture, but the very culture itself."*

The Making of Europe *is nearly a half-century old, and yet is as fresh and full of insight as ever. Dawson demonstrated one of his own sayings, "one of the great merits of history is that it takes us out of ourselves," it is the great corrective to provincialism. On the other hand, he was persuaded that the Catholic had a special advantage when it came to understanding this era. As he put it in the Introduction, "to the Catholic they are not dark ages so much as ages of dawn, for they witnessed the conversion of the West, the foundation of Christian civilization, and the creation of Christian art and Catholic liturgy."*

The book is divided into three parts with five chapters in each of the first two parts and four chapters plus a conclusion in the third part. The selection that follows consists of the first and last chapters (11 and 14) of the third part, plus the conclusion. The reason for drawing from this third part is obvious; Part One deals with "The Foundations," Part Two with "The Ascendancy of the East," while Part Three is "The Formation of Western Christendom." It is thus in Part Three that the basic development is described which must be grasped if Western culture is to be understood. The conversion of the barbarians led to that union of "Teutonic initiative and Latin order" which is the source of the whole mediaeval development. The common Anglo-American bias to start Western history with the Renaissance and Reformation is totally inadequate for appreciating the real roots and values of our culture, and no one has provided more help for overcoming that bias than Christopher Dawson. Later divisions and controversies should not be allowed to obscure the vital role played by the Catholic Church in "the making of Europe."

THE MAKING OF EUROPE

T he fall of the Western Empire in the fifth century did not result in the immediate formation of an independent cultural unity in Western Europe. In the sixth century Western Christendom was still dependent on the Eastern Empire, and Western culture was a chaotic mixture of barbarian and Roman elements which as yet possessed no spiritual unity and no internal principle of social order. The temporary revival of civilisation in the sixth century was followed by a second period of decline and barbarian invasion which reduced European culture to a far lower level than it had reached in the fifth century. Once again it was on the Danube that the crisis developed. The second half of the reign of Justinian had seen a progressive weakening of the frontier defences and the Balkan provinces were exposed to a series of destructive invasions. The Gepids, an East German people allied to the Goths, had taken the place of the Ostrogoths in Pannonia, while the Kotrigur Huns held the lower Danube and carried their raids to the very gates of Constantinople. In their wake came the Slavs, who now for the first time emerge from the prehistoric obscurity that envelops their origins. Faced by so many dangers, the imperial government found itself unable to defend its frontiers by military means and fell back upon diplomacy. It egged on the Utigurs of the Kuban steppe to attack the Kotrigurs, the Herules and the Lombards against the Gepids, and the Avars against the Gepids and the Slavs. Thus in 567, after the death of Justinian, the Avars united with the Lombards to destroy the Gepid kingdom, and the government of Justin II, hoping to recover Sirmium for the Empire, left the Gepids to their fate. But here the Byzantines overreached themselves, for Bayan, the great Khan of the Avars, was no petty chieftain to be made the catspaw of imperial diplomacy, but a ruthless Asiatic conqueror of the type of Attila and Genghis Khan. In place of a relatively stable Germanic state, the Empire now had to deal with a people of warlike nomads whose empire extended from the Adriatic to the Baltic. Under its pressure the Danube frontier finally gave way, and the Illyrian provinces, which had been for nearly four hundred years the foundation of the military strength of the Empire and the cradle of its soldiers and rulers, were occupied by Slavonic peoples who were dependent on the Avars.

But the Empire was not the only power to suffer. All Central Europe fell a prey to the Asiatic conquerors. Their raids extended as far as the frontiers of the Frankish kingdom. The Northern Sueves were forced to evacuate the lands between the Elbe and the Oder, and Eastern Germany was colonised by the Slavonic subjects of the Avars. Thus of the East German peoples who had formerly ruled Eastern Europe from the Baltic to the Black Sea, there remained only the Lombards, and they were too wise to try conclusions with their Asiatic allies. Immediately after the fall of the Gepid Kingdom they evacuated their lands on the Danube and marched on Italy. Here again the Empire was powerless to protect its subjects. Lombardy and the whole of the interior of the peninsula was occupied by the invaders, and the Byzantines only preserved their hold upon the coastal districts—the Venetian Islands, Ravenna and the Pentapolis, the Duchy of Rome, and Genoa, Amalfi and Naples.

This was the last blow to the declining civilisation of Italy, and we cannot wonder that to the men of that age the end of all things seemed at hand. The writings of St. Gregory the Great reflect the appalling sufferings and the profound pessimism of the age. He even welcomes the pestilence that was devastating the West as a refuge from the horrors that surrounded him. "When we consider the way in which other men have died we find a solace in reflecting on the form of death that threatens us. What mutilations, what cruelties have we seen inflicted upon men, for which death is the only cure and in the midst of which life was a torture!" He sees Ezekiel's prophecy of the seething pot fulfilled in the fate of Rome: "Of this city it is well said 'The meat is boiled away and the bones in the midst thereof'. . . . For where is the Senate? Where is the People? The bones are all dissolved, the flesh is consumed, all the pomp of the dignities of this world is gone. The whole mass is boiled away."

"Yet even we who remain, few as we are, still are daily smitten with the sword, still are daily crushed by innumerable afflictions. Therefore let it be said, 'Set the pot also empty upon the coals.' For the Senate is no more, and the People has perished, yet sorrow and sighing are multiplied daily among the few that are left. Rome is, as it were, already empty and burning. But what need is there to speak of men when, as the work of ruin spreads, we see the very buildings perishing. Wherefore it is fitly added concerning the city already empty, 'Let the brass thereof be hot and melt.' Already the pot itself is being consumed in which were first consumed the flesh and the bones. . . ."

But the worst had not yet come. In the seventh century the Arabs conquered Byzantine Africa, the most civilised province of the West, and the great African Church, the glory of Latin Christianity, disappears from history. Early in the eighth century the tide of Moslem invasion swept over Christian Spain and threatened Gaul itself. Christendom had become an island isolated between the Moslem south and the Barbarian north.

Yet it was in this age of universal ruin and destruction that the foundations of the new Europe were being laid by men like St. Gregory, who had no idea of building up a new social order but who laboured for the salvation of men in a dying world because the time was short. And it was just this indifference to temporal results which gave the Papacy the power to become a rallying-point for the forces of life in the general decadence of European civilisation. In the words of the inscription which Pope John III set up in the Church of the Most Holy Apostles: "In a straitened age, the Pope showed himself more generous and disdained to be cast down though the world failed."

At the very moment of the fall of the Empire in the West, St. Augustine, in his great book *Of the City of God,* had set forth the programme which was to inspire the ideals of the new age. He viewed all history as the evolution of two opposite principles embodied in two hostile societies, the heavenly and the earthly cities, Sion and Babylon, the Church and the World. The one had no final realisation on earth, it was *"in via,"* its *patria* was heavenly and eternal; the other found its realisation in earthly prosperity, in the wisdom and glory of man; it was its own end and its own justification. The State, it is true, was not condemned as such. In so far as it was Christian, it subserved the ends of the heavenly city. But it was a subordinate society, the servant and not the master: it was the spiritual society that was supreme. The moment that the state came into conflict with the higher power, the moment that it set itself up as an end in itself, it became identified with the earthly city and lost all claims to a higher sanction than the law of force and self-interest. Without justice, what is a great kingdom but a great robbery—*magnum latrocinium?* Conquering or being conquered does no one either good or harm. It is pure waste of energy, the game of fools for an empty prize. The terrestrial world is unsubstantial and transitory, the only reality worth striving for is that which is eternal—the heavenly Jerusalem—"the vision of peace."

This ideal of the supremacy and independence of the spiritual power found its organ of expression above all in the Papacy. Already before the fall of the Empire the Roman bishop possessed a unique position as the successor and representative of St. Peter. Rome was the "Apostolic See" *par excellence,* and in virtue of this authority it had intervened decisively against both Constantinople and Alexandria in the doctrinal struggles of the fourth and fifth centuries. The decline of the Empire in the West naturally enhanced its prestige, for the process by which the bishop became the representative of the Roman tradition in the conquered provinces was far more accentuated in the case of the ancient capital. The old imperial tradition was carried over into the sphere of religion. In the fifth century St. Leo the Great, addressing his people on the Feast of SS. Peter and Paul, could say, "These are they, who have brought thee to such glory as a holy nation, a chosen people, a royal and priestly city that thou mightest be made the head of the world by the Holy See of St. Peter, and mightest

36

bear rule more widely by divine religion than by earthly dominion."

The Pope was still a loyal subject of the Emperor and regarded the cause of the Empire as inseparable from that of the Christian religion. The Liturgy couples together "the foes of the Roman name and the enemies of the Catholic Faith," and the Roman Missal still contains a prayer for the Roman Empire "that God may subdue to the Emperor all the barbarous nations, to our perpetual peace." But after the Lombard invasion and the age of St. Gregory, the actual authority of the imperial government in Italy was reduced to a shadow, and it was on the Pope that the responsibility fell for the safety of Rome and the feeding of its inhabitants. Rome became, like Venice or Cherson, a kind of semi-independent member of the Byzantine state. It remained an open door between the civilised East and the barbarised West; it was a common meeting-ground to both, without exactly belonging to either.

This anomalous position was very favourable to the exercise of papal influence in the barbaric kingdoms of the West, since the Papacy enjoyed the prestige of its connection with the Eastern Empire without any danger of being considered an instrument of imperial policy, and thus the Frankish kings raised no objection to the Bishop of Arles receiving the office of Apostolic Vicar for the Church in Gaul. Nevertheless, the power of the Papacy, and with it that of the Universal Church, was greatly limited by the inherent weakness of the local churches. The Church of the Frankish kingdom, especially, suffered from the same process of barbarisation and cultural decadence that affected the whole society.

The bishop became a territorial magnate, like the count, and the greater was his wealth and power, the greater was the danger of the secularisation of the office. The monarchy had no direct intention of interfering with the prerogatives of the Church, but it naturally claimed the right of appointing to an office which took such an important share in the administration of the kingdom, and its candidates were often of very dubious character, like the "robber bishops," Salonius and Sagittarius, whose exploits are described by Gregory of Tours (*Lib.* IV, *cap.* 42; V, *cap.* 20). Moreover, the transformation of the state into an agrarian society and the progressive decline of the city had a most deleterious effect on the Church, since the influence of the barbarous and half pagan countryside came to predominate over that of the cities. For while in the East Christianity had penetrated the countryside from the first, and the peasantry was, if anything, more Christian than the townspeople, in Western Europe the Church had grown up in the towns and so had failed to make a deep impression on the peasants and countryfolk. They were *pagani*, the "pagans," who clung after the manner of peasants to their immemorial customs and beliefs, to the rites of seedtime and harvest, and to the venerations of their sacred trees and springs.

Yet the fundamental ethos of the new religion was in no way alien to the peasant life. Its first beginning had been amongst the fishermen and peasants of Galilee, and the Gospel teaching is full of the imagery of the field and the fold and the vineyard. Christianity only needed a new organ besides the city episcopate in order to permeate the countryside. Now at the very moment when the conversion of the Empire was binding the Church closer to the urban polity, a new movement was drawing men away from the city. The heroes of the second age of Christianity, the successors of the martyrs, were the ascetics—the men who deliberately cut themselves off from the whole inheritance of city cultures in order to live a life of labour and prayer under the simplest possible conditions.

In the fourth century the deserts of Egypt and Syria were peopled with colonies of monks and hermits which became schools of the religious life for all the provinces of the Empire, and the neighbouring peoples of the East. But in the West, though its fundamental ideals were the same, the difference of social conditions forced the monasteries to take up a different attitude towards the society that surrounded them.

In the rural districts of the West the monastery was the only centre of Christian life and teaching, and it was upon the monks rather than upon the bishops and their clergy that the task of converting the heathen or semi-heathen peasant population ultimately fell. This is evident even as early as the fourth century in the life of the founder of Gallic monasticism, the great Martin of Tours, but its great development was due to

the work of John Cassian, who brought Gaul into direct contact
with the tradition of the monks of the Egyptian desert, and to
St. Honoratus, the founder of Lerins, which became the greatest
monastic centre of Western Europe in the fifth century and the
source of a far-reaching influence.

But it was in the newly-converted Celtic lands of the far
West that the influence of monasticism became all-important.
The beginnings of the monastic movement in this region dates
from the fifth century, and probably owes its origins to the influence of Lerins, where St. Patrick had studied in the years
before his apostolate and where in 433 a British monk, Faustus,
had held the position of abbot. But though St. Patrick had introduced the monastic life into Ireland, his organisation of the
Church followed the traditional lines of episcopal organisation,
as did that of the British Church in Wales. Since, however, the
Roman bishop was always the bishop of a city, the normal
system of ecclesiastical organisation possessed no natural
social basis in the Celtic lands, where the social unit was not the
city but the tribe. Consequently, the great extension of monastic influence and culture in the sixth century led to the
monastery's taking the place of the bishopric as the centre of
ecclesaistical life and organisation. The movement started in
South Wales, where the monastery of St. Illtyd on Caldey
Island became a great school of the monastic life after the
model of Lerins early in the sixth century. From this centre
the monastic revival was diffused throughout western Britain and Brittany by the work of St. Samson, St. Cadoc of
Llancarvan, St. Gildas and St. David. Moreover, the great
development of Irish monasticism that took place in the sixth
century under the "Saints of the Second Order" was closely
related to this movement. St. Finnian of Clonard (d. 549),
the chief inaugurator of the new type of monasticism, was
in close relations with St. Cadoc of Llancarvan and with St.
Gildas, and it was through him and his disciples, above all St.
Ciaran of Clonmacnoise (d. 549), St. Brendan of Clonfert,
and St. Columba of Derry and Iona, that the monastic tradition of St. Illtyd and his school was diffused in Ireland. The
importance of this movement was literary as well as ascetic,
for the school of St. Illtyd and St. Cadoc cultivated the tra-

ditions of the old schools of rhetoric, as well as those of purely ecclesiastical learning, and encouraged the study of classical literature.

This is the origin of the movement of culture which produced the great monastic schools of Clonard and Clonmacnoise and Bangor, and made Ireland the leader of Western culture from the close of the sixth century. It is, however, probable that its development also owes something to native traditions, for the Irish, unlike the other barbaric peoples, possessed a native tradition of learning, represented by the schools of the poets or *Filid*, which enjoyed considerable wealth and social prestige. The new monastic schools entered in a sense into the inheritance of this native tradition, and were able to replace the old druidic and bardic schools as the intellectual organs of Irish society. By degrees the imported classical culture of the Christian monasteries was blended with the native literary tradition, and there arose a new vernacular literature inspired in part by Christian influence but founded in part on native pagan traditions. Although this literature has come down to us mainly through Middle Irish versions of mediaeval date, there can be no doubt that its original creation goes back to the seventh and eighth centuries—the Golden Age of Irish Christian culture—and that the literary tradition of mediaeval Ireland has its roots deep in the prehistoric past. The most striking example of this is the great prose epic or sage—the *Tain Bo Cualgne*—which takes us back behind the Middle Age and behind the classical tradition to the heroic age of Celtic culture, and preserves the memory of a stage of society resembling that of the Homeric world. Thus there was no sudden break between the old barbaric tradition and that of the Church, such as occurred elsewhere, and a unique fusion took place between the Church and the Celtic tribal society entirely unlike anything else in Western Europe. The hierarchic episcopal organisation of the Church, which was common to the rest of Christendom, was here completely subordinated to the monastic system. Bishops of course continued to exist and to confer orders, but they were no longer the rulers of the Church. The monasteries were not only the great centres of religious and intellectual life; they were also centres of ecclesiastical jurisdiction.

The abbot was the ruler of a diocese or *paroechia,* and usually kept one or more bishops in his community to perform the necessary episcopal functions, except in those cases in which he was a bishop himself. Still more extraordinary is the fact that this kind of quasi-episcopal jurisdiction was sometimes exercised by women, for the see of Kildare was a dependency of St. Bridget's great monastery and was ruled jointly by bishop and abbess, so that it was in the phrase of her biographer "a see at once episcopal and virginal."

The monasteries were closely connected with the tribal society, for it was the prevailing if not the universal custom for the abbot to be chosen from the clan to which the founder belonged. Thus the *Book of Armagh* records in the ninth century that the Church of Trim had been ruled for nine generations by the descendants of the chieftain who endowed the see in the days of St. Patrick. In the same way the early abbots of Iona belonged to the family of St. Columba, the royal race of the northern Ui Niall.

In organisation and way of life the Irish monks closely resembled their Egyptian prototypes. They rivalled the monks of the desert in the rigour of their discipline and the asceticism of their life. Their monasteries were not great buildings like the later Benedictine abbeys, but consisted of groups of huts and small oratories, like the Egyptian laura, and were surrounded by a *rath* or earthwork. Moreover, they preserved the oriental idea of the eremitical life as the culmination and goal of the monastic state. In Ireland, however, this ideal assumed a peculiar form that is not found elsewhere. It was common for monks to devote themselves to a life of voluntary exile and pilgrimage. The case recorded in the Anglo-Saxon Chronicle (*s.a.* 891) of the three monks "who stole away from Ireland in a boat without any oars because they would live in a state of pilgrimage for the love of God, they recked not where," is typical of this development. It led to a movement of travel and exploration which is reflected in a legendary form in the adventures of St. Brendan the Navigator. When the Vikings first discovered Iceland they found that the Irish "papas" had been there before them, and every island of the northern seas had its colony of ascetics. The informants of Dicuil, the Carolingian geographer, had even sailed beyond Iceland and reached the frozen Arctic seas.

But the real importance of this movement lies in the impulse that it gave to missionary activity, and it was as missionaries that the Celtic monks made their most important contribution to European culture. The monastic colonies of St. Columba at Iona, and of his namesake Columbanus at Luxeuil, were the starting points of a great expansion of Christianity. To the one was due the conversion of Scotland and of the Northumbrian kingdom, to the other the revival of monasticism and the conversion of the remaining pagan elements in the Frankish kingdom. Luxeuil, with its six hundred monks, became the monastic metropolis of Western Europe, and the centre of a great colonising and missionary activity. Very many of the great mediaeval monasteries not only of France, but of Flanders and Germany, owe their foundation to its work—for example, Jumièges, St. Vandrille, Solignac and Corbie in France, Stavelot and Malmedy in Belgium, St. Gall and Dissentis in Switzerland, and Bobbio, the last foundation of Columbanus himself, in Italy. All through Central Europe the wandering Irish monks have left their traces, and the German Church still honours the names of St. Kilian, St. Gall, St. Fridolin and St. Corbinian among its founders.

It is easy to understand what an influence this movement must have exercised on the peasants. It was essentially rural, avoiding the towns, and seeking the wildest regions of forest and mountain. Far more than the preaching of bishop and priest from the distant city, the presence of these colonies of black-robed ascetics must have impressed the peasant mind with the sense of a new power that was stronger than the nature spirits of the old peasant religion. Moreover, the Irish monks were themselves countrymen with a deep feeling for nature and for the wild things. The biographer of Columban relates how, as he went through the forest, the squirrels and the birds would come to be caressed by him, and "would frisk about and gambol in great delight, like puppies fawning on their master." Indeed, the legends of the monastic saints are full of an almost Franciscan feeling for nature. It is true that the Celtic monastic ideal was that of the desert; they loved the forest or, better still, uninhabited and inaccessible islands, like Skellig Michael, one of the most impressive of monastic sites, just as the Eastern monks to-day still choose Mount Athos or the Meteora. Nevertheless, the monastic settlements were forced by necessity to take up the peasants' task, to clear the forest and to till the ground. The lives of the monastic saints of the Merovingian period, whether Gallic or Celtic, are full of references to their agricultural labours—their work of clearing the forest and of bringing back to cultivation the lands that had been abandoned during the period of the invasions. Many of them, like St. Walaric, the founder of St. Valery-sur-Somme, were themselves of peasant origin. Others, though noble by birth, spent their whole lives working as peasants, like St. Theodulph, the abbot of St. Thierry near Rheims, who would never cease from labour and whose plough was hung up in the church as a relic by the peasants.

These were the men to whom the conversion of the peasants was really due, for they stood so near to the peasant culture that they were able to infuse it with the spirit of the new religion. It was through them that the cultus that had been paid to the spirits of nature was transferred to the Saints. The sacred wells, the sacred trees and the sacred stones retained the devotion of the people, but they were consecrated to new powers, and acquired new associations. The peasants near Rheims paid honour to a holy tree, which was said to have sprung miraculously from the ox-goad which that same St. Theodulph thrust into the earth. In the West the stone crosses of the saints replaced the menhirs of the heathen cult, just as the great tumulus of Carnac has been crowned by a chapel of St. Michael, and a dolmen at Ploucret has been turned into a chapel of the Seven Saints. It was only with difficulty that the Church succeeded in putting down the old pagan customs, and it was usually done by providing a Christian ceremony to take the place of the heathen one. The statement in the *Liber Pontificalis* that St. Leo instituted the ceremonies of Candlemas in order to put an end to the Lupercalia is perhaps erroneous, but the Great Litanies and processions of April 25th seem to have taken the place of the Robigalia, and the feast of the Collection or *Oblatio* that of the opening of the Ludi Apollinares. Still more remarkable is the correspondence between the Ember Days and the seasonal pagan Feriae of the harvest, the vintage and the seedtime. The liturgy for the Advent Ember Days, especially, is full of references to the seedtime, which it associates with the mystery of the Divine Birth. "The Divine seed descends, and whereas the fruits of the field support our earthly life, this seed from on high gives our soul the Food of Immortality. The earth has yielded its corn, wine and oil, and now the ineffable Birth approaches of Him who through His mercy bestows the Bread of Life upon the Sons of God."

But this liturgical transfiguration of the spirit of the Vegetation Religion was too spiritual to reach the mind of the peasant. In spite of all the efforts of the Church the old pagan rites still survived and all through Europe the peasants continued to light the midsummer fires on St. John's Eve and to practise the magic ritual of fertility in spring. Even to-day, as Maurice Barrès has shown in *La Colline Inspirée*, the sinister powers of the old nature religion are still latent in the European countryside and are apt to reassert themselves whenever the control of the new order is relaxed. Nevertheless it is remarkable that it is just in those regions where the external survivals of pagan customs are most noticeable, as in Brittany and the Tirol, that the Christian ethos has affected the life of the peasant most deeply. For Christianity did succeed in remoulding the peasant culture. The old gods disappeared and their holy places were reconsecrated to the saints of the new religion. It is true that the cult of the local sanctuaries and their pilgrimages gave occasion to all kinds of strange survivals, as we see in the Breton Pardons to this day. But it was this very continuity of culture—this association of the old with the new—which opened the peasant mind to Christian influences that it could not receive in any other way. And the disappearance of the old peasant customs in later times has often been accompanied by a relapse into paganism of a far deeper kind than the paganism of archaeological survivals.

But the evangelisation of rural Europe during the Merovingian period is only one among the services which monasticism rendered to European civilisation. It was also destined to be the chief agent of the Papacy in its task of ecclesiastical reform

44

and to exert a vital influence on the political and cultural restoration of European society. The same period that saw the rise of Celtic monasticism in Ireland was also marked by a new development of monasticism in Italy which was to have an even greater historical importance. This was due to the work of St. Benedict "the Patriarch of the Monks of the West," who founded the monastery of Monte Cassino about the year 520. It was he who first applied the Latin genius for order and law to the monastic institution and who completed that socialisation of the monastic life which had been begun by St. Pachomius and St. Basil. The ideal of the monks of the desert was that of individual asceticism and their monasteries were communities of hermits. That of the Benedictine was essentially co-operative and social: its aim was not to produce heroic feats of asceticism, but the cultivation of the common life, "the school of the service of the Lord." In comparison with the rules of Pachomius and St. Columban, that of St. Benedict appears moderate and easy, but it involved a much higher degree of organisation and stability. The Benedictine monastery was a state in miniature with a settled hierarchy and constitution and an organised economic life. From the first it was a landowning corporation which possessed villas and serfs and vineyards, and the monastic economy occupies a larger place in the rule of St. Benedict than in any of the earlier rules. Hence the importance of co-operative labour which filled so large a part of the life of the Benedictine monk, for St. Benedict was inspired by the ideals which St. Augustine had set forth in his treatise *De opere monachorum* and had an equal detestation of the idle and "gyrovagous" monks who had done so much to bring monasticism into disrepute in the West.

But the primary duty of the monk was not manual labour, but prayer, above all the common recitation of the Divine Office, which St. Benedict terms "the work of God." Nor was study neglected. It was the monasteries which kept alive the classical tradition after the fall of the Empire. In fact the last representative in the West of the learned tradition of the Roman civil service—Cassiodorus—was also a founder of monasteries and the author of the first programme of monastic studies. It is true that the ostentatious literary culture of the old rhetorician at Vivarium was alien from the stern simplicity and spirituality which inspired the Benedictine rule, but Western monasticism was to inherit both traditions. Under the influence of the Papacy the rule of St. Benedict became the Roman standard of the monastic life and finally the universal type of Western monasticism. After the Celtic expansion came the Latin organisation.

The beginning of this Benedictine world mission was due to the action of St. Gregory, himself a Benedictine monk. It was from the Benedictine monastery on the Caelian that St. Augustine and his monks set out on their mission for the conversion of England, and the Benedictine monastery at Canterbury, probably the earliest Benedictine foundation outside Italy, became the starting point of a movement of religious organisation and unification which created a new centre of Christian civilisation in the West.

The appearance of the new Anglo-Saxon culture of the seventh century is perhaps the most important event between the age of Justinian and that of Charlemagne, for it reacted with profound effect on the whole continental development. In its origins it was equally indebted to the two forces that we have described—the Celtic monastic movement and the Roman Benedictine mission. Northern England was common ground to them both, and it was here that the new Christian culture arose in the years between 650 and 680 owing to the interaction and fusion of the two different elements. Christianity had been introduced into Northumbria by the Roman Paulinus who baptised King Edwin in 627 and established the metropolitan see at the old Roman city of York, but the defeat of Edwin by the heathen Penda and the Welsh Cadwallon led to the temporary ruin of the Anglian Church. It was re-established by King Oswald in 634 with the help of St. Aidan and the Celtic missionaries whom he brought from Iona to Lindisfarne, and throughout his reign Celtic influence reigned supreme. It was not until the synod of Whitby in 664 that the Roman party finally triumphed, owing to the intervention of St. Wilfrid, who dedicated his long and stormy life to the service of the Roman unity. It is to him and to his friend and fellow-worker, St. Benedict Biscop, that the establishment of Benedictine monasticism in Northern England is due. Nor was their activity solely of ecclesiastical importance; for they were the missionaries of culture as well as of religion, and they were responsible for the rise of the new Anglian art. They brought back from their many journeys to Rome and Gaul skilled craftsmen and architects, as well as book, pictures, vestments and musicians, and their abbeys of Ripon and Hexham, Wearmouth and Jarrow, were the great centres of the new culture. At the same time in the South, a similar work was being carried out by the Greek-Syrian archbishop, Theodore, and the African abbot, Hadrian, who were sent from Rome in 668. In them we can trace the appearance of a new wave of higher culture from the East, which does much to explain the rise of Anglo-Saxon scholarship and the superiority of the Latin of Bede and Alcuin to the barbarous style of Gregory of Tours or the Celtic author of the *Hisperica Famina.* The higher culture had survived far more in the Byzantine provinces of Africa and the East, and the storm of Arab invasion had brought an influx of refugees to the West, who played somewhat the same part in the seventh century as the Greek refugees from Constantinople in the fifteenth. From 685 to 752 the Roman see was occupied by a succession of Greeks and Syrians, many of them men of considerable character, and the oriental influence was at its height, not only at Rome but throughout the West. In the Anglian art of this period, the oriental influence is especially well marked. From about the year 670—probably as a result of the activity of Benedict Biscop—we find in place of the old Germanic art, a new school of sculpture and decoration, purely oriental in inspiration, and based on the Syrian motive of a vinescroll interwoven with the figures of birds or beasts, as we see it in the great series of Anglian crosses, especially the famous ones at Ruthwell and Bewcastle, which probably date from the beginning of the eighth century. That an Irish school of art also existed in Northumbria is proved by the magnificent Lindisfarne Book of Gospels, but there is no trace of its influence on architecture or sculpture. On the other hand the art of Saxon England is much more composite and shows the influence not only of the oriental style both in its Northumbrian and its Frankish Merovingian forms, but also that of Irish art.

Nevertheless, behind all these foreign influences there lies a foundation of native culture. The same age and district that produced the Anglian crosses also saw the rise of Anglo-Saxon literature. It was the age in which the old pagan story of Beowulf received its literary form, and even more characteristic of the time were the Christian poets, Caedmon, the shepherd of Whitby Abbey, whose romantic story is preserved by Bede, and Cynewulf, the author of several surviving poems, including *Andreas, Elene, Juliana* and, perhaps, also of the noble *Dream of the Rood,* a quotation from which is sculptured on the Ruthwell cross.

The rise of this vernacular literature no doubt owes something to the influence of Ireland where, as we have seen, a remarkable development of vernacular Christian culture was taking place at this time. But Anglo-Saxon literature has a very distinctive character which is neither Celtic nor Teutonic but all its own. It is marked by a characteristic melancholy which has nothing in common with the "Celtic melancholy" of literary tradition. It is the melancholy of a people living among the ruins of a dead civilisation whose thoughts dwell on the glories of the past and the vanity of human achievement.

But this native tradition is not necessarily Anglo-Saxon: it may go back further than that. Mr. Collingwood has explained the sudden flowering of Anglian art as due to a renaissance of the genius of the conquered people, and this seems even more probable in the case of the leaders of religion and culture. The almost entire absence of any remains of heathen Anglian settlements north of the Tees in Bernicia, the centre of Northumbrian power in the days of St. Oswald, is specially noteworthy. It suggests the probability of the survival of native elements in the very region that played so large a part in the history of the Anglian culture, *i.e.,* Tyneside and the east end of the Roman wall.

And the same holds good to a lesser degree of Wessex, both Aldhelm and Boniface being natives of regions not occupied by the Saxons in early times. The enthusiasm of the newly converted Anglo-Saxons for the Latin culture and the Roman order cannot have been merely fortuitous. A man like Bede, who represents the highest level of culture in the West between the fall of the Empire and the ninth century, cannot have been an artificial product of an Italian mission to Germanic barbarians; the appearance of such a type in Denmark, for example, even after its conversion, is inconceivable. The conversion of the Anglo-Saxons produced such a vital change in England because it meant the reassertion of the old cultural tradition after the temporary victory of barbarism. It was the return of Britain to Europe and to her past.

This was the reason why the Christian and monastic culture attained in England an independence and autonomy such as it did not possess on the continent except for a time in Spain. In the Frankish dominions the kingdom still kept some of the prestige of the ancient state, and exercised, as we have seen, considerable control over the Church. In England, the Church embodied the whole inheritance of Roman culture as compared with the weak and barbarous tribal states. It was the Church rather than the state that led the way to national unity through its common organisation, its annual synods and its tradition of administration. In the political sphere the Anglo-Saxon culture was singularly barren of achievement. The Northumbrian state fell into weakness and anarchy long before the fall of the Anglian art and culture. The popular conception of the Anglo-Saxon as a kind of mediaeval John Bull is singularly at variance with history. On the material side Anglo-Saxon civilisation was a failure; its chief industry seems to have been the manufacture and export of saints, and even Bede was moved to protest against the excessive multiplication of monastic foundations which seriously weakened the military resources of the state.

But, on the other hand, there has never been an age in which England had a greater influence on continental culture. In art and religion, in scholarship and literature, the Anglo-Saxons of the eighth century were the leaders of their age. At the time when continental civilisation was at its lowest ebb, the conversion of the Anglo-Saxons marked the turn of the tide. The Saxon pilgrims flocked to Rome as the centre of the Christian world and the Papacy found its most devoted allies and servants in the Anglo-Saxon monks and missionaries. The foundations of the new age were laid by the greatest of them all, St. Boniface of Crediton, "the Apostle of Germany," a man who had a deeper influence on the history of Europe than any Englishman who has ever lived. Unlike his Celtic predecessors, he was not an individual missionary, but a statesman and organiser, who was, above all, a servant of the Roman order. To him is due the foundation of the mediaeval German Church and the final conversion of Hesse and Thuringia, the heart of the German land. With the help of his Anglo-Saxon monks and nuns he destroyed the last strongholds of Germanic heathenism and planted abbeys and bishoprics on the site of the old Folkburgs and heathen sanctuaries, such as Buraburg, Amoneburg and Fulda. On his return from Rome in 739 he used his authority as Papal Vicar in Germany to reorganise the Bavarian Church and to establish the new dioceses which had so great an importance in German history. For Germany beyond the Rhine was still a land without cities, and the foundation of the new bishoprics meant the creation of new centres of cultural life. It was through the work of St. Boniface that Germany first became a living member of the European society.

This Anglo-Saxon influence is responsible for the first beginnings of vernacular culture in Germany. It is not merely that the Anglo-Saxon missionaries brought with them their custom of providing Latin texts with vernacular glosses, nor even that the earliest monuments of German literature—the old Saxon *Genesis* and the religious epic *Heliand*—seem to derive from the Anglo-Saxon literary tradition. It is that the very idea of a vernacular culture was alien to the traditions of the continental Church and was the characteristic product of the new Christian cultures of Ireland and England, whence it was transmitted to the continent by the missionary movement of the eighth century.

But in addition to this, Boniface was the reformer of the whole Frankish church. The decadent Merovingian dynasty had already given up the substance of its power to the mayors of the palace, but in spite of their military prowess, which saved France from conquest by the Arabs in 735, they had done nothing for culture and had only furthered the degradation of the Frankish Church. Charles Martel had used the abbeys and bishoprics to reward his lay partisans, and had carried out a wholesale secularisation of Church property. As Boniface wrote to the Pope, "Religion is trodden under foot. Benefices are given to greedy laymen or unchaste and publican clerics. All their crimes do not prevent their attaining the priesthood; at last rising in rank as they increase in sin they become bishops, and those of them who can boast that they are not adulterers or fornicators, are drunkards, given up to the chase, and soldiers, who do not shrink from shedding Christian blood." Nevertheless, the successors of Charles Martel, Pepin and Carloman, were favourable to Boniface's reforms. Armed with his special powers as Legate of the Holy See and personal representative of the Pope, he undertook the desecularisation of the Frankish Church.

In a series of great councils held between 742 and 747, he restored the discipline of the Frankish Church and brought it into close relations with the Roman see. It is true that Boniface failed to realise his full programme for the establishment of a regular system of appeals from the local authorities to Rome and for the recognition of the rights of the Papacy in the investure of the bishops. But, though Pepin was unwilling to surrender his control over the Frankish Church, he assisted St. Boniface in the reform of the Church and accepted his ideal of co-operation and harmony between the Frankish state and the Papacy. Henceforward the Carolingian dynasty was to be the patron of the movement of ecclesiastical reform, and found in the Church and the monastic culture the force that it needed for its work of political reorganisation. For it was the Anglo-Saxon monks and above all, St. Boniface who first realised that union of Teutonic initiative and Latin order which is the source of the whole mediaeval development of culture.

CHAPTER XIV

THE RISE OF THE MEDIAEVAL UNITY

The storm of barbarian invasion that fell upon Europe in the ninth century seems sufficient of itself to explain the premature decline of the Carolingian empire and the dissolution of the newly-acquired Western unity. Nevertheless, it is easy to exaggerate its importance. It was far from being the only influence at work; indeed, it is almost certain that the fortunes of the Carolingian Empire would have followed a similar course even if it had not had to undergo the attacks of the Vikings and the Saracens.

The germs of decay were inherent in the Carolingian state from its origins. For in spite of its imposing appearance, it was a heterogeneous structure without an internal and organic principle of unity. It claimed to be the Roman Empire, but it was in fact the Frankish monarchy, and so it embodied two contradictory principles, the universalism of the Roman and Christian traditions on the one hand, and the tribal particularism of barbaric Europe on the other. Consequently, in spite of its name, it bore little resemblance to the Roman Empire or the civilised states of the old Mediterranean world, it had much more in common with those barbaric Empires of the Huns and the Avars and the West Turks which were the ephemeral products of military conquest and which succeeded one another so rapidly during these centuries on the outskirts of the civilised world.

The Roman Empire of the Carolingians was a Roman Empire without the Roman law and without the Roman regions, without the City and without the Senate. It was a shapeless and unorganised mass with no urban nerve centres and no circulation of economic life. Its officials were neither civic magistrates nor trained civil servants, but merely territorial magnates and semi-tribal war leaders. And yet it was also the embodiment and representative of an ideal, and this ideal, in spite of its apparent failure, proved more durable and persistent than any of the military or political achievements of the period. It outlived the state to which it had given birth and survived through the anarchy that followed, to become the principal of the new order which arose in the West in the eleventh century.

The champions of this ideal were the great Carolingian churchmen, who played so large a part in the administration of the Empire and the determination of the imperial policy from the time of Charles the Great to that of his grandson Charles the Bald.

While the counts and secular magnates for the most part represented local and territorial interests, the leaders of the ecclesiastical party stood for the ideal of a universal Empire as the embodiment of the unity of Christendom and the defender of the Christian faith. Agobard of Lyons even ventures to attack the traditional Frankish principle of personal law and to demand the establishment of a universal Christian law for the universal Christian commonwealth. In Christ, he says, there is neither Jew nor Gentile, Barbarian nor Scythian, neither Aquintanians, nor Lombards, nor Burgundians, nor Allemanni. "If God has suffered in order that the wall of separation and enmity should be done away and that all should be reconciled in His Body, is not the incredible diversity of laws that reigns not only in every region or city, but in the same household and almost at the same table, in opposition to this divine work of unity?"

Thus the Emperor was no longer the hereditary chieftain and war leader of the Frankish people; he was an almost sacerdotal figure who had been anointed by the grace of God to rule over the Christian people and to guide and protect the Church. This involves, as we have seen, a strictly theocratic conception of kingship, so that the Carolingian Emperor was regarded, no less than the Byzantine Basileus, as the vicar of God and the head of the Church as well as of the state. Thus Sedulius Scotus (c. 850) speaks of the Emperor as being ordained by God as His vicar in the government of the Church and as having received power over both orders of rulers and subjects, while Cathulf goes so far as to say that the king stands in the place of God over all his people, for whom he has to account at the Last Day, while the bishop stands in the second place as the representative of Christ only.

But the Carolingian theocracy differed from the Byzantine in that it was a theocracy inspired and controlled by the Church. There was no lay bureaucracy such as existed in the Eastern Empire; its place was taken by the episcopate, from whose ranks the majority of the Emperor's advisers and ministers were drawn. Consequently, as soon as the strong hand of Charles the Great was removed, the theocratic ideal led to the exaltation of the spiritual power and the clericalisation of the Empire rather than to the subordination of the Church to the secular power.

The leaders of the clerical party were men who had played an important part in the inauguration of the new Empire, above all, Charles the Great's nephews, Adalhard and Wala of Corbie, and Agobard of Lyons. During the early years of Lewis the Pious, in spite of the temporary disgrace of Adalhard in 814, their ideals were in the ascendant. In 816 the sacred character of the Empire was solemnly reaffirmed by the coronation of Lewis by Pope Stephen at Rheims, and in the following year the unity of the empire was secured by the Constitution of Aix, which set aside the old Frankish rules of succession in favour of the Roman principle of undivided sovereignty. Lothair was to succeed his father as sole Emperor, and though his brothers Pepin and Lewis received in appanage kingdoms in Aquitaine and Bavaria, they were strictly subordinated to the imperial supremacy.

This settlement represented the triumph of the religious ideal of unity over the centrifugal forces in the national life; and consequently when Lewis, under the influence of his second wife, the Empress Judith, attempted to set it aside, so as to provide a third kingdom for their child, Charles, he met with the determined resistance not only of Lothair and the other interested parties, but also of the leaders of the ecclesiastical party. For the first time the Church intervened decisively in European politics by the part that it played in the dramatic events which culminated in the temporary deposition of Lewis the Pious in 833. The importance of this episode has been obscured by the natural sympathy that historians have felt for the unfortunate Lewis, deserted by his followers and humiliated by his children after the manner of King Lear, and they have consequently seen in the events of Colmar, "the Field of Lies," nothing but a shameful act of treachery dictated by selfishness and greed. Nevertheless, the movement of opposition to Lewis was not simply the work of time-serving prelates and courtiers; it was due to the action of idealists and reformers who stood for all that was highest in the Carolingian tradition; men such as Agobard, and Wala, Paschasius Radbertus, the theologian, Bernard of Vienne, and Ebbo of Rheims, the apostle of the North. The disinterestedness and sincerity of these men is evident from the writings of St. Agobard himself and of Paschasius Radbertus, who was also a personal witness of the events and whose life of Wala—the *Epitaphium Arsenii*—is regarded by Manitius as one of the most remarkable works of the Carolingian age.

Agobard was the representative of the Western tradition of Tertullian and St. Augustine in its most uncompromising form, and he is remarkable for the vigour with which he denounced popular superstitions, such as the belief in wizards and the practice of the ordeal, and maintained the rights of the Church and the supremacy of the spiritual power. Wala equally stood for the same principles, but in a less uncompromising fashion. He regarded the misfortunes of the Empire as due above all to the growing movement of secularisation that caused the Emperor to usurp the rights of the Church, while the bishops devoted themselves to affairs of state. This, however, did not prevent him from intervening in the question of the imperial succession, for the unity and peace of the Empire was in his eyes no mere question of secular policy. It was a moral issue, and therefore one on which it was the right and the duty of the Church to pronounce, even if this involved passing judgment on the Emperor himself. Consequently, when Pope Gregory IV, who had accompanied Lothair to Colmar, hesitated to infringe the traditional Byzantine conception of the imperial prerogative, it was Wala and Radbertus who reassured him by reminding him of his right as Vicar of God and St. Peter to judge all men and be judged by none, and eventually persuaded him to take the leading part in the proceedings which culminated in the deposition of the Emperor.

This episode marks the emergence of a new claim to the supremacy of the spiritual over the temporal power; and to the Church's right of intervention in the affairs of the state, which foreshadows the later mediaeval development. And it is significant that it originated not with the Papacy itself, but with the Frankish clergy, and was closely connected with the new theocratic conception of the state that was implicit in the Carolingian Empire. The state was no longer regarded as something distinct from the Church with independent rights and powers. It was itself a part, or rather an aspect, of the Church, which was, in the words of the letter of the bishops to Lewis the Pious in 829, "a single body divided under two supreme figures—that of the king and that of the priest." Thus the state could no longer be identified with the world and regarded as essentially unspiritual; it becomes itself an organ of the spiritual power in the world. Nevertheless, the older conception had entered so deeply into Christian thought, above all through the writings of St. Augustine, that it could not be entirely superseded, and thus throughout the Middle Ages, while the state insisted on its divine right as the representative of God in temporal affairs, it was always apt to be regarded by religious minds as a profane and worldly power that had no part in the sacred inheritance of the spiritual society.

In the Carolingian age, no doubt, so long as the Empire remained united, the Emperor was actually regarded as the representative of the principle of unity and the leader of the whole society. But with the division of the Carolingian inheritance among the sons of Lewis this ceased to be the case, and henceforward it was the episcopate that became the guardian of the imperial unity and the arbitrator and judge between the rival princes. The chief representative of this tendency in the second half of the ninth century was the great metropolitan of the West Frankish kingdom, Hincmar of Rheims, who was a redoubtable champion alike of the rights of the Church against the secular powers and of the cause of peace and unity in the Empire. But the same principles were admitted by the rulers themselves, notably by Charles the Bald, who recognises his dependence on the ecclesiastical power in the most unequivocal terms in the manifesto that he issued in 859, when an attempt was being made to depose him. He appeals to the sacred character of the authority that he had received as anointed king, and adds, "From this consecration I ought to be deposed by none, at least not without the hearing and judgment of the bishops by whose ministry I have been consecrated king, for they are the Thrones of God on whom God sits and by whom He passes judgment. To their paternal correction and chastising judgment I have always been ready to submit and do at present submit myself."

Here we see the coronation ceremony which had previously been of very secondary importance elevated into a new position as the ultimate basis of the royal power. In fact it is on this that Hincmar himself bases his argument for the supremacy of the spiritual power, for since it is the bishops that create the king, they are superior to him, and his power is an instrument in the hands of the Church, to be guided and directed by it towards its true end. But Hincmar's ideal of a theocratic Empire controlled by an oligarchy of metropolitans involved a conflict on the one hand with the universal authority of the Holy See, and on the other with the independent claims of the local episcopate. It was in the interests of the latter that the False Decretals, issued under the name of Isidore Mercator, were compiled, probably at Le Mans or elsewhere in the province of Tours between the years 847 and 852. These are the most important of all the forgeries of the Carolingian period, but they are by no means an exceptional phenomenon, for the scholars of that age devoted themselves to the forgery of ecclesiastical and hagiographical documents with no less enthusiasm and no more moral scruple than the Renaissance scholars showed in imitating the works of classical antiquity. Their attitude to history was indeed so radically different from our own that it is equally difficult for us to condemn or to excuse them. In the case of the False Decretals, however, the motive is clear enough. The author wished to establish by detailed and unequivocal evidence the rights of the local episcopate to appeal directly to Rome against their metropolitans, and to safeguard the indpendence of the Church against the secular power. But great as was their importance for the subsequent development of canon law and for the progress of ecclesiastical centralisation in the Middle Ages, it is impossible to regard them as directly responsible for the increased prestige of the Papacy in Western Europe in the ninth century. They were a result rather than a cause of that development, which had its roots in the conditions that we have just described.

And still less can we attribute any real influence on Papal policy to the other great forgery of the period—the Donation of Constantine—for it seems to have been unknown to the Popes of the ninth century, and it was not until the middle of the eleventh century that it was first used at Rome in support of the wider papal claims. It is indeed still very uncertain when or where it was composed and for what object. The old view that it was concocted at Rome in the eighth century (c. 775) in order to secure the independence of the states of the Church, is now sometimes questioned, and it seems possible that it dates from the same period as the False Decretals. Perhaps the most plausible view is that it was the work of that able and sinister man, Anastasius the Librarian, during the period after 848, when he was in exile from Rome and was intriguing with Lewis II for the papal chair. Such an act agrees well enough with the measureless ambition and the historical interests of that unscrupulous scholar, though at first sight it seems inconsistent with his connection with Lewis II. Nevertheless, the latter was ready enough to exalt the Papacy when it served his purpose, especially against the rival claims of the Byzantine Empire, and it was actually he who first asserted the view, adopted by the later mediaeval canonists, that the Emperor owes his dignity to his coronation and consecration by the Pope.

Thus the new position of social hegemony in Western Europe that the Papacy acquired at this period was thrust upon it from without rather than assumed by its own initiative. As Dr. Carlyle writes with regard to the rise of the Temporal Power, "Any one who studies the Papal correspondence and the Liber Pontificalis in the eighth century will, we think, feel that the leadership of the Roman *respublica* in the West was forced upon them (the Popes) rather than deliberately sought. It was only slowly and reluctantly that they drew away from the Byzantine authority, for after all, as civilised members of the Roman state, they preferred the Byzantine to the barbarian." In the same way in the ninth century the Papacy submitted to the control of the Carolingian Empire and even accepted the Constitution of 824, which made the Emperor the master of the Roman state and gave him practical control over the appointment of the Pope. Nevertheless, the bond of association with Carolingian Empire of itself increased the political importance of the Papacy, and as the Empire grew weaker and more divided, the Papacy came to be regarded as the supreme representative of Western unity. Thus there was a brief period between the political effacement of the Papacy under Charlemagne and Lothair and its enslavement to local factions in the tenth century, when it seemed prepared to take the place of the Carolingian dynasty as the leader of Western Christendom. The pontificate of Nicholas I (858-867) foreshadows the future achievements of the mediaeval Papacy. He withstood the greatest men of time, the emperors of the East and West, Hincmar, the leader of the Frankish episcopate, and Photius, the greatest of Byzantine patriarchs, and he successfully asserted the spiritual authority and independence of the Holy See even when the Emperor Lewis II attempted to impose his will by the use of armed force.

His successors were incapable of maintaining so lofty a position. Nevertheless, under John VIII (872-882), the Papacy was the one remaining bulwark of the Carolingian Empire, and it was due to the personal initiative of the Pope that Charles the Bald was crowned Emperor in the year 874, and Charles the Fat in 881. This final restoration of the Empire was, however, little more than an empty gesture. It was as different from the Empire of Charlemagne as the feeble and epileptic Charles the Fat was unlike his magnificent ancestor. In fact, the Empire no longer represented political realities and was in no position to act as the guardian of the Church and of civilisation. "We have looked for light," wrote the Pope, "and behold darkness! We seek succour, and we dare not emerge from the walls of the city in which there reigns an intolerable storm of persecution, because neither our spiritual son, the Emperor, nor any man of any nation brings us help." In 882 John VIII fell a victim to his enemies and Rome became the scene of a carnival of murder and intrigue which reached its climax in the ghoulish farce of 896, when the corpse of Pope Formosus was dragged from its tomb and submitted to a mock trial by his successor Stephen VI, who was himself to be murdered a few months later. Thus

Papacy and Empire alike slid down into the abyss of anarchy and barbarism which threatened to engulf the whole of western civilisation.

It is difficult to exaggerate the horror and confusion of the dark age that followed the collapse of the Carolingian experiment. The acts of the synod of Troslé in 909 give us some idea of the despair of the leaders of the Frankish Church at the prospect of the universal ruin of Christian society. "The cities," they wrote, "are depopulated, the monasteries ruined and burned, the country reduced to solitude." "As the first men lived without law or fear of God, abandoned to their passions, so now every man does what seems good in his own eyes, despising laws human and divine and the commands of the Church. The strong oppress the weak; the world is full of violence against the poor and of the plunder of ecclesiastical goods." "Men devour one another like the fishes in the sea."

In fact the fall of the Empire involved not only the disappearance of the scarcely achieved unity of Western Europe, but the dissolution of political society and the breaking up of the Carolingian states into a disorganised mass of regional units. Power fell into the hands of anyone who was strong enough to defend himself and his dependents from external attack. This was the origin of the new local and semi-national dynasties that make their appearance in the latter part of the ninth century owing to the work of men like Robert the Strong, the founder of the Capetian house, who fought strenuously against the Vikings of the Loire and the Seine; like Bruno, Duke of Saxony, who defended his land against the Danes and the Wends; or Boso of Provence, who was crowned king by the bishops and nobles of Burgundy in 879, because they needed a protector against both the Vikings of the North and the Saracens of the Mediterranean. But these kingdoms were no less weak and insecure than the Carolingian states, since they were exposed to the same centrifugal forces that destroyed the Empire. During the second half of the ninth century the local officials had emancipated themselves from the control of the central government, and the office of count and duke had become hereditary benefices and usurped all the privileges of royalty. In fact the count was for all practical purposes the king of his *pagus*, or canton. The one principle of the new society was the law of force and its correlative—the need for protection. Personal freedom was no longer a privilege, for the man without a lord became a man without a protector. Thus fealty and homage became the universal social relations, and the ownership of land became bound up with a complex of rights and obligations, both personal, military and juridical. In the same way the churches and monasteries were forced to find protectors, and these "advocates"—*Vögte, avoués*—acquired practical control over the lands and tenants of their clients. In short, the state and its public authority had become absorbed in the local territorial power. Political authority and private property were merged together in the new feudal relation, and the rights of jurisdiction and the duty of military service ceased to be universal public obligations and became annexed to the land as privileges or burdens of a particular tenure.

But though this evolution towards feudalism was the characteristic feature of the age, the feudalism of the tenth century was far from being the elaborately organised and symmetrical system that we find in Domesday Book or in the Assizes of Jerusalem. It was a much looser and more primitive organisation, a kind of compromise between the forms of an organised territorial state and the conditions of tribal society. The artificial administrative centralisation of the Carolingian period had disappeared, and there remained only the bare elements of barbaric society—the bonds of land and kinship and that which united the chief and his warriors. Thus the social bond that held feudal society together was the loyalty of warriors to their tribal chieftain rather than the public authority of the state; indeed, the society of the tenth century was in some respect more anarchic and barbarous than the old tribal society, for except in Germany, where the ancient tribal organisation still preserved its vitality, the traditional law and social spirit of the tribal society had disappeared, while the culture and political order of the Christian kingdom was too weak to take their place.

Nevertheless, the Church remained and continued to keep alive the traditions of higher civilisation. In so far as intellectual culture and civil life still survived, they existed in close dependence on the ecclesiastical society. For the state had lost all contact with the urban tradition and had become completely agrarian. The kings and nobles lived a semi-nomadic existence, subsisting on the resources of their lands and passing on from one estate to another in turn. Such a society had no use for towns, save for purely military purposes, and the so-called towns that came into existence at this period, like the *burgs* of Flanders and Germany and the *burhs* of Anglo-Saxon England, were in fact primarily fortresses and places of refuge, like the tribal strongholds of an earlier period. The old cities, on the other hand, were now almost wholly ecclesiastical in character. In the words of Professor Pirenne, "a theocratic government had completely replaced the municipal regimen of antiquity." They were ruled by the bishop and owed their importance to his cathedral and court and to the monasteries that lay within the city walls, or like St. Germain-des-Prés at Paris, and Westminster in London, in their immediate vicinity. They were the centre of administration of the diocese and of the episcopal and monastic estates, and their population consisted almost entirely of the clergy and their dependents. It was to provide for their needs that the market existed, and the great feasts of the ecclesiastical year attracted a large influx of population from outside. It was in fact a sacred city rather than a political or commercial organism.

In the same way, it was the Church, not the feudal state, that was the true organ of culture. Learning, literature, music and art all existed primarily in and for the Church, which was the representative of the Latin tradition of culture and order as well as of the moral and spiritual ideals of Christianity.

Moreover, all the social services which we regard as natural functions of the state, such as education and poor relief and the care of the sick, were fulfilled, in so far as they were fulfilled at all, by the action of the Church. In the Church every man had his place and could claim the rights of spiritual citizenship, whereas in the feudal state the peasantry had neither rights nor liberty and was regarded mainly as property, as part of the livestock that was necessary for the equipment of an estate.

Christopher Henry Dawson

It is impossible to understand early mediaeval culture on the analogy of modern conditions, which are based on the conception of the single all-inclusive society of the sovereign state. There were in fact two societies and two cultures in early mediaeval Europe. On the one hand, there was the peace-society of the Church, which was centred in the monasteries and episcopal cities and inherited the tradition of later Roman culture. And, on the other hand, there was the war-society of the feudal nobility and their following, whose life was spent in incessant wars and private feuds. Although the latter might be affected personally by the influence of the religious society, whose leaders were often their own kinsmen, they belonged socially to a more primitive order. They were the successors of the old tribal aristocracies of barbarian Europe, and their ethos was that of the tribal warrior. At the best they preserved a certain rude measure of social order and protected their subjects from external aggression. But in many cases they were purely barbarous and predatory, living in their strongholds, as a mediaeval chronicler writes, "like beasts of prey in their dens," and issuing forth to burn their neighbours' villages and to hold the passing traveller to ransom.

The vital problem of the tenth century was whether this feudal barbarism was to capture and absorb the peace-society of the Church, or whether the latter could succeed in imposing its ideals and its higher culture on the feudal nobility, as it had formerly done with the barbarian monarchies of the Anglo-Saxons and the Franks.

At first sight the prospects seemed even more unfavourable then they had been in the age that followed the barbarian invasions, for now the Church itself was in danger of being engulfed in the flood of barbarism and feudal anarchy. Princes and nobles took advantage of the fall of the Empire to despoil the churches and monasteries of the wealth that they had accumulated during the previous period. In Bavaria, Arnulf carried out a wholesale secularisation of church lands, as Charles Martel had done in the Frankish kingdom at the close of the Merovingian period, and the Bavarian monasteries lost the greater part of their possessions. In the West things were even

63

worse, since the monasteries had been almost ruined by the ravages of the Northmen; and the feudalisation of the West Frankish kingdom left the Church at the mercy of the new military aristocracy, who used its resources to create new fiefs for their followers. Hugh Capet was lay abbot of most of the richest abbeys in his dominions, and the same policy was followed on a smaller scale by every local potentate.

Thus the development of feudalism had reduced the Church to a state of weakness and disorder even greater than that which had existed in the decadent Merovingian state before the coming of St. Boniface. Bishops and abbots received investiture from the prince like other feudatories and held their benefices as "spiritual fiefs" in return for military service. The higher offices had become the prerogative of the members of the feudal aristocracy, many of whom, like Archimbald, the tenth-century Archbishop of Sens, wasted the revenues of their sees on their mistresses and boon companions. Even in the monasteries the rule of chastity was no longer strictly observed, while the secular clergy lived openly as married men and often handed on their curés to their sons.

Worst of all, the Church could no longer look to Rome for moral guidance and spiritual leadership, for the Papacy itself had fallen a victim to the same disease that was attacking the local churches. The Holy See had become the puppet of a demoralised and truculent oligarchy, and under the rule of Theophylact and the women of his house, above all, the great Marozia the Senatrix, mistress, mother and murderess of Popes, it reached the lowest depths of degradation.

Nevertheless, the state of affairs was not so hopeless as one might conclude from the spectacle of all these scandals and abuses. They were the birth-pangs of a new society, and out of the darkness and confusion of the tenth century the new peoples of Christian Europe were born. The achievements of the Carolingian culture were not altogether lost. Their tradition remained and was capable of being applied anew to the circumstances of the regional and national societies wherever there was any constructive force that could make use of them. Above all, the forces of order found a rallying-point and a principle of leadership in the Carolingian ideal of Christian royalty. The kingship was the one institution that was common to the two societies and embodied the traditions of both cultures. For while the king was the lineal successor of the tribal chieftain and the war leader of the feudal society, he also inherited the Carolingian tradition of theocratic monarchy and possessed a quasi-sacredotal character owing to the sacred rites of coronation and anointment. He was the natural ally of the Church, and found in the bishops and the monasteries the chief foundations of his power. And this dual character of mediaeval kingship is represented by two sharply contrasted types of ruler. There are the war-kings, like Sweyn of Denmark, or Harold Hadrada, whose nominal profession of Christianity does not prevent them from following in all things the traditions of the barbarian warrior; and there are the peace-kings and royal saints, like Wenceslas of Bohemia, and Edward the Confessor, and Robert II of France, who are entirely the servants of the spiritual society and live the life of crowned monks. But it is rare to find either element existing in so pure a form as in these examples, and the normal type of mediaeval royalty embodies both characters, as we see in the case of monarchs like St. Olaf and Canute, the Saxon emperors, and the great kings of Wessex.

The last are of peculiar importance, since they were the first to attempt the task of national reconstruction in the spirit of the Carolingian tradition and to inaugurate that alliance between the national monarchy and the national church which is the characteristic feature of the period. So complete was the fusion in Wessex that the synods and councils of the Anglo-Saxon church became merged in the secular assemblies, and the ecclesiastical legislation of the tenth and eleventh centuries is the work of the king and his council, in which, however, the churchmen took the most prominent place. In the same way it was the king who took the initiative in the reform of the Church and in the restoration of monastic life which had been almost destroyed by the Danish invasions. Moreover, it is in Wessex, even more clearly than elsewhere, that we can trace the growth of a new vernacular culture on the basis of the Carolingian tradition under the patronage of the national monarchy. For King Alfred's remarkable translations of St. Gregory and Orosius and Boethius and Bede, which he carried out with the help of foreign scholars, "Plegmund my archbishop, and Asser my bishop, and Grimbald and John, my mass priests," actually represent a deliberate attempt to adapt the Christian classical culture, which had been confined to the international world of Latin culture, to the needs of the new national culture. "For it seems good to me," he writes in his preface to St. Gregory's *Pastoral Care,* or *"Herd Book,"* "that we also should turn some of the books that all men ought to know into that language that we can all understand, and so bring it about, as we easily may with God's aid if only we have peace, that all the youth of England, sons of free men who have the wherewithal, shall be set to learning before they are fit for other things, until they can read English writing well; and let those whom one wishes to educate further and to advance to a higher rank afterwards be instructed in the Latin language."

The work of restoration which was inaugurated by Alfred and his successors in the Anglo-Saxon kingdom was carried out on a far larger scale and with more permanent results by the Saxon kings in German. Indeed it is possible that the latter owed something to the example of their English predecessors, for Henry the Fowler allied himself to the house of Alfred by the marriage of his son Otto I with the daughter of Athelstan, and there are features in his policy in which historians have seen the influence of Anglo-Saxon precedents. Nevertheless, Henry himself was an unlettered barbarian, who cared nothing for culture, who showed little favour to the Church, and who ruled Germany as the warrior leader of a tribal confederation. His power rested not on the universal claims of the Carolingian monarchy, but on the loyalty of his fellow Saxons, who still preserved their old tribal organisation and traditions in a purer form than any of the other peoples of Germany. The strength of this tribal feeling may be seen in Widukind's *History of the Saxons,* which is inspired throughout by a spirit of purely tribal patriotism, although it is the work of a monk of Corvey, the headquarters of ecclesiastical culture in the region, and dates from after the revival of the empire.

Christopher Henry Dawson

It was Henry's son Otto I who was the first to recover the Carolingian tradition and unite it with the tribal patriotism of the Saxon people. In contrast to his father, he was not satisfied with his election by the secular magnates, but took care to be crowned and anointed according to the solemn ecclesiastical rites at Aix, the old capital of the Empire, and he inaugurated the policy of close co-operation with the Church which was to make the episcopate the strongest foundation of secular government. For the bishop was no longer merely a coadjutor and overseer of the local count; he had begun to acquire the dual character of the mediaeval prince-bishop, the ruler of an ecclesiastical principality. This system was, of course, irreconcilable with the spiritual independence of the Church and the canonical principle of episcopal election, since it was essential for the ruler to keep the appointment of bishops in his own hands, as they had become the only reliable instruments of royal administration. In Lorraine, for example, the dukedom was held by Bruno, the Archbishop of Cologne, the brother of Otto I, and it was the bishops who controlled the disorderly feudal nobility and maintained the royal authority throughout the whole territory.

Nevertheless, this fusion between the Church and the royal power did not merely result in the secularisation of the former; it also lifted the monarchy out of the restricted environment of the tribal polities and brought it into relation with the universal society of Western Christendom. The Papacy, for all its weakness and degradation, remained the head of the Church, and the ruler who wished to control the Church, even in his own domains, was forced to secure the co-operation of Rome. And even apart from this the whole weight of Carolingian precedent and tradition forced the new kingdom towards Rome and the imperial crown.

Modern nationalist historians may look on the restoration of the Empire as a regrettable sacrifice of the true interests of the German kingdom to an impracticable ideal. But for the statesmen of the time, Christendom was just as much a reality as Germany, and the restoration of the Carolingian monarchy in Germany found its natural fulfillment in the restoration of the Christian Empire. It is true that an interval of thirty-seven years had gone by since the death of the last nominal emperor, but for the greater part of that time Rome had been in the power of Alberic, the greatest of the house of Theophylact, who had been strong enough to keep possible rivals at a distance and to appoint a succession of Popes who were not unworthy of their office. His son, the infamous Pope John XII, was however, incapable of taking his father's place and was driven to follow the example of the Popes of the eighth century, and call on the German king for help against the kingdom of Italy.

Consequently Otto I was undertaking no novel adventure, but merely treading a well-worn and familiar path when he answered the appeal of the Pope, like so many rulers before him, and entered Italy in 961 to receive the imperial crown. But none the less his coming produced a profound change in the European situation. It brought Northern Europe once more into contact with the civilised world of the Mediterranean from which it had been so long divorced. For Italy, in spite of its political disorder, was now at last entering on a period of economic and cultural revival. The rich trading cities of the South and the Adriatic—Naples, Amalfi, Salern, Ancona and Venice—were in close relation with the higher civilisation of the Eastern Mediterranean and were largely Byzantine in culture, and their influence had a stimulating effect on the economic and social life of the rest of the peninsula, especially on the cities of the Lombard plain and of Romagna.

And this revival of Italian culture was accompanied by a reawakening of national feeling and of the old civic traditions. Venice was arising in the splendour of her youth under the first of her great doges, Peter Orseolo II, while even rulers like Alberic and Crescentius attempted to recall the memory of Rome's past greatness.

In the cities of Italy the old traditions of secular culture still survived. They alone in the West still possessed lay schools in which the grammarians kept alive the old ideals of the classical schools of rhetoric. They produced scholars, such as Liudprand of Cremona, Leo of Vercelli, and Stephen and Gunzo of Novarra, who rivalled the monastic scholars of the North in their learning, and far surpassed them in the quickness of their wits and the sharpness of their tongues, as we see in the amazing epistle in which Gunzo overwhelms an unlucky monk of St. Gall, who had ventured to criticise his grammar, with a torrent of mingled erudition and abuse. The persistence of classical and even pagan influences in Italian culture is also shown in the curious story of Vilgard, the grammarian of Ravenna, who was a martyr to his belief in the literal inspiration of the sacred poets, Horace, Virgil and Juvenal, and appears in a more attractive form in the charming little poem, *"O admirabile Veneris idolum"* composed by an unknown clerk of Verona. No doubt this only represents one aspect of Italian culture, which was by no means lacking in religious elements. The very poet whom I have just mentioned was, according to Manitius, also the author of *"O Roma Nobilis,"* that classic expression of the Christian ideal of Rome, and the same ideal inspires the remarkable poem on the procession on the feast of the Assumption—*Sancta Maria quid est?*—dating from the time of Otto III, which is almost the only literary product of the Roman culture of that age which we possess.

Nevertheless, as in the fifteenth century, the revival of Italian culture and its complete independence of the North were undoubtedly accompanied by a movement of religious decline and moral disorder. The holy See had become the slave of nepotism and political factions, and had lost its international position in Christendom. And its situation was the more perilous inasmuch as the Church north of the Alps was being affected by the new moral ideals of the movement of monastic reform and had begun to set its own house in order. At the council of Saind-Basle de Verzy in 991 the French bishops openly declared their belief in the bankruptcy of the Papacy. "Is it to such monsters (as Pope John XII or Boniface VII), swollen with their ignominy and devoid of all knowledge human or divine, that the innumerable-priests of God throughout the world who are distinguished by their knowledge and virtues should lawfully be submitted?" asks their spokesman, Arnoul of Orleans. "We seem to be witnessing the coming of Antichrist, for this is the falling away of which the apostle speaks, not of nations but of the churches."

If Italy had remained isolated from Northern Europe, Rome would have naturally gravitated towards the Byzantine Empire, as was indeed the deliberate policy of Alberic and other leaders of the Roman aristocracy, and there would have been a real danger that the eleventh century would have witnessed a schism, not between Rome and Byzantium, but between the old world of the Mediterranean and the East and the young peoples of Northern Europe. Actually, however, this danger did not materialise. The Northern movement of reform did not turn against the Papacy, as in the sixteenth century, but became its ally and co-operated with it to renew the religious life of Western Christendom; and the first representative of this movement to occupy the Papal chair and to prepare the way for the new age was the very man who was the representative of the Gallican party at the council of Saint-Basle and recorded its anti-Roman pronouncements, Gerbert of Aurillac.

This change, however, could never have taken place had it not been for the existence of the Western Empire. It was the coming of the Empire that rescued the Papacy from its servitude to local factions and restored it to Europe and to itself. It is true that the restoration of the Empire seemed at first to mean nothing more than the subjugation of the Papacy to a German prince in place of a local magnate. Nevertheless, the new conditions inevitably changed the horizon of imperial policy and brought with them wider and more universal aims. The Empire gradually lost its Saxon character and became an international power. Otto I married the Burdundian-Italian Queen Adelaide, while their son Otto II was the husband of a Greek princess, Theophano, who brought with her to the West the traditions of the Byzantine imperial court. Thus the offspring of their marriage, Otto III, united in his person the twofold tradition of the Christian Empire in its Carolingian and Byzantine form. From his mother and from the Calabrian Greek, Philagathus, he received the influence of the higher culture of the Byzantine world, while his tutor, Bernward of Hildesheim, at once a scholar, an artist and a statesman, represented all that was best in the Carolingian tradition of the North. Moreover, he was intensely sensitive to the higher spiritual influences of the time as we see from his personal friendship with St. Adalbert of Prague, and his relations with the leading ascetics of Italy, St. Romuald and St. Nilus.

With such a character and such an upbringing it is not surprising that Otto III should have conceived an imperialism that was Byzantine rather than Germanic, and that he should have devoted his life to the realisation of its universal claims and ideals. It was in pursuance of this end that he broke with the tradition of centuries by making his youthful cousin Bruno Pope, instead of a member of the Roman clergy. But it was not in Bruno, but in Gerbert, the most learned and brilliant scholar of the age, that he found a true kindred spirit who was capable of co-operating with him in his life's work. Hitherto he had been conscious of the inferiority of Western culture in comparison with Greek civilisation and refinement. It was Gerbert who taught him that it was the West and not Byzantium that was the true heir of the Roman tradition and who inspired him with the desire to recover this ancient inheritance. "Let it not be thought in Italy," wrote Gerbert, "that Greece alone can boast of the Roman power and of the philosophy of its Emperor. Ours, yea ours, is the Roman Empire! Its strength rests on fruitful Italy and populous Gaul and Germany and the valiant kingdoms of the Scythians. Our Augustus art thou, O Caesar, the emperor of the Romans who, sprung of the noblest blood of the Greeks, surpasses the Greeks in power, controls the Romans by right of inheritance and overcomes both alike in wisdom and eloquence."

Consequently when the early death of Bruno made it possible for Gerbert to succeed him as Pope Sylvester II, Otto proceeded with his help to carry out his plans for the renewal of the Empire and the restoration of Rome to its rightful place as the imperial city and the centre of the Christian world. His attempt, and still more the Byzantine forms in which it was embodied, has, it is true, aroused the derision of modern historians, who see in it nothing but a piece of childish make-belief, cloaked in Byzantine forms. But in reality Otto's policy, though without political results, had far more historical significance than any of the practical achievements of contemporary politicians, for it marks the emergence of a new European consciousness. All the forces that went to make up the unity of mediaeval Europe are represented in it—the Byzantine and Carolingian traditions of the Christian Empire and the ecclesiastical universalism of the Papacy, the spiritual ideals of monastic reformers, such as St. Nilus and St. Romuald, and the missionary spirit of St. Adalbert, the Carolingian humanism of Gerbert, and the national devotion of Italians like Leo of Vercelli to the Roman idea. Thus it marks the point at which the traditions of the past age flow together and are merged in the new culture of the mediaeval West. It looks back to St. Augustine and Justinian, and forward to Dante and the Renaissance. It is true that Otto III's ideal of the Empire as a commonwealth of Christian peoples governed by the concordant and interdependent authorities of Emperor and Pope was never destined to be realised in practice; nevertheless, it preserved a kind of ideal existence like that of a Platonic form, which was continually seeking to attain material realisation in the life of mediaeval society. For the ideal of Otto III is precisely the same ideal that was to inspire the thought of Dante, and throughout the intervening centuries it provided an intelligible formula in which the cultural unity of mediaeval Europe found conscious expression. Nor was it as sterile in practical results as it is usually supposed, for the short years of Otto and Gerbert's joint rule saw the rise of the new Christian peoples of Eastern Europe. It was due to their action, inspired in part by Otto's devotion to the memory of his Bohemian friend, St. Adalbert, that the Poles and the Hungarians were freed from their dependence on the German state-church and given their own ecclesiastical organisation which was the indispensable condition for the independence of their national cultures.

This marks a vital modification in the Carolingian imperial tradition. The unity of Christendom was no longer conceived as the unity of an imperialist autocracy, a kind of Germanic Tsardom, but as a society of free peoples under the presidence of the Roman Pope and Emperor. Hitherto conversion to Christianity had involved political dependence and the destruction of national tradition, and this is the reason why the Wends and the other Baltic peoples had offered so stubborn a resistance to the Church. But the close of the tenth century saw the birth of a new series of Christian states extending from Scandinavia to the Danube. The eleventh century saw the passing of Northern paganism and the incorporation of the whole of Western Europe into the unity of Christendom. And at the same time the long winter of the Dark Ages had reached its end, and everywhere throughout the West new life was stirring, new social and spiritual forces were awakening, and Western society was emerging from the shadow of the East and taking its place as an independent unity by the side of the older civilisations of the oriental world.

CONCLUSION

It is impossible to draw an abrupt line of division between one period and another, above all in the history of so vast and complex a process as the rise of a civilisation; and consequently the date which I have chosen to mark the end of this survey is a matter of practical convenience rather than of scientific definition. Nevertheless there is no doubt that the eleventh century marks a decisive turning-point in European history—the end of the Dark Ages and the emergence of Western culture. The previous revivals of culture in the age of Justinian and that of Charlemagne had been partial and temporary, and they had been followed by periods of decline, each of which seemed to reduce Europe to a lower stage of barbarism and confusion than it had known before. But with the eleventh century a movement of progress begins which was to continue almost without intermission down to modern times. This movement shows itself in new forms of life in every field of social activity—in trade and civic life and political organisation, as well as in religion and art and letters. It laid the foundations of the modern world not only by the creation of institutions that were to remain typical of our culture, but above all by the formation of that society of peoples which, more than any mere geographical unit, is what we know as Europe.

This new civilisation was, however, still far from embracing the whole of Europe, or even the whole of Western Europe. At the beginning of the eleventh century Europe was still, as it had been for centuries, divided up between four or five distinct culture-provinces, of which Western Christendom appeared by no means the most powerful or the most civilised. There was the Nordic culture of north-western Europe, which was just beginning to become part of Christendom, but still preserved an independent tradition of culture. In the South there was the Western Moslem culture of Spain and North Africa, which embraced practically the whole basin of the Western Mediterranean. In the East, the Byzantine culture dominated the Balkans and the Aegean and still possessed a foothold in the West through South Italy and the Adriatic and the Italian trading cities, such as Venice and Amalfi and Pisa; while further north, from the Black Sea to the White Sea and the Baltic, the world of the Slavs, the Balts and the Finno-Ugrian peoples was still mainly pagan and barbarous, though it was beginning to be affected by influences from the Byzantine culture of the South, the Nordic culture of Scandinavia and the Moslem culture of Central Asia and the Caspian.

Thus the culture that we regard as characteristically Western and European was confined in the main within the limits of the former Carolingian Empire, and found its centre in the old Frankish territories of Northern France and Western Germany. In the tenth century it was, as we have seen, hard pressed on every side and even tended to contract its frontiers. But the eleventh century saw the turn of the tide and the rapid expansion of this central continental culture in all directions. In the West the Norman Conquest took England out of the sphere of the Nordic culture that had threatened for two centuries to absorb it, and incorporated it into the continental society; in the North and East it gradually dominated the Western Slavs and penetrated Scandinavia by its cultural influence; while in the South it embarked with crusading energy on the great task of the reconquest of the Mediterranean from the power of Islam.

In this way the peoples of the Frankish Empire imposed their social hegemony and their ideals of culture on all the surrounding peoples, so that the Carolingian unity may be regarded without exaggeration as the foundation and starting-point of the whole development of mediaeval Western civilisation. It is true that the Carolingian Empire had long lost its unity, and France and Germany were becoming more and more conscious of their national differences. Nevertheless they both looked back to the same Carolingian tradition, and their culture was compounded of the same elements, though the proportions were different. They were still in essence the Western and East Frankish realms, though, like brothers who take after different sides of their family, they were often more conscious of their difference than of their resemblance. In both cases, however, the cultural leadership lay with the intermediate regions—the territories of the Empire that were most Latinised, and those in France where the Germanic element was strongest: Northern France, Lorraine and Burgundy, Flanders and the Rhineland. Above all, it was Normandy, where the Nordic and Latin elements stood in sharpest contrast and most immediate contact, that was the leader of the movement of expansion.

It was this middle territory, reaching from the Loire to the Rhine, that was the true homeland of mediaeval culture and the source of its creative and characteristic achievements. It was the cradle of Gothic architecture, of the great mediaeval schools, of the movement of monastic and ecclesiastical reform and of the crusading ideal. It was the centre of the typical development of the feudal state, of the North European communal movement and of the institution of knighthood. It was here that a complete synthesis was finally achieved between the Germanic North and the spiritual order of the Church and the traditions of the Latin culture. The age of the Crusades saw the appearance of a new ethical and religious ideal which represents the translation into Christian forms of the old heroic ideal of the Nordic warrior culture. In *The Song of Roland* we find the same motives that inspired the old heathen epic—the loyalty of a warrior to his lord, the delight in war for its own sake, above all the glorification of honourable defeat. But all this is now subordinated to the service of Christendom and brought into relation with Christian ideas. Roland's obstinate refusal to sound his horn is entirely in the tradition of the old poetry, but in the death scene the defiant fatalism of the

Nordic heroes, such as Hogni and Hamdis, has been replaced by the Christian attitude of submission and repentance.

"Towards the land of Spain he turned his face, so that Charles and all his army might perceive that he died as a valiant vassal with his face towards the foe. Then did he confess him in right zealous wise and hold forth his glove to heaven for his transgressions."

It is true that the heroic ideal had already found expression in the literature of the Christian peoples, above all in the noble Lay of Maldon with its great lines: "Thought shall be harder, heart the keener, courage the greater, as our might lessens." But here there is as yet but slight trace of Christian sentiment. The old tradition still survives intact. Indeed, throughout the Dark Ages, Western Society had been characterised by an ethical dualism that corresponds to the dualism of culture. There was one ideal for the warrior and another for the Christian, and the former still belonged in spirit to the barbaric world of northern paganism. It was not until the eleventh century that the military society was incorporated into the spiritual polity of Western Christendom by the influence of the crusading ideal. The institution of knighthood is the symbol of the fusion of Nordic and Christian traditions in the mediaeval unity, and it remains typical of Western society from the time of *The Song of Roland* to the day when its last representative Bayard, "the good knight," died like Roland with his face to the Spaniards at the passage of the Sesia, in the age of Luther and Machiavelli. For the Middle Ages are the age of Nordic Catholicism, and they endured only as long as the alliance continued between the Papacy and the North—an alliance which had been inaugurated by Boniface and Pepin and consolidated by the work of the northern movement of ecclesiastical reform in the eleventh century, which had its source in Lorraine and Burgundy. This alliance was first broken by another Boniface and another king of the Franks at the close of the thirteenth century, but though it never wholly recovered its strength it remained the corner-stone of Western unity, until the time when the Papacy became completely Italianised and the peoples of the North ceased to be Catholic.

Christopher Henry Dawson

But though mediaeval culture was the culture of the Christian North, its face was turned, like Roland's, to the Islamic South, and there was not a land from the Tagus to the Euphrates in which the northern warriors had not shed their blood. Norman princes ruled in Sicily and Antioch, Lorrainers in Jerusalem and Edessa, Burgundians in Portugal and Athens, Flemings in Constantinople; and the ruins of their castles in the Peloponnese and Cyprus and Syria still bear witness to the power and enterprise of the Frankish barons.

This contact with the higher civilisation of the Islamic and Byzantine world had a decisive influence on Western Europe and was one of the most important elements in the development of mediaeval culture. It showed itself, on the one hand, in the rise of the new aristocratic courtly culture and the new vernacular literature, and, on the other, in the assimilation of the Graeco-Arabic scientific tradition and the rise of a new intellectual culture in the West. And these influences remained in the ascendant until they were checked by the Renaissance of the classical tradition, which coincided with the Turkish conquest of the East and the separation of Western Europe from the Islamic world. With the ending of the Middle Ages, Europe turned its back on the East and began to look westward to the Atlantic.

Thus the mediaeval unity was not permanent, since it was based on the union of the Church and the Northern peoples, with a leaven of oriental influences. Nevertheless its passing did not mean the end of European unity. On the contrary, Western culture became more autonomous, more self-sufficient and more *occidental* than ever before. The loss of spiritual unity did not involve the separation of the West into two exclusive and alien cultural units, as would almost certainly have been the case if it had occurred four or five centuries earlier. In spite of religious disunion, Europe retained its cultural unity, but this was now based on a common intellectual tradition and a common allegiance to the classical tradition rather than on a common faith. The Latin grammar took the place of the Latin Liturgy as the bond of intellectual unity, and the scholar and the gentleman took the place of the monk and the knight as the representative figures of Western culture. The four centuries of Nordic Catholicism and oriental influence were followed by four centuries of Humanism and occidental autonomy. To-day Europe is faced with the breakdown of the secular and aristocratic culture on which the second phase of its unity was based. We feel once more the need for spiritual or at least moral unity. We are conscious of the inadequacy of a purely humanist and occidental culture. We can no longer be satisfied with an aristocratic civilisation that finds its unity in external and superficial things and ignores the deeper needs of man's spiritual nature. And at the same time we no longer have the same confidence in the inborn superiority of Western civilisation and its right to dominate the world. We are conscious of the claims of the subject races and cultures, and we feel the need both for protection from the insurgent forces of the oriental world and for a closer contact with its spiritual traditions. How these needs are to be met, or whether it is possible to meet them, we can at present only guess. But it is well to remember that the unity of our civilisation does not rest entirely on the secular culture and the material progress of the last four centuries. There are deeper traditions in Europe than these, and we must go back behind Humanism and behind the superficial triumphs of modern civilisation, if we wish to discover the fundmental social and spiritual forces that have gone to the making of Europe.

Romano Guardini
1885-1968

Romano Guardini was born in Verona, Italy, but grew up mostly in Mainz, Germany, where his father was Italian consul. This combination of Italian and German elements has often been pointed to in partial explanation of the fruitful tension characterizing his thought. In a time of increasing specialization he remained a remarkable universalist with a commitment to the totality of the life of the mind.

Chemistry and economics were his first pursuits at the university, but then he turned to theology and was ordained a priest in 1910. By then he had studied at three great universities: Tübingen, Berlin, and Freiburg. His doctoral dissertation was on St. Bonaventure's doctrine of redemption. He was already well aware of the current of Western thought in which he was most at home, that which leads from Plato to Augustine on to Bonaventure. This stream with its mystical strain and sensitivity to value and perfection he balanced with his concern for the realities of history. The dialectical nature of his thought was evident as early as 1914 when he published The Antithesis, *dealing with the problem of knowledge.*

From 1923 to 1939 he occupied a chair created for him at the University of Berlin. He was "Professor for the philosophy of religion and the Catholic worldview" until terminated by the Nazis. After the war he was for a short time at Tübingen, but in

1948 went to Munich where he remained until his retirement in 1963.

Guardini was one of the giants inspiring the Catholic renewal that got under way between the wars. With The Spirit of the Liturgy *in 1918 and* The Church and the Catholic *in 1923 he proved himself one of the earliest and most influential of the precursors of Vatican II. His opening words to the latter book became famous: "A religious process of incalculable importance has begun—the Church is coming to life in the souls of men." He had a knack for identifying and clearly expressing precisely those aspects of spirituality that evoked the most positive response among the people of his time.*

In an era when the understanding of the Church was largely in juridical terms, Guardini called for a deeper theology. "The Church," he insisted, "is the original principle from which the life of the individual comes; it is the ground which supports him, the atmosphere which he breathes . . . The Church is a living whole which penetrates the individual." All types of individualism or provincialism are anti-Christian. "It is time to realize that all divisions have only a methodological value . . . It is time for us to consider the whole as a whole. In the process we shall preserve all that has been won in the long, sustained effort of previous centuries."

The Church and the Catholic *consists of five chapters and an epilogue. The selection that follows contains chapters 3 and 4. Written nearly forty years before Vatican II, their spirit is clearly much closer to the work of that Council than of Vatican I. Guardini was one of that handful of people who raised the sights and the tempo of Catholic theology until the movement for renewal gathered enough momentum to result in a new vision for all.*

THE CHURCH
AND THE CATHOLIC

CHAPTER 3

THE WAY TO BECOME HUMAN

We propose to consider the meaning of the Church. I have already attempted to sketch it in general outline. For the individual the Church is the living presupposition of his personal perfection. She is the way to personality. Before, however, we go into details, allow me to make a preliminary observation. When I tried to explain the Church's significance for individual personality, objections, perhaps, came into your minds. Your inner glance saw many defects confronting it. Your thought travelled back to many personal disillusionments, and therefore you possibly felt that what I said was untrue. You thought that what I said was indeed true of the ideal, of a spiritual church, but that the actual Church is not, and does not accomplish, what I was maintaining. I owe you an answer to this objection. Those who could speak of the meaning of the Church must also speak of her defects. Even the Church cannot escape the tragedy inherent in all things human, which arises from the fact that infinite values are bound up with what is human and consequently imperfect. Truth is bound up with human understanding and teaching; the ideal of perfection with its human presentation; the law and form of the community with their human realisation; grace, and even God Himself—remember the Sacrifice of the Mass—bound up with actions performed by men. The Infinitely Perfect blends with the finite and imperfect. This, if we dare say it, is the tragedy of the eternal Himself, for he must submit Himself to all this if He is to enter the sphere of humanity. And it is the tragedy of man, for he is obliged to accept these human defects, if he would attain the Eternal. All this is as applicable to the Church, as to every institution that exists among human beings. But in her case it has an additional poignancy.

For the highest values are here involved. There is a hierarchy of values, and the higher the value in question, the more painfully will this tragic factor be felt. Here, however, we are concerned with Holiness, with God's Grace and truth, with God Himself. And we are concerned with man's destiny which depends on this Divine Reality—the salvation of his soul. That the State should be well ordered is, of course, of great importance, and so is a well-constructed system of the natural sciences; but in the last resort we can dispense with both. But the values bound up with the Church are as indispensable on the spiritual plane as food in the physical order. Life itself depends upon them. My salvation depends upon God; and I cannot dispense with that. If, however, these supreme values, and consequently the salvation of my soul, are thus intimately bound up with human defects, it will affect me very differently from, for instance, the wrecking of a sound political constitution through party selfishness.

But there is a further consideration. Religion stands in a unique relation to life. When we look more closely, we see that it is itself life; indeed, it is fundamentally nothing but that abundant life bestowed by God. Its effect, therefore, is to arouse all vital forces and manifestations. As the sun makes plants spring up, so religion awakens life. Within its sphere everything, whether good or bad, is at the highest tension. Goodness is glorified, but evil intensified, if the will does not overcome it. The love of power is oppressive in every sphere, but in the religious most of all. Avarice is always destructive, but when it is found in conjunction with religious values or in a religious context, its effect is peculiarly disastrous. And when sensuality invades religion, it becomes more stifling than anywhere else. If all this is true, the human tragedy is intensified in religion, since any shortcoming is here a heavier burden and more painfully felt.

Yet a further point. In other human institutions the realisation of spiritual values is less rigid. They leave men free to accept or refuse a particular embodiment. The value represented by a well-ordered political system, for instance, is indeed bound up with particular concrete states. But every man is free to abandon any given state and to attach himself to another, whenever he has serious grounds for taking the step. In the Church, however, we must acknowledge not simply the religious value in the abstract, nor the mere fact that it is closely knit with the human element, but that it is bound up with this, and only this particular historic community. The concrete Church, as the embodiment of the religious value, demands our allegiance. And even so, we have not said enough. The truth of Christianity does not consist of abstract tenets and values, which are "attached to the Church." The Truth on which my salvation depends is a Fact, a concrete reality. Christ and the Church are that truth. He said: 'I am the truth.' The Church, however, is His Body. But if the Church is herself Christ, mystically living on, herself the concrete life of truth and the fulness of salvation wrought by the God-man; and if the values of salvation cannot be detached from her and sought elsewhere, but are once and for all embodied in her as an historical reality, the tragedy will be correspondingly painful, that this dispenser of salvation is so intimately conjoined with human shortcomings.

Therefore, just because the Church is concerned with the supreme values, with the salvation of the soul, because religion focuses the forces of life and thus fosters everything human, both good and bad, because we are here confronted with an historical reality which as such binds us and claims our allegiance, the tragedy of the Church is so intense. So intense is it that we can understand that profound sadness which broods over great spirits. It is the *'tristezza così perenne,'* which is never dispelled on earth, for its source is never dry. Indeed, the purer the soul, the clearer its vision, and the greater its love for the Church, the more profound will that sorrow be.

This tragedy is an integral part of the Church's nature, rooted in her very essence, because 'the Church' means that God has entered human history; that Christ, in His nature, power and truth, continues to live in her with a mystical life. It will cease only in Heaven, when the Church militant has become the Church glorified. And even there? What are we to say of the fact that a particular man who should have become a saint and who could have attained the full possession of God, has not done so? And who will dare to say that he has fully realised all he might have been? We are comforted here by one of those ultimate enigmas before which human thought is impotent. Nothing remains but to turn to a Power which is bound by no limits, and whose creative might 'calleth those things that are not, as those that are'—the Divine Love. Perhaps the tragedy of mankind will prove the opportunity for that love to effect an inconceivable victory in which all human shortcomings will be swallowed up. It has already made it possible for us to call Adam's fault 'blessed.' That the love of God exceeds all bounds and surpasses all justice is the substance of our Christian hope. But for this very reason what we have already said remains true.

To be a Catholic, however, is to accept the Church as she is, together with her tragedy. For the Catholic Christian this acceptance follows from his fundamental assent to the whole of reality. He cannot withdraw into the sphere of pure ideas, feelings, and personal experience. Then, indeed, no 'compromises' would be any longer required. But the real world would be left to itself, that is, far from God. He may have to bear the reproach that he has fettered the pure Christianity of the Gospel in human power and secular organisation, that he has turned it into a legal religion on the Roman model, a religion of earthly ambitions, has lowered its loftiest standards addressed to a spiritual élite to the capacity of the average man, or however the same charge may be expressed. In fact he has simply been faithful to the stern duty imposed by the real world. He has preferred to renounce a beautiful romanticism of ideals, noble principles and beautiful experiences rather than forget the purpose of Christ—to win reality, with all that the word implies, for the Kingdom of God.

Paradoxical as it may seem, imperfection belongs to the very essence of the Church on earth, the Church as an historical fact. And we may not appeal from the visible Church to the ideal of the Church. We may certainly measure her actual state by what she should become, and may do our best to remove her imperfections. The priest is indeed bound to this task by his ordination, the layman by Confirmation. But we must always accept the real Church as she actually is, place ourselves within her, and make her our starting point.

This, of course, presupposes that we have the courage to endure a state of permanant dissatisfaction. The more deeply a man realises what God is, the loftier his vision of Christ and His Kingdom, the more keenly will he suffer from the imperfection of the Church. That is the profound sorrow which lives in the souls of all great Christians, beneath all the joyousness of a child of God. But the Catholic must not shirk it. There is no place for a Church of æsthetes, an artificial construction of philosophers, or congregation of the millenium. The Church man needs is a church of human beings; divine, certainly, but including everything that goes to make up humanity, spirit and flesh, indeed earth. For 'the Word was made Flesh,' and the church is simply Christ, living on, as the content and form of the society He founded. We have, however, the promise that the wheat will never be choked by the tares.

Christ lives on in the Church, but Christ Crucified. One might almost venture to suggest that the defects of the Church are His Cross. The entire Being of the mystical Christ—His truth, His holiness, His grace, and His adorable person—are nailed to them, as once His physical Body to the wood of the Cross. And he who will have Christ, must take His Cross as well. We cannot separate Him from it.

I have already pointed out that we shall only have the right attitude towards the Church's imperfections when we grasp their purpose. It is perhaps this—they are permitted to crucify our faith, so that we may sincerely seek God and our salvation, not ourselves. And that is the reason why they are present in every age. There are those indeed who tell us that the Early Church was ideal. Read the sixth chapter of the Acts of the Apostles. Our Lord had scarcely ascended to Heaven when dissention broke out in the primitive community. And why? The converts from paganism thought that the Jewish Christians received a larger share than they in the distribution of food and money. This surely was a shocking state of affairs? In the community through which the floods of the Spirit still flowed from the Pentecostal outpouring? But everthing recorded in Holy Scripture is recorded for a purpose. What should we become if human frailties actually disappeared from the Church? We should probably become proud, selfish and arrogant; æsthetes and reformers of the world. Our belief would no longer spring from the only right motives, to find God and secure eternal happiness for our souls. Instead, we should be Catholics to build up a culture, to enjoy a sublime spirituality, to lead a life full of intellectual beauty. The defects of the Church make any such thing impossible. They are the Cross. They purify our faith.

Moreover, such an attitude is at bottom the only constructive type of criticism, because it is based on affirmation. The man who desires to improve a human being must begin by appreciating him. This preliminary acknowledgment will arouse all his capacities of good and their operation will transform his faults from within. Negative criticism, on the contrary, is content to point out defects. It thus of necessity becomes unjust and puts the person blamed on the defensive. His self respect and justifiable self-defence ally themselves with his faults and throw their mantle over them. If, however, we begin by accepting the man as a whole and emphasise the good in him, all his capacities of goodness, called forth by love, will be aroused and he will endeavour to become worthy of our approval. The seed has been sown, and a living growth begun which cannot be stayed.

We must, therefore, love the Church as she is. Only so do we truly love her. He alone genuinely loves his friend who loves him as he is, even when he condemns his faults and tries to reform them. In the same way we must accept the Church as she is, and maintain this attitude in everyday life. To be sure we must not let our vision of her failings become obscured, least of all by the artificial enthusiasm aroused by public meetings or newspaper articles. But we must always see through and beyond these defects her essential nature. We must be convinced of her indestructibility and at the same time resolved to do everything that lies in our power, each in his own way and to the extent of his responsibility, to bring her closer to her ideal. This is the Catholic attitude towards the Church.

My introduction has been lengthy. But it was important; so important indeed that I believe that what follows will seem true to you, only in proportion to your agreement with what has been said hitherto.

We saw in the last lecture that the problem we have to face is not the alternative 'the Church or the individual?' It concerns rather the relation between these two realities. In theory our aim must be a harmony between the two in which of course the precedence of the Church is fully safeguarded. But the intellectual and spiritual current of a period always flows in a particular direction. Harmonious syntheses are achieved only in brief periods of transition between two different epochs, for example when an age whose outlook is extremely objective and in which the social sense is powerfully developed is yielding to an epoch of individualism. Soon, however, one tendency predominates, and moreover, that which is opposite to the former. The Catholic attitude does not preclude the emphasis being laid on one aspect, otherwise it would be condemned to a monotonous uniformity and would deprive man of history. It demands only that the other aspect shall not be rejected, and coherence with the whole be preserved. That is to say, a particular aspect brought into prominence by the historical situation is emphasised, but is at the same time brought into a vital and organic relationship with the whole. A door is left open to the particular disposition of the historical present, but it is attached to the whole, which always in a sense transcends history. This whole is less actual, but in return it partakes of eternity. It is less progressive, but instead wise, and in the depths is alone in accordance with reality.

Our age is in process of passing from the individualistic and subjective to the social and objective. A stronger emphasis will therefore be laid on the Church. And these lectures will do the same. They will enquire how individual personality, by surrender to the Church, becomes what it should be. My lecture to-day will show how the Church is the way to individual personality. And I shall proceed from the fact that the Church is the spiritual locality where the individual finds himself face to face with the Absolute, the power that effects and maintains this confrontation.

* * * * *

Let us try to realise how deeply we are sunk in relativism, that is, the attitude of mind which either denies an Absolute altogether, or at any rate tries to restrict it within the narrowest limits.

We have lived through the collapse of an edifice which we expected to endure for an incalculable period of time, the collapse of the political structure of our country and its power, of the social and economic order existing hitherto, and with it of much besides. We can watch the social sense changing. And our mental attitude towards objects and life in general is equally changing. These changes go too deep to be dismissed with a few words. Artistic vision has changed; the expressionism, which had gradually become familiar, is already yielding, and the desire is springing up for a new classicism. A scientific and philosophical view of the universe is forming, which strives to attain a loftier and a freer understanding of objects in accordance with their essential nature.

Faced with these profound changes we become rather more acutely conscious of what in truth is always happening—that the attitude of the soul towards itself, its environment, and the first principles of being, is continually shifting. The forms of human life, economic, social, technical, artistic and intellectual, are seen to be in a state of steady, if slight, transformation.

We live in a perpetual flux. As long as this flux is not too clearly perceived, as long as a naive conviction ensures a strong underlying reserve of vitality, or deeply-rooted religious beliefs balance the increase of knowledge, life can endure it.

But in periods of transition, and when centuries of criticism have worn away all fixed belief, the flux forces itself on the mind with an evidence from which there is no escape. The condition ensues which ten years ago was universally predominant, and is still widespead to-day; a sense of transitoriness and limitation takes possession of the soul. It realises with horror how all things are in flux, are passing away. Nothing any longer stands firm. Everything can be viewed from a thousand different angles. What had seemed secure disintegrates, on closer inspection, into a series of probabilities. To every thing produced there are many possible alternatives. Every institution might equally well have been ordered otherwise. Every valuation is only provisional.

Romano Guardini

Man thus becomes uncertain and vacillating. His judgments are no longer steady, his valuations unhesitating. He is no longer capable of action based on firm conviction and certain of its aim. He is at the mercy of the fashions prevalent in his surroundings, the fluctuations of public opinion, and his own moods. He no longer possesses any dignity. His life drifts. He lacks everything which we mean by character. Such a man is no longer capable of conquest. He cannot overcome error by truth, evil and weakness by moral strength, the stupidity and inconstancy of the masses by great ideas and responsible leadership, or the flux of time by works born of the determination to embody the eternal values.

But this spiritual and intellectual poverty is accompanied by a colossal pride. Man is morbidly uncertain and morbidly arrogant. The nations are confused by pride, parties are blinded by self-seeking, and rich and poor alike are the prey of an ignoble greed. Every social class deifies itself. Art, science, technology—every separate department of life considers itself the sum and substance of reality. There is despairing weakness, hopeless instability, a melancholy consciousness of being at the mercy of a blind irrational force—and side by side with these a pride, as horrible as it is absurd, of money, knowledge, power, and ability.

Impotence and pride, helplessness and arrogance, weakness and violence—do you realise how by the continued action of these vices true humanity has been lost? We are witnessing a caricature of humanity. In what then does humanity in the deepest sense of the term consist? To be truly human is to be conscious of human weakness, but confident that it can be overcome. It is to be humble, but assured. It is to realise man's transience, but aspire to the eternal. It is to be a prisoner of time, but a freeman of eternity. It is to be aware of one's powers, of one's limitations, but to be resolved to accomplish deeds of everlasting worth.

What is a complete humanity? When neither of these two essential aspects is obscured, but each is asserted and developed; when they neither destroy each other nor drive each other to extremes, but blend in an evident unity replete with inner tension yet firm, imperilled, yet assured, limited, yet bound on an infinite voyage, this is a complete humanity. And a man is human in so far as he lives, consciously, willingly, and with a cheerful promptitude as a finite being in the midst of time, change, and the countless shapes of life—but at the same time strives to overcome all this flux and limitation in the eternity, and infinity, which transfigure them. A man is human in so far as he truly and humbly combines these two essential aspects. Herein lies the inexpressible charm of all things human—a mystery pregnant with pain and strength, desire and confident hope.

* * * * *

Well then—the Church is always confronting man with the Reality which creates in him the right attitude of mind: namely, the Absolute.

She confronts him with the Unconditioned. In that encounter he realises that he himself is dependent at every point, but there awakens in him the yearning for a life free from the countless dependencies of life on earth, an existence inwardly full. She confronts him with the Eternal, he realises that he is transitory, but destined to life without end. She confronts him with Infinity, and he realises that he is limited to the very depths of his being, but that the Infinite alone can satisfy him.

The Church continually arouses in him that tension which constitutes the very foundation of his nature: the tension between actuality and a task to be accomplished. And she resolves it for him by the mystery of his likeness to God and of God's love, which bestows of its fulness that which totally surpasses the nature. He is not God, but a creature, yet he is God's image and therefore capable of apprehending and possessing God. *Capax Dei*, as St. Augustine says, able to grasp and hold the Absolute. And God Himself is love. He has made the creature in His own image. It is His will that this resemblance should be perfected by obedience, discipline, and union with Himself. He has redeemed man, and by grace has given him a new birth and made him god-like. But all this means that God has made man for His living kingdom.

But observe this encounter with the Absolute, in which man faces the Infinite and sees clearly what he is, and what It is; but which at the same time awakens the longing for this Absolute Godhead and the confident expectation of its fulfilment by His love—this fundamental experience of Christianity, truth, humility, yearning love, and confident hope in one, is the moment in which for the first time in the spiritual sense man becomes truly human.

This transformation of a creature into man in the presence of the Absolute is the work of the Church.

* * * * *

She accomplishes it in various ways. In the first place, through her very existence, through that character which Jesus compared to a rock, the living self-revelation of the eternal God in her.

But in particular there are three essential expressions of the Absolute in the Church—her dogma, her moral and social system, and her liturgy.

The thought of modern man is relativist. He sees that historical fact is at every point conditioned by something other than itself, and everything, therefore, appears subject to change. Experimental research has made him extremely cautious, and he is wary of drawing conclusions. He has become accustomed to critical thinking, and does not readily venture beyond hypotheses and qualified statments. Statistics have taught him conscientious regard for exactitude, and he is apt to demand of any conclusion a complete experimental proof which is unattainable. He has thus become uncertain and hesitant where truth is concerned.

At this point the Church comforts him with dogma. We shall not discuss its detailed content. We are solely concerned with the fact that we are here presented with and apprehend truths unconditionally valid, independently of changing historical conditions, the accuracy of experimental research, and the scruples of methodical criticism. Nor shall we consider the factor of Catholic doctrine which is itself temporally conditioned and therefore changeable. We are dealing only with its unchangeable content, with dogma in the strict sense. He who approaches dogma in the attitude of faith will find in it the Absolute. He thus comes to realise how extremely unreliable is his own knowledge. But he is confronted by Truth divinely guaranteed and unconditional. If he honestly assents to it, he becomes 'human.'

He has a correct valuation of himself. His judgments are clear, free and humble. But at the same time he is aware that there is an Absolute, and that it confronts him here and now in its plenitude. By his faith he receives the Aboslute into his soul. Humility and confidence, sincerity and trust unite to constitute the fundamental disposition of a thought adequate with the nature of things. Henceforward the unconditional organises the believer's thought and his entire spiritual life. Man is aware of something, which is absolutely fixed. This becomes the axis upon which his entire mental world turns, a solid core of truth which gives consistency and order to his entire experience. For it becomes the instinctive measure of all his thinking even in the secular sphere, the point of departure for all his intellectual activity. Order is established in his inner life. Those distinctions are grasped without which no intellectual life is possible—the distinction between certainty and uncertainty, truth and error, the great and the petty. The soul becomes calm and joyful, able to acknowledge its limitations yet strive after infinity, to see its dependence, yet overcome it.

This is what is meant by becoming human.

Moral purpose is relative; ideals of perfection, standards of goodness, and codes of individual and of social behaviour are fluctuating and unstable. Effort is thus crippled, and the will, powerless when important decisions must be made, will in compensation give a free rein to arbitrary impulse in some particular sphere.

The Church confronts man with a world of absolute values, an essential pattern of unconditional perfection, an order of life whose features bear the stamp of truth. It is the Person of Christ. It is the structure of values and standards which He personified and taught, and which lives on in the moral and hierarchical order of the Church.

The effect thus produced is the same, as before, though now in the field of valuations and moral judgment, in the life of practice and production; man is confronted with what is unconditionally valid. He faces and acknowledges his own essential limitation. But at the same time he sees that he can attach his finite life at every point to God's Infinite Life, and fill it with an unlimited content. He there finds rest. He rejoices in the fact that he is a creature, and still more that he is called to be a 'partaker of the divine Nature.' His inner life becomes real, concentrated around a fixed centre, supported by eternal laws. His goal becomes clear, his action resolute, his whole life ordered and coherent—he becomes human.

Men envisage their relationship with God in various and shifting fashions. One man beholds God in every object, in tree and stone and sea. To another He speaks from the rigid and sublime laws of thought and duty. A third sees Him as the Great Organiser and Architect. Yet another finds him in the life of the community, in love and in neighbourly assistance. One man has a clear conception of God; for another He is a vague entity, the Great Incomprehensible; to a third He is an abstraction. Indeed the same man may have different conceptions of God according to his age, experience, or moods. The danger thus arises that man may make God in his own image, and so form a finite and petty conception of Him; that his longing and prayer may no more reach out freely beyond himself, but may degenerate into a dialogue with an enlargement of his own portrait.

In the liturgy the Church displays God as He really is, clearly and unmistakable, in all His greatness, and sets us in His presence as His creatures. She teaches us those aboriginal methods of communion with God which are adapted to His nature and ours—Prayer, Sacrifice, Sacraments. Through sacred actions and readings she awakes in us those great fundamental emotions of adoration, gratitude, penitence and petition.

In the liturgy man stands before God as He really is, in an attitude of prayer which acknowledges that man is a creature and gives honour to God. This brings the entire spiritual world into the right perspective. Everything is called by the right name and assumes its real form—face to face with the true God, man becomes truly man.

* * * * *

That man should see with perfect clearness what he is, a creature; but that he should rejoice in this fact, and regard it as the starting point of his ascent to the Divine, that he should be humble, but strive after the highest; sincere, but full of confidence, and so for the first time be truly human; is the work of the Church. She tells man everywhere, 'Thou art but a creature, yet made in God's image, and God is Love. Therefore He will be thine, if only thou dost will it.'

CHAPTER 4

THE ROAD TO FREEDOM

When the Catholic Christian handles a vital issue theoretically or practically, the situation should be immediately altered. It should be as when something is brought out from a false light into the full and clear light of day; or an object previously held in the violent grasp of some boorish bully has been released from his possession and passes into the hands of one who can respect and appreciate it. Every object brought into the Catholic sphere of influence and subjected to the Catholic spirit should recover its freedom and once more fully realise its nature. The Catholic spirit should impose the true standard, the great should appear great, and the petty, petty; and light and shadow put in the right place. . . . Yes—so it would be if one were really Catholic! Then indeed we should possess that true Goodness which sees all things as they are, and brings freedom. And life, which everywhere is suffering violence, would again breathe freely in all that we are and do, and all things be made new!

This is certainly expected of the Catholic Christian by those who are looking on at him from without. They do not expect him to talk brilliantly, or to live in an exceptional fashion remote from life, arbitrary and one-sided. There is an intelligentsia which in an intellectual fashion does violence to life more brilliantly and more significantly than he. These onlookers do not expect this from the Catholic. They expect him to possess something of Adam's pure vision, and that creative power with which the first man named all things according to their nature. They expect to find in him a glance which proceeds from the centre of the soul and penetrates the heart of objects, and to which they reveal themselves completely; that great love which redeems the silent misery of the world.

But we are not really Catholic, if the term is to be understood in its full and exacting implication, and it is our great, if painful, good fortune that we realise how little we are Catholic. But to be truly Catholic is the real, indeed the only genuine form of human existence, its way of life dictated at once by man's deepest nature and by divine revelation. It is a way of looking at things and of thinking about them which becomes instinctive. This, however, can be formed only in the operation of a long tradition, when the personal attitude of individuals has taken shape in objective forms, customs, organisations, practical achievements, and these exert a formative influence upon individuals, to be in turn remoulded by them. The Reformation and the *Aufklärung* have wrought incalculable destruction; we are all under the influence of the individualistic, naturalistic, and liberal spirit.

We are, therefore, no doubt taking a risk when we speak about human life, without being really Catholic. But we do it tentatively, and well aware that the greatest merit we can achieve is to be forerunners. Our master is St. John the Baptist, who said that after him One was to come Whom the Holy Spirit would baptise with fire. It is only after us that there will come those who will think, feel, produce and speak, out of the fulness of Catholic life. Ours must be the meagre joy of being allowed to prepare their way.

* * * * *

We are going to speak about one of the supreme treasures of life—about freedom.

How shop-soiled this word has become, and yet it is one of the most noble! How often have we Catholics allowed the most intimate of our possessions to be taken from us; and filled with the spirit of error, and then listen suspiciously to what our soul should utter with the deep accents of her native speech! Freedom—what a dubious connotation the word has acquired! Yet it contains the sum of what Christ has brought us. It is one of those royal words with which the spiritual masters of the Middle Ages described the majesty of God. 'God the free,' they called Him.

* * * * *

What then is freedom? What sort of man, exactly, is the free man?

To answer that freedom is the absence of external constraint, the power to choose, according to one's own will, among several possible courses, gives no notion of the wealth comprised in the term. For it cannot be contained in a short phrase.

Let us try to bring to light something of this treasure.

Each one of us possesses a pattern of his being, the divine idea, in which the Creator contemplated him. It comprises not only the universal idea of human nature, but everything besides, which constitutes this particular individual. Every individual is unique, and a unique variety of human nature. Indeed, the Rembrandt-German could say truly, could even maintain, strictly speaking, that a number of people should not be counted together, because in reality each is unique, and cannot be compared with the rest.

When this unique quality of a man's individual being is allowed to emerge, and determines all his existence and activities; when he lives from the centre of his own being, not, however, putting an artificial restraint upon himself, but naturally and as a matter of course, he is a free man. He is free who lives in complete harmony with the divine idea of his personality, and who is what his Creator willed him to be. He has achieved a complete equilibrium, the effect of a tension but

96

a resolved tension, a powerful yet gentle rhythm of life, a life at once rich and concentrated, full yet restrained.

All this, however, is but a part of true freedom. The free man must also see things as they are, with a vision not clouded by mistrust, nor narrowed by prejudice, nor distorted by passion, whether hatred, pride, or selfishness; must see them in the fulness of their objective reality, and in their genuine measure. He must see them in their entirety, rounded off, displayed on all sides, in their true relations with other objects, and in their right order. He will thus see them from the standpoint of their divine idea, just as they are. His glance will pierce from the centre of his soul to the centre of its objects. His love, issuing from an entire heart, will embrace their entire fulness. And his action, supported by a personality not divided against itself, grasps the world steadily and draws from it that which had awaited the hand of God's child, to be brought pure and complete into the light.

That man should respond to the true nature of things with the integrity of his own nature and in the unique fashion of his divinely ordained individuality, that the divine idea within and that without encounter each other in his personal life—this is freedom.

* * * * *

But freedom is even more than this. A man is free when he can see the great as great, and the small as small; the worthless as worthless and the valuable as valuable; when he views correctly the distinctions between different objects and different conditions; the relations between objects and their measure. He is free when he recognises honestly the hierarchy of objects, and their values, placing its base and its apex, and each intermediate point in its right position. He is free when he apprehends the idea in its purity, but contemplates in its light the complete reality; when he sees everyday life with all its rough and tumble and all its shortcomings, but also what is eternal in it. He is free when his vision of the idea does not blind him to reality, and everyday existence does not make him oblivious of the idea, when he 'can gaze upon the stars, but find his way through the streets.'

To see all this, to hold fast to the vision with stout heart and unswerving will, and act in accordance with it amid the confusion of appearances and passions—this is freedom.

But he must do this not because a compulsion is upon him, but because he himself is resolved upon it; not merely as the laborious and painful application of principles, but because the impulse and volition of his own nature impel him, and because the very heart of his personality is thereby fulfilled— thus and not otherwise is he free.

Freedom is a great thing—the supreme fulfilment and the purest standard of worth, truth and peace.

And with all that we have said we still have not plumbed the ultimate depth of freedom. It is that the man who is truly free is open to God and plunged in Him. This is freedom for God and in God.

You will ask, if that is freedom, are we free? Outwardly, of course, we are often free. We can resist a palpable restraint. Psychologically also, for we can choose between right and left. But freedom in the comprehensive sense which we have given? No, we must certainly acknowedge that we are slaves.

Here once more we encounter the mission of the Church —she, and she alone, conducts us to this freedom.

* * * * *

What are the bonds which a man must break to win this complete freedom?

There are in the first place those external circumstances which impede a man's development. These can be very strong; but if his energy is sufficient, he will in the end overcome them, either outwardly, by altering them, or inwardly, by a free renunciation which raises him above them.

The intellectual environment binds more potently, through current opinions, customs and tradition; through all those imponderable but constantly operative forces of example and of influence, mental and emotional. These things penetrate to the profoundest depths of the spirit. Even genius cannot wholly break their spells. And we average people are all subject to these influences, whether we consent to them or oppose them.

Just consider for a moment the extent of their sway. What cannot be effected by a slogan if the environment is favourable? No one can altogether escape its power. How powerful are the intellectual tendencies of an epoch! So potent can they be that ideas which are simply incomprehensible when the intellectual situation has changed may receive the unquestioning credence due to dogmas of faith. Do we not ask ourselves with amazement to-day how certain ideas of Kant's could have been accepted as so many dogmas, disagreement with them regarded as a proof of intellectual weakness? Remember, too, how powerful a compulsion is exercised by highly developed forms of art if the cultural environment is congenial. Think of the manifold ways, often so subtle as to defy discovery, in which certain political, social, or economic forms, for example, democracy or capitalism, mould a man's entire psychology; how a type of humanity recognised as ideal, for example, the knight, the monk, or the traveller, shapes men by its influence to the very core of their being. Against such forces the individual is powerless.

Reflect how, under the spell of such a general tendency, a particular age, the Renaissance, for example, with the decision born of the sense of an immeasurable superiority, rejects what another age—in this case the Middle Ages—had ardently embraced, how we are only now beginning to regard the Renaissance and what followed it as a disaster, and the Middle Ages as—rightly understood—our future. And bear in mind that this was no mere change of externals, but of man's attitude to essentials, values and ideas. In view of all this we have only one choice. Either we must canonize relativism in one shape or another, whether in its cruder form, the doctrine of the milieu, or in the form given to it by Keyserling, psychologically more profound and resting on a metaphysical basis, or embrace with our whole soul a power which can emancipate us.

It is the Church.

* * * * *

In the Church eternity enters time. Even in the Church, it is true, there is much which is temporal. No one acquainted with her history will deny it. But the substance of her doctrine, the fundamental facts which determine the structure of her religious system and the general outlines of her moral code and her ideal of perfection, transcend time.

In the first place, of her very nature she thinks with the mind, not of any one race, but of the entire and Catholic world. She judges and lives, not by the insight of the passing moment, but by tradition. The latter, however, is the sum total of the collective experience of her past. She thus transcends local, national and temporal limitations, and those who live and think with her have a *point d'appui* above all such restricted fields of vision, and can therefore attain a freer outlook.

The Church of her nature is rooted, not in particular local conditions or particular historical periods, but in the sphere above space and time, in the eternally abiding. She enters, of course, into relation with every age. But she also opposes each. The Church is never modern. This was the case even in the Middle Ages. We have only to read between the lines of the *Imitation* to detect it. The present always reproaches the Church with belonging to the past. But this is a misconception; the truth is that the Church does not belong to time. She is inwardly detached from everything temporal, and is even somewhat sceptical in her attitude to it.

And she has also had to endure the constant charge that she is not national, that she represents foreign nations, not the particular nation in question. It is a misconception of the truth. In the last resort she is not concerned with nations, but with humanity as a whole, and individual men and women. These, however, are the two expressions of humanity which touch eternity, while everything lying between them, and in particular political and national organisations, are bound to time.

The Church, therefore, stands amid the currents of intellectual fashion like a vast breakwater. She is the power which resists the spell of every historical movement, no matter what. She opposes the strength of her misgivings to every force which threatens to enslave the soul—economic theories, political slogans, human ideals of perfection, psychological fashions—and repudiates their claim to absolute validity. The Church is always the opponent of the contemporary. When an idea is new, it exercises a special attraction. It is fresh and novel; opens up to the mind unexplored avenues of thought, and thus arouses far more enthusiasm than its intrinsic value merits. And when a people becomes acquainted with a culture previously unknown and the conditions are favourable, it takes an irresistible hold upon that people, as Asiatic culture, for example, is affecting us to-day. In the same way new tendencies in art, new political principles, indeed novelties in every sphere down to such externals as fashions of dress and the conventions of social intercourse. If the environment is receptive, everything new is double potent, like oxygen *in statu nascendi*. Very often its power bears hardly any proportion to its true value, with the result that our picture of it is falsified to the point of distortion. The present, therefore, is always to a certain extent an hallucination and a prison. It has always attacked the Church, because it is over-excited, and her timeless calm resists its petulant importunacy; because it is one-sided, and her comprehensiveness transcends its limited vision. And the Church has always been the foe of the present, because its unspiritual violence enslaves the soul and its obtrusive clamour drowns the voice of eternity. In every age the Church opposes what is Here and Now for the sake of For Ever; the contemporary tendencies and 'politics,' for the sake of those aspects of humanity which are open to eternity—individual personality and mankind. When this has been understood, a great deal becomes clear.

He who lives with the Church will experience at first an impatient resentment, because she is constantly bidding him to oppose the aims of his contemporaries. So long as he regards what is being said everywhere, the public opinion prevalent at the moment, as the last word on any question, and makes parties or nations his criteria of value, he will inevitably feel himself condemned to obscurantism. But once the bandage has been removed from his eyes, he will acknowledge that the Church always releases those who live in her from the tyranny of the temporal, and to measure its values gives him the standard of abiding truth. It is a remarkable fact that no one is more sceptical, more inwardly independent of 'what everyone says' than the man who really lives in the Church. And as a man abandons his union with her, to the same degree does he succumb to the powerful illusions of his environment, even to the extent of sheer superstition. And surely the decision between those two attitudes involves the very roots of human culture. The Church is indeed the road to freedom.

* * * * *

But we have not spoken so far of the strongest bonds of all, those imposed by a man's own character.

There are, in the first place, psychological characteristics common to all men as such, passions, for example, and tendencies of the will. Only if we could conceive knowledge as the purely logical operations of a purely logical subject, as a kind of intellectual mechanism, which always functions smoothly, and which can immediately be set in motion under any conditions, would it be possible to regard it as unaffected by the other psychological functions. But the subject of thought is not an abstract, logical subject, but a living man; thought is a vitally real relation between man and the object of his thought. In the function of thinking all his other activities and states participate, fatigue, for example, and energy strung to the tensest pitch, joy and depressions, success and failure. The experience of every day proves that our intellectual productivity, the direction of our thoughts, and the nature of our conclusions, are influenced by the vicissitudes of daily life. Our psychological states may assist, hamper or completely prevent acts of knowledge, strengthen or weaken the persuasiveness of arguments. Desire, love, anger, a longing for revenge, gratitude— anyone who is honest with himself must admit how enormously the force of an argument, apparently purely logical, fluctuates in accordance with his prevalent mood, or the person who puts it forward. Even the climax of the cognitive process—the evidence, the subjective certainty of a judgment, a conclusion, a structure of reasoning—is to an enormous extent subject, as you can see for yourselves, to the influence of psychological states and the external environment. It is a strange chapter in practical epistemology.

So far we have been speaking only of speculative thought. There remains the whole order of values, judgments, pronouncements about good and evil, the lawful and the unlawful, the honourable and the dishonourable, the valuable, the less valuable, and the worthless. How enormously these judgments depend on the fact that the man who forms them acknowledges, esteems, and loves the value in question, or rejects, hates and despises, and on his general attitude towards men and things; whether he is receptive or self-contained, trustful or suspicious, has keener eyes for good or evil.

When you reflect upon all this, you must admit that our thought and valuations are permeated to the depths by the influences of a man's personal characteristics, his stage of development, and his experiences.

By this I do not mean that our thought and judgments are merely a product of our internal and external conditions; no reduction of thought and valuation to psychological and sociological processes is implied. Their nucleus is intellectual, but it is embedded in those processes. Thought has an objective reference, and is always striving to realise it more purely, that is to say, to grasp more perfectly objective truth. It has an objective content, this very truth—and becomes more perfect as this content becomes richer and more distinct. In spite of this, however, thought is life, and valuation is life—a vitally real relation between man and the object. And everything which affects that man or the object plays its part in the process.

What will bring us release from this imprisonment? Most certainly no philosophy; no self-training, no culture. Man can be set free only by a power that opens his eyes to his own inner dependence and raises him above it, a power that speaks from the eternal, independent at its centre of all these trammels. It must hold up unswervingly to men the ultimate truths, the final picture of perfection, and the deepest standards of value, and must not allow itself to be led astray by any passion, by any fluctuations of sentiment, or by any deceits of self-seeking.

This power is the Church. As contrasted with the individual soul she may easily give an impression of coldness and rigidity. But to the man who has grasped her essence, she becomes pure life. Certainly it is a life so abundant that the weakly, irritable man of to-day cannot easily experience it. The Church clears the path to freedom through the trammels of environment and individual psychology. In spite of all her shortcomings, she shows man truth seen in its essence, and a pure image of perfection adapted to his nature.

He is thus enabled to escape his personal bondage.

* * * * *

Once more we must delve deeper, and at last we shall reach our conclusion.

We have spoken of the inner pattern contained in every individual personality which determines its unique quality. The individual is not a human being in general, but bears a stamp peculiar to himself. He embodies a distinctive form in virtue of which he realises human nature in a special way. It is the organic ideal and fundamental law of his entire being and activity. It is expressed in everything he is or does; it determines his disposition and external attitude. It is, however, that task of the individual—we shall return to this point later—to acknowledge this individual form, bring it out, see its limitations, and place it in its due relation to the world as a whole. The strength of the individual lies in this unique quality. It represents what God desires him to be, his mission and his task. But at the same time it is the source of his weakness.

Consider first those more general mental types which classify men into distinct groups, that is to say, fundamental types of character. Thought is determined by them, the way in which things are seen, will and emotion, and the attitude towards self, man, the world, and God.

We shall sketch one example of these types of character, though only in general outline. We shall call it the synthetic type. A man of this type is interested in similarity and combination. This is already evident in his own nature. There thought, will, activity and emotion strongly tend towards unity and effect a thoroughgoing harmony. Such a man gets quickly into touch with things, and can easily pass from one to another. In objects he sees first of all their similarities, the connecting links and numerous transitions between them. He is powerfully aware of their unity, and if he gives a free rein to his native temper he will reach some type of monism, that is to say, a conception of the universe based wholly on the tendency to likeness and unity which pervades reality. He is, of course, aware of the distinctions between things, but regards them as of secondary importance and is disposed to relegate them increasingly to the background and to explain them away as mere stages of development, transitional forms, and modes of the one great unity. He will even by degrees transform the relation between God and the universe into a unity, and regard Him as simply the Energy at work in all things, maintaining and animating them. And his practice will correspond with his thought. His fundamental attitude will be one of conciliation unless, indeed, as a result of the law of psychological ambivalence, he devlops a passionate antagonism towards external objects, which, however, is at bottom determined by his sense of affinity with them. In every sphere he seeks a compromise. He explains evil as due to accidental imperfections, or as a necessary step in the development of good. Thus in practice and theory he is a monist, though his monism may wear a rationalist, æsthetic or religious colour.

A man of this type proves and disproves, unaware of the extent to which he is in the power of his own disposition. He persistently selects from reality those features which suit his nature, and passes over or distorts those which are opposed to it. In the last resort his entire view of the world is an attempt to establish his personal preference by rational proofs.

The opposite temper may express itself similarly. It gives birth to that fundamentally critical attitude which in any sphere notices past and present unlikenesses, what differentiates one object from another, their limitations and dividing lines. For men of this type the world is dissolved into isolated units. The distinctive qualities of objects stand out sharply side by side; the classifications made by thought are not linked up with sensation and desire. The distinctions between what is and what ought to be, between duty and right, and moral choices stand out rigid and inexorable. Conflicts, the decision between alternatives, are universal.

If this type of man follows his bent to the full, he also is enslaved. He, also, chooses, values, and measures in accordance with 'his own mind,' and is convinced that the result is objective truth. When the intellectual processes of a mind dominated by its period are listed in the light of their psychological presuppositions, the effect is peculiarly devastating. A host of affirmations, chains of reason and systems of valuations, apparently purely rational, prove but the slightly veiled expression of a particular psychological temperament. One of the most striking instances of this is Kant. His writings develop a system of thought at first sight as purely objective as could be conceived. But simultaneously they reveal their author's most intimate personality. To us, whose mentality is so utterly different, this latter aspect stands out clearly, like the original writing of a restored palimpsest, and we cannot understand how a philosophy so largely the self-expression of a genius could be mistaken for a discovery of the fundamental nature of objective reality. But unless some higher sources of truth safeguards us against the danger, we shall inevitably yield credence to some other teacher who proclaims as objective truth what is but the expression of his own mentality, or formulate as serious fact, and with a great display of reasoning, matters which we have devised to express our personal attitude to life.

To return to the two types we described above—neither is free. First and foremost both are slaves as men, as human types. For there exists in every human being, side by side with his predominant mentality, its opposite. Therefore, the synthetic type of mind is also capable of criticism, and the critical type is not devoid of the power of synthesis. But in each case the complementary disposition is weaker; the mentality takes its character from the predominant tendency. But every living organism is subject to a law we may term the economy of force. It tends to use those organs which are particularly developed, so that the rest become increasingly atrophied. Each type, therefore, should develop its complementary aspect to the utmost of its power. Only by this mutual balance it will achieve complete and harmonious development. But the man who is left to himself develops one-sidedly. The predominant trait of his inner psychological composition increasingly asserts itself and thrusts the rest into the background. Over-developed in one direction he is stunted in another. Such a nature, however, is an enslaved nature, for only a being which has developed freely and harmoniously all its native capacities is free.

Moreover, a man whose development is thus one-sided is not free in relation to his environment. For of the rich abundance of its concrete reality he can see only one aspect—that aspect which is adapted to his particular temperament, and for which the powers he has specially fostered have given him a peculiarly acute vision and comprehension. He is thus held captive by it, and incapable of taking an all-round view of reality.

Such men do not live with their full nature, nor in accordance with the idea of their personality, which, whatever its particular emphasis, is always a whole, but merely with a fragment of their true selves. And their life is not in contact with objects as concrete wholes, but merely with artificial selections from them. Each, however, by a singular delusion, maintains that he is complete and his attitude the right one, his impoverished and mutilated world God's free world of full reality.

There are other types and corresponding ways of regarding the world. Each is a power, each the way to a distinctive outlook. But each is also a net liable to entangle the man who casts it. The different types mingle, and the degree of their combination varies. Their energy, warmth and wealth vary. To these must be added national, local and vocational characteristics, and those derived from heredity or environment. And finally, there are those enigmatic qualities which may be said to constitute the colouring, idiosyncrasy or mannerism of the individual, that wholly unique something which belongs to the one individual alone. All these blend with his fundamental type and foster its independent development.

Remember, also, that the instincts of self-preservation, self-love, and the sense of honour, feed a man's predominant disposition, that all his personal experiences are viewed in its light and adjusted to it. You will now be able to gauge its strength.

How then can a man thus in bondage to his disposition be set free?

He must acknowledge, and to the very core of his being, that reality includes all its possible aspects, is all-round. He must recognise that this reality can be grasped only by a subject equally comprehensive in his knowledge, his valuations and his activities; and that he himself does not possess this comprehensiveness, but is fragmentary, the realisation of one possibility of human nature among a host of others. He must recognise the errors which this one-sidedness produces, and how they narrow the outlook and distort the judgment.

He must indeed fully accept his own special disposition, for his nature and his work are based upon it. But he must also fit it into the entire scheme of things. He must correct his own vision of the world by the knowledge of others, complete his own insights by those of other men, and thus stretch out beyond himself to the whole of reality; and this not only in his knowledge, but in his judgments of value and practical conduct.

That is to say, he must not efface his distinctive character and attempt to make his life a patchwork externally sewn together. His distinctive character must always remain the foundation. But character must become vocation, a mission to accomplish a particular work, but within an organic whole and in vital relation to it. Then one-sidedness will become fruitful distinction, bondage be replaced by a free and conscious mission, obstinate self-assertion by a steadfastness in that position within the whole which a man recognises to be his appointed place.

Anyone who honestly attempts this task quickly realises that he cannot accomplish it by himself. Then is the moment of decision. Will he abandon the attempt? Will he acquiesce in the impossibility? Will he become a sceptic? Or will he arrogantly endeavour to make his inner impotence tolerable by declaring it the only right attitude? In either case, he remains the slave of his own inner bonds, in the deepest sense a Philistine, however eloquent the language with which he proclaims his servitude. Or else his determination to possess truth, reality, the whole, is ready for the sacrifice which alone will lay the way open, ready 'to lose his soul, in order to save it.' If this is his disposition, he will experience the Church as the road to freedom.

Of her nature the Church is beyond and above these bonds, and he who 'surrenders his soul to her, in her shall win it back,' but free, emancipated from its original narrowness, made free of reality as a whole.

* * * * *

The Church is the whole of reality, seen, valued, and experienced by the entire man. She is co-extensive with being as a whole, and includes the great and the small, the depths and the surfaces, the sublime and the paltry, might and impotence, the extraordinary and the commonplace, harmony and discord. All its values are known, acknowledged, valued and experienced in their degree and this not from the standpoint of any particular type or group, but of humanity as a whole.

The whole of reality, experienced and mastered by the whole of humanity—such, from our present standpoint, is the Church.

The problems with which we are faced here involve experience as a whole. No part of it may be detached from the whole. Every partial question can be correctly envisaged only from the standpoint of the whole, and the whole only in the light of a full personal experience. For this, however, a subject is required which itself is a whole, and this is the Church. She is the one living organism which is not one-sided in its essential nature. Her long history has made her the repository of the entire experience of mankind. Because she is too great to be national her life embraces the whole of humanity. In her men of diverse races, ages, and characters think and live. Every social class, every profession and every personal endowment contribute to her vision of the whole truth, her correct understanding of the structure of human life. All the stages of moral and religious perfection are represented in the Church up to the summits of holiness. And all this fulness of life has been moulded into a tradition, has become an organic unity. Superficialities are subordinated to deeper realities; intermediate values take precedence of the trifling and the accidental. The fundamental questions of man's attitude to life have been the meditation of centuries; so that the entire domain of human experience has been covered and the solution of its problems matured. Institutions have had to be maintained through vicissitudes of period and civilisation, and have reached a classical perfection. Consequently, even from the purely natural point of view, the Church represents an organic structure of knowledge, valuation and life, of the most powerful description. To this we must add her supernatural aspect. The Holy Ghost is at work in the Church, raising her consistently above the limits of the merely human. Of Him it is said that He 'searcheth all things.' He is alone the Spirit of discipline and abundant life. To Him 'all things are given.' He is enlightenment and Love. He awakens love, and love alone sees things as they are. He 'sets in order charity' and causes it to become truth with a clear vision of Christ and His Kingdom. He makes us 'speak the truth in love.' Thus the Church is sovereign above man and above the world, and can do full justice to both.

Dogma that is revealed and supernatural truth binding our assent, is the living expression of this living organism. The entire body of religious truth which it records is seen by a complete man. And it determines the attitude towards truth of the individual Catholic.

And that form of religion in which the entire man enters into a supernatural communion with God—namely, the liturgy—is another living expression of this living orgainism. It determines the Catholic attitude towards religion in the stricter sense.

Finally, the Church's discipline and constitution—her moral law and ideal of perfection—are yet another living expression of this organism. They determine the Catholic attitude towards ethics.

The Church holds up before man this truth, this scale of values, and this ideal of perfection; and not as merely possible or advisable, but as obligatory. She calls upon man to rise above his narrowness and grow up to this complete truth, this comprehensive ideal and universal rule of life. She commands it, and disobedience is sin. Only thus does the demand receive sufficient weight to counterbalance human selfishness, with its exaggerated and tenacious self-assertion.

If man obeys and accepts the fundamental sacrifice of self-surrender and trusts himself to the Church; if he extends his ideas to the universal scope of Catholic dogma, enriches his religious sentiment and life by the wealth of the Church's prayer, strives to bring his conduct into conformity with the lofty, complete pattern of perfection, a pattern, moreover, which moulds the private life of the spirit presented by her communal life and her constitution, then he grows in freedom. He grows into the whole, without abandoning what is distinctively his own. On the contrary, for the first time he sees his individuality clearly when it is confronted with all the other human possibilities to be found in the Church. He sees its true significance to be a member of the whole. He perceives it as a vocation, a God-given task, the contribution made possible by his unique character as an individual, which he has to make towards the great common task of life and production.

Thus man develops into a personality. It is rooted in his individuality, but essentially related to the whole. It involves an individual outlook the consequence of its uniqueness, but this individual outlook is harmonised at every point with the outlook of others because it never loses sight of the whole. It involves also a joyful determination to realise its own nature, but within the framework of the entire organism. Thus the outlook of the genuine personality is comprehensive and recognises other men's points of view. He divines their meaning, and views his own vocation in relation to the whole. Such a man will not display instant enmity towards a personality of different type to his own, as one species of animals is hostile to another. On the contrary, he will co-ordinate both within the superior unity to which both belong, in the performance of a common task in which each supplements the other. He evinces that great power of acceptance which finds room for other types, and is therefore able to share their life. Thus his wealth increases, for what belongs to others is also his.

My attention has been drawn to a saying of St. Paul's in which the Christian's consciousness of this supreme freedom of his entire being finds striking expression: 'The spiritual man judgeth all things: and he himself is judged of no man.' (I Cor. ii. 15) The true Christian is sovereign. He possesses a majesty and a freedom which remove him from the jurisdiction of the unbeliever. He cannot on principle be subject to his judgment, since the unbeliever cannot focus the Christian within his field of vision. The vision of the former, on the contrary, embraces 'all things,' and his standard is absolute. How remote is the impoverished consciousness of our Catholicity from this attitude of St. Paul, in which perfect humility—all his Epistles reveal it—is united with the knowledge that he possesses, not one point of view among others, but the unique and absolute point of view; genuine humility combined with the sublime consciousness of absolute and perfect supremacy.

This is the meaning of *'sentire cum Ecclesia'*—the way from one-sidedness to completeness, from bondage to freedom, from mere individuality to personality.

Man is truly free in proportion as he is Catholic. But he is Catholic to the extent that he lives, not within the narrow confinement of his purely individual and separate existence, but in the fulness and integrity of the Church, to the extent, that is to say, that he has himself become identified with 'the Church.'

Charles Journet
1891-1975

*Charles Journet was born in Geneva, Switzerland, in 1891.
He was ordained in 1917 and published a couple of books in
the 1920s about Protestant-Catholic relations in Switzerland.
But it was as professor of theology at the Grand Seminaire in
Fribourg, Switzerland, that he established his reputation as
scholarly theologian, especially in ecclesiology. The selection
that follows is from the first volume of his work,* The Church
of the Word Incarnate, *which appeared in French in 1941.
It immediately associated him in the minds of many with
Yves Congar and Henri de Lubac, the other French-speaking
theologians who were breaking new ground in understanding
the Church.*

*This work was not translated into English until 1955. By
then Journet had completed his second volume, copies of
which he sent to Pope Pius XII and his Secretary of State
G. B. Montini (later Pope Paul VI) in 1952. Montini assured
Journet in a thank-you letter that "you are to be congratulated
on having carried out successfully a work which will help many
of our contemporaries to get a firmer grasp of this mystery of
the Church, which perpetuates through the centuries and the
vicissitudes of history the very mystery of the Word Incarnate."*

*In 1947 Journet published an introduction to theology,
translated into English in 1952 as* The Wisdom of Faith. *In*

1948 came The Dark Knowledge of God *and in 1953* The Primacy of Peter. The Meaning of Grace *in 1959 and* The Meaning of Evil *in 1960 were followed in 1961 by a work in which he cooperated with his friend Jacques Maritain on the topic of the sin of the angels. He was a consultor to the Swiss bishops during Vatican II and in 1965 Pope Paul VI made him a cardinal archbishop.*

In many ways Charles Journet was a transitional figure. As a Neo-Thomist he had absorbed the Scholastic method and tradition thoroughly, but he was also open to the new. His comprehensive, speculative approach is not much in favor today, but still provides evidence of the great faith and energy of the one who utilized it. His initial plan was to produce four volumes on the Church, one on each of the four "causes" constituting it: efficient, material, formal, final. The astounding wealth of information and analysis which he provides set him head and shoulders over the ordinary manualists of the scholastic method.

As Journet analysed it, the efficient cause of the Church is the "Apostolic Hierarchy." In an amazing tour de force he elaborates on that proposition in ten chapters, covering 560 pages provided with extensive documentation. What follows is merely the first of those chapters, enough to see an unusual man in action, sketching his vision of the Church he loved.

Journet was a shy, soft-spoken teacher, beloved by the seminarians whom he taught for most of his adult life, and sought after by many who desired spiritual counsel. When he died on April 15, 1975, Pope Paul VI wired condolences to the Swiss bishops on losing so exceptional a colleague. His priorities come through in one of his statements in the introduction to The Church of the Word Incarnate: *"I am enough in love with speculative theology to give it the greater part of my time; but I am well aware that a higher wisdom exists, one which St. Thomas speaks of on the very threshold of his* Summa, *and which consists, he tells us, in 'suffering' divine things."*

114

THE CHURCH
OF THE WORD INCARNATE

CHAPTER I

THE PHASES OF THE ACT GENERATIVE OF THE CHURCH, OR, THE SUCCESSIVE DIVINE REGIMES OF THE CHURCH

T he first act of the divine omnipotence is that by which it creates the universe from nothing, and maintains the substantial being of things by virtue of an unceasing immediate contact. "Now in each thing," says St. Thomas, "there is a proximate and immediate effect of God. For we proved ... that God alone can create. Also, in each thing there is something caused by creation: in bodies, there is primary matter; in incorporeal beings there is their simple essence ... Accordingly God must be present in all things at the same time: especially since those things He called into being from non-being, are continually preserved in being by Him. Wherefore it is said [Jeremias xxiii. 24]: *I fill heaven and earth;* and [Psalm cxxxviii. 8 (Vulg.)]: *If I ascend into heaven, Thou art there: if I descend into hell, Thou art present."*

The second act of divine omnipotence is even more astonishing. It is that by which it seeks to invest and enrich human persons with gifts so wonderful and so pure that these persons can become, in union with each other and with God, a collective living abode in which God Himself will delight to dwell. When, in the Old Testament, Wisdom speaks, it is to say: "And in all these [peoples and nations] I sought rest, and I shall abide in the inheritance of the Lord" (Ecclus. xxiv. II (Sept.)). Similarly, towards the end of the Apocalypse, the Church appears to St. John as "the holy city, the new Jerusalem"; and he hears a great voice coming from the throne and saying: "Behold, the tabernacle of God with men, and he will dwell with them. And they shall be his people: and God himself with them shall be their God" (xxi. 2-3).

Now what are we to say of this act by which God has produced the Church, His abode among men—whether we call the

Church a miserable hovel on account of human sin, or a temple on account of the Guest it shelters? Has it known but a single form, unchanged down all the ages? Did God from the beginning produce His Church as it stands to-day, and has time no other part to play than to lend endurance to what was perfect from the start?

The answer is clear. The divine act that produced the Church has been marked by several phases. These might be called the various divine regimes under which the people of God have lived during the course of the ages, the divine regimes of the Church. For God led the Church through various successive states, and the purpose of time is to enable this Church not only to endure, but also to progress till it reaches that state which is to be the last one in this world, the state in which it enters the era of the Incarnation and the Pentecost.

Let us briefly recall the succession of the divine regimes of the people of God and of the Church.

I. The Regime Prior to the Church

The Angelic Doctor teaches that God originally decided to act upon men directly, that is to say without any intermediary cause, to invest them with the grace of innocence and so to make of them the living abode in which He would come to dwell upon earth. In that respect the first regime of the people of God was profoundly different from those that followed the Fall and with which the Church properly so-called was to begin her course. Neither the mediation of Christ, nor that of any instrumental causes such as the sacramental or jurisdictional powers, was then in question at all.

It is clear in fact that the supernatural gifts of grace and truth with which the first man was to be endowed, could not pass by way of Christ, since the Word was not yet incarnate. We must go further. These supernatural gifts were not even given *in view of* the future sufferings of Christ, since, had man not sinned, God would not have had to redeem him by His sufferings; since indeed, as St. Thomas thought towards the end of his life, had man not sinned God would never become incarnate. Consequently, neither the grace conferred on the first man, nor that conferred on the angels, could, properly speaking, be the grace of Christ,

gratia Christi. In connection with this point however, to which
we shall return, there is a difference between the grace of the
first man and the grace of the angels. While on the one hand the
grace of innocence had to be lost in order to give place to that
of redemption, to which it was ordered only indirectly and
materially, the grace of the angels was ontologically preaccorded
(both intensively and extensively) to the perfect grace that was
to fill the soul of Christ when the Word should eventually become incarnate. Consequently, when man's sin had shattered
the harmony of innocence and the Word had resolved to become
incarnate so as to die on the cross, the plenary grace created at
that instant in His heart became the centre of reference, the
locus, of all the graces that existed beforehand in the angels,
just as the centre marked afterwards in an already existing circle
becomes the locus of every point in the circumference. We can
go further along this road and add that as soon as the incarnation
of the Word was accomplished, the angels began to receive,
through the physical intermediation of the humanity of Christ,
those graces which hitherto they had received immediately. Thus
Christ is indeed the King of angels, now distributing to them the
essential grace they have always possessed and the accidental
graces superadded thereto.

It is clear furthermore, according to the doctrine of St.
Thomas, that had mankind continued in innocence the supernatural gifts of grace and truth would have reached them without
passing through instrumental causes such as the sacramental or
jurisdictional powers. The law of innocence meant in fact that
spiritual life would flow from God to the soul and from the
soul to the body: it would have been a breach of this law if grace
and truth had come to the soul, which is spiritual, by way of
sensible means or signs.

Thus the divine omnipotence was the sole cause of the
people of God in its first form. Doubtless the ministry of angels
was already in operation to fortify men against the wiles of the
devil and to bring them the divine commands; but the object of
this mediation, which, in any case, was wholly spiritual, remained
accidental. The essential gifts of grace and truth came immediately from God. Thus the divine government, prior to the coming
of the Church, excluded all corporeal or visible intermediaries.

2. The First Regime of the Church

Why did God allow the state of innocence to be destroyed? We know the answer: God permits evil only to make of it the occasion for a greater good. To the regime of creation, which might appear perfect, succeeds the regime of redemption which, on the whole, is to be better still. These two regimes differ profoundly. That of creation excluded every visible mediator; that of redemption was to be essentially the regime of a Mediator, awaited, then recognized, "the man Christ Jesus, who gave himself a redemption for all" (I Tim. ii. 6). The first regime gave birth to the first form of the people of God. The regimes that followed were to give birth to the Church properly so-called, which was not to be a people of God pure and simple, but a people of God marked with the sign of the redemptive Incarnation, a people of God called the "Body" of Christ, a people whose vocation it would be to prolong in space and time His temporal life.

Immediately after the Fall the first of the regimes of the Church began. Grace and truth were not to be dispensed through a visible mediation.

The *grace* bestowed on souls from then onwards was that same grace which the Redeemer would one day merit by His love and pay for by His sufferings. In this sense it was already the grace of Christ, *gratia Christi.* And that is why it worked inwardly not only to begin the organization of the new people of God, but to lead this people gradually through the vicissitudes of their history towards the concrete and definitive status which it was to receive from Christ Himself.

To make it obscurely felt from the very outset that it came by anticipation from the mystery of the redemptive Incarnation, that is to say from the mystery of a God who made Himself visible and came down into our flesh, this grace was now given in dependence on visible signs, on outward actions, which theologians were to call sacraments. These sacraments were doubtless rudimentary. They were not yet, as they were to become under the New Law, the instrumental means and causes of grace; they were merely practical signs of it, serving to designate those on whom God in His mercy sent His grace immediately, provided

118

they were rightly disposed. These sacraments existed already under the law of nature, but their number and importance was to be laid down in detail under the Law of Moses. As the history of the people of God unfolds, and the work of salvation progresses, we shall see the sacramental principle coming more and more to the fore.

An analogous course was followed in the preaching of divine truth. First of all the primitive revelation was transmitted exteriorly by the organ of a magisterium essentially fallible. God contented Himself with inwardly enlightening each particular soul by hidden inspirations. But under this regime the dangers besetting the work of salvation outweighed its advances. Then God raised up men whose mission was not merely to recall the content of the primitive revelation, but also to make it more explicit and more precise as time went on. These were the prophets. With them the principle of an exterior infallible teaching, first oral, then written, as a normal means of divine government, entered history for the first time.

Thus, in the measure in which the work of salvation procceeds, the importance of a visible mediation appears more and more clearly. Immediation is a sign of inferiority, mediation a sign of perfection and of progress. Why this law, at once so general and so mysterious? The answer is not far to seek. Visible mediation does not mean that God relaxes His care for the governing of men; it means on the contrary that His condescension begins to be more urgent, more helpful to a human nature wounded by sin. The moment it is introduced the immediate and direct solicitations of love, far from diminishing, become more abundant than ever. We may lay down the principle that for every outward promulgation of the law, there corresponds an inward inpouring of grace. These things are clear enough to anyone who understands that the regime of visible mediation is, from its very inception, a sort of adumbration and luminous shadow of the mystery of the Incarnation.

It remains true however that so long as this regime lasted, the visible mediation involved was still too imprecise to allow the act productive of the Church to bring with it the fullness of its effects of grace and truth:

I. Grace still came down directly from God to man. It did not pass through the humanity of Christ, so that it was not yet that rejoicing love which was to be concentrated first in the heart of the Word made flesh as the love with which the Father loved Christ, to overflow thence on all other men. Nor did it pass through the sacraments, which at this state merely signified it but did not cause it: hence it still lacked the virtue and riches of those sacramental graces by which Christ was to establish His Church in its perfect state.

2. Moreover, supernatural truth, in the absence of a fully developed visible mediation, was neither completely revealed nor perfectly preserved.

Hence the first regime of the Church in its various realizations under the natural or the legal state, represents only a preparatory phase of the act productive of the Church.

3. The Existing Regime of the Church

It was only when God, inaugurating the final era of history, chose to pour out at last upon men the supreme favours reserved for them from all eternity, that He established the Church in its definitive temporal status by bringing the regime of visible mediation to its highest point of perfection. This brought with it at once the deepest joy and the most effective help, but also the hardest trial and the most exacting exercise of our faith: the greatest joy and help, because there is nothing so connatural to man as to receive divine things humanly; the hardest trial and effort, because there is no more surprising mystery than this collaboration of the uncreated with the created, of omnipotence with indigence, of eternity with time, of immensity with place.

First the Word is sent from heaven into our flesh, and then, having promised the help of the Spirit, He sends His own disciples into the world: "As the Father hath sent me, so also I send you" (John xx. 21). Hence the perfect regime of the Church militant involves a double visible mediation: that of the Incarnation and that of the hierarchy.

A. *The Mediation of the Incarnation*

The first and principal mediation is that of the human nature of Christ which from the moment of the Incarnation

120

became the organ of the Divinity, the instrument by which the divine action is to fill the world with the good things of grace. Henceforth, all gifts that come down to us from the abyss of the Deity first pass into the heart of Christ; it is of His fullness that all men—and even angels, as we have seen—receive. But how then can the human nature of Christ, which is finite and circumscribed by reason of the body, extend its influence over all men in the world, and even to the angels? Just as an instrument can produce, in virtue of the principal agent, an effect that surpasses its own powers and bears the stamp of the principal agent, so the created nature of Christ, by becoming the instrument of the divine immensity, can overleap its natural boundaries and receive a virtue beyond all limits. And it is precisely because Christ is able to pour the rays of His charity upon all men without exception, because He can knock at the door of every soul, and play a part in the inner drama of each individual conscience, that God has made Him the absolutely universal instrument for the sanctification of the world to the exclusion of all others, so that, since His coming, no saving grace is ever given apart from Him. Hence it is that divine grace—now rightfully called the grace of Christ not only because it was merited by His charity and sufferings, but also because it passes through His heart before reaching us—brings with it new privileges.

For it delivers men for the first time from the penalty of original sin, opening the gates of heaven for them without further delay. That could not be said of the grace given by anticipation to the just men of the Old Law.

Grace moreover, while of its own nature it divinizes men, does this now by "christening" them, that is to say by working to conform their lives more and more to that of Christ. It is true that the human nature of Christ acts as an organ of the Divinity and that, in a general way, effects resemble their principal cause rather than the instrument; but the human nature of Christ, being henceforth united to the Person of the Word as a human hand is united to a human person, possesses all the fullness of the life that it pours out on other men. It became on this account a privileged instrument, *speciale divinitatis instrumentum*, causing our salvation "as by its own proper virtue", not by a virtue transmitted as a "separated" instrument does, and as a minister, even a sinful minister, can do. That is why it was that from the Incarnation onwards, more than in earlier times, grace tended to draw men to God by conforming them to Christ.

B. The Mediation of the Hierarchy

The second visible mediation, wholly subordinate to the first, is the mediation of the hierarchy.

I. THE TRUE EXPLANATION

I. Christ, in the course of His temporal life, could, as physical instrument of the divine power, act in two different ways: either from a distance, or by sensible contact.

This can be seen in the case of the bodily cures. When the Jewish official begs Him to come down to Capharnaum where his son lies dying, Christ sends him back comforted, and straightway the child is healed (John iv. 46-54). When the centurion expressly asks that his servant may be healed by a single word spoken from afar, his prayer too is heard (Matt. viii. 5-13). When the Syrophœnician woman goes home she sees her child already freed from the devil (Mark vii. 29-30); and when the ten lepers are on the way to show themselves to the priests they find themselves suddenly cleansed (Luke xvii. 14). The cures however are, for the most part, wrought in a more direct way, by bodily contact. Our Lord touches a leper in Galilee (Mark i. 41); He spits on the eyes of a blind man at Bethsaida and lays hands on him twice (Mark viii. 23-25); He touches the eyes of two blind men at Capharnaum (Matt. ix. 29); and again at Jericho (Matt. xx. 34); He allows the woman with the issue of blood to touch the hem of His garment (Luke viii. 44); He takes Jairus' daughter by the hand (Luke viii. 54); He touches the bier on which a dead youth is carried (Luke vii. 14); He makes them take away the stone which separates Him from Lazarus (John xi. 39), and so on. Further, Jesus seems to go out of His way, at one time to insist on the value of this sensible contact (as when He puts His fingers into the ears of the deaf-mute to signify that He is going to open them, and moistens his tongue to signify that He will unloose it (Mark vii. 33)); at another, to make His virtue pass by poor and altogether disproportionate material means (as when He puts clay on the eyes of the blind man of Siloë (John xi. 6));

and again to extend its range by the use of words (as when He commands the paralytic to rise (Mark ii. II), or Lazarus to come forth (John xi. 43)). Why finally, did He deliberately prolong an absence without which Lazarus need not have died (John xi. 21 and 32), if not to help us to realize the virtue of His bodily presence?

These bodily cures are, above all, the symbols of spiritual ones. As soon as Jesus appeared, His heart radiated grace to illumine the world from afar. It was from afar that He knew Nathanael under the fig-tree (John i. 48-50), and His glance travels yet farther to all the true adorers in spirit and in truth (John iv. 23), and all the sheep not yet in the fold of Israel (John x. 16). But He acted in a still more marvellous manner on those who approached Him; He slaked their thirst: "If any man thirst, let him come to me and drink" (John vii. 37); He comforted them: "Come to me all ye that labour and are burdened, and I will refresh you" (Matt. xi. 28); He absolved them: ". . . but she with ointment hath anointed my feet. Wherefore I say to thee: Many sins are forgiven her, because she hath loved much" (Luke vii. 46-47); He touched their hearts with penitence: "And the Lord, turning, looked on Peter. And Peter remembered . . . and going out wept bitterly" (Luke xxii. 61); He put new heart into them: "Was not our heart burning within us, whilst he spoke in the way?" (Luke xxiv. 32); He met their love with love: "Now there was leaning on Jesus' bosom one of his disciples whom Jesus loved" (John xiii. 23). Here too we shall see Him use the spoken word to enlarge the field of this sanctifying contact. A word casts out the unclean spirit in the synagogue of Capharnaum (Mark i. 25), and among the Gerasenes (Mark v. 8), and takes away the sins of the paralytic (Mark ii. 5), and cleanses the adulteress (John viii. II).

It thus appears that in the days of His mortal life Jesus acted in two ways: He scattered His graces far and wide, and that is *action from a distance*; and He communicated them in a more intimate manner to those whom He could touch, and that is *action by contact*. Certainly such contact is no indispensable means to His action; but it is His *connatural* means, the means to which He draws our attention, and for which He takes care to provide all possible opportunity by moving about through

Galilee, Samaria, Judea, Decapolis and even to Phœnicia. And if we want the ultimate reason for this procedure we must seek it not merely in the principle (still too general) that direct contact between agent and patient favours the full efficiency of physical action (for when it comes from God through the heart of Christ, physical action can be perfect even at a distance), but above all in the *fact*, much more immediate, that inasmuch as our nature is wounded, it stands in need of a sensible stimulus to awaken it connaturally to the life of grace. And that explains why the perfection of heaven, where man will be glorified, will not be incompatible with Christ's action from a distance; whereas the perfection of earth, where man remains wounded, requires the action of Christ by sensible contact.

2. Jesus has now been "taken up into heaven", He "sits on the right hand of God" (Mark xvi. 19), and is fully associated with His Father's power. Is His action to be restricted, from now onwards, to action from a distance? Is this the end of His action by contact? No: for before He left us He willed that there should always be among us certain men invested with divine powers, by whom the action that He initiates from heaven may be sensibly conveyed to each of us and may continue to reach us in the only way connatural to us—through direct contact. These are the hierarchic powers. Far from being substituted for Christ's action they are subordinated to it so as to carry it, in some sort, through space and time: like those mists left behind by the rain which continue to refresh the earth when the rain has ceased, they come to birth from the mystery of the Incarnation to perpetuate its blessings among us. These powers are essentially ministerial, that is to say, transmitters; they would be without effect if the divine power, passing into the heart of Christ, did not perpetually come to touch them into life. They comprise two kinds of powers: the jurisdictional power, transmitting truth, and the sacramental power, transmitting grace. Our Lord Himself announced, prepared and instituted them while He was still visible in our midst: He first sent the twelve Apostles into Galilee (Luke ix. I), then the seventy-two disciples into Judea (Luke x. I), and finally the "Eleven" with a mission to teach all nations until the consummation of the world (Matt. xxviii. 16-20). He baptized, or had baptized, all who came to

Him (John iii. 22; iv. 2) and He willed that after His ascension all nations should be baptized (Matt. xxviii. 16-20). And we have a sign, at once mysterious and manifest, that in these hierarchic powers He seeks to establish sensible contact with us. It appears in this, that the end of the highest of these powers, the power of order, is to give us His very presence itself, real and corporeal, under the sacramental veils.

Doubtless God could have saved us without becoming incarnate. Probably even in that case He would have established a visible hierarchy—an opinion that finds support in reasons of a general order, such as the fact that providence habitually rules lower things through higher. Such general reasons cannot content us when others, more precise and immediate, are at hand. We know that it was the desire to come into immediate touch with us that led God to become incarnate. And we know that Christ, after a short time in this world, was taken up into heaven where He sits at the right hand of the Father. How then can sensible contact between Him and ourselves be maintained? There is only one solution: namely that Christ, when about to leave the earth, founded here a visible hierarchy, assisted by Himself, directed by Himself, a hierarchy which, living in our midst, could serve as His instrument in establishing contact with us. He continues then to make contact with us by His action, but under the appearances of the hierarchy; as, in the greatest of the sacraments, He continues to make contact with us by His substance under the appearances of bread and wine. Such is the direct and immediate explanation of the institution of the Christian hierarchy.

2. FALSE EXPLANATIONS

To those who seek an explanation of the origin of the hierarchy but fail to rise to this level, it can hardly appear to be more than the product of a process of human self-divinization. We may here recall Chestov's reflections on what he calls the "power of the keys". In this he sees a hand uplifted against the transcendence of God, a progressive attempt at a hellenization of the biblical revelation. For Chestov, Socrates was the first who clearly enunciated the formidable idea that the keys of heaven are on earth, at the disposal of men. The Christians tore this power from the hands of the idolators, and to-day it is the scientific spirit that makes bold to grasp it. "Scratch a modern European, and whether he be positivist or materialist you soon discover under his skin the old medieval Catholic, convinced of his exclusive right to open the gates of heaven . . . If God Himself came to tell us that the *potestas clavium* belonged to Him alone the mildest of us would revolt." We may find a very similar idea on the significance of our ecclesiastical hierarchy in Karl Barth.

At the bottom of the outlook of these thinkers there lies a fatal misconception of the relations between God and man. They suppose that if God conferred some of His powers on man He would have to resign these powers Himself; that what man possesses ministerially as instrumental cause, God must cease to possess sovereignly as First Cause; that there is, in a word, a concurrence or conflict between the *potestas* of the Creator and the *potestas* of His creatures, so that something given to them is something taken from Him. In such an hypothesis, it is evident that the salvific powers—but also all powers in general, even down to the act of existence itself—cannot belong to God *and* to man; we must choose whether we shall attribute them to God *or* to man.

Those who reason thus are the victims of an univocal metaphysic. We do not attribute one and the same power of the keys both to God and to His ministers. The notion of the power of the keys is proportional, analogical. There are the keys of authority (*clavis auctoritatis*) which are the prerogative of the Holy Trinity; the keys of excellence (*clavis excellentiae*) which are proper to Christ, in that His human nature is the organ of the Divinity; and finally the keys of the ministry (*clavis ministerii*) which alone are communicated to the Church and subsist in dependence on the two foregoing as if suspended from them. The first keys contain the second, and the second the third, as the ocean contains all its currents. It is a metaphysical error which falsifies in advance all attempts at exegesis, to imagine that the divine power cannot communicate itself to men by contact without losing something of itself in the process, that it ceases to be sovereign master of the goods it bestows. That the hierarchic powers, along with the created subjects in which they reside, remain in uninterrupted dependence on the divine power,

Charles Journet

is asserted by the author of the *Imitation of Christ*. Expressing the common doctrine on the most sublime and mysterious of these powers, that of consecrating the Body and Blood of the Saviour, he writes: "The priest is God's minister, using God's word, by God's own command and institution; but it is God who is here the principal Author and invisible Operator, to whom is subject all that He wills, and who is obeyed in all that He commands."

3. THE CHARACTERISTICS OF THE HIERARCHIC ACTION

The virtue coming from God through contact with a visible hierarchy—which therefore might be called "hierarchic virtue" or, again, "apostolic virtue"—will have for its proper effect the formation of the Church. It will bear the marks of its double origin, divine and visible. And that is why it will possess characteristics apparently opposed; for instance, it will be perfect, but yet will call for completion; it will be universal, but yet in need of something to supply for it.

It is *perfect* because it alone confers those sanctifying effects which are to bring the Church militant to her perfect historical age, to her ultimate specific form, which are to make her the completed Body of Christ, the community having Christ for Head and Christians for members, the marvellous abode in which God dwells somewhat as He dwells in Christ Himself. And yet it has need of *completing* graces over and above itself to prepare souls for it in the first place, and to perpetuate its effects. How, to start with, would the action of the hierarchy be welcomed by adults if they were not interiorly prepared by hidden influences coming from Christ without mediation to predispose them towards it, and continuing to stir them up afterwards to new progress? And since the hierarchy can only operate by individual acts, from time to time, in a way that is *morally* continuous of course, but yet *physically* discontinuous, how could its divine effects in souls—such as the sacramental character and sacramental grace, which nothing else could supply—be kept continuously in existence save by a continuous and secret influx? Certain gifts of plentitude, necessary for the constitution of the Church, could never be given to man without the contact of the hierarchy; but to ensure the acceptance of these gifts and their continuous

127

persistence in time, requires the action of a power of completion, also coming from Christ, but without mediation and wholly invisibly.

Furthermore, the hierarchic virtue is *universal*, since it is to extend to all nations and to endure for all time: "Going therefore teach ye all nations: baptizing them . . . and behold I am with you all days even to the consummation of the world" (Matt. xxviii. 19-20). But the hierarchy reaches men through sensible contact. Can such a contact be really universal? Undoubtedly it can. First of all *de jure*, because the hierarchy is the unique visible instrument chosen by God to form His Church here below and communicate the fullness of grace and evangelical truth to the world; and *de facto* as well, for on the day of Pentecost the hierarchy established contact with a multitude of men of all conditions, classes and tongues. Yet this factual universality of the hierarchy will be never fully achieved. Conditions for preaching the Gospel can always become more favourable; there can always be a greater readiness to receive it, more active zeal to spread it abroad. To suppose that the universality of the hierarchy will one day reach its theoretical maximum, is to suppose it to make contact not only with each of the great categories of mankind, but also with each subordinate group contained in those categoreis. That, in fact, is the utmost perfection of universality which we have any right to expect of a visible and social instrument of salvation. Even supposing it achieved, the hierarchy would not necessarily have made contact with each individual of each group; any individual might still be in invincible (non-culpable) ignorance of its divine character. Now we know on the other hand that God "will have all men to be saved, and to come to the knowledge of the truth" (I Tim. ii. 4), and that no human person, no man endowed with reason and freedom, will ever be abandoned by Him; even though, by no fault of his own, he wholly misses or misconceives the hierarchy. Such a man, living beyond its reach, will at least be visited as from afar by hidden redemptive influences, and only one who knowingly rejects these express invitations will be definitively condemned. We have said: only the outpouring of grace that comes of visible contact with the hierarchy will enable the Church to attain to its final specific state and grow to the fullness of the Body of

Christ in this world. But this outpouring, though plenary and *universal* in its order, calls for another, altogether spiritual and effected from a distance; an outpouring whose normal purpose it will be to complete the former, but whose extraordinary purpose it will also be in a certain measure to supply for it.

Consequently, two influences from Christ are to be recognized. The first is exerted through *contact* with the hierarchy. It is perfect. It is universal both *de jure* and *de facto,* but still in a particular genus, in that way namely in which a hierarchy, a visible and social instrument of salvation, can be said to be universal, i.e. by reaching every class of men, not necessarily each man in each class, *genera singulorum, non singula generum;* let us call it if you will, "collective universality". The second influence, *action from a distance*, is universal with the universality possible to a pure ray of the spirit: it enters freely into each human conscience, normally as completing, i.e, as disposing it to receive the hierarchical impulse and retain its effects; but exceptionally, when this latter is lacking, as supplying for it, and filling up in a measure what it lacks. This we may call "individual universality".

4. ACTION FROM A DISTANCE AS SUPPLEMENTARY

The divine power of Christ makes use exclusively of the contact of the hierarchy to constitute the Church in her last historical epoch, to give men the sacramental characters, the sacramental graces, and the right orientation of their thought and action. And yet the divine power of Christ is not confined to the use of visible instruments. It can dispense with them. It sends into each human conscience from afar, if not the same gifts, at least the elementary grace of salvation. Of this action from a distance, in so far as it is called upon exceptionally to *supply for* action by contact, I must here say a few words.

It will always be granted till the consummation of the world. For in this world there will always be men who, by no fault of their own, will live in ignorance or misconception of the hierarchy. They will not receive the graces that make them full members of the Church; yet none of them will be deprived, save by his own fault, of the grace of salvation.

If they refuse this grace, they condemn themselves. If they are docile to it to the point of living in love, they are Christ's sheep. They are not yet visibly united to the flock that Peter has to feed. They are sheep still scattered, souls still in exile.

But the grace that comes to their souls is, in itself, a grace bearing them towards the Church. It orientates all men secretly towards the one flock of Christ. It does not always succeed in bringing them in effectively. Many, by no fault of their own, may die without reaching the end of their journey. They are not yet, but nevertheless they can be, of the Church. They are not yet of her in any stable or definitive way, but they can be so in a precarious and provisional way; they are not yet wholly members in achieved act, *re*, but they can be so incompletely, in virtual act, *voto*; they are not yet qualified to receive the efficient causal influence of the hierarchic powers, but they can be already *en route*—perhaps without knowing it, perhaps superficially against the grain—towards regions illuminated and fecundated by the hierarchical powers. So that in a sense there is really only one flock upon earth already, gathered together by Christ and for Christ, and entrusted by Christ to Peter—a flock to which many faithful belong consciously, openly, visibly, and many other faithful unconsciously, secret and invisibly.

4. The Future Regime of the Church

The visible mission of the Word, on the day of the Incarnation, gave the Church Christ for Head; the visible mission of the Spirit on the day of Pentecost gave her the faithful for body; with these missions, the Church entered on her definitive economy. What was inaugurated at that time—which the Apostles insistently called "the last days" (Heb. i. 2) and "the last times" (I Peter i. 20)—was destined to endure for eternity. For indeed all the riches that God had reserved for us in His heart since the beginning of the world were then really given us. In this world we possess them only under veils and in a nature still gravely injured by sin. But later, when all veils are torn away, we shall possess them fully and openly, in a nature glorified and transfigured. Thus, even in the definitive economy of the Church, we have to distinguish two successive regimes: the regime of earth and the regime of heaven.

130

The beatifying vision and love of the angels and of the elect plunge them directly and *immediately* into the very Godhead Itself. The strength by which they know God as He knows Himself and love Him as He loves Himself still comes to them *mediately*, by way of the human nature of Christ, the eternal King of men and angels; but in heaven, with all our weaknesses healed, the difference between action by contact and action from a distance is of no great importance. The one will penetrate us with the same ease and the same connaturality as the other.

The visible hierarchy will not then be needed any more. Its whole purpose was to continue that sensible contact by which Christ touched our wounds to heal them. That is why the Fathers and Doctors of the Church were so fond of presenting the mediation of the hierarchy in the light of a remedy. It has no *raison d' être* in the state of original justice. It will have less still in the state of glorified nature: "When the consummation is come the use of sacraments will cease; for the blessed in celestial glory have no longer any need of the sacramental remedy. They endlessly rejoice in the presence of God, contemplating His glory face to face and, transformed from brightness to brightness in the abyss of Deity, they taste the Word of God made flesh as He was in the beginning and will be for ever."

Émile Mersch
1890-1940

Émile Mersch was born in Marche, Belgium, in 1890 and joined the Jesuits in 1907. His theological studies coincided with the First World War (1914–1918), and in 1920 he was assigned to teach philosophy at Namur, where he remained until 1935. He was stationed in Louvain from 1936 and when the Nazis invaded Belgium in 1940, Mersch was asked to lead a group of elderly Jesuit priests to safe haven somewhere. He made arrangements in various villages for all but two. With them he secured transportation in a crowded automobile that was heading for France. He somehow became separated from them and ended up in Lens and was given lodging at the local pastor's home. The town was under heavy air attack and two soldiers informed Mersch the next day that many wounded lay along the Douai highway. He went to see if he could be of help and a few hours later his body was found beside the road, apparently the victim of one of the bombing raids. He was two months short of his fiftieth birthday.

Seldom is a particular book so closely identified with the entire life of its author as The Theology of the Mystical Body is with Mersch. He presented a paper in 1917 in a seminar on the subject, and spent the rest of his life working out in detail the project of grouping all Christian teaching around this as the central idea. His determination in doing the fullest patristic *research resulted in his two-volume historical work of 1933,* The Whole Christ. *But this was ever viewed as preliminary, the necessary groundwork for the theological synthesis he wanted to construct on this foundation. The first draft took up all his available time from 1929 to 1935, but in that time he had himself matured to the point that he was dissatisfied with the product and began to rewrite it completely. The second draft was finished in 1939. He began a third draft and had told friends a few weeks before his death that it was about ready for the press.*

Mersch took that precious third draft of his life's chief labor with him in the automobile with the two elderly priests, and lost it with the rest of his luggage when he got separated from them. Only one briefcase containing eleven chapters was found. The other ten chapters of the revision were lost. An editorial board of former friends and associates worked loyally to get the manuscript ready for the publisher, combining the different drafts to make as coherent a whole as possible. It was finally published in 1944 and in 1951 the English translation by Cyril Vollert, S.J., appeared.

The name of Emile Mersch must thus be added to those of Congar, de Lubac, Journet, Adam, and Guardini as the ones responsible between the wars for the renewal of Catholic thinking about the Church. His premature death prevented him from seeing his approach vindicated by the important encyclical of Pope Pius XII in 1943, Mystici Corporis. *On the other hand, his work certainly contributed to making that encyclical possible. If ecclesiology has moved on into still another phase with the events of Vatican II, that should not obscure the value of the very real progress which Mersch's work represents.*

Mersch's synthesis organized all the major concerns of Christian theology into five books: 1) Theological and Philosophical Introduction, where he lays down his principles; 2) The Coming of Christ, treating of creation, sin, and mariology; 3) Christ, dealing with Christology and redemption; 4) The Blessed Trinity, including treatment of revelation and the Holy Spirit; and 5) In Christ, on the supernatural, the Church, and Grace. What follows is chapter 16, taken from this fifth book, on "The Nature and Notes of the Church."

THE THEOLOGY OF
THE MYSTICAL BODY

CHAPTER XVI

I. NATURE OF THE CHURCH

T he ordinary procedure followed in studying the Church is to consider it as it appears in itself. But we can also study the Church by considering it in the light of Christ. This is the procedure we shall adopt in these pages. Such a study of the Church will not expose us to the danger of losing sight of it as it is in itself, but will rather lay open to us its inner principle and cause. The Church is the continuation of Christ, for it is His mystical body.

A remark seems to be in order here. Although we may nearly always regard the terms, Church and mystical body, as interchangeable, it does not follow that the two expressions have exactly the same shade of meaning in every case and from every point of view. We believe that we would be forcing the sense of the Pauline text, "the Church, which is His body," and of several similar passages, if we claimed to find in them an affirmation of such identity. However, some authors are of this mind, and they even go so far as to declare that the mystical body in the strict sense of the word is exclusively the Church militant.

In this contention they are quite orthodox. Yet we are of the opinion that the Apostle's doctrine is not completely decisive on this point, and tradition has taken a wider view of the teaching. In the ordinary language of the Church, "mystical body" connotes the entire multitude of those who live the life of Christ, with a life that admits of degrees, whereas the word "Church" represents the society of the baptized faithful as organized under their lawful pastors.

The two realities are closely related, and the present chapter will show how the one necessarily involves the other. But the two are not absolutely identified on this earth. A person can be a member of the visible society of the Church without actually living the life of Christ as a perfect member of the mystical body; this is the case with a Catholic hardened in sin. Likewise, one can truly live the life of Christ without being actually attached to the visible society that is His Church; an example is a pagan who would have received grace and charity without being aware of the Church, or a fervent catechumen.

It is quite true that the Church visible alone, as established over the entire earth, fully represents what Jesus Christ desires. But it is also true that the visible Church is far from having achieved that position, and Jesus Christ foresaw this. Accordingly the great number of souls effectively living the life of Christ is one thing, and the visible Church is another; in a matter so delicate, dealing with such important objects, we shall find it useful to have two different words to designate two realities that differ *de facto,* however closely they may be related *de jure.*

As we perceive, the two notions, while involving the same truths, line them up differently and stress different points. These notions are the product of different thought-processes and theological elaborations; they correspond to different questions and preoccupations. By forcibly reducing them to each other we should be renouncing a traditional heritage of meditations and studies, and the apparent simplification resulting might turn out to be an impoverishment, instead of having two shades of thought, we should have nothing more than two synonymous terms. This would be the more regrettable inasmuch as the particular notion of the mystical body, in spite of a certain indefiniteness which detracts from its maneuverability for purposes of controversy, has a special tonality and resonance that fit it for some theological expositions, for example, those that undertake to make clear to Christian people the nature of their life and its mysteriousness.

Besides, it has the advantage, which is often important, of being but slightly weighed down with Latin or juridical terms, and of having preserved almost the same meaning for many of our separated brethren as for ourselves. By safeguarding its particular significance, we keep alive the possibility of conversations, of exchanges of views, and even, perhaps, of formulas of union. Providence cannot but have some reason for preserving it and for thrusting it into the foreground in our day.

In any case, to return to the subject of the present chapter, our purpose is to study the Church regarded as the body of Christ and its continuation here on earth. Our aim is not to construct a treatise *On the Church* for its own sake; many excellent ones are at hand. Our wish is rather to see, at least in bold outline, how an ecclesiology that is nothing but a continuation of Christology would take shape. If the Church is the continuation of Christ, should not the science that describes it be a continuation of the science that describes Christ?

Christ continues Himself in the whole of mankind that is susceptible of salvation, that is, mankind as living in heaven in purgatory, and on earth. This threefold continuation corresponds to a threefold Church: the Church triumphant, the Church suffering, and the Church militant. With regard to the earth in particular, Christ is continued—if we can speak of continuation in this connection—during the centuries that preceded Him as well as during those that have followed Him. Hence there is a Church of the Old Testament and a Church of the New Testament.

During the centuries that preceded Him, Christ pre-existed as a man pre-exists in the human line that prepares and announces him. However He pre-existed not only as an effect issuing from its causes, but as a principle giving rise to this whole line regarded as progressing toward the God-man and presaging His holiness. This pre-existence is the community of Israel which we may call the Church of the Old Testament, and in a wider sense is all that is truly religious in all the religions of ancient times.

During the centuries that follow Him, Christ is to perpetuate Himself in a new form, which is the new way of existing He gives to the human race. This is the life of the Church in the strict sense, the Church militant properly so called—the Church that is the object of discussion in this chapter.

Every man survives himself to some extent in the wake he leaves behind. This wake is the more clearly marked and enduring the more intensively the man himself has lived and acted.

It will have supreme intensity for the sacred humanity of Christ, for He lived and acted with supreme intensity. In other words, it will derive its most characteristic traits from Him and will be closely connected with His humanity. To be the continuation of Christ's humanity in this way, it must be constituted as the sacred humanity is constituted, and must, so to speak, be the continuation of the sacred humanity's constitution.

But Christ's humanity was both an empirical thing and a mysterious reality. Viewed from the outside by the eyes of the body, it was a humanity like all others, carried along by the same tides, lashed by the same winds and rains, subject to the same laws of the universe with their ordinary lack of concern for the individual. It was a humanity as visible as all others and open to the same processes of observation. From within, this empirical humanity was mysteriously divinized with a superabundant fullness, so as to possess, in the manner of a universal source, the supernatural life and divinization of all mankind.

The second of these two aspects, divinization, exists only in the hypostatic union with the divinity; it comes from this union and exists for this union. Hence the temptation may arise to say that this second aspect is the divinity. The formula would evidently be inexact; the divinity is not an aspect of the humanity. Yet we would be able to interpret it in an acceptable sense.

As these two aspects are found in Christ's humanity, they will also be found in the mystic perpetuation of that humanity which is the Church. The Church will likewise be an empirical thing and a mysterious reality.

First, it will be an empirical, concrete, visible, tangible thing, like all human realities that prolong themselves in some form of continuation; for it is a human institution, a human society. And it is a society quite visibly and tangibly; its sociology and canon law can be written down; it has its clearly defined members and its definite seat: it is the Church of Rome, as Jesus Christ was Jesus of Nazareth. As a society it is perfect in its kind, with a firm and well-delineated structure, as befits a thing that is the perpetuation of the God-man.

Secondly, the Church will be an invisible reality: a life of thought, love, and grace that is infused into souls, a divinization and adoptive sonship which, in the unity of the only-begotten, incarnate Son is diffused throughout all mankind so deeply as to be inaccessible to natural consciousness, and which, in the depths thus reached, unifies mankind in itself and attaches it to God.

Through this second aspect, that is, the divinization conferred on it, the Church is a theandric reality, a divine-human reality, as many authors aptly put it. The reason is not that the Godhead is one of its elements or aspects, or that the Church has its own union with the Godhead independently of Christ and His hypostatic union, but only that it is the perpetuation of the theandric humanity, the humanity fully divinized and subsisting in the Word, the humanity of the God-man.

This second aspect is what makes the Church the new mankind, the mankind that exists otherwise and more perfectly, by a new and more efficacious contact with pure Being, and with a new and more intimate aspect of Being than that which constitutes simple mankind. This mankind is not the result of the impress of the divine hands, but exists in its divine head, in the most interior of unions with the divine life.

We call it the new mankind, for in it is realized, like a new human form or a new human act, its supernatural, "filial," Trinitarian form. It is mankind par excellence. It is not a replacing but a renovation of the old mankind, and is henceforth the only admissible form of mankind, the form to which all mankind is directed by the divine vocation and by the work which grace begins to perform in it. For this reason the Church, like mankind, will have two aspects, one external and visible, the other internal and invisible. But these two aspects are joined and make up a single new mankind.

The two aspects of the Church, the visible and the invisible, are often called the soul and the body of the Church. This manner of speaking may have disadvantages, and they are brought out in our day; but it greatly facilitates certain explanations. Hence we may profitably devote some consideration to it.

The body of the Church, as we see at once, is the external aspect, the empirical society which is the Church of Rome. The word "body" does not have here the precise sense it has in the term "mystical body." For the expression "mystical body" designates the mysterious and interior element of the Church; even for those who identify the Church militant with the mystical body, it does not designate the external aspect, the "body," except so far as it is the outward manifestation of the interior soul, which consists in such a mystery.

The soul of the Church must clearly be the factor that makes this society a living organism; it is the first general principle of a collective and unified life in all the members. This factor can be nothing else than the grace which causes all these members to be living members of Christ, the divinizing grace that is infused into all by one and the same Christ. Or else we may say that it is Christ, the Son of the Father, regarded as the principle of life in the whole supernatural organism because of this infusion: "a certain universal principle in the genus of such as have grace," as St. Thomas says, "a universal principle for bestowing grace on human nature."

Christ's humanity cannot be such a principle in the Church unless His divinity is an interior source of supernatural fullness and teeming life in it. In this sense we may say that the divinity and in particular, by appropriation, the Holy Spirit, is in some way a soul with respect to the grace and divinization of Christ's humanity, and hence that it is also a sort of soul, the soul of the soul, the life of the life of the Church. We can be still more precise and say that the divinity, as possessed by the person of the Son, has this function by a causality of union, that it is a sort of quasi-formal cause, or rather a quasi-actuating cause imparting subsistence, and also that the Godhead and the Trinity and in particular the Spirit have the same function by way of efficient causality or production. These considerations, which we propose in passing, may serve to round out what we said in chapter 14 about the soul of the mystical body.

In any case we should note well that the soul of the Church, together with the body, forms a total entity, a single Church of Christ, just as soul and body constitute a single man or as the empirical aspect and the fullness of divinization

140

make up a single Christ. Christ's divinity and humanity are united *inconfuse et incommutabiliter*, though also *indivise et inseparabiliter*; in an analogous way His humanity and the transcendent divinization of it that is brought about by union with the divinity are united without confusion but also without division; they are distinct but inseparable. This union existing in this distinction passes on to the Church. Because of Christ, the two aspects that perpetuate the two aspects of Christ's sacred humanity, the aspect of empirical society and the aspect of fellowship in grace and divinization, are indissolubly united in the Church, without on that account being identified.

The Church knows only too well that they are not identical, for she is aware of the presence of sin, and that she herself, the sacred body of Christ, is in exile, "absent from the Lord." The empirical organism which is the outer aspect of the Church has not yet fully assimilated the grace, the unity, and the holiness whereof it lives and whose totality is found in it germinally, truly possessed but not yet completely realized. Just as the life of grace in each Christian depends on union with God, so the unity, the substance, and the essence of the Church regarded as an empirical society depend on union with Christ, with His grace, and with God who gives grace in Christ; yet the Church is not formally this grace nor Christ, for they are not empirical.

But this way of regarding the Church is nothing more than a mental precision. In reality, the main thing is the union we have been speaking of; although the united elements are distinct, even as elements they exist through this union and in this union. When our view of the visible aspect of the Church comprises it as it actually is, we perceive perfect intercommunion and inseparability: "what God hath joined together, let no man put asunder."

Some say that this union is the most marvelous trait of the Church; others say that it is the scandal of the Church; in any case it is the mystery of the Church. In the same way the union between the divine nature and the human nature is the characteristic feature of Jesus, a fact that spells ruin for some and resurrection for others; but in any case it is a sign of contradiction. That the divine nature is a mystery, will be readily conceded. But that a reality which is of this world and is even, at times, too much of this world, should be a mystery, appears irritating. The Church is a society like other societies, granted; or it is an ideal entity, a fellowship in love of God and one's neighbor, granted again; but its claim to be both together, to belong to time and to eternity, to possess the qualifications needed to administer its property and to have the mission of dispensing divine life, this is what bands idealists and positivists against it—and is also the very things that enables it to gather both these parties within its embrace. The Church does indeed make this claim and has to; otherwise it would be false to it self and would cease to be the perpetuation of the God-man.

This is a paradox, if you will; assuredly it is a mystery—the Christian mystery par excellence, the mystery of the Incarnation, must understand this mystery; indeed, they do not have to understand anything else. It alone explains them to themselves, and it alone is the adequate object of their knowledge. This will become clearer in the light of what we have to say about the note of the Church.

II. THE NOTES OF THE CHURCH

A. Theory of the notes in the mystical body. The two aspects we have been discussing are so closely united that details of the one are reflected in details of the other, and that the exterior of the Church is an indication of its interior nature. This leads to a theory about the notes of the Church, a subject interesting to consider at this juncture. Our point of view is not that of apologetics, and we shall propose no explicit apologetic. Our concern is with the theological significance of the notes, especially as viewed in the light of the theology of the mystical body.

If the Church is actually the mystical continuation of Christ Himself, its method of making itself known and of proposing itself for men's belief, will be a continuation of Christ's method. Accordingly if we wish to know what the Church and its notes are, we have to consider Christ and the credentials He presented about His mission. Therefore we shall study Jesus Christ at some length; this will also afford us an opportunity for getting to know Him better.

The great proof Jesus Christ gave of His mission and teaching is He Himself. This is as it should be. That which is first in any genus does not depend on that genus for anything whatever. Christ is the first in the order of grace and of the new mankind, in the order that sums up and transfigures the whole of the ancient order. Nothing in the new order or in the old order was a proportionate authentication or proof of Him.

He was a man who was a person and an empirical individual by being the Word; and that was enough. Appointed by God for the salvation of all men, He took part in their misery and intervened in their tendency toward God. He is the sanctuary in which the Trinity gives itself to mankind, the precise point of direct passage from the human to the divine, the living way, the entrance that beckons, the path that leads to the heart of God and lies open to the heart of man. He is the road that lifts and carries those who travel on it, and which therefore invites and attracts with the attractiveness of God Himself.

If the assumed humanity was to be this offer of the invisible even in its visible form, if it was to subsist in this donation of the necessary even in its visible form, if it was to subsist in this donation of the necessary even in its flesh and blood, it had to reveal some outwardly perceptible reflection of this invisible and necessary, this imponderable but intensely meaningful property, which to this very day it retains in the Gospel narratives like some quality that endows a countenance with living expression and that is everything or nothing according to the will of each observer. Although this property is phenomenal and empirical, it exists only through a mystery and in a mystery, and is not really perceptible except in the perception of this mystery. It is something that leads the beholder to faith and blesses his eyes with faith; for, although it appears in the domain of natural vision, yet it is profoundly rooted in the supernatural, that is, the domain of faith.

Between this vague something and the grace that is everywhere offered and everywhere active, there were harmony and proportion; indeed, there were even affinity and continuity. Did not Christ's sacred humanity, empirical as it was, contain the transcendental totality and the visible form of grace, and did not something in it have to reveal this excellence that constituted it? Between this something and the life of grace which God in His universal goodness formed or sketched or tried to sketch in every soul, there were always this proportion and participation that could be discerned as though by intuition and connaturality.

Since it existed in the experimental domain, this quality was necessarily perceptible in some degree by natural knowledge. But it was open to natural knowledge in a very restricted and imperfect fashion, like an insoluble problem and a sign of contradiction. Because of the total divinization it expressed, it pertained essentially to a different order and required a different kind of knowledge: supernatural knowledge, the knowledge that belongs to grace and faith.

If we desire greater precision, we may say with St. Jerome that the quality we are speaking of must have been a certain radiance of mien, a certain majesty of attitude; or we may recall what some of the Fathers have said of Christ's beauty. In our opinion, however, we shall do better to leave to the supernatural its ineffable character. Let us confine ourselves to the assertion that this visible man was God who was giving Himself, and that those to whom the Father gave the grace that "drew" them could in some way discern immediately the glory of God shining in the face of a man, the glory which the Father sheds over His only-begotten Son: "Philip, he that seeth Me seeth the Father also."

Accordingly Christ was His own sign, His own proof, His "note." He is the way, and needs no other way to lead to Him. He is the perfect mediator, and supposes no other mediator to introduce men to Him. The truth is the judge of itself and of falsehood. As the truth is its own criterion, and as light is its own demonstration, Christ presented Himself through Himself: "He signs Himself with His own light."

This is the way we see Him teaching in the Gospel, without basing His words on anything but Himself, without proving anything, without appealing to authorities; He is content to manifest Himself and to live most nobly the message that is really He, the gift of the Trinity to mankind. This procedure is particularly striking in the case of His moral teaching, which is not a set of rules deduced from certain principles; it is not even a system that prevails because of its coherence or its appeal to the lofty sentiments of His hearers. It is He, the God-man and the incarnate Son, who is the living formula of all divinization and access to the Trinity. He has only to be Himself without keeping anxious watch over His words or restraining Himself, He has only to act and react frankly and simply in the presence of the Twelve and the multitude, to voice His preferences, His indignation, and His approval, in a word, to express Himself, in order to formulate the code of supernatural perfection for all mankind.

To be sure, He appeals to His miracles and prophecies by way of authentication. But these miracles are He, so strongly does He assert Himself in them; and the prophecies are also He, for He is the key to them and their fulfillment.

He presents His miracles more as a mark of His spirit, as a revelation of His mission, His goodness, and the gift of God in Him, that is, as the sign we spoke of before, than as an external guaranty designed to overpower all rationalist explanations. Does not He Himself reprehend the evil and adulterous generation that demands miracles as a condition for faith? In any case, His great argument, the essential motive on which He bases faith and for which He exacts so much confidence, is He Himself, His word, "But I say to you," and His works: "Believe the works." The supreme sign He gives is He Himself in His love for the Father and His obedience to the Father, that is, He Himself as the Son. He is there, He is God, and He gives Himself to the world; no need to seek outside of Him for an authentication of His message.

What He thus was in Himself, He is also in the Church; and the Church is the same in Him. Like Him and because of Him, the Church has its miracles and prophecies; does not St. Augustine say that the prophets foretold the Church even more clearly than they foretold Christ? But the miracles of the Church are not its chief argument. May we not even say that they are not in the front rank of argument? These miracles of goodness, mercy, and kindness seem rather designed to exalt charity, to foster love and devotedness toward others and generosity toward God, than to furnish an irrefutable minor for a syllogism to be used in controversy.

The great argument of the Church, as of Christ, must be the Church itself in Christ and Christ in the Church; for in the Church Christ continues to be God who gives Himself, and in Christ the Church continues to be the point at which God unites Himself to men and the emergence of the divine in the human. The Church cannot be all this in its empirical exterior, in its outer aspect as a visible institution, without some of its inner nature becoming manifest to the eyes of men.

In Jesus Christ, as we have said, this external appearance had the character of a sign and a note. According to the well-known text of St. Leo the Great, each of Christ's two natures, acting in conjunction with the other, revealed the other by its own way of acting; and therefore the incarnate Word manifested His divinity in His risen body when He exhibited His pierced hands, "to induce us to acknowledge that the divine and the human natures remained each in its own individuality, and thus to perceive that the Word is not the flesh, but rather to confess that the one Son of God is both the Word and the flesh."

The same, by analogy or rather by continuation, must be true of the Church. The Church continues Christ even in its visible exterior; hence this visible exterior must be modeled on Him, so that they who are able to read the delicately drawn but eloquent signs may discover Christ when they look at the Church. The Church, like Christ and in Christ, is an empirical reality and a transcendent mystery; yet it remains one; in the Church, therefore, as in Christ, a close union between the two must obtain. Since the Church, in its empirical aspect, is truly the body and the exterior of a divinization that diffuses itself, something in the empirical aspect must reveal this divinization.

As the redemption is still going on and as the persons to be divinized are sinners, this trait will ordinarily not be brilliant or glorious, and will not be completely decisive on the experimental level; on the contrary, it will be humble and hidden, though captivating. To the extent that it exists in the empirical order, it will be an object of natural knowledge, and can be fashioned into a science; this science is apologetics.

Yet its empirical exterior reveals only half of what it is, for it is essentially the expression of a transcendental divinization. It

146

will not be wholly perceptible unless this divinization is also perceived; hence an act of faith elicited with the help of grace is needed. Generally speaking, therefore, it will be a path leading to faith. It is a perpetual offer of the grace of faith, for in Christ it is the body and the expression of the divinization that is perpetually being given. In itself, when taken in its totality, it is a complete and sufficient sign that needs no other sign or introduction, a sign suitable for every soul. Such is the teaching of the Vatican Council:

> The Church itself, by reason of its admirable extension, its eminent holiness, and its inexhaustible fruitfulness in all good, its Catholic unity and unshakable stability, is a great and perpetual motive of credibility and an irrefutable witness of its own divine mission. And therefore, like a standard set up before the nations, it beckons to itself those who do not yet believe, and assures its children that the faith they profess rests on a most secure foundation. And a power from on high confirms this testimony. For our most gracious Lord stirs up and helps with His grace even those who wander astray, that they may "come to the knowledge of the truth" (I Tim. 2:4), and strengthens with His grace those whom He has brought "out of darkness into His marvelous light" (I Pet. 2:9), that they may persevere in this light; and He never deserts those who do not desert Him.

This passage describes the double action of Providence, internal and external, that gives an outer sign and grants interior grace for the understanding of the sign. The two matching gifts, or rather the single but twofold gift, is suited to the twofold nature in man and is like the twofold action exercised by Christ's humanity: the action of His word without and the action of His grace within.

Thus the Church itself is a sign of itself, perpetuating across the centuries the witness that Christ gives of Himself and of His prolongation in mankind, and continuing also the witness given of Christ by the Father. "The Church itself," says the Council; the Church itself is seen in its own light, in Christ;

the Church itself attracts those who are as yet its sons only by divine vocation; the Church itself retains its children, and confirms and consolidates their faith.

The science of apologetics, which considers the Church from outside, from the point of view of those who as yet remain beyond its doors, can discern the notes only from without. Accordingly these notes appear only on the surface, not in their essence, as marks sufficiently proclaimed by Christ and sufficiently discernible in themselves to set the Church apart from all other Christian confessions. But these marks, as such, are arbitrary, without a necessary connection with what they indicate; Christ could have chosen others, or could have made them express something else.

But in the theology of the mystical body, which considers the Church from within, the notes are also considered from within. This does not diminish their visibility; do we see the windows of a cathedral less clearly when we look at them from inside? The notes remain decisive signs and unimpeachable witnesses; they are such intrinsically, for they contain what they express, and they also contain Christ, who expresses the same thing; for they are ways of making known the presence of Christ in the Church. Once we perceive them distinctly, we need no longer speculate about Christ's past intentions or about the meaning He wished to give to these characteristics; they speak for themselves. Moreover, what they manifest in the interior of the Church is identical with what grace accomplishes in the interior of souls. At one stroke they teach the necessity of the Church for the inner life of Catholics and the essentially ecclesiastical nature of this inner life.

The list of the notes is well known. The Vatican Council gives it in the passage quoted above, even while insisting on the interior character of the guaranty which the Church is in itself. In the details mentioned by the Council, the "unshakable stability" may be taken as corresponding to apostolicity, for it signifies that the Church still is and always will be what it was at its origin at the time of the apostles. Thus we have the four traditional notes: unity, holiness, catholicity, and apostolicity.

And in fact, as we should observe, these four notes are exactly what we would expect of the society of grace in which

Christ and His characteristics are perpetuated. Christ's humanity receives its complete holiness and divinization directly from its union with God. This unparalleled perfection makes it the unity that contains, as in a source, the entire supernatural work accomplished by God among men over the surface of the earth and throughout the duration of the centuries. These four characteristics, unity, holiness, universality throughout space, and duration throughout time, are possessed by Christ's humanity regarded as the head of a mystical body. Therefore Christ's humanity will possess them in the society that is His body, and this society will likewise possess them. And these are the four notes of the Church regarded as the perpetuation of Christ: unity, holiness, catholicity, and apostolicity.

We may comment on this group of four notes by referring to what we have said about the Church, the new, supernatural mankind. Mankind has a certain unity by its very nature, an imperfect unity that gropingly seeks self-realization here on earth. It has a certain moral value or holiness, of which it possesses the norm in its natural law and which it must work out in detail. It also has a certain universality of its own, so that it finds self-expression only by spreading out indefinitely in space and time.

Mankind must likewise have unity, holiness, and spatial and temporal universality in its new, supernatural form, but in a new way and under a supernatural form; it must possess these properties in Christ, as it has its new form in Christ. And thus once again we have the four notes mentioned in the Creed: "one, holy, catholic, and apostolic Church."

One, holy, catholic, apostolic: these are the four traditional notes with which we associate the characteristics possessed by the Church as the body of Christ. But we repeat that we need not envisage them here formally as notes, as apologetic proofs. We can find elsewhere all the discussions of this subject that may be desired. We wish rather to present a theology of them in function of the doctrine of the mystical body. We are not concerned here with what the exterior of the Church is *de facto* or with the reasoning processes for which that fact can furnish a foundation; our purpose is to examine what this exterior is *de jure*, what is means for the faith, and accordingly what exactly we may expect to find there.

B. Unity. The first of the notes, unity, is perhaps the one that appears to be most prominent to the outside world and that best makes the Church known. It is also the note that is most explicitly brought out by Christ's words. Hence we shall have to consider it attentively.

Even infidels have been struck by this unity and by the marvelous organization that builds up the new Jerusalem into a unique whole so solidly cemented that neither the inevitable clash of human self-interests nor earthly or infernal forces have been able to make a breach in the impregnable structure.

However, he who sees nothing but this exterior has not as yet seen anything; such a unity is but the unity of a machine. If that is all we extol, we run the risk of repelling those who believe in life and its spontaneous freedoms. The unity of the Church is something much more and much better; it is the visible expression and the social body of an interior unity that is its soul and life, the visible side of a great invisible deification by which God in Christ unites all men with one another and with Himself. As the soul is the living principle and the explanation of the body, this invisible unity gives meaning to the visible unity; to understand the latter we have to understand the former.

We have already spoken of the soul and the body of the Church. Here we need but apply these notions to the idea of unity, especially of social unity. Every society may be said to have a soul, a collective soul, which makes it a living organization and is the form by which the multiplicity of members receives the collective unity that constitutes it a society. This soul is neither a complete substance nor a spiritual substance; its only reality consists in the social activities of the individuals it unites in the common end, means, and aspirations that bring them together. The more perfect a society is, the more perfect its soul will be. If the society has a supernatural perfection, as the Church has, its soul will likewise have a supernatural perfection. In the case of the Church, as we said before, this soul is the humanity of Christ regarded as a universal principle of divinization.

This soul of the Church which is the humanity of Jesus has an absolute unity, for it is one with the unity of a divine person, and at the same time, by reason of this divinity, it is the interior source of life, unity, and supernatural inwardness of each member. Hence it is simultaneously transcendent and immanent. In the same way, we may point out as a comparison, man's soul is one in itself because it has its own act and is a spirit, and it is also one with all parts of the body, imparting unity to all, because it is the form of the body.

We shall first consider the attribute of transcendence. Through Christ, the unity of the Church has its ultimate principle in one of the divine persons. This ultimate unity and nothing less is what Christ desired for His followers: "That they may be one, as We also are one," He repeated over and over. He conferred this ultimate unity on them by incorporating them into Himself, and no other ultimate unity is found in Him than the person of the Word. As His followers are one in Him, He Himself is one in the Word. Hence they must be one in Him, the Word, and therefore in God as triune.

Accordingly this is a sacred unity, an essentially supernatural unity. To get some idea of it, we may have recourse to natural analogies, such as comparison with well-regulated states or with families or the organism of living beings. Nothing is more legitimate; yet we must go beyond such figures. We are dealing with a fellowship that is definitely above all this, a fellowship with the mystery of absolute unity.

In the preceding chapter, when discussing grace, we spoke of a new kind of being, supernatural being, that exists through union with the very interior of Being. We must speak in similar fashion of supernatural unity. The Church is one with a unity that no finite being can bestow on itself or receive from the Creator by way of creation; a unity that cannot exist except by interior union with the inner unity of Being, that is, with Trinitarian unity. In the humanity of Christ, this is the hypostatic union; in the rest of mankind, it is mystical union with Christ's humanity.

This union cannot be known in itself alone, any more than it can exist by itself alone. Either we do not see it as it really is, or else we perceive in it Him who, through union, makes it what it is: Christ who is present in His members, the Son whom the Father sends to all mankind, the Trinitarian unity. This, and nothing less, is what Jesus desired for His members: a unity that comes incessantly from the Trinity and that incessantly carries those who contemplate it toward the Trinity. "That they all may be one, as Thou, Father, in Me and I in Thee; that they also may be one in Us; that the world may believe that Thou hast sent Me . . . . I in them and Thou in Me; that they may be made perfect in one, and the world may know that Thou has sent Me." This unity is a note, a sign, and we do not see it fully unless we believe in Christ as He is in the Trinity and in His humanity.

The primacy of such a unity is evidently absolute. It is not the product of the members it joins together, in the way that the unity of natural societies is a product of the tendency toward union found in men, whether such union is imposed by nature or sought by free choice. Rather the members are the product of it, and it makes them one in itself; for Christ by His influence causes Christians to be Christians, and they cannot live unless they are all united to Him. Thus the Church exists more truly in Christ, its unity, than it exists in the multiplicity of His members; for in Christ it exists in its source.

Yet that is the very reason why it exists so perfectly in each of Christ's members; it is as immanent in them as it is transcendent over them. For Christ, in whom it resides perfectly, resides deeply and supernaturally in each member. Compared with this unity, the unity of natural societies is superficial and external, and consists in a certain common end and means, a certain imitation of nature that cannot have full self-consciousness or take full possession of itself; for it is not in contact with the root of being.

The Church alone is so perfectly one in Christ that it has all its unity in all its parts, in the way that the human soul is present whole and entire in every part of the body. St. Peter Damian says that every Christian soul is the whole Church, and that the Church is also every human soul: "The Church of Christ is held together by such a strong bond of charity that it is mysteriously one in all men and whole in each man. Deservedly, then, the whole universal Church is regarded as the one spouse of Christ, and through the sacramental mystery each soul is considered to be the whole Church."

Émile Mersch

The unity of the Church is not a fitting together of parts, but a union of persons; and since these persons are wholes, they are united to one another as wholes, by an interior bond. The Church is one in this way because it is a society of men, but much more because it is a society of men sanctified in that Man who is the person of the Word; and therefore, as we said above, this Man supernaturally brings all the others together in Himself as persons.

We cannot argue from this totality of the Church in each of its members, that it exercises all its functions in each. "If the whole body were the eye, where would be the hearing? If the whole were hearing, where would be the smelling?" A unity that would suppress variety would no longer be a multiplicity, and if differentiated organs were lacking, the organism would cease to exist. Specialization and distinction must always be present, as we shall show later at greater length. But this specialization is for the benefit of the union; the various members, though not possessing the totality of functions, will perform their respective tasks, each in its own way, for the life of the whole and through the life of the whole. The very variety of operations bears witness to the unity of the Spirit and of Christ, as St. Paul declares.

What we have to conclude from this totality is that the principle of ecclesiastical unity may not be taken in too narrow a sense so far as it affects each Christian soul. Otherwise the supposition would have to be denied. Christ is the bond of inner unity in each member, as He is the bond of collective unity in the whole assemblage. Is Christ divided, so that we may ask if a member situated on one side is better than a member situated on the other side? In a very real sense, there is no more in the whole Church than in a single member of the faithful, as there is no more in heaven than in a person who receives Holy Communion. The difference is that Christ is in the Church for certain functions, and is in the believer to make him live and act. He is the same in one and the other, and we should explain the mystery of unity very badly were we to split it into sections in order to compare the fragments.

Unity of this sort will find its clearest expression in love or charity, the great unifying force. Is not this unity the perpetuation, in the limitless human race, of that loving embrace that was and forever is the Incarnation? This is an infinitely close and efficacious embrace, because the love poured out in it is infinitely ardent; it is the embrace with which God, in His incarnate Son, presses mankind so strongly to His heart in love and for love that He makes men one among themselves and with Him. "God so loved the world as to give His only-begotten Son, that whosoever believeth in Him may not perish, but may have life everlasting."

This is the way the Fathers regarded our unity; for them it was a sweet and good unity, a gentle and motherly unity, a unity of love, charity, and devotedness. This is also what Jesus wanted. He had no use for a unity expressed in overlordship and flattery. He said quite unmistakably: "The kings of the Gentiles lord it over them; and they that have power over them, are called beneficent. But you not so!" He required a unity of mutual service, respect, and love. In the discourse in which He spoke at greatest length and indeed exclusively about unity, His theme was restricted to love. This is the discourse after the Last Supper, and was uttered after the institution of the sacrament of unity and charity. In His thoughts unity and charity are linked, and He speaks of them together; they are equally His sign, His commandment, His supreme concern. In His eyes, unity and charity are identical.

That is exactly what our unity is: "One Christ, loving Himself." The one Christ gives Himself unreservedly to all His members by giving them to one another and to God. This unity proceeds from eternal charity. Consequently it must not only be anchored in charity but must also inspire and vitalize charity; it must make each man look upon all other men as being one with him, as the pupil of his eye, as being one in calling and in fact with God and Christ, as those whom he must save at all costs in order to save himself.

We need scarcely remark that such a unity differs to the point of contrast from a simple centralization. Of course a certain centralization is indispensable in the Church, as in every human society. But its importance should not be exaggerated; indeed, it is the product of a gradual formation, and varies with different epochs. At the Vatican Council, for example, a certain bishop could maintain without heterodoxy that centralization was excessive in the Church; he could not have said the same of unity without offending against the faith.

Unity in Christ is life and a condition for life. Centralization is an abstract formula that can lead to death if carried too far. By forcing life too much to the center, it runs the risk of lopping off members and of killing the organism. Two things so different cannot be identified.

Ecclesiastical unity, moreover, exhibits seeming paradoxes at some essential points of its structure which clearly mark out its originality as compared with other kinds of unity obtaining among men. For instance, the inequality resulting from the duty to command that is found in some and the duty to obey that is found in others, leaves intact the equality that levels them all in the eyes of the one supreme Pastor, whose sheep they all are.

Ecclesiastical superiors exercise their leadership as public personages, and their superiority, which is genuine as regards their office, vanishes when their private life is in question. They interpret the law of Christ with authority deriving from Christ, and they alone have such power; but the law they alone interpret has to be observed by them in common with all the rest. True, they dispense the means of sanctification; but, like all the others, they need the sacrament of penance if they sin, the Eucharist if they wish to have life in them, and extreme unction when they come to die. From this point of view they are part of the faithful, no less than their subjects. The pope, like any other Catholic, has to go to confession, and he needs a priest to administer the sacrament. As a private person he too is one of the sheep of the flock he leads in his capacity of public person.

I may be mistaken, but this combination of radical equality with radical inequality seems to me to indicate the point at which the Church differs from natural societies. Natural societies fluctuate between absolute monarchy that always threatens to degenerate into a despotism incompatible with the multitude's personal autonomy, and an unsociable egalitarianism prone to deny the unity that ought to organize the masses in a hierarchical order. The Church speaks with an authority which it receives from its head and which is stronger than that of any king, for it is the authority of God and is always exercised under God's direction. No account has to be rendered to anyone on earth, and no one demands an account, for all are persuaded that what that authority does it does well. At the same time, the Church speaks with perfect equality; all have sinned and have the same need of a Savior and a Teacher, for all alike are children in His eyes.

The center of each soul and the center of the whole organism coincide in Christ. The formulas that may seem to imply centralization actually signify reverence for the interior life, and formulas of supernatural personalism become formulas of interior Catholicism and union.

That is the theory. In practice, it is carried out imperfectly, at times very imperfectly indeed. But even this has its foundation in theory: the Church and its unity are still in formation, and this formation progresses in an order of redemption, that is, in the midst of sin and evil. Unity is realized only little by little, in the neverending struggle against its contrary that is ever springing up within the growing unity.

We shall come back to this point in a moment. Indeed, we could come back to it at every moment, in connection with each noble attribute we shall have to extol in the Church. To avoid repetition, we may here emphasize the matter once for all, so that we shall not have to say the same thing over again whenever important occasions demand reference to it.

One of these occasions occurs precisely at this juncture. While discoursing on unity, we have to consider the contradiction which a divided Christianity offers to Christ's prayer, "That they may be one." The scandal has its explanation, and the explanation touches the essence of Christianity: the unity of Christianity is the unity of a redemption that has to be achieved step by step. Sin remains in the world and in the Church, and sin is a breaking-away and secession, the source of narrow egoisms, of suspicious individualisms, and of shattering lusts. The work of unity has to be accomplished in a process of separation and disintegration; it is a struggle for unity in the Church militant; a struggle against a multiplicity that, from within and without, is ever springing up again with resurging sin.

For the evil that makes its appearance in schism is found in all mankind and in the heart of every believer. In the matter of unity, neither the world nor Christianity nor each soul realizes the ideal. The world is rent apart in a profusion of religions when there should be but one; the hosts of those who cleave to Christ and sincerely desire to cleave to Him are divided among a great number of Christian confessions, although Christ founded only one Church; and the faithful keep aloof from one another in various ways, although they ought to foster union and charity in Christ. These three gaps are connected; the cleavage showing up in various places comes from the same evil, the same practical forgetfulness of the immensity, the catholicity, the charity, and the unity of Christ. The fissures will not be repaired at their base unless we are sharply aware of this evil.

Any attempt to seek the source of this evil in others is fruitless. We have no more right to judge them than we have power to change them. We perform a salutary work if we ferret out the evil in ourselves and in our own people, for we have the duty to be humble and the power, God aiding, to become better. Catholics especially, who can make no concessions in the matter of doctrine, ought to be eager to make concessions about their persons. Their Church, their leaders, and they themselves enjoy so many privileges that are the good of Christ in them, that they ought to be happy to emphasize their personal shortcomings as wretched sinners; no one, certainly not they themselves, should be tempted to look on these privileges as personal glories.

God Himself teaches them in Sacred Scripture to make such acknowledgments. Scripture narrates how the first bishops, but recently consecrated, were all guilty of defection through fear: "The disciples all leaving Him, fled." After this example, Catholics need not be afraid to avow that in the course of the centuries, at times of persecution, bishops have led their people into heresy and schism. In the apostles' desertion, Scripture focuses its inexorable light on Peter's abandonment, and so strongly stresses his denial, his break with unity, and his failure to make a public profession of faith that, as we behold the foundation stone crumbling, we are bound to realize that the firmness it will have later on is not a quality of the rock itself. And with reference to this same Peter, Scripture reports the altercation at Antioch. Peter, invested with the full power of the papacy after the Ascension and Pentecost, in the seeming opportunism of drawing back from the wearisome task of dealing with a separatist clique, holds himself aloof from the great Church and thus furthers secessionist tendencies. This harsh fact is found in the sacred text. And Paul, under the inspiration of the Holy Spirit, insisted on relating this weakness on the part of him who ought to have been the pillar of the Church, just as he wished then and there to reproach Peter to his face; for Peter was pulling away from Christian life and unity.

What Scripture does, Christians can do without treachery to piety, and indeed with the joy of humility. They can acknowledge that they themselves and their pastors have carried God's treasure in a fragile vessel. They should glory religiously in all that God has wrought through their Church; but they should be even readier to proclaim that they have contributed precious little, and should add that, if God has in all essentials preserved the bond of unity in their leaders, personal shortcomings have counteracted the miraculous work of unity by many an act of petty selfishness. Let them fear to put their hopes in any man or even seem to do so.

All this was inevitable, and Jesus foresaw it; the human heart is so easily duped and so quickly befuddled. There had to be and there has been the sort of pride that identifies august functions with banal personalities; there had to be and there have been opportunist insincerities, abuses of power, and inability to understand; and in such human constrictions the splendid unity of Catholicism could not display all its grandeur and attractiveness. The astounding thing is not that egoism and narrowness have entered the sanctuary, for Jesus has opened it to men, but that they have not penetrated farther.

In turning such matters over in our minds, let us guard against the conceited and sordid joy of finding our superiors at fault. Under pretext of exalting unity, this would degenerate into a spirit of secession. "Hypocrite, cast out first the beam out of thy own eye" (Matt. 7:5). The evil is a human evil; all men, whether they are priests or religious or laymen are soiled by it, and the first task of the grace that heals it is to show to each man the center of infection in him.

Do we not have to confess, to our shame, that in many religious environments the faithful abandon Catholic practices, piety, life, and even religion, because those in authority make these matters so exclusively their own affair that private individuals no longer see what part is left for them? In many places is it not true that defections, secessions, and petty schisms are owing to the imperious airs of the clergy, whether secular or regular, to their perpetual interfering, their perfidious opportunism, their mania for identifying docility to grace with respect for the soutane, in a word, to the egoism and the vanity that make some churchman instead of Christ the center of religion and substitute an odious vaunting of self for the witness that ought to be borne to the unity of all mankind?

Do not the faithful, who are likewise men, as all priests are numbered among the faithful, have to admit that they are quick to believe in their own superiority and the bad faith of others—a trait hardly calculated to attact these others—and that they scarcely show the rest of men that the unity whereof they live, Catholic unity, is the unity of the whole human race? How many of them care, if only a little, about the union of the Churches and the conversion of the world? And yet Christ who is in them has ardently desired and still desires such unity; and countless of their separated brothers long for it with passionate weeping.

If that unity does not come, may not the reason be, in part, that we obstruct it? If it does not appear attractive, is not the reason that we defile it under our leprosy? And if upright souls do not discern it, is not the fault also in us who keep it hidden? That is what we have to recognize before we can apply a remedy; it is not our job to weigh the responsibilities incurred by Photius or Henry VIII. We need collective humility, ecclesiastical humility, the humility of sincerity and love that cries out its deficiencies in the public squares for fear lest men saddle them on the unity of Christ, humility that is the mark of Christ and the true service of unity.

If Catholics, the faithful and their pontiffs, would let Christ display in them all that He is and all that the Church is in Him, the path leading to the union of Christian Churches would soon be smoothed. And if other Christians would let Christ show forth in them all that He is and all that Christianity is in Him, all the love, the sincerity, and truth, the unity that He is, the religious unity of the earth would soon come to be a reality.

But if man's sin does not allow this supernatural unity to display all its glory in the redemption that is still going on, sin cannot keep it from existing, for it is indefectible, and even in the divisions caused by sin, cannot prevent it from being a seed, a force, an inception of the perfect unity it actually is. Although the Catholic Church is made up of men and hence of divergent individualities, it is not on that account less but rather more a magnificent spectacle of unity for those who have eyes to see. In spite of everything, ourselves included, the unity of all mankind in Christ is found in us. Little by little it will make us less unworthy of bearing witness to Him.

The unity of all mankind and of all Christianity in Christ is found even in the divisions of the Christian confessions. More deeply than human lack of understanding, Christ with His unity lives in all His followers who have not sinned against the light and against charity; and such followers are numerous, and Christ's life is in them. As we write this we are thinking respectfully of the Christians of the Russian Church and of the Protestants of the German confessions who, during the Second World War, remained faithful to Christ even at the cost of life. The faith that they all have, despite the faulty formulation they give to it, is a participation in the God-man's knowledge; their hope is a longing anticipation of the unity of all men with God in Christ; their charity is a communication of the love that embraces all mankind in the incarnate Son; their grace is the same eternal life that flows from the same source and is diffused over all, bringing them all together by the very principle that gives life to them as individuals. Hence unity exists in all Christianity; it is disfigured on the surface, but is real at the center. It exists, and therefore the effective and visible union of all, which otherwise would seem utopian, must be said to be capable of realization. Unity comes at the first springing up of all Christian life, for Christ sends it along with all His love. In our efforts to achieve it outwardly, we have an invincible ally within.

To dedicate themselves to the realization of this aim in the way open to them, Catholics have only to be Catholics, or rather to become ever better Catholics. They must rid themselves more and more of an ever resurging individualism, nationalism, and of all particularist pride of culture, temperament, and mentality. To the greatest extent possible, they must be living witnesses to God's gift to all mankind in Christ.

Those men who remain outside as well as those who are inside may fail to perceive all that is implied in the one true Church. But that does not make its lines less clear. In desiring to draw near to God, they really desire what the God-man alone has to give and what His Church, which has a particular pope and a definite canon law, unceasingly holds out to them.

When God delivered Himself up to mankind in Christ, He drew no limits; the believer who has eyes to see, knows that the Savior's human nature is mystic and catholic: "Christ is all and in all" (Col. 3:11). Likewise, when Christ delivered Himself up to His Church, to Peter and the apostles, He did so without reserve or restriction, and His Church is a mystical and universal "body." Wherever He may have gone after that, to take His place at the right hand of the Father or in the depths of souls, He remains the Christ of His Church and of Peter; and the first steps of His approach to any heart and the first touches of His grace that is never idle in any part of the world, is also the first moment of His residence in men.

The vast extension which the body of the Church receives from its soul is comparable to the extension which the human body receives from the human soul. As the form of the body, man's soul is limited in time and space, for the body is thus limited. As a spirit, however, the soul is so superior to time and space that, far from being contained in them, it rather contains them, as is evidenced by its power to give intelligible expression to them. But this soul, this spirit, constitutes with the body a single being that is man. The soul imparts existence to the body and is its act, its ultimate interior principle; and the body is the realization and expression of the soul on the level open to experience. Accordingly, if the body on its part limits the soul in time and space by its own limitation, the soul, on its part and because of its own illimitation, confers on the body a certain independence of time and space. We may ponder, for example, the boundless expanses attained by certain of man's acts that in themselves depend on his animal life, such as the act of imagining or the act of seeing. They take place in the organism and through the organism, and yet they reach objects at the immense distances where these objects are located, and at will bring forth in interior vision vast regions with their limitless spaces. And in an act such as this man sees also himself: an infinitesimal speck, almost indiscernible, clambering up a mountain or losing itself in a crowd. This clearly brings out both the smallness of the body in itself, and the greatness it has as an instrument and as the body of such a soul; it is a limited body of an unlimited soul, and hence is in its own way unlimited.

We may say that the body of the Church presents an analogous case. It likewise is the body of something unlimited, the body of a soul that is the universal gift of the Infinite to men in Christ. In its own way, therefore, it must share in this illimitation. The body realizes and expresses such illimitation on the empirical level, as we have said. And this illimitation in turn impresses itself on the body, conferring a certain illimitation on it as an empirical thing, but with reference to the supernatural attitudes entailed by such illimitation. However, the body's illimitation is only a sharing in the soul's illimitation, and is discerned only when the latter is apprehended by faith.

Nevertheless the Church is a society with a limited exterior. But when we contemplate the infinite gift which God offers to all men in this Church, we may discover, discern, or conjecture some influence exercised by the Church whenever some effect of this gift allows itself to be discovered, discerned, or conjectured; we may apprehend certain derivations or coincidences that are sometimes extraordinary, sometimes quite natural. Such presages and inklings are found wherever grace works and man cooperates, however little, with the divine advances. Even non-Christian religions, to single out those that seem farthest removed from the body of the Church, may be regarded, by what is essential to them as human religions, as the collective responses which mankind, left to itself and without special graces, but still in the grip of sin that continues to wreak havoc in it and all its works, even the fairest, has given as best it could to the divine vocation that takes in the whole race of men after the Fall. But the Church is not that same response, for it is the absolute and last response, the blameless, sure, integral response that a special Providence has called forth, the response made by God Himself and subsisting in God Himself, although made also by men and by a man who is the God-man.

May we not say that the Church is great with all the extension of those religions, that is, with all the extension of the religious phenomena in mankind, though with an expansion that is still to be achieved and still to be freed of the encumbrance of matter and of sin? May we not say that the Church is one in their immense multiplicity? Thus we may behold the one Church in them all, just as, when we know how to look, we can discover the one sun in scattered rays, or the full glory of the opened flower in the midst of the drooping leaves that surround it.

If the Church is thus the "body" whose soul is Christ, and if it is union with God and the vehicle of the universal salvific will, it must be necessary with the necessity of Christ, of God, and of God's universal will to save. Therefore we must insist that salvation is not to be found outside the Church, and that submission to the Roman Pontiff is necessary for the salvation of every human creature.

This does not mean that adherence to the Church is just one more condition to fulfill in order to achieve salvation, but that the Church is salvation such as it is offered today; not that the Church is an added intermediary between God and man, any more than Christ is such an intermediary, but that it is the pure gift of God to men which is always present in the way that is needed for men. Christ is mediator, not as a third person placed between two conflicting parties, but as God who lives with man in the unity of His unique divine person. In like manner the Church is not a mechanism placed between Christ and the faithful, but is Christ Himself who has come to live in mystical union with the faithful.

Thus the Church, which is necessary as Christ is necessary, is intolerant as Christ is intolerant. Christ is essentially intolerant; since He is the way, the truth, and the life, whatever is cut off from Him is deviation, error, and death. And in Christ, the Church is also essentially intolerant. Christ continues to be in the Church what He is in Himself, the way, the truth, and the life; outside the Church, consequently, men can only lose themselves, deceive themselves, and die.

Although this intolerance is essential to the Church, it is not disdainful or arrogant, any more than Christ's intolerance is. Christ readily admitted that a man might be upright, holy, and acceptable to God before knowing Him and becoming His disciple. He admitted this and rejoiced at it: "I have not found so great faith in Israel"; "I say to you that the publicans and the harlots shall go into the kingdom of God before you." But He was the union of God and man, and He regarded all such reconciliations of man with God as reconciliations with Himself. The Church does the same. It does not pretend that the persons of whom it is composed, whether they are its visible heads or its members, are of themselves a road to God; it says that Christ is in them fully enough that, although they may be less noble than their task, He is never unequal to His mission. The Church does not say that no holiness can come to light outside its visible frontier; but it claims that holiness, whereever it may spring up, is always hers. Any degree of holiness that may be realized, is found fully in the Church alone. Hence the Church can admire such holiness, without ceasing to believe in its own unique excellence. Without in any way abating its intolerance, and even when pushing its intolerance to the extreme limit, the Church can be free from all aggressiveness and can ever throw open its doors in warm welcome.

Every source of saintliness on earth, even in schism or paganism, belongs to the Church, for holiness springs up only from a seed that has retained something of the Church or is linked with the Church in virtue of the grace of God whose visible form is the Church. The Church is still fertile in those separated fragments. As St. Augustine points out, it sometimes happens that a vine has pushed its way into brambles, and that a traveler sees a bunch of grapes hanging in the tangle of briars; he gathers the fruit but avoids the thorns: "Pluck the grapes, avoid the thorns, but notice the root"; the traveler knows well from what root the cluster comes.

This teaching does no violence to souls, and it is not an irking imperialism usurping power to regulate the torrents of grace or imprison its flood within alien banks. Life itself gives notice of its exigencies in order to develop its greatness, and requires full attachment to the body in order that the blood may richly nourish all its parts.

Therefore, when the Church declares that men must have her for their mother, as otherwise they will not have God for their Father, she merely expresses in words what grace silently urges in the hearts of those who have received grace but have not clearly understood its demands. The Church does not roar with the haughty tones of a martinet, but pleads with the anguished insistence of love. Her intolerance is exacting but sweet; it is the intolerance of unyielding truth.

C. Holiness. After unity comes the mark of holiness; we believe in "one holy Church." As we have already spoken of holiness in various connections, little remains to be said. The holiness of the Catholic Church as expressed in its moral code and its cult, its sacraments and its teaching, is well known. Everyone is acquainted with the schools of sanctity, similar in the midst of variety, that are the religious orders nurtured in her bosom: missionary and hospital congregations, Carthusians and Little Sisters of the Poor. We observe the magnificent procession of saints whom the Church sends forth to meet the Lamb; and we should note that they are saints because they belong to the Church and have lived the teaching of the Church with love.

We should like to dwell on this truth. What makes the saints heroes? This has to be understood, and we would miss their meaning were we to pay homage to them by turning aside from the masses of their fellow men. The saints manifest what the people are, and point out the treasures of holiness found among them, somewhat as miracles, according to St. Augustine, have the purpose of drawing attention to the marvels that daily occur throughout the world but that become commonplace because of their very frequency: *assiduitate viluerunt.*

The saints repeat this lesson often. Their humility, their occasional deficiencies, a certain lack of achievement, even the perfections that are found in them but are received from others, bring the truth home to us. They are saints because of the environment in which they live and because of Christ from whom everything comes to them and who continues to live on in the whole Church. Their holiness was rooted in the common soil before it became their own. Therefore it bears witness to the Catholic holiness of the Church and not, properly speaking, to their own sanctity.

This common holiness is the outstanding as well as the greatest miracle wrought by the all-holy God. It is a human holiness, prosaic like ordinary human life; a holiness suited to every man and even to every sinner, since every man is a sinner. This miracle is more striking and significant than any other, for, being the message of divinization for all men, it is more precisely the pure message of the God-man, the message addressed to all mankind. The message gains a hearing from every man, for every man perceives that it describes a perfection meant for him; it tells of a holiness, a divinization he can actually possess, and grace operating from within informs him of his need of it.

We need not demonstrate the existence of this miracle in these pages; we have only to give the theological theory, which in turn will effectively aid us to ascertain its existence. The principle in this theory is the Christological dogma, which also governs ecclesiology, that Christ is perfectly God, perfectly man, and perfectly one; and hence that He is the type and ideal of divinized man, who is man as he actually is, Adam's progeny. The conclusion arrived at is the formula of common, universal human holiness: to be divinized in Christ, man, whoever he may be, is exactly as he ought to be; his sluggish heart, his intermittent courage, and his barely awakened intelligence are just what are required; even his sin, with all the miseries it leaves in its wake, is so far from being an obstacle that it is precisely what a continuing redemption presupposes.

This description of man in Christ's redemption and in the holy Church which is a redemption indicates how man ought to unite himself to God's will and freely to let himself be formed by this will. With man's free cooperation and even through such cooperation, in all that man can do and suffer, God will beget him as His adopted son in His incarnate Word. Everything can help toward this. Our very difficulties and past faults will teach us patience, humility, filial dependence, prayer, obedience, and adherence to God in love. The poor human effort, so short of breath and power, is exactly what God needs in order to insert His own all-powerful effort that can make sons of Abraham out of stones and children of God out of wretched men, by utilizing their very miseries.

This holiness can always be realized, because the precept to be holy is measured by one's inner capacity and light. It is universal, because all men, with their human resources, have all that is needed for receiving it. It is transcendent, because it is inserted as a member into the holiness of the God-man, the Redeemer, and because it makes Christians perfect as the heavenly Father is perfect, thus imitating Christ who is the consubstantial image of the Father. And it is a collective holiness in which the holiness of each individual combines with that of all the others to form a single holiness of the whole body, and in which each is begun, developed, completed, explained, influenced, and supported by every other; like the Christian life and the quality of membership in Christ, each man's holiness is interior to each, yet is connected in solidarity with the holiness of all. Such sanctity may not seem very remarkable when regarded in its apparent isolation, but is magnificent when regarded in its connection with the whole, for then it is splendid with the splendor of the whole.

To see it thus we need grace, the *gratia redemptoris* that corresponds to the holiness. This grace is precisely the grace which holiness makes manifest and of which it is the outer body, the grace contained in the reserves of holiness under pressure, so that it is always ready to gush forth. And in order that no one may distractedly and indifferently wander past the sight of holiness and grace that are so near, a more striking holiness breaks forth at points, posing in an inescapable way the perpetual question: "What think you of the Church?"

The holiness in question is conferred by the redemption. We believe that we have to meditate deeply on Christ the Redeemer if we wish to understand the universal holiness of His work. The great wonder is not that God raises up saints, but that He makes saints out of the poor sinners that we are, by means of the consequences of our sins and in an environment continually ravaged by sin. The task is earthly and humble; it is the march of rational animals, heavy-footed and soiled, toward God. But that makes it all the more splendid and moving; it is the work of repeated repentance and forgiveness, of a cult that is partly material and is always accompanied by the letter that weighs down the spirit. But in general this magnificence remains invisible even to those in whom it is realized, and the glorious image that is slowly formed in the souls of the just will not be seen until the day when all veils are parted.

For God, who assists His holy Church to be the Church militant on earth, does not assist it to be the Church triumphant on earth. He helps it to fight against the sin that still remains in the heads as well as in the members, the sin that keeps it from being what it ought to be and what it already is in seed and hope, in Christ.

The holy Church humbly proclaims this fact in her prayer and teaching. In the liturgy and the psalms the officiating priest who speaks in the name of the Church unceasingly avows his guilt; and in her teaching the Church affirms with all her might that sinners are indeed members, and her priests and pontiffs, though laden with faults, are nevertheless priests and pontiffs. "No flesh should glory in His sight." Neither the faithful of the Church nor the hierarchy may appropriate to themselves the glory that is due to God alone. They do so to some extent; that seems to be inevitable for poor human nature. Yet no man ought thus to glory; the genuine holiness which is dogmatically defined must be universally human and truly catholic.

D. Catholicity. In the ordinary sense, the catholicity of the Church means its universal diffusion. Universal diffusion belongs rightfully to the Church, for the Church is the message of salvation addressed to every man; universal diffusion is also a fact, for the Church is established everywhere or almost everywhere. The Church has always been aware of its vocation to cover the earth; scarcely was the Church born than it set about its duty of converting the Roman Empire, and even spread beyond that Empire's frontiers. It has always returned to this work, and after the persecutions and reversals it suffered, began again both to repair its ruins and to invade the universe.

Even more astonishing than this expansion are the resistance of the Church to the disruptive influence of distension and the fact that while ever spreading, it remains intrinsically one.

> Though spread over the earth, the Church everywhere carefully guards the same faith, as if it occupied but a single house. It believes the same dogmas, as though it had but one heart and one soul. It announces this teaching with a single voice, and transmits it as though it had only one mouth. The languages spoken over the earth may vary; but the power of tradition remains the same. The Churches founded in Germany do not differ from other Churches in their beliefs or traditions; nor do the Churches that are in Spain, or those found among the Celts or in the East or in Egypt or in Libya.

Space does not conquer the Church, but the Church conquers space. The whole universe, and it alone, is big enough for the Church.

We have only to scrutinize this catholicity with attention to find in it the particular truth that is the theme of these pages. The paradox of this immense extension is that it leaves the unity of the Church intact. Over the whole earth the Church remains a single entity, the one mystical body of the Savior. The universality of its expansion corresponds exactly to the central characteristic of its constitution. Besides having a positive commission, it has a need to expand in order to be itself, just as a tree, in order to live, has to spread its branches over the surrounding land.

Jesus commanded the Church to teach all nations. This order merely expresses the structure He gave it. And this structure in turn is merely the expression of Jesus Himself in the society where He continues to live. Thus we come back again to the Incarnation, the point of departure and the orientation of all Christianity. As we said before, the Incarnation heightened the perfection native to Christ's humanity by endowing it with the personality of the Word; yet it remains human, or rather becomes fully human, so far as a human nature can be made fully human in God and by the power of God. Therefore it is universally human and the principle of life for the whole human race.

Christ does not change. In the Church, which is His body, He retains His fullness of humanity. Because of Him, the Church is perfectly, transcendentally, surpassingly human; and all mankind is needed to express concretely the human perfections contained in the Church, the mystical body of Christ.

In consequence, the property of catholicity does not merely prove that the Church is endowed by God with powerful forces, or that it is supported by God's all-powerful assistance. It is the sign that the Church is human with a divine perfection, and that it is the mystical body of Him in whom all mankind can and ought to be recapitulated. It is a "note" informing us, by God's grace, that the Church is even more than a society founded by Christ; for it is Christ continued.

The observable fact that the Church fills the earth is a strong argument in its favor. But the thousand indications demonstrating that it remains the same in this immense expansion, and that this appropriation of the universe is the act by which it achieves its full growth, giving to Christ all mankind that is His plenitude and to mankind the supernatural physiognomy it can receive from Christ alone, is a more decisive proof that it is the Church of the Lord; for thus it is His body.

The Greek word for Church, *Ekklesia,* is derived from a root meaning "call." May we not interpret the name as the great call, the limitless vocation God offers to the whole human race which in principle He assumed in Christ?

The catholicity of the Church is an inner catholicity, a radical and constitutive catholicity, of the whole Church and of each of its members. The external catholicity is but the expression of this internal catholicity. The external catholicity expresses the internal catholicity, first, as we have said, in a certain universal adaptability. The religion of the God-man is suited to every man in the formula of universal holiness it proposes and the universal realism in which, as the continuation of the redemption, it admits and can admit the multitude of sinners, that is, the multitude making up actual mankind. Everything in this religion is to be theirs, not by sufferance but by right.

Sin is obviously the reason why the Church has not yet been able to impress its catholicity on all mankind. Too much sin bars its expansion. Even so the internal catholicity finds expression, though only in a sort of anguish and torment and in the ardent pressure that impels the Church to attain its true size and to become in fact all mankind.

To be true to itself, the Church must become completely universal. So long as it has not yet arrived at this goal, it does not outwardly correspond to what Christ is within it. There are certain kinds of union with God and types of sanctity which are genuinely human and truly belong to the Church, but which the Church has not yet presented to God or the world because they are peculiar to some particular nations, races, and cultures that have not yet entered the Church. In other words, certain genuinely religious attitudes have been drained off by other religions; we are not referring to other Christian sects, in which this truth is quite evident. Yet such attitudes properly belong to Christ, as we have tried to show.

All this variety of temperaments and mentalities is needed to bring out the unique holiness possessed by the Church as the mystical body of Christ. Catholicity, holiness, and unity are not mutually exclusive but rather mutually complementary. Since the Savior's holiness is transcendent, it requires the universality of men to display in detail all that it contains in unity. The Church will not have its full perfection until the peoples of all the nations have entered its doors. Meanwhile it possesses only by right and in compressed energy the power for good that cannot operate at full efficiency except in the totality of the human race. In the same way we cannot see all that a child is capable of until he becomes a man.

As a universal society and the unity of mankind, the Church cannot realize the perfection of its unity save in a magnificent variety. Man, always essentially one, is also essentially diverse according to the various epochs, environments, climates, and circumstances in which he lives. Since the Catholic religion is the religion of man and of the God-man, it does not have to be uniform to be unified. In its teeming life, every shade of humanity, every people, every race, and every century has its own peculiar, rightful place and its particular, individual Catholic luster.

This unity in variety, this living catholicity can be only the work of centuries and of a long, patient labor that assimilates everything without suppressing anything. In the beginning, missionary effort is geographically restricted and inevitably establishes a certain uniformity that is the product of centralization. But time passes, and the Spirit who peoples the Church over all the earth has in our day made more clearly manifest the divine commission of supernatural universalism, and so we have native clergies, hierarchies, languages, arts, and outlooks. The Spirit suggests more and more unmistakably to the Church the variety, the flexibility, the adaptation, and the multiplicity of human preferences it can allow. The unity of the Church is a living unity, like the Spirit's own unity, for its unity is that of Christ; it is a unity so immensely human that it cannot well find expression except in the immensely variegated unity of mankind. To tell the truth, a different kind of unity, a unity achieved by rigidity, monotony, and conformism would be clearer, easier to conceive mathematically, and to organize juridically; but it would be dead and inhuman; it would not be a unity vitally organized to form a living thing; it would not be the mysterious, catholic unity of the Church. The day is coming, and we see it approaching, when the catechism will be thoroughly Indian in the Indies, Malaysian in Malaysia, and Russian in Russia, as it is Latin among the Latin races; and it will be all the more profoundly one on that account. We need not add that, although such a work can be begun by missioners, it cannot be carried through to completion except by the indigenous Churches themselves.

Faced by these bold initiatives of the Spirit and also by threats of deep cleavages among the peoples, certain cautious souls entertain misgivings about unity. As if the unity of the Church, that has to have external expression, had its source in externals! As if, in itself and its inner principle, it were in any way a product of external regulations! All the bishops and all Christians might be walled off from one another in unconnected reservations; nevertheless Catholicism would be one; they might all speak different languages; yet Christ, the life of them all, would still be one. There are neither Jews nor Gentiles; all men are one in Christ. And the inner unity would reproduce outer unity by adapting it to circumstances; for men do not make this inner unity; it makes itself, and Christ makes it by making Christians His members. Such is its life and energy that man can oppose it by trying to force it into his own categories as well as by rising up against it to cleave it; strangling causes death no less efficiently than dismemberment. The unity of the Church is not a formula but a life, the life of Christ, first principle of the new humanity, who makes it more supernaturally one in its very humanity, and hence more supernaturally varied, by bringing it into living unity.

God can intervene as He pleases; but in the Christian economy which He has made His own, He performs His actions through men. Men are responsible for the coming of salvation to all mankind for whom it is destined, and men set the limits of this salvation by the degree of their cooperation. External activity, the departure of missioners, and even financial resources are needed in this collaboration; but they are not the essential thing. The essential thing is the source of all this, which is charity, love and devotedness toward others, ardent concern for the salvation and happiness of all, inner zeal for the kingdom of God; the main thing is intense living of the true Christian life, that is, the life of Christ; not the life He lives in Himself, but the life men let Him live in them; both the full life He lives in the Church, and the mysterious, inceptive life He endeavors to live by grace everywhere in mankind.

That is the inner fire; and it is Christ present here on earth in His members and in the charity of men. The irradiation of the heat that is to spread over the world depends on the flames of this fire.

E. Apostolicity. The Church exists everywhere and always. Its life resists time as well as space, or rather dominates time and space, and from so high a vantage point that it takes in all the successive generations of men as it comprises their geographical expansion.

THE CATHOLIC TRADITION: The Church

The thing that is now the Catholic Church began with Adam. The first to be a member of Christ was Adam, or else Abel, as is said more often, to preserve the parallelism between the two heads of mankind. The Church endures forever, and is always the same since its origin. But at this first beginning the Church was in a preparatory stage; it was not fully established until after the life and death of Jesus, or, more precisely, after Pentecost. As Christ, head of the whole mystical body, is not, properly speaking, a member of that body, according to the ordinary teaching of theology, we must hold that the Church, as the mystical body, began with the apostles. In this sense it has the characteristic, or note, of being apostolic.

This note has been emphasized from the origins of Christianity. The Fathers declare that Christian preaching is true because it is the same as the preaching of the apostles; the demonstration of a truth is its connection with the teaching of the apostles. The vindication the Church gives of itself is that which we still, in our day, mention when we address God Himself: "Peter the apostle and Paul the teacher of the nations are they, O Lord, who have taught us Thy law."

In the works of the Fathers as well as in modern controversial treatises, this vindication takes the form of a historical argument: the point is to establish lists of bishops. Such lists are our guaranty that today's teaching is the same as that of the beginning.

This establishing of identity that continues throughout all the passing centuries in spite of the variations and lapses that occur everywhere, is also a sign of God's assistance. It is an unmistakable mark of a unique life that is tremendously resistant and that wears out time itself. The latter point of view is the one that specially interests us in this book. As we see, it is a particular and partial way of regarding apostolicity. We believe that, if it does not comprise all that is implied in the note, it at least allows us to perceive more clearly, from the point of view of these pages, what this note signifies.

When we discover in the Church of today the same life, the same reactions, the same beliefs, and the same attitudes as in the apostolic Church, we are manifestly confronted with a life that is unequaled in its kind and is more excellent than any

174

human life. Such a mystical, living being, that gathers to itself the centuries, bears its own witness that it is more man than man himself, if we may so express our thought; we mean that it is man, but man with a superhuman perfection received from the divine assistance and from union with God.

This Man, who is man to the limit of human capacity, is Christ, the head of a mystical body, the God-man. Furthermore the Church, whose continuity is clearly contemporaneous with all the centuries, bears witness that it is Christ continued. Its note of apostolicity flows directly from the thing signified, that is, the close relation existing between the Church and Christ whose body it is.

To convince ourselves that the Church remains always the same, we have only to study its doctrine at different periods, its cult, and its history. We shall speak of its doctrine when we come to investigate its teaching office.

The cult practiced in the Church likewise gives testimony to a perpetual identity. It remains always the same, and always consists in conferring a sort of perpetuity on the actions of Jesus. The cross is unceasingly raised up at Mass; the Savior's death and resurrection are continually being renewed in baptism; the Redeemer's blood still flows in the sacrament of penance. In a word, Christ is the one who continually confers the sacraments through the ministry of His priests. The life of Christ is the perennial inspiration of the liturgical year. Advent, Christmas, Lent, and Easter are His own history that is perpetually unfolding among the Christian people.

Moreover, when we meditate on the history of the Church, we see that it presents striking resemblances with the history of Jesus. Benson has brought them out clearly in a very suggestive book. We shall not undertake to perform a task which has rendered superfluous. Let us merely recall that the thought is by no means new, and that Athanasius based his apologetic work, *Against the Greeks* and *On the Incarnation of the Word,* on this view of the notes of the Church. The vitality of the Church is proof that it lives a superior life, a life that flows into it from a risen Savior, a life of resurrection. Indeed, from the very beginning, Catholicism has had the destiny of going from agony to agony and from resurrection to resurrection.

There have always been Herods and Pilates, executioners, and also, alas, Judases, as well as apostles and holy women. What happens in the Church is the continual renewal, or rather the continuation, of what took place in Christ.

Christ's history, consequently, unfolds in time, because, like us who are still living our mortal life, He is in time. But as it unfolds, this history bears witness, with numberless signs, that it remains unchanged, whereas time is nothing but change. The history of Christ is still today what it was at its origin; we observe the same actions, the same events, the same life, whereas time exists only on the condition of ceasing to exist.

Henri de Lubac
1896-

Henri de Lubac was born in 1896 and joined the Jesuits in 1929. His first major work, entitled Catholicism, a study of the corporate destiny of mankind, *appeared in 1937. In the 1940s he joined Jean Daniélou in editing a first-rate series of translations of the Fathers, and also cooperated in bringing out a wide-ranging series of works of historical theology. The third volume in this series was his own* Corpus Mysticum *(1943), in which he traces historically the use of the phrase "mystical body" as meaning the Eucharist in earlier writers, then gradually the shifting of the term to mean the Church.*

In 1946 de Lubac published a book called The Supernatural, *which became the center of a great controversy. His biblical-patristic-historical approach had already brought so much new material to light that his work seemed "dangerous" to conservative critics. This "new theology" came under suspicion as possibly in conflict with the tradition, and some alleged that de Lubac was one of the objects of Pope Pius XII's censure in* Humani Generis *(1950). Throughout these trying years he maintained an admirable demeanor. Temporarily exiled from the classroom and forbidden to publish, his reaction is best seen in the selection presented here from his* Splendor of the Church *(1956). He wrote the book to share with others, despite all his troubles, "the pricelessness of that good which consists, quite simply, in belonging to the Church."*

De Lubac's scholarship is of such breadth as to defy synthesis. Paradoxes *(1947),* The Drama of Atheist Humanism *(1950),* Aspects of Buddhism *(1954),* Teilhard de Chardin, the Man and His Meaning *(1964) are but a few of his contributions that became well known in English.*

Central to the thought of de Lubac is the solidarity of mankind. His vision unifies God, mankind, and the Church in a way that rejects the artificial barriers of nationalism, race, culture, etc. All have a common origin and a corporate destiny and anything that obscures that fact is anti-Christian. An inveterate humanist, it is his theory that results in the kind of stance taken by Pope John XXIII and the Church of Vatican II in entering into sympathetic dialogue with the world and everyone in it. Anything that separates people, whatever divides mankind, all obstacles to open communication, these are appropriate areas for Christian concentration in the attempt to bring reconciliation, atonement.

Unlike his much-admired confrere Teilhard de Chardin, Henri de Lubac has lived to see his basic vision vindicated. He has become for many a symbol of the Catholic revival itself: he devoted his vast energies to penetrating to a deeper understanding of Catholic tradition, he bore admirably the brunt of hostility and criticism from less gifted contemporaries, and he rejoiced in the events that brought about Vatican II with its endorsement of the reforms required by the renewed vision of the Church.

THE SPLENDOUR
OF THE CHURCH

CHAPTER VIII

OUR TEMPTATIONS CONCERNING THE CHURCH

L ove should, of course, be our only reaction to our
Mother the Church; yet in fact there are many temptations which trouble us with regard to her. Some are
clear enough, and violent; others are less clear, and all the more
insidious. There are some that are perennial, and some that are
peculiar to our time, and they are all too varied—even to the
point of mutual opposition—for any one of us ever to think
himself sheltered from the threat which they constitute.

There will always be men who identify their cause with
that of the Church so totally that they end by equating the
Church's cause with their own, and this in all good faith. It
does not occur to them that if they are to be truly faithful
servants they may have to mortify much in themselves; in their
desire to serve the Church, they press the Church into their
own service. It is a "dialectical transition", inside-out from
pro to *contra*, as easy as unobtrusive. From them the Church
is a certain order of things which is familiar to them and by
which they live; a certain state of civilization, a certain number
of principles, a certain complex of values which the Church's
influence has more or less Christianized but which remain none
the less largely human. And anything which disturbs this order
or threatens this equilibrium, anything which upsets them or
merely startles them, seems to them to be a crime against a
divine institution.

Where there is a question of a muddle of this sort, we are
not always involved with those crude forms of "clericalism"
which estimate the amount of honour paid to God by the
privileges accorded to His ministers or measure the progress
of divine rule over souls, and the social reign of Christ, by the
influence, either hidden or open, of the clergy on the course

of secular affiars. Here the whole order of thinking may well
be on the loftiest plane—as when Bossuet, towards the end of
his life, adjusted the whole Catholic order in accordance with
a Louis-Quatorze pattern of things, and was unable to see
anything but a threat to religion in the mixed forces which began to disintegrate that particular synthesis, which was, of
course, a brilliant one, but was also matter for questioning in
some aspects at least—a thing contingent, and by essence
perishable. Against those forces he made his stand, and that
with every ounce of his strength.

Bossuet was as perceptive as he was forthright; yet his per-
ceptiveness did not go the whole way. "Together with an
imperious will, he had a spirit by nature timid." He wanted
to maintain for ever (though courageously condemning certain
faults and criticizing certain abuses) the mental and social world
in which his genius found a natural ground for its unfolding.
He could not imagine how the faith could survive it—rather like
those ancient Romans (among whom were even some Fathers
of the Church) for whom the collapse of the Empire could not
be anything other than the heralding of the end of the world,
so great an impression had the Roman power and majesty made
upon the mind of the time. But since Bossuet's dream was of
something which was in fact impossible, he found himself involving with the moribund world in question the Church whose
business it was to free herself from it in order to bring life to
the coming generations. The inadequate defences he threw up
against the oncoming evil buried beyond hope of germination
the seeds of the future; he was apparently victorious on every
field which he fought but it was irreligion which profited from
the way in which he won his victories.

In the same way, we are sometimes all the more self-con-
fident and strict in the judgments we pass in proportion as the
cause we are defending is the more dubious. It is possible that
we sometimes forget in practice something we know well
enough in principle—that the intransigence of the faith is not a
passionate unbendingness in the desire to impose upon others
our personal tastes and personal ideas. A tight-clenched hard-
ness of that kind is fatal to the supple firmness of truth, and is
no defence to it whatsoever; a Christianity which deliberately

takes up its stand in a wholly defensive position, closed to every overture and all assimilation, is no longer Christianity. Sincere attachment to the Church can never be used for the purpose of canonizing our prejudices, or making our partialities part of the absolute of the universal faith. It may thus be pertinent to recall that a certain confidence and detachment are part of the Catholic spirit. At the right time, the Church can find in the very shrines of the devil things to beautify her own dwelling; that particular miracle is always something new and unforeseen, but we know that it will happen again. However rooted in history the Church may be, she is not the slave of any epoch or indeed of anything whatsoever the essence of which is temporal. The message which she is bound to pass on and the life which she is bound to propagate are never integral parts of "either a political regime or a social polity or a particular form of civilization", and she must forcefully remind people of the fact, in opposition to the illusive evidence to the contrary which in fact derives simply from the bonds of habit. She repeats for us, in their widest possible sense, the words of St. Augustine: "Why are you dismayed when earthly kingdoms pass away?" for she is founded upon no rock other than that of Peter's faith, which is faith in Jesus Christ; she is neither a party nor a closed society. She cannot resign herself to being cut off from those who do not yet know her simply for the sake of the comfortableness of those who make up her traditional faithful. She desires no opposition from the reality in men, since they are all her sons, at least virtually; on the contrary, she will make it her aim to set them free from all evil by giving them their Saviour.

We should therefore ourselves get into this frame of mind, which was that of Christ, and we should if necessary impose on ourselves the mortifications fitted to this end. Far from failing in the intransigence of the faith, we shall in this way alone sound its depths. We must not relax in any way our zeal for Catholic truth, but we should learn how to purify it. We must be on guard against turning into those "carnal men" who have existed since the first generation of Christians and who, turning the Church into their own private property, practically stopped the Apostles from announcing the Gospel to the Gentiles. For if we do that we lay ourselves open to something yet more calamitous—collaboration with militant irreligion, by way of making it easier for it to carry out its self-assigned task of relegating the Church and her doctrine to the class of the defunct; we provide irreligion with a clear conscience, as it were, for it has no understanding of the actuality of the eternal. Its attitude is: "Let the Church remain what she is" (and one knows what sort of petrifaction such a wish implies)—and then "she will receive all the appreciation always accorded to historic relics". An irreligion of this type mixes up at will cases of the most widely differing kinds, confusing with dogma opinions or attitudes inherited from situations which have ceased to be, and takes up a firm stand over "concessions" in which it detects "bad faith or irresponsibility". It establishes its own lists of what is suspect—in the fashion of religious authority itself—and is ready to call that authority to order, if need be. Having made up its mind once and for all that there can be nothing reasonable in Christian beliefs, it brands as "liberalism" or "modernism" every effort made to disentangle Christianity in its real purity and its perpetual youth, as if this were an abandonment of doctrine. It can never see in the thought of men like Justin or Clement of Alexandria or their modern disciples anything but the concessions of an apologetic which sacrifices the "tough" element in dogma to the desire to please those whom it wishes to win over; Tatian and Hermias are the favourites, and their method alone is regarded as the only Christian one. It maintains that "the Church can never cut loose from her past . . . religion is a whole which must not be touched . . . as soon as you reason about it, you are an atheist". The principle is "All or nothing"—provided that the "all" is understood in the terms dictated—which are not those of the Church; thus, for example, Renan, making the Catholic faith involved for ever with the historicity of the Book of Daniel and other things of the same kind. And it is a day of rejoicing in this quarter when voices are raised within the very heart of "this poor and aged Church" which sound like approval. A false intransigence can certainly cause an enormous amount of harm in this way—quite in opposition to its own intentions.

The vistas opened up by all this should be yet one more notive for our distrusting ourselves. We should be wary of a certain kind of humility which borders on pride, cultivating a healthy fear of sacrilegious usurpation, and taking to heart the exhortation of St. Augustine to his fellow-fighters in the thick of the Donatist controversy: "Take your stand upon the truth without pride." We have to bear in mind that our knowledge is always partial and that in this world we only glimpse the divine truth "through a glass in a dark manner", like Newman, instead of settling ourselves into the Church as our private property and personal possession and more or less identifying her with ourselves, we should rather make it our business to identify ourselves with the Church, and without expecting any personal triumph from it.

But there is another temptation from the opposite direction, which is certainly more frequent today, and sometimes more aggressive in the provocation which it offers—the critical temptation. This also very frequently advances itself cunningly under the camouflage of the good; it can easily put itself forward to the apostolically-minded as a necessary concern for clarity. And for this reason it cannot, in most cases, be avoided save by a preliminary "discernment of spirits".

The very word "criticism" means discernment, and there is of course, a kind of criticism which is good—particulary self-criticism. That kind is a striving for realism in action—a determination to bar all that cannot justify its claim to genuineness. It is an examination carried out in humility, capable of recognizing the good achieved, but arising out of an essentially apostolic discontent and a perpetually restless spiritual dynamism. It is born and grows from attitudes such as the inability to be satisfied with work done and a burning desire for the best; integrity of judgment on matters of method; independence of will to break with customs that cannot be justified any more, to get out of ruts and put right abuses; above all, a lofty idea of the Christian vocation and faith in the mission of the Church. It stimulates an intensified activity, inventive ingenuity and a sudden outburst of exploration and encounter which must, doubtless, be brought under control on occasion—and which certainly often disturbs our habits a little too rudely. Criticism of this type is hard on the illusions which it tracks down, but can induce others which will soon be in turn the object of similar criticism. Yet how very much better it all is, still, than the naive self-complacency which admits of no reform and no healthy transformation—that certain comfortableness which gradually digs itself deeper and deeper into its dream-world, that obstinacy which thinks that it is preserving things when all it is doing is piling up the ruins of them.

We should be wrong if we wished to prevent on princple all public expression of this kind of criticism. When the Church is humble in the persons of her children she is more attractive than when they show themselves dominated by the all-too-human concern for respectability. Jacques Maritain once said, not entirely without his tongue in his cheek, that many Christians of today find any admission of our deficiencies "somehow indecent". "It will be said," he adds, "that they are afraid of putting difficulties in the way of apologetic . . . The ancient Jews and even the Ninivites didn't stand on ceremony in that way." No more did the saints in the past. Think of St. Jerome's famous address to Pope Damasus, or St. Bernard's broadsides against bad pastors and the programme of reform which he outlines in his *De Consideratione*, or diatribes like that of St. Catherine of Siena against certain highly-placed ecclesiastical dignitaries: "O men who are no men but rather devils incarnate, how you are blinded by your disordered love for the rottenness of the body, and the delights and bedazzlements of this world!" Or again, remember for a moment people like St. Brigid, and Gerson, and St. Bernardino of Siena, and St. Thomas More; or, to come nearer to our own day, St. Clement Hofbauer. Or think of the struggles of the "Gregorians" to tear the government of the Church free from the system which was enslaving it; or the audacity of a man like Gerhoh of Reichersberg, addressing to Pope Eugenius III his work *On the Corrupt State of the Church*, like St. Bernard; or Roger Bacon, demanding of Clement IV that he should "purge the Canon Law" and cast out of the Church the pagan elements which had been brought into her with the ancient Civil Law; or of William Durandus publishing his treatise *De Modo Celebrandi et Corruptelis in Ecclesia Reformandis*; of the Carthusian Peter of

Leyden exhorting the Roman Pontiff at the opening of the edition which he issued in 1530 of the works of his fellow-Carthusian Denys. This last example evokes the whole great movement of Catholic reform which is all too inadequately described under the name of the Counter-Reformation; an enterprise of that kind could not even have been outlined without an effective determination on self-criticism, of which history shows us more than one brilliant example.

Yet for every constructive complaint and each clear-headed and fruitful analysis there is all too much excess and recklessness. Each really courageous act is counterpoised by a mass of futile agitation. There is all too much purely negative criticism. Sanctity is not common, and the sincerest goodwill has neither the same rights nor the same privileges. And both competence and opportunity may be lacking; even if a given criticism is a fair one, we are nevertheless, not always justified in making it. In addition, we have to bear in mind this important fact; that today we do not have the same situation as existed in what we call the Christian centuries. Then, everything happened within the family circle, as it were; and irreligion was not perpetually on the lookout to turn this, that and everything to account in argument. Today, when the Church is in the dock, misunderstood, jeered at for her very existence and even her sanctity itself, Catholics should be wary lest what they want to say simply in order to serve her better be turned to account against her. We have to be on our guard against misunderstandings of a fatal kind; and this is a filial delicacy which has nothing to do with prudery or hypocritical calculatingness. It is not possible to give a hard-and-fast rule, but the Holy Spirit will not be miserly with the gift of counsel to the really "ecclesiastical" man, as I have tried to depict him above—that is, to the man who cannot but be truly spiritual.

We must in any case make a distinction between healthy self-criticism, even when it is excessive or ill-directed, and all sterile complaining—everything that stems from a loss, or even a diminishing, of confidence in the Church. It would certainly be impious to use one or two unfortunate occurrences as an excuse to run down "contemporary Christianity's excellent and laborious task of diagnosing its own deficiences, and trying to understand, love and preserve all that has grown up of value outside its own direct influence, and to venture out into the storm to collect the first materials for its new dwelling." But if an attempt of this kind is to be carried out and bear fruit, we have to be careful that it is not contaminated by the breath of a spirit very different from that which is its own principle.

There are certain times when one sees springing up in every direction the symptoms of an evil which catches on like an epidemic—a collective, neurasthenic crisis. To those who are afflicted by it, everything becomes matter for denigration, and this is not just a case of the irony, quarrelsomeness of bitterness which are at all times a perpetual threat to a certain kind of temperament. Everything gets a bad construction put upon it, and knowledge of all kinds, even when accurate, only serves to intensify the evil. Half-digested new discoveries and clumsily used new techniques are all so many occasions for believing that the traditional foundations of things have gone shaky. The spiritual life goes but limpingly—so much so that nothing is really seen in the light of it any more. People think themselves clear-headed when all the time it is precisely the essential that they have overlooked. We are no longer capable of discovering, sometimes on our very doorsteps, the fresh flowerings of the Holy Spirit's innumerable inventions—that Holy Spirit which is always in Its own likeness and always new. And thus discouragement creeps in by a thousand and one different ways; things that might have given us a healthy shock simply have the effect of paralysing us. Faith may stay sincere, but it is undermined here, there and everywhere, and we begin to look at the Church as if from outside, in order to judge her; the groanings of prayer become an all-too-human recrimination. And by this movement of Pharisaism—a sort of interior falling-away—which may be unadmitted but is one the less pernicious for all that, we set foot on the road which may end in open denial.

That this should be realized in time and that the appropriate reaction should take place, is something devoutly to be hoped for. There is no question of blinding oneself to inadequacies; those are always only too real. And there is no question of not feeling the painfulness of them; indifference can be much worse than excess of emotion. The total and burning loyalty of our holding to the Church does not demand of us a puerile admiration for every possible thing that can be, or be thought, or done, within her. Christ wished His Bride to be perfect, holy and without spot; but she is this only in princple. If she does indeed shine with a spotless radiance, it is "in the sacraments with which she begets and nurtures her children; in the faith which she preserved ever inviolate; in the holy laws which she imposes on all, and in the evangelical counsels by which she admonishes; and, finally, in the heavenly gifts and miraculous powers by which out of her inexhaustible fecundity she begets countless hosts of martyrs, virgins and confessors." Her soul is the Spirit of Christ but her members are men, all the same; and we know well that men are never up to the level of the divine mission which is entrusted to them. They are never wholly amenable and submissive to the inspirations of the Spirit of Christ, and if they do not succeed in corrupting the Church— since the source of her sanctifying power does not lie in them— she, on the other hand, will never succeed in stopping completely the source of evil in them—at least, as long as the conditions of this world hold good. Their good will is no guarantee of their intelligence, and intelligence is not always accompanied by strength. The best among them will always be setting up innumerable obstacles to the good which God wants to bring about through them; so that we may as well get it well into our heads to start with that nothing which they do should surprise us—a lesson which is most healthily rammed home by history.

Yet we are all men, and there is none of us but is aware of his own wretchedness and incapacity; for after all we keep on having our noses rubbed in our own limitations. We have all, at some time or other, caught ourselves red-handed in the very act of contradiction—trying to serve a holy cause by dubious means. And we must add that our most serious shortcomings are those very ones that escape our notice; from time to time, at least, we see that we are without understanding in the face of the mystery which we are called upon to live out. So that there are scanty grounds for making exceptional cases of ourselves; and none at all for the withdrawal implied in a grimly-judging eye. If we behave in that way we fall into an illusion like that of the misanthrope, who takes a dislike to humankind, for all the world as if he himself were not a part of it; "In order to attain to a deep understanding with humanity it is enough to be a part of it, to cleave to the whole mass of it and all the intermingling of its members"—then "we have no more grievances left, no more standing-back, no more judgments and no more comparisons." Then the staring contrast between the human wretchedness of those who make up the Church, and the greatness of her divine mission, will no longer be a scandal to us; for we shall first have become painfully aware of it in ourselves. Rather, it will become a stimulus. We shall understand how a certain sort of self-criticism which is always directed outwards may be nothing more than the search for an alibi designed to enable us to dodge the examination of our consciences. And a humble acceptance of Catholic solidarity will perhaps be more profitable to us in the matter of shaking us out of some of our illusions. It will perhaps help us to fall in love once more, from a new standpoint, with those elements in the wisdom and the institutions and the traditions and the demands of our Church which we were coming near to understanding no longer.

Today, however disquite often takes forms more precise than this, and the most lowly of active Catholics does not entirely escape it. He may ask himself with painful anxiety: Is the Church's action on our age properly adapted to it? Surely indisputable experience shows that it is tragically ineffective? For some time past at least that kind of question has been asked in many quarters, and we should not underestimate its seriousness, or dismiss it hastily as if we refused to look at it. If we do that we shall only add to the troubles of those who (perhaps because they are more wide awake than we) are at grips with it in a real "dark night." But here again we must make a sober effort at the discernment of spirits.

In many quarters people are asking themselves questions as to the real value, not, of course, of Christianity itself, but of many of the parts that go to make up, as it were, the religious instrument, as the centuries have forged it. They find its efficiency at too low a level, and point grimly to the worn cogs and tired springs; many practices are put in the dock and there is talk of out-of-date methods and institutions. It will scarcely be a matter for surprise if there is in all this more than one illusion of the inside-out kind, and if certain errors creep into both the diagnosis of the evil and the choice of remedies for it; a genuine intuition of new needs may be accompanied by inadequate knowledge and a certain lack of grip on reality. It is not always possible to make an accurate distinction between what ought to be preserved and what ought to be changed, at the first shot; sometimes we are over-quick to despair of forms which, though apparently dead, are capable of reanimation. However, if our inspiration is sound we shall not find it difficult to make the necessary adjustments to a programme rather hastily drawn up, and to round out a somewhat one-sided effort by others more calculated to balance it.

But it is that inspiration, precisely, which stands in need of control. For here the worst may go cheek by jowl with the best. What is the real source of this concern for adaptation, or—which is very much the same thing—the need felt for what is often called a more effective "incarnation"—a concern in itself wholly justified and frequently encouraged of set purpose by the supreme authority of the Church? Is it pure overflowing of charity, as in the case of St. Paul who, following the example of Christ, wanted to make himself all things to all men? Or is there some admixture in it of this illusion, all too natural to the professional man which every priest must inevitably be to a certain extent—that it is enough to make a change of method, as all human undertakings may do, to obtain results which primarily suppose a change of heart? Realistic views, objective enquiry, statistics, the elucidation of sociological laws, the drawing up of methodical plans, breaks both big and small with the forms of apostolate belonging to the past, the perfecting of new techniques—all these things may be made use of by zeal that is really pure and upright, and anyone who belittled them puts himself in the right with a facility somewhat suspect if he makes a mere opposition between them and the methods of the Curé d'Ars. Yet all these things have to be kept in their proper place, in the service of the Spirit of God alone.

But—and this is something more serious—it may well be that there is mingled with our disquiet in some more less subtle way a certain timidity, a certain deep-seated lack of assurance and secret revulsion against the tradition of the Church. We may, when we see ourselves as setting ourselves free from what seems a spirit of senility, and as struggling against ankylosis and sclerosis, be putting ourselves in the way of contracting "childish ailments"; what we take for an awakening of the personality may in point of fact be the end-product of a blind aberration, and we may set ourselves to judge all things in accordance with criteria which are superficially "modern" and no more. The secular values which the world spreads before our eyes may begin to dazzle us, and in the presence of those who stand for them we may, bit by bit, allow ourselves to be affected by an inferiority complex. Where things that should be most sacred to us are concerned, we may be on the way to accepting ideas about them held by men whose blindness should in fact be matter for our sorrow. We may be stupidly allowing ourselves to be imposed upon by the manifestations of the "pride of life"; to put it in a nutshell, although our faith may not be flagging, we may be beginning to lose our faith in our faith, if one may put it so.

This should be an occasion for recalling with greater explicitness certain constant truths. "I, when I have been lifted up from the earth, will draw all things unto me"—those words of Christ are not, doubtless, an invitation to literal imitation, and we are not Wisdom personified that we should be able to be content to say: "Come over to me all that desire me: and be filled with my fruits." St. Paul, conformed to Christ, travelled the world over, the precursor of a whole army of apostles, and the Church will always be a missionary. And this is at least the symptom of a certain spirit; in other words, we are quite right not to want to be separated from men who are to be led to Christ—if by that we understand the necessity of breaking down the barriers which would be put between them and ourselves by forms of living or thinking which are superseded, and even more so by ways of behaving whose sole justification is an ideal of comfortableness or peace and quiet. We are quite right not to allow ourselves to be shut up in any sort of ghetto, by ourselves any more than by anybody else. But we have to be on our guard against misunderstanding both the truly central position which our faith guarantees us, to the degree of its own strength, and that essential condition of being "set apart" from the world which belongs to every Christian, let alone every priest. If we are really "turned to God" we have "abandoned idols" and cannot "bear the yoke" with those who are deceived by them. And if we show real vitality in this sacred operation and the joyful practice of all that it imposes on us, others will certainly be drawn to this source of life and will not want to be separated from us. The miracle of the drawing power of Christ will continue in and through our lives.

We should, then, have no inhibitions about feeling a profound sympathy with the men who surround us. We should be fully human, for we are obliged to that by our duty of interior sincerity as well as of brotherly love; or rather, that disposition should be something so natural and congenital to us that there is no need to go looking for it. We ought not to get our loyalty to the eternal mixed up with an attachment to the past which is mischievous and even morbid. Yet at the same time we should beware of modern self-sufficiency; we should be wary of making our own the weaknesses and infatuations, the pretentious ignorance and the narrowness of the surrounding milieu, and of giving a welcome to worldliness, whether it be proletarian or middle-class, refined or vulgar. Or rather, we should be always extricating ourselves from it—for unfortunately we are always getting involved in it to a greater or a lesser degree. To sum up. we should always be adapted, and that as spontaneously as possible; but we must do it without ever allowing ourselves, either in behaviour or thought, to adapt Christianity itself in the least—that is to say, to de-devinize it or lower it, make it insipid or twist it out of shape. We should have a great love for our age, but make no concessions to the spirit of the age, so that in us the Christian mystery may never lose its sap.

For some, this difficulty is made more acute at the intellectual level, and the pain more piercing at the depth of the soul, when it seems that in spite of every possible effort of adaptation the action of the Church remains far from effective, through causes which make all effort powerless. Far from making a perpetual advance, she goes back. Even where she is in apparent control and her influence is recognized and encouraged, she does not bring about the reign of the Gospel and the social order is not transformed according to her principles. Yet the tree is surely to be judged by its fruits; and that, surely, provides grounds for believing that the Church has shot her bolt? It seems that we must fear that she can never realize other than symbolically what others feel confident of being able to realize eventually in truth; and the conclusion would appear to be that we should transfer elsewhere the confidence which we once reposed in her.

There is much equivocation in the process of reasoning, apparently so simple. it is obvious that if each member of the Church were all that he ought to be, the Kingdom of God would progress at a very different rate, though always through a perpetual piling-up of obstacles—as we saw earlier on—and always invisible to eyes which are not enlightened by God. And it is equally true that this or that historical happening and this or that social context can, independently of the will of the individual, create unfavourable conditions, deep-reaching misunderstandings and divergences, and thus set formidable problems. But if we are to have a change of solving these—or at least of maintaining our confidence, even if we have to concede that some of them are, for the time being, insoluble—then a great many latent equivocations must be exposed. We will leave on one side all considerations of the sociological order, for it is with the preliminary "discernment" that we must concern ourselves to begin with.

When the Church is in question we must not judge of advance and retreat, success and frustration, as we should do in the case of things which are of time. The supernatural good which the Church serves in this world is something that reaches its totality in the invisible order, and finds its consummation in the eternal. The communion of saints grows from generation to generation. And we should not regress into any dream of a Church exteriorly triumphant, for the Church's Head did not promise her dazzling and increasing success. If we say of the Church, as did Pascal, that she is destined to be in her agony until the end of the world, like Christ, this is not a relapse into mere rhetoric or the enjoyment of a romantic emotional luxury. We must not forget the demands of the "redeeming wisdom". We should watch her at work in the life and action of Jesus; that will help us to be patient in even our very anxiety. It will help us to pass through our disquiet and arrive on the other side, rather than drag us back to the hither side of it in a sort of resignation which may be a fall in itself. The apostolically-minded must know how to wait, and the priest has often occasion to know how to accept the sense of being helpless; he *must* accept the fact of being nearly always misunderstood.

Above all, we must not get the wrong idea about the Kingdom of God which is the end of the Church and which is her mission to anticipate. Here the whole of the faith is involved; without in any way underestimating the urgency of the urban problem or the irreplaceable part which the Church must play in the solution of it, it is impossible to lose sight of the fact that her desire is to solve a problem no less urgent, but at a higher level and more far-reaching, more constant and more all-embracing. Like sicknesses that evolve in some germ-breeding environment, waging war on the remedies applied to them and cropping up again under a new form every time we think we have got them under control, the root evil which man carries in his depths flares up again, always the same in itself, under forms that change perpetually as society changes. Psychologies, customs, and social relationships change; man remains, with his evil. This does not mean that we ought not to try everything in our search for betterment; the tenacity of evil can be nothing other than a challenge to a yet more determined and sustained struggle. But suppose for a moment something which we are, unfortunately, far enough away from—a more or less perfect functioning of society; that is, not an economic or political machine more or less adequately powerful, but an exterior order which is as human as possible. With all that granted, the Church's work would not, in a sense, have even started. For her business is not to settle us in comfortably in our earthly existence, but to raise us above it. Her bringing to us of the redemption of Christ means that she wants to tear us free from the evil that is in us and lay us open to another existence; and the other side of the same fact is that if she were to give temporal effectiveness top priority, that very thing would not be granted to her. If she were to wait, in order to carry out in the world the work of salvation, for temporal conditions to undergo an eventual improvement (whatever the terms in which the ideal state of affairs were actually conceived), she would be playing false to her mission, which is to bring safely home not a future humanity at some time to come, but the whole of humanity throughout time—not a mythical humanity but the actual men of each generation.

If, then, we want to be realistic, it is none the less indispensable that our realism should not mistake its object. And if we are anxious to be effective, it is essential that we should not build our foundation on means which are too extrinsic and thus calculated to turn us aside from our end. If we rightly may, and sometimes should, be strict with those who call themselves Catholics—with ourselves—it is essential that we should understand what we do and do it with reference to valid standards. We must not lose sight of the essential.

This essential, which cannot remain as even a distant objective on our horizon if we do not find a place for it in the heart of our present activity, is not something which can be judged from a quantitative point of view. God brings about the saving of us according to laws which are hidden from us as far as their concrete application is concerned, but which are imposed on our faith in principle—the mysterious laws of the community of salvation. And today the prayer of intercession and the sacrifice of charity have lost none of their secret power; moreover, the existence of one saint alone would be sufficient witness to the divine value of the principle by which saints live. But the question is whether our sight is clear enough, and whether we have sufficient knowledge of where to look, to discern among ourselves, in this order of sanctity, the effectiveness of the Church? Let us at least try to catch a glimpse of it. Massive appearance should not hide from us the central reality, nor noisy ideological debate prevent us from hearing the silent breathing of the Spirit. At a time when he was head of a community which was made up of none but the poor and uneducated, and was without appreciable influence on the destinies of the Empire, the great St. Cyprian said: "As for us, we are philosophers not in word but in act; we do not say great things but we do live them." And that saying remains true, in all its proud humility. The essential is very rarely something that can be much talked about; Christian vitality is in every age very much less dependant on all that is discussed and done and picked to pieces on the world's state than we are often led to believe. There is a life which it is almost impossible to judge of from the outside; and that life keeps itself going, passes itself on and renews itself under all the turmoil of politics, all the swirl of public opinoin, the currents of ideas and the controversies, far removed from the scene of public debate, unsounded and untabulated. The blind see, the deaf hear, the dead are raised to life and the poor have the Gospel preached to them; the Kingdom of God shines in secret. Here and there there are sudden glimpses; patches of light break through, widen, and join up with others. A point of light or two in the night suddenly shines more brightly; sometimes there will be patches of blood, to draw our attention. All are so many hearalding signs.

Today, when there is so much discussion about Christianity and so much complaining about its "ill-adeptedness" or "ineffectiveness", we should always be returning again and again to these very simple considerations. The best Christians and the most vital are by no means to be found either inevitably or even generally among the wise or the clever, the intelligentsia or the politically-minded, or those of social consequence. And consequently what they say does not make the headlines; what they do does not come to the public eye. Their lives are hidden from the eyes of the world, and if they do come to some degree of notoriety, that is usually late in the day, and exceptional, and always attended by the risk of distortion. Within the Church itself it is, as often as not, only after their deaths that some of them acquire an uncontested reputation. Yet these are responsible, more than anyone else, for ensuring that our earth is not a hell on earth. Most of them never think to ask themselves whether their faith is "adapted" or "effective". It is enough, for them, to live it, as reality itself, and reality at its most actual; and because the fruit of all this is often enough a hidden fruit it is none the less wonderful for that. Even if such people are themselves not engaged in external activity, they are the source of all initiative and action, all spadework which is not to be fruitless. It is these people who are our preservation and who give us hope, and it would be a bold man who said that they are less numerous and less active today than in the past.

We should not become blind to the real fruitfulness of our Mother the Church for the sake of a dream of efficiency which may be no more than a mirage.

But there is another temptation yet. This again is not that of the simple soul, and it is the most serious of all.

Its point of entry is by way of an observation which was made as early as in St. Paul's day: "For see your vocation, brethren, that there are not many wise according to the flesh, not many mighty, not many noble." The wise, the powerful and the noble were to come, certainly, but the Apostle's words retain their profound and many-sided truth none the less for that. Like her Master, the Church cuts in the eyes of the world the figure of a slave; on this earth she exists "in the form of a slave". And it is not only the wisdom of this world, in the crude sense, that is lacking in her; it is also—in appearance at least—the wisdom of the spirit. She is no exclusive club for spiritual geniuses or supermen, no academy of the clever; in fact, she is the very opposite. The warped, the sham and the wretched of every kind crowd into her, together with the whole host of the mediocre, who feel especially at home in her and everywhere set the tone of things. Her most magnificent advances merely serve to accentuate this characteristic, both in the average run of her members and in the stuff of her day-to-day existence; to show how, in detail, would be only too easy. And as a consequence it is hard, not to say entirely impossible, for the "natural man" to find in such a phenomenon the consummation of the saving *kenosis* and the awe-inspiring traces of the "humility of God"—that is, in so far as his inner-most thoughts have not been changed in direction.

The Church has always drawn down on herself the contempt of the élite. There are many philosophers and devotees of the spiritual life, much concerned about the sources of spiritual vitality, who refuse her their adherence; some of them are openly hostile to her, disgusted, like Celsus, by "this scrape-together of simple minds", and they turn aside from her, either with the Olympian serenity of a Goethe or in the Dionysiac fury of a Nietzsche. It is as if they said: "So you claim to be the Body of Christ, do you?—the Body of God? Could the Body of God really be made of such coarse stuff as that? And to start with, how can Divinity have a body anyhow?"

196

There are others among these sophisticated men who feel that they are doing the Church full justice and protest when they are described as her adversaries. After all, they would stand up for her if need were; they think she plays a very useful part. "What!" says one of them, replying to some friends who considered him too favourable to the Christian schools. "Do you want me to explain Parmenides to my cook?" But they keep their distance; they don't want for themselves a faith which would make them one with all the wretched creatures above whom they rank themselves in virtue of their aesthetic culture, their powers of rational reflection and their concern with the things of the spirit; they are an aristocracy who don't see themselves mixing with the herd. In their view, the Church leads men by ways that are altogether too well-trodden. They willingly concede her her skill in presenting higher truth under the veil of imagery; but they distinguish themselves as those who know, from the mass of "those who believe", and claim to know the Church better than she knows herself. They "place" her, condescendingly, and grant themselves the power of disentangling the deeper meaning of her doctrines and actions—without her consent—by virtue of a "metaphysical transposition". They place their own intuition above her faith, as they would place the absolute above the relative, or direct and active participation. One might describe them as "specialists of the *logos*"— but specialists who have not read, in St. Paul how the Logos repulses "every height that exalteth itself against the knowledge of God". They are the wise—but not wise enough to see how for twenty centuries the prophecy has been worked out: "I will destroy the wisdom of the wise." They are the rich who have never taken in the first beatitude. Some of them, setting themselves up as the leaders of schools or sects, add to the attraction of the promise of knowledge that of the secret— like Valentine in the early days, or that Faustus under whose influence St. Augustine suffered for a time, or, to quote an example from our own day, René Guénon—for the mirage of initiation has a fascination for minds at every level. Yet others remain in their solitude; and that is not always in virtue of a diabolical refusal—sometimes, and much less mysteriously, it is quite simply an absurd pretentiousness. It may be merely a case of the disgust felt by a lofty intelligence for ways of thinking and living which would get him mixed up with the common crowd; or the shivering recoil of the "sensitive soul". And thus there develops a "distinguished individualism which is, however, a closed one, admitting at most only a few chosen beings to a friendly sharing in interior experience". There is a fear that just as the Church would hamper the freedom of investigation and put the curb on the adventurousness of spiritual impulse, so also strict adherence to her would surely involve something like regimentation and a kind of pigging in with the herd.

The Christian consciousness itself can give out a faint echo of these objections and this repugnance. Faith may not be shaken by them, but all the same they sometimes have the effect of straining the bonds that bind us into the Church and lessening their strength and holding power. Without going as far as making an actual break, we can come to forget the close correlation of ecclesiastical faithfulness and religious faithfulness, for the fact is that Christianity may, at the level of truth, emerge triumphant from the challenge, and the Church yet not appear correspondingly justified; at least, the theoretical justification may now win a down-right victory over an experienced repugnance. Impartial enquiry may indeed establish that the wisdom she offers and infuses does not, in fact, consist of that collection of "puerile futilities" which St. Augustine believed it to be before the preaching of St. Ambrose opened his eyes. It may lead a man to discover the solidity of her dogma, even to get a glimpse of the depth of her mysteries, and the orthodox interpretation of them given by the great Doctors of the Church. It may bring him to admire the artistic splendours and the cultural riches which have glorified the human aspect of her, at certain periods at least. But all that does not change the obvious commonness of the binding medium which all Catholic living has to use from day to day and in which we must ourselves be set.

André Malraux, confronted with the pictures in the Roman catacombs and their first graphic expression of the Word which was heard in Christ, was driven to exclaim: "How badly these poor figures answer to that voice, and all its depths!"

—a reaction we may develop further. Won't it be so, and fatally so, with every expression of the Catholic reality, whatever its mode and its nature? What, in fact, does happen to revelation in current preaching—what becomes of the summons of God in the popular mind, or of the Kingdom of God in many an imagination among the devout or the theologically-minded? What becomes of the holy love of unity in hearts which are all too inadequately purified of human passion, or of mystery— all too often—in our textbooks? Pascal was much impressed by the fittingness of maintaining two extremes while covering the whole space that lies between, and thus uniting so many truths, "which seem repugnant and yet all subsist in a wonderful order"—yet in practice this dynamic synthesis very often transforms itself into some flat-foot formula of the happy medium. The wonderful *complexio oppositorum* held out to us by every aspect of Catholicism does, in point of fact, cause considerable alarm and despondency in a great many believers. The Church herself does not as a rule encourage overbold thought or too-high-flying spirituality; for the forms which she approves most willingly must be such as can be accepted by the average Catholic environment—and that, one must admit, is always "something somewhat insipid and somewhat mediocre"—which all provides perpetually rich matter for the *irrisio infidelium*, even from among the educated. And in truth, if we look at it realistically, not in the rarefied atmosphere of pure idea but in concrete reality, the Church is—as Newman pointed out—a humiliated body which calls forth insult and impiety, sharp revulsion or at best an indulgent reserve, from men who do not live by faith.

There is no question of simply suffering in silence the really destructive elements in all this, or of accepting it wholesale as something to be desired; it is a matter of *assuming* it, of taking it all upon ourselves, and that with a loyalty which will not deserve the name if it is of the surface only. There is no "private Christianity", and if we are to accept the Church we must take her as she is, in her human day-to-day reality just as much as in her divine and eternal ideality; for a separation of the two is impossible both in fact and by right. Loving the Church means loving her in the full massiveness of her tradition, all repugnance overcome, and burrowing deep, so to speak, into the massiveness of her life, as the seed goes deep into the earth. Equally, it means giving up the insidious drug of religious philosophies which would take the place of our faith, or offer to transpose it. For such is the Catholic way of losing oneself in order to find oneself. The mystery of salvation cannot reach us or save us without this final mediation; we have to push to its conclusion the logic of the Incarnation, by which Divinity adapts itself to human weakness. If we are going to have the treasure, then we must also have the "earthern vessels" which contain it and outside which it evaporates. We have to accept what St. Paul, who knew all about the contrary temptation, called "simplicity in Christ". We must be "the common people of God" with no reservations made. To put it another way: the necessity of being humble in order to cleave to Christ involves the necessity of being humble in order to seek Him in His Church and add to the submission of the intellect "brotherly love."

He alone participates in Christ who keeps himself united to all the members of His body. Insofar as he is rich, he does not say to the poor man: "You are not necessary to me." Insofar as he is strong he does not say that to the weak: insofar as he is wise, he does not say it to the foolish . . . He is a part of the Body of Christ, which is the Church. And it is necessary that he should know that those who, in the Church, appear weak, poor, foolish—like the sinners—should be surrounded with all the greater honour and watched over with all the more exacting care. On that condition he will be able to say to himself: "I am one of those who fear the Lord." It is necessary that he should have compassion on men of this kind, as opposed to showing himself embarrassed by them; that he should suffer with those who suffer, in order to learn by experience that we are all one Body with many different united members.

Such is the price of a good thing which cannot have any price set upon it—Catholic communion. The point was made as early as by St. Clement of Rome, one of the earliest among

Peter's successors, who thus went at one stroke to the very heart of the meaning of the Church: "Christ belongs to all those who have a humble attitude and to to those who set themselves above the flock."

As far as the superior type of man can see, everything in the Church is low-grade. But "power sorts well with this poor quality"—in fact it sorts well with it alone. The idealized forms in which that kind of man finds such satisfaction seem higher and purer to him only because they are the product of his own thought. It does not matter whether he is seeking in them an instrument for the fashioning of a rich personality which is both integrated and forceful; or a reference frame for interpreting the universe with; or a springboard from which to project himself beyond the limits which enclose the human condition. In each and every case they are equally powerless; they cannot even begin to change his own heart. For all its apparent sublimity the thought of the superior man is no more than a mirror in which he admires himself and which in consequence holds him hypnotized in vanity. It sets up an idol in his heart and when he throws himself into the arms of it his embrace finds nothingness—the One which is pure only if it is not being, or the Universal Possibility from which the multiple states of being are derived: "Id vanitate sentit humana non veritate divina." We know all to well—unfortunately—that the profession of Catholicism, even militant Catholicism, does not automatically confer sanctity, and we must admit that amongst us (and even in surroundings distinguished by fervour and freedom from contamination) much human narrowness often places obstacles in the way of the action of the Spirit. Yet we also know well that the humblest of our saints is freer, interiorly, than the greatest of our masters of wisdom. The former speaks modestly of salvation while the latter is all ready to talk about deliverance; but it does not take long to see which of the two is, in point of fact, "delivered." The noblest and sincerest efforts, thrown awry by an initial *hubris*, end up in the hollowest of pretensions; the only depths which are not deceptive are those which the Spirit Himself hollows out within a man, and they presuppose the ground of the common faith, accepted without second thoughts and never abandoned. There, and there only, is the royal road.

"O humility, O sublimity! House of clay and palace of the king, body of death and temple of light! A thing of scorn to the proud, and spouse of Christ." In all her apparent crudity the Church is the sacrament—the true and effective sign—of those "depths of God." And by the same token there are opened to us the depths of man—"deep calls to deep." That is why the passage from St. Paul commented on earlier is at one and the same time the statement of a scandal to the "natural man" and a cry of triumph to the believer—"For see your vocation, brethren, that there are not many wise according to the flesh, not many mighty, not many noble. But the foolish things of this world hath God chosen, that he may confound the wise: and the weak things of this world hath God chosen, that he may confound the strong. And the base things of the world and the things that are contemptible, hath God chosen; and things that are not, that he might bring to nought things that are: that no flesh should glory in his sight."

It takes a miracle of grace to enable us to see things so; without it, the most edifying sentiments and the richest spiritual gifts are merely obstacles, making men like the cedar of Lebanon which has not yet been broken by the Lord—they feed pride and close the heart to charity. And as we have said, they can become a temptation even in the heart of the Church itself. If something of the sort ever becomes the case with us, perhaps we shall benefit from recalling to mind the example of men who have heroically overcome such a situation, together with the concrete circumstances under which they did it.

When Newman, driven by an interior logic which was something much more than a "paper logic", knelt at the feet of Father Domenico Barberi and asked him to receive him into the Church, it was not just that he sacrificed a situation, and habits dear to him, and delightful friendships, and a spiritual home loved with a certain melancholy but always tenderly, and a reputation which was already a glorious one. The situation was even more unfavourable than that. It was an autumn evening in the year 1845, toward the end of the pontificate of Gregory XVI; to Newman, Catholicism had everywhere the appearance of a thing beaten by life, and all the sorrier a figure because it trailed after it so many ironic relics of a recent splendour. It could have no human attraction whatsoever for the one-time Fellow of Oriel; as he wrote later: "Ours is not an age of temporal glory, of dutiful princes, of loyal governments, of large possessions, of ample leisure, of famous schools, of learned foundations, of well-stored libraries, of honoured sanctuaries. Rather, it is like the first age of the Church, when there was little of station, of nobility, of learning, of wealth, in the holy heritage; when Christians were chiefly of the lower orders; when we were poor and ignorant, when we were despised and hated by the great and philosophical as a low rabble, or a stupid and obstinate association, or a foul and unprincipled conspiracy. It is like that first age, in which no saint is recorded in history who fills the mind as a great idea, as St. Thomas or St. Igantius fills it, and when the ablest of so-called Christian writers belonged to heretical schools. We certainly have little to show for ourselves; and the words of the Psalm are fulfilled in us: 'They have set fire to thy sanctuary, they have defiled the dwelling-place of thy name on earth. Our signs we have not seen; there is no prophet . . .' " Indeed, Newman found nothing attractive about Roman Catholics; he admitted that he did not find himself attuned to them, and that he expected little from them, and that in becoming one of their number he had made himself an outcast—he had, as he put it, turned to the wilderness. And, of course, at that time he could not know of all the other thorns which were to tear at him in the course of his long trek across that wilderness. Yet to his soul, full of faith, the step was inevitable, and he was never to regret it for a moment.

Again, we may read what St. Augustine has to say in the eighth book of the *Confessions.* He had the story from his friend, Simplicianus, and it is well known how deep an impression it made upon him at the moment when he also was in the process of making a similar decision. The aged Victorinus was a philosopher, "skilled in all the liberal disciplines"; yet he, who had taught so many noble senators and who, as a famous thinker, had seen his own statue set up in the Forum, eventually "thought it no shame to make himself the slave of Christ and bend his neck beneath the yoke of humility and his brow under the shame of the cross." But that did not come about without a long resistance, strengthened by a superb incomprehension—for which the example is none the less fine:

O Lord, Lord, who dost bow down Thy heavens and descend, dost touch the mountains and they smoke, by what means didst Thou find Thy way into that breast? He read, so Simplicianus said, Holy Scripture; he investigated all the Christian writings most carefully and minutely. And he said, not publicly, but to Simplicianus privately, and as one friend to another: "I would have you know that I am now a Christian." Simplicianus answered: "I shall not believe it, nor count you among Christians unless I see you in the Church of Christ." Victorinus asked with some faint mockery: "Then is it the walls that make Christians?" He went on saying that he was a Christian, and Simplicianus went on with the same denial, and Victorinus always repeated his retort about the walls. The fact was that he feared to offend his friends, important people and worshipers of . . . demons, he feared their enmity might fall heavily upon him from the height of their Babylon-dignity as from the cedars down. But when by reading in all earnestness he had drawn strength he grew afraid that Christ might deny him before his Angels as if he were ashamed to confess Christ before men. He felt that he was guilty of a great crime in being ashamed of the sacraments of the lowliness of Your Word, when he had not been ashamed of the sacrilegious rites of those demons of pride whom in his pride he had worshipped. So he grew proud towards vanity and humble towards truth. Quite suddenly and without warning he said to Simplicianus, as Simplicianus told me: "Let us go to Church. I wish to be made a Christian." Simplicianus, unable to control his joy, went with him. He was instructed in the first mysteries of the faith, and not long after gave in his name that he might be regenerated by baptism . . .

If Victorinus had not made up his mind to take this decisive step and lose himself among the humble flock of the "practising" faithful, we should doubtless still remember him as a distinguished philosopher. Perhaps we should be able to admire him still as the thinker who first conceived the elements of that internal theory of the Trinity for which St. Augustine was to provide the West with the definitive formulae. We may even imagine that he would have been capable, without entering the Church, of composing his hymns to the Trinity, in which case his name would also live among those of the poets of dogma. But if all that were so he would still have no better title than the one which he has, for he would not have deserved to be called by a name which is common indeed and in the eyes of many without distinction, yet is the finest of all when its significance is understood; he would not have been a "Catholic".

John Tracy Ellis

1905-

John Tracy Ellis was born in 1905 in Seneca, Illinois, and attended St. Viator College in Bourbonnais, Illinois. Upon graduation in 1927, he entered the Catholic University in Washington, D.C., to do graduate work in history, and he was granted the doctorate in 1930. He then taught as a layman in St. Teresa's, St. Benedict's and St. Viator College until deciding to pursue studies for the priesthood. That brought him back to Catholic University in 1935, where he also taught part-time. He was ordained as a priest of the Winona diocese in 1938 and thereupon received an appointment as full-time instructor of history at Catholic University, the start of his real career.

In 1940 Ellis was asked to take over the graduate courses of Peter Guilday, a pioneer of American Catholic history, who was in declining health. To prepare himself more adequately for this task, Ellis requested a year's leave of absence, most of which he spent at Harvard where he audited the courses of Arthur M. Schlesinger, Sr., and others. He subsequently referred to this as his "Harvard interval," a time that had a considerable impact on his academic orientation.

It was while he was at Catholic University in the 1950's that Ellis came into his own as a nationally recognized historian of American Catholicism. He wrote the two-volume biography of James Cardinal Gibbons that appeared in 1952, and American

Catholics and the Intellectual Life *in 1956. And for two decades (1941-1961) he served as secretary of the American Catholic Historical Association and as managing editor of the* Catholic Historical Review. *From 1964 to 1976 he was professor of church history at the University of San Francisco, but during those years he also took time to serve as visiting professor at Brown, Notre Dame, Graduate Theological Union (Berkeley), as well as at both the Gregorian and the Angelicum universities in Rome. In 1976 he returned to Catholic University as professorial lecturer, teaching a course in exchange for room and board.*

Made a domestic prelate by Pope Pius XII in 1955, Monsignor Ellis won the Gilmary Shea prize the following year for the book American Catholicism, *from which the following selection is taken. What especially caught the attention of reviewers was the way in which Ellis could bring all his scholarship to bear on his narrative, providing factual material and critical interpretation, yet keeping it brisk and readable. The work is divided into the four chronological periods: 1) The Church in Colonial America, 1492-1790; 2) Catholics as Citizens, 1790-1852; 3) Civil War and Immigration, 1852-1908; 4) Recent American Catholicism, 1908-1956.*

In May of 1978 the National Catholic Reporter *carried a wide-ranging interview with the 73 year-old Monsignor Ellis. When asked who his "heroes" are, he spontaneously replied with four names: his patron, John the Evangelist, then John Henry Newman, Thomas More, and Teresa of Avila. And when asked what he would most like to see happen in the Church in America in our time, his reply was "I would like to see a mitigation and a dimunition . . . of the divisiveness in the Catholic family." Insofar as accurate information and clear insight about the past contribute to a unified perspective from which to view the future, John Tracy Ellis has done more than his share to bring that about.*

AMERICAN CATHOLICISM

CHAPTER I

THE CHURCH IN COLONIAL AMERICA
1492–1790

C olumbus' conversation with the friar at La Rábida is the starting point of modern history. The past had ruled the world till then—what began that day was the reign of the future." Thus did Lord Acton characterize the fateful change of plans brought about by the Italian navigator's visit to the former confessor of Queen Isabella; for it was Fray Juan Perez who convinced Columbus that he should await the results of another approach to the Spanish sovereigns before turning to France. With that change of plans the destiny of every one of us was in a remote way connected by the voyage of 1492 which opened the real history of the world we inhabit.

In this discussion of colonial America I should like to dwell upon several principal aspects of the threefold penetration of the Western Hemisphere by the Catholic Church in the two and one-half centuries before the United States was born. I say "several" for this reason, as the reader will understand: a brief survey of such a lengthy span of years can afford only a very restricted treatment. The development of the subject is determined by the association of the Church in three quite distinct relationships, that is, with the colonizing enterprises of Spain, France, and England. There were, moreover, differences as to time and place of colonization. Spain preceded France and England by almost a century in planting permanent settlements. The Spanish Empire embraced Central and South America, the French occupied what is today Canada, and all three powers ultimately assumed a stake in the islands of the Caribbean. But with the history of these distant outposts we are in no way concerned; our sole purpose here is to deal with certain features of colonial Catholicism that occurred within the borders of what is now the United States.

THE CATHOLIC TRADITION: The Church

If we Americans of the mid-twentieth century do not understand as well as we should the varied pattern of our colonial past, the reason is not far to seek. Until about forty years ago the *leyenda negra*, or the "black legend" of Spain, so completely possessed the national mind that pioneers like Adolph Bandelier and others who sought to win a hearing for the case of Spain were shouted out of court by those bred in the tradition of sixteenth-century England. The historians of that tradition succeeded to a remarkable degree in passing on to generations of Americans a thoroughly biased view of Spain's accomplishments in the New World. In spite of the recently increasing number of solid studies in American historiography, I should say that students interested in the history of ideas will still find it piquant to trace the manner in which the Whig approach to Spanish history captured the American historical profession and held it firmly in its grip until a generation or more ago.

The man to whom, above all others, the credit is owed for a broader and more enlightened view is Herbert Eugene Bolton, who searched restlessly in Spanish archives on both sides of the Atlantic until his death in 1953. As Bolton uncovered the documentary riches, he became more and more convinced, not only of the defective method of many who had preceded him, but of the necessity for Americans to know the history of Spanish America if they were fully to understand their own past. It was an approach that slowly won a considerable audience; and by the time Bolton delivered his presidential address before the American Historical Association at Toronto in 1932 on a subject he entitled "The Epic of Greater America," it was realized that this sympathetic yet objective treatment could serve a highly useful purpose for the Good Neighbor policy of the American government, for the world view of history that even then was beginning to force itself upon our notice, and, too, for the cause of true historical scholarship.

With regard to Catholicism in the Spanish colonies, there are, I think, certain prime postulates that one should keep in mind. First is the fact that at the dawn of colonization and for a century thereafter Spain was a nation more united in its religious faith, perhaps, than in any other single way. The recent conquest of the Moors, the concessions granted to the Spanish crown by

210

the Holy See over the management of ecclesiastical affairs, and the fact that Spain was unquestionably the greatest Catholic power of Europe set in conflict with the rising Protestant states—all helped to stamp upon every Spanish enterprise the seal of Catholic energy. Such zeal appears, indeed, in the first entry that Columbus made in his famous journal, where he remarked that among the principal aims of his voyage one was to contact the native peoples so that he might observe what he termed "the manner in which may be undertaken their conversion to our Holy Faith." It is likewise evident in almost every major patent granted by the crown for settlement in the New World; for example, when Charles V in June, 1523, outlined for Vasquez de Ayllón the objectives he was to pursue in his conquest of Florida, the conversion of the Indians to Catholicism was described as "the chief motive you are to bear and hold in this affair, and to this end it is proper that religious persons should accompany you."

Not only was the religious motive high among the objectives of Spanish colonization, as to a lesser extent it was with both the French and English, but in no other country was the State's control over the Church quite so complete as in the case of Spain. A decade before the discovery of America there had begun with Pope Sixtus IV a series of concessions to the kings of Spain which culminated in Julius II's bull *Universalis ecclesiae* of 1508, which made necessary the State's approval for every church, monastery, and religious house opened in the colonies and which gave to the state the right to nominate in perpetuity to every ecclesiastical benefice in the colonial empire. This exceedingly close union of Church and State was, then, both the greatest strength and the predominant weakness of Catholicism in Spanish America. The interests of the political and ecclesiastical orders frequently clashed over control of the Indians, and as a consequence Spanish colonial records through the three centuries from Juan Ponce de León's entry into Florida in 1521 to the opening of the last California mission at San Francisco Solano in 1823 are filled with the strife between Church and State.

However, this combination produced more than sterile quarrels. Within the immense arc which the Spaniards gradually drew around the rim of the United States from Florida on the east to upper California on the west, they had to deal with primitive and savage peoples, and in so doing they found no more effective instrument than the Catholic mission system. The missionaries, dependent upon the civil and military authorities for financial support and physical protection, likewise realized that they could never press their claims too far. As a result the *real patronato*, the term used to describe the State's control over the Church, continued to the end of Spanish rule with many a dispute referred to superiors in Mexico City and Madrid for lengthy adjudication that gave ample time for fiery Spanish tempers on the frontier to cool. No informed person would endeavor to maintain that the churchmen were always in the right, but by the same token no one can deny that they were generally on the side of the angels in their treatment of the Indians. It was the outraged voice of a friar, Bartolomé de las Casas, which first made Europe aware of the fate that had befallen thousands of the natives in enslavement by the Spanish conquerors. And it was the agitation aroused by Las Casas and his kind that prompted Pope Paul III in 1537 to issue the bull *Sublimis Deus* in which he declared: "The said Indians and all other people who may later be discovered by Christians, are by no means to be deprived of their liberty or the possession of their property, even though they be outside the faith of Jesus Christ."

There was an element of compassion for the red man as a child of God in the ideology of the Spanish missionaries that was entirely lacking in the attitude of most of the English settlers along the Atlantic Coast. It was the conviction that he had a soul worth saving that inspired their extraordinary sacrifices in his behalf. That, and that alone, will explain the dogged persistence with which the missionaries pushed on in the face of repeated setbacks and tragedies such as the murder of Fray Juan de Padilla, their protomartyr, on the plains of Kansas in 1542. How otherwise can one accóunt for the fact that so many highly gifted priests like the Tyrolese Jesuit, Eusebio Kino, and Junipero Serra, the Franciscan from Majorca, both university-trained men, should abandon their cultivated surroundings to dedicate their lives to the moral and material uplift of these savage people? Failure they knew aplenty, but they also knew success, as, for example, when the Franciscan superior in New Mexico reported in 1630 that there were then 35,000 Christian Indians living in ninety pueblos grouped around twenty-five missions. Two centuries later when the blow of secularization fell upon the twenty-one missions of California, a like number of peaceful and diligent red men were in possession of nearly 400,000 head of cattle, over 300,000 hogs, sheep, and goats, 62,000 horses, and farms that yielded over 120,000 bushels of grain plus the products of orchards, gardens, wine presses, looms, shops, and forges. In California alone between 1769 and 1845, there were 146 Franciscans who gave all or a portion of their adult lives to this difficult task. There were contributions the like of which could be duplicated in no other area of colonial America, and it was no romantic impulse when Bolton spoke of the missions of the Spanish Jesuits and Franciscans as "a force which made for the preservation of the Indians, as opposed to their destruction, so characteristic of the Anglo-American frontier."

In all these colonial missions—and there were at one time as many in Texas as in California, more than that number in Florida, and twice California's twenty-one in New Mexico—the Franciscans, Jesuits, and other priests were not only ministers of religion. They were agents of the Spanish crown, and as such they supported the policies of the government whenever those policies did not run counter to the principal business of the missionaries, which was to save souls. For example, the news of Spain's declaration of war on Great Britain in June, 1779, was long in reaching California, but when Serra learned of it, he dispatched a circular letter to all the missions on June 15, 1780, in which he informed the friars of what had happened, reminded them of the generosity of Charles III's government to their missions, and emphasized the interest which they should take in the matter. There was nothing that the Franciscans in California could do to hasten Spain's victory over England but to pray, and with that in mind Serra said, "Of each and every one of Your Reverences I most earnestly ask in the Lord that as soon as you receive this letter you be most attentive in begging God to grant success to our arms." Little did the American rebels on the Atlantic Coast realize that over 3,000 miles to the west a Spanish friar was ordering prayers to be said for the defeat of their common enemy!

As an important part of the colonizing methods of Spain in the New World, the numerous missionary establishments of the Church were, as has been said, closely linked with the civil and military administration. The missionaries were in every sense agents of both Church and State, for it was from the State that they received—if often irregularly—their annual stipends. It was likewise the State that furnished troops from neighboring presidios for the protection of the missions. The civil government usually paid an initial grant equivalent to $1,000 for equipping the missions with items such as bells, sacred vessels and vestments for religious services, and tools for the workshops. But the priests more than earned their keep by their disciplining and civilizing of the natives. It was the missionaries who taught the Indians the rudiments of learning within the mission compound, instructed the women how to cook, sew, spin, and weave, and the men how to plant the crops, to fell the forests and to build, to tan leather, run the forge, dig ditches, shear the sheep, and to tend the cattle. It was they who introduced to these distant frontiers almost every domestic plant and animal then known in Europe, and it was they who taught the savages how to make the best possible use of husbandry for profit and enjoyment.

No one acquainted with the history of Catholicism in the Spanish borderlands will deny that there were at times defects and abuses. One of the chief sources for the defects in the system was the *real patronato*, a set of privileges that had been conceded to the Spanish kings by the Holy See almost a century before the establishment of the first enduring mission in the future United States. Out of the State's patronage of ecclesiastical affairs, there arose endless disputes between the two authorities, which in turn led to serious division in the Spanish settlements and to a general weakening of colonial government. The scandal given the Indians by these quarrels was real, for they often found themselves the bewildered victims of contests between the civil and military on the one hand and the missionaries on the other. Consequently, there ensued a demoralizing effect on the natives and a lessened respect for the Catholic faith which they had been asked to embrace. The differences arose at many points where the jurisdictional lines between Church and State were dim, and in one form or another they existed throughout the entire colonial period. The military, for example, often tried to win the natives for their selfish purposes by plying them with liquor, a practice which the missionaries fought vigorously, as they likewise resisted the civil officials' attempts from time to time to profit by Indian labor. On the other hand, from time to time a missionary would overstep the bounds of his jurisdiction and encroach upon the civil domain. Thus the friction was more or less constant, revolving, as a historian of New Mexico has said, around fundamental issues ever the same: "rivalry for control of the destiny of the Indians, problems of mission discipline, the conflict of economic interests, the question of ecclesiastical immunity, the authority of the custodian as ecclesiastical judge ordinary, the proper exercise of ecclesiastical censures, and interference of the clergy in strictly secular matters."

Today hardly more than a chain of place names, stretching from St. Augustine, Florida, the first Catholic parish established in 1565 within the present United States, through San Antonio, Los Angeles, and on to San Francisco, remains to remind Americans of the three centuries of Spanish rule on the borderlands of their country. Yet the mission system was the most successful institution for dealing with the aborigines, and its builders gave a style of architecture to the Southwest and California that is as characteristic of those regions as the colonial design is to New England. It was likewise by virtue of elaborate accounts of explorations through uncharted areas and detailed maps made by missionaries like Father Kino that the cartography of the West was advanced. Through the missionaries' grammars and dictionaries of the native dialects and their preservation of Indian artifacts, which one sees in the museums of the Southwest, anthropologists were furnished with knowledge of the languages and customs of the Indians that would otherwise have perished. This old Christian civilization of the borderlands endured far beyond the age of Spanish greatness, and when the Americans arrived in those areas in the mid-nineteenth century, it afforded a link entirely absent from the plains and valleys to the north, with which to bind the old with the new order. It was facts such as these that Herbert Ingram Priestley had in mind when he said, "It is of prime importance for the life of America today that the first white men to settle on these western shores were Spaniards and Roman Catholics, representatives of a powerful nation that was the citadel of a united faith."

In the case of France, the other major power through whose agency Catholicism entered North America, many characteristics of its colonial missions resembled those of Spain. Here, too, Church and State were at the time united, and since the concordat signed by Pope Leo X and Francis I in 1516 the crown had enjoyed the right of nominating to vacant bishoprics and to newly established sees. But the Gallican tendencies which by the time of Louis XIV had brought about so tight a control over the Church in France were never able to effect quite the same results in North America. In no small measure this was due to the precedents set by the first bishop in New France, Francois de Montmorency Laval, a man of iron will and determination, who after his arrival in the colony in 1659 gave battle at every turn to the officials of the State when the rights of the Church were threatened. A recent writer has said of the bishop: "In all, Laval guided the destinies of the Church in New France for thirty-four years, ruling in a more authoritarian and absolute fashion than any representative of the all-powerful Sun King. He left more of a mark upon the colony than any governor except the great Frontenac, with whom he had quarreled violently." The union of Church and State in New France was nonetheless real, and it was the basis for many a contest waged between the two throughout the North American experience of France in the seventeenth and eighteenth centuries.

But apart from political matters, there were other similarities between Spain and France in the New World. The same concept, of the Indian as a man whose soul had equal value in the sight of God with that of the white man, motivated the French Jesuit and Récollet around the Great Lakes and through the Mississippi Valley as much as it did their Spanish brethren farther south. Father Jean de Brébeuf, for example, lived nearly three years among the Hurons for the sole purpose of learning

216

their language and gaining a knowledge of their customs. Enriched with this background, he wrote out in 1637 a set of instructions for his confrères who were to evangelize the tribe, and if any of the future missionaries had thought that his superior education would impress the red men, Brébeuf was quick to disillusion him: "Leaving a highly civilized community, you fall into the hands of barbarous people who care but little for your Philosophy or your Theology. All the fine qualities which might make you loved and respected in France are like pearls trampled under the feet of swine, or rather of mules, which utterly despise you when they see that you are not as good pack animals as they are." Fully cognizant as he was of what was in store for him, Brébeuf yet continued his Indian ministrations through the next twelve years up to that day in March, 1649, when he was captured by the Iroquois near Georgian Bay and submitted to a series of tortures that has made many a modern reader recoil in horror. Francis Parkman detailed his last hours and remarked of Brébeuf: "He came of a noble race,—the same, it is said, from which sprang the English Earls of Arundel; but never had the mailed barons of his line confronted a fate so appalling, with so prodigious a constancy. To the last he refused to flinch, and 'his death was the astonishment of his murderers.' "

As Spain's high missionary zeal in the sixteenth century had been quickened by the triumph over the Mohammedans and the contest with the Protestant north, so a century later the compelling faith that carried the French missionaries to North America was fired by one of the most resplendent periods in the Catholicism of France, the age that produced a St. Francis de Sales, a St. Vincent de Paul, a Jacques Olier, a Cardinal Bérulle, and a host of other striking figures in religious thought and action. In France, too, the union of Church and State facilitated the arrangement for joint undertakings in the distant colonies, even if it later often hindered their execution. But there was a difference between the Spanish and French ecclesiastical regimes. After 1659 there was a bishop at Quebec in the person of the forceful Laval who, once admitted to the governing council of New France, powerfully barred the encroachments of the civil arm against the Church. Though distances were great and travel slow between the Great Lakes and Louisiana, the official position and high ecclesiastical rank of Laval and his successors told with more effect when disputes arose between the missionaries and civil officials than was true of the remonstrances of bishops in Mexico and Cuba.

For a century and a half, Jesuits, Récollets, Capuchins, and the diocesan priests of New France traversed the heart of the continent in pursuit of a goal that often eluded them. If the souls of these steadfast priests had not been kindled by a deep and abiding faith, they would soon have despaired; the story of the sufferings of the Jesuits alone during the 1649's at the hands of the savages remains one of the most heroic tales in our colonial past. From the time that Isaac Jogues, after incredible tortures, was felled beneath the ax of an Iroquois near the little village of Auriesville, New York, in October, 1646, to the murder of Brébeuf and Gabriel Lalemant on Georgian Bay in March, 1649, the slaughter continued. Then the insensate hate of the Iroquois against the Hurons and their friends seemed for a time to abate.

The Huron mission, it is true, had failed, but the Blackrobes did not quit New France. Instead they directed their eyes westward toward Lake Superior where Isaac Jogues had traveled as early as 1641. These were the years that saw a renewal of war in Europe and a more aggressive policy upon the part of France once Louis XIV had assumed personal control of the government in 1661. As rivalry for the mastery of North America intensified, Jean Talon, the royal intendant of New France, laid plans to forestall competition in the heart of the continent. On June 4, 1671, Simon Francois Daumont, Sieur de Saint Lusson, acting as Talon's representative, took formal possession of the entire western country in the name of God and Louis XIV. In this ceremony at Sault Ste Marie, to which the chiefs of all the neighboring tribes had been invited, Father Claude Alloüez, already a veteran in those parts, played a prominent role. After the cross and the standard of the king had been raised aloft as the symbols of the dual auspices of the undertaking, Alloüez preached a sermon in which he explained to the savages the doctrine of Christ's redemption of mankind on the cross. Then pointing to the royal banner, he said, "But look likewise at that other post, to which are affixed the armorial bearings of the great Captain of France whom we call King. He lives beyond the sea; he is the Captain of the greatest Captains, and has not his equal in the world." Thus were Church and State joined at that remote spot on Lake Superior to advance the policies of Louis XIV, Colbert, and Louvois.

The years that followed bore greater fruit for the Jesuits' missions than they had hitherto known, and by 1673 there were 1,800 refugee Ottawas and Hurons resident at St. Ignace Mission on the north shore of the Straits of Mackinac. South and west from these northern bases, the Blackrobes fanned out into the future states of Michigan, Wisconsin, and Illinois, and as the civil and military arms of France advanced upon the Mississippi they were either in the vanguard alike Alloüez—tracking for thirty years over the prairies and through the forests of the Old Northwest—or like Jacques Marquette, in company with Louis Jolliet, reaching down to the borders of the Southwest. During the time that Marquette had spent at La Pointe de Saint Esprit on the south shore of Lake Superior, he had received visits from tribesmen, including the Illinois, who spoke to him of a great river and asked that he come among them. The thought of establishing a missions for these Indians was uppermost in his mind, therefore, when in May, 1673, he set out with Jolliet on their famous expedition. In the long and arduous months that lay ahead, the missionary was sustained by his hopes for the conversion of the Illinois and by his deep and abiding faith in God and the Mother of Christ. No one has written more majestically of this personal devotion of Marquette for the Blessed Mother than Parkman, who, although he in no way shared in the Jesuit's sentiments, appreciated the beauty and elevation of his thoughts. Parkman said of Marquette:

> He was a devout votary of the Virgin Mary, who, imaged to his mind in shapes of the most transcendent loveliness with which the pencil of human genius has ever informed the canvas, was to him the object of an adoration not unmingled with a sentiment of chivalrous devotion. The longings of a sensitive heart, divorced from earth, sought solace in the skies. A subtle element of romance was blended with the fervor of his worship, and hung like an illumined cloud over

the harsh and hard realities of his daily lot. Kindled
by the smile of his celestial mistress, his gentle and
noble nature knew no fear. For her he burned to dare
and to suffer, discover new lands and conquer new
realms to her sway.

Before this great missionary gave up his life in May, 1675, near
where the river that bears his name empties into Lake Michigan,
he had the joy of opening the mission of the Immaculate Conception for the Illinois near the present village of Utica. Although
his failing health permitted only a brief stay, others came to
spread a network of Jesuit stations on the shores of the Great
Lakes and the banks of the rivers of the Middle West.

Meanwhile, members of other orders appeared in these in-
land regions to supplement the Society of Jesus in affording
religious ministrations to the white settlers in the wilderness and
to seek converts among the red men. It was a Récollet, Louis
Hennepin, who explored the upper Mississippi in 1680 as far
north as the present site of Minneapolis and named the Falls of
St. Anthony. Hennepin's confrères, Gabriel de la Ribourde and
Zénobe Membré, who visited the tribes of northern Illinois, met
violent deaths, the former in September, 1680, at the hands of
the Kickapoo near Seneca, and the latter with a fellow religious,
Maxim le Clercq, in January, 1689, as a member of LaSalle's
ill-starred venture on the coast of Texas. Diocesan priests trained
at the seminary of Bishop Laval at Quebec also played a part as
missionaries to the Indians of the Middle West and as pastors of
the infant parishes in the frontier towns. Authorized in May,
1698, to open missions for certain tribes along the Mississippi,
these priests often became pastors to the French, as, for example,
did Henri Rolleux de la Vente, who in September, 1704, was
installed as first pastor of the Church of the Immaculate Conception at Fort Louis, the forerunner of the present city of Mobile.
After the French had established the new colony of Louisiana
in the early years of the eighteenth century, an agreement in
May, 1722, brought the Capuchins, who endured throughout
the century and beyond the time of Louisiana's purchase by the
United States.

It was fortunate for Catholics that the Récollets, Capuchins, and diocesan priests had been enrolled, for the disaster

which befell the Jesuits in the colonies of Spain had been visited even earlier upon their French brothers. When in July, 1763, the superior council at New Orleans ordered Jesuits banished from Louisiana and the Illinois country, a most dismal page was added to the history of the Church in colonial America. The harshness with which the civil officials acted and the manner in which they profaned even the symbols of religion justified the comment of the old Jesuit who described the episode: "One might have thought that it was the enemies of the Catholic religion who had caused it."

To understand the persistence of the French missionaries in the face of so many apathetic or hostile Indians, one must remember that they not only were trained for hardship and disappointment but were schooled as well for failure in the sense that the world reckons failure. To the Jesuits, for example, it was not a failure for more than three hundred of the finest specimens of French manhood to expend their lives in converting a few Indians and in the end to be ruthlessly expelled from America by the government that had brought them here. To men imbued with a living faith in the supernatural and in the philosophy of the cross, this type of failure was akin to that of the martyrs of the pagan Roman Empire out of whose sufferings in the first three centuries of the Christian era the Church of Europe was born. It is the kind of attitude toward failure that we have been hearing almost monthly since 1950 as the missionaries expelled from Communist China reach Hong Kong only to declare that they will re-enter China at the first opportunity. It is an exceedingly difficult thing to convey a spirit of this kind to paper, but Parkman caught something of its meaning when he wrote of Father Marquette, and even such moderns as Charles and Mary Beard, to whom the New World empires were mainly predatory operations, remarked: "The heroic deeds of Catholic missionaries, daring for religion's sake torture and death, bore witness to a new force in the making of world dominion."

French Catholics in colonial America were less successful than the Spaniards in converting Indians, but they were, perhaps, more successful in planting permanent settlements in the wilderness. At towns like St. Louis, Vincennes, Detroit, New

Orleans, and Mobile the Church continued to play a leading part in the restricted lives of the inhabitants down to the time of the American Revolution. Amid the rough surroundings of the frontier the spirit of religion often burned very low, but it was never completely extinguished.

When these frontier posts were later engulfed in the stirring events of the Revolution and the War of 1812, the French Catholic population was found loyal to the American cause. George Rogers Clark and his Virginia militiamen experienced that loyalty at firsthand when they took Kaskaskia in 1778 and received aid from Father Pierre Gibault, the village priest. It was Gibault's influence that won Cahokia, and it was he, too, who tracked through the forests to help deliver Vincennes and its Indians into American hands. Father Gabriel Richard at Detroit was so noticeably attached to the United States in the War of 1812 that the British ordered his house arrest.

Throughout the western expanse traversed by the missionaries of France and settled by its Catholic people before the American nation was born, a litany of cities, towns, and rivers tells of who once settled there. There is Vincennes, there is Marquette, and there is St. Louis, named to commemorate the saintly Louis IX. There is Dubuque, named for a Canadian descendant of the French. There is Louisville, called after Louis XVI, and Marietta, Ohio, after Marie Antoinette. To these settlements the refugee French priests fled after 1790 before the whirlwind of revolution that had broken over France. In the wilderness these priests kindled anew the fire of religious faith and enriched the lives of all—Catholic and non-Catholic alike— with their cultured manners and minds. D. W. Brogan has said that the old towns of the Middle West are more American and more touching to the historical imagination than the large cities. Vincennes and Bardstown were once, as Brogan stated, "centres of civilization, of learning, of religion, of commerce." In both Vincennes and Bardstown, a cathedral and a college were staffed by bishops and priests from France before the advancing frontier had passed their doors. Here, then, was a significant stabilizing factor in the maturing process of the newborn states, an ancient and fixed tradition to mellow the rough and raw elements of the West.

John Tracy Ellis

What a different world one enters when he turns to the English settlements along the Atlantic Coast! Within the areas subjected to the rule of Spain and France no other Christian belief than that of Catholicism ever held sway; it was unchallenged by any but pagan Indian cults. To the English colonists, however, a century of official hostility had made Catholicism more hated than any other Christian faith. In fact, so thoroughly had the job been done that, as a student of English expansion remarks, "With such conviction did they preach this doctrine that Englishmen at length accepted it as their imperial destiny."

For present purposes the history of the Catholic Church in colonial English America may be reduced without too great simplification to four main points. First, a universal anti-Catholic bias was brought to Jamestown in 1607 and vigilantly cultivated in all the thirteen colonies from Massachusetts to Georgia. Second, the small body of Catholics, mostly English and Irish, who settled on the Atlantic seaboard after more than a century of active persecution and handicap clung to their religious faith. Third, the Catholic minority in their brief tenure of power in two colonies introduced the principle of religious toleration. Finally, the absence of domination by any one of the different Protestant churches fostered the principle of religious freedom for all, a principle to which the Catholics gave full assent.

The first point scarcely needs much documentation, since the proscription against Catholics in the colonial charters and laws is too well known to require emphasis, and the sermons, religious tracts, books, and gazettes of the period with monotonous regularity bore the same spirit and intent. The Anglican ministers of Virginia and the Puritan divines of Massachusetts Bay were often worlds apart in their theology, but there was nothing that would cause them to close ranks more quickly than a supposed threat from the Church of Rome. That is why one finds so much similarity between Virginia's law against Catholics of March, 1642, and the enactment at Massachusetts Bay five years later. It may be said that this transplantation of English religious prejudice to America thrived, though carried thousands of miles from its place of origin, and struck such enduring roots in new soil that it became one of the major traditions in a people's religious life. In a recent work Louis

Wright states that, for better or for worse, Americans have inherited the basic qualities of their culture from the British. The thought prompts him to say: "For that reason we need to take a long perspective of our history, a perspective which views America from at least the period of the first Tudor monarchs and lets us see the gradual development of our common civilization, its transmission across the Atlantic, and its expansion and modification as it was adapted to conditions in the Western Hemisphere." Apace with the influences exercised by other national strains in the generation of American civilization, the British has yet remained the strongest and has assimilated most of the others. Americans are not Englishmen, but, as Wright concludes, "we cannot escape an inheritance which has given us some of our sturdiest and most lasting qualities." Certainly the anti-Catholic bias brought to this country with the first English settlers has proved one of the sturdiest and most lasting of these qualities. The viability of that tradition would have astonished even Edmund Burke, who understood so well how the hatred of Catholics had operated in his native land. It was Burke who in a famous letter on the penal laws against the Catholics of Ireland remarked:

> You abhorred it, as I did, for its vicious perfection. For I must do it justice; it was a complete system, full of coherence and consistency, well digested and well composed in all its parts. It was a machine of wise and elaborate contrivance, and as well fitted for the oppression, impoverishment, and degradation of a people, and the debasement, in them, of human nature itself as ever proceeded from the perverted ingenuity of man.

That the penal codes of the American colonies did not reach the tyrannical perfection noticed by Burke elsewhere was no hindrance to holding the few colonial Catholics in thorough subjection.

What made the laws against Catholics in colonial America seem so absurdly harsh was the fact that at no time was more than an insignificant minority of the population Catholic. Protestants outnumbered Catholics among the 200 to 300 colonists who settled Maryland in 1634, and a census of that colony in 1708 turned up only 2,974 Catholics in a total population of 33,833. In Pennsylvania, the other colony where Catholics were concentrated, the census of 1757 recorded about 200,000 inhabitants, of whom 1,365 were Catholics. Even as late as 1785, when the new United States contained nearly four million people, there were scarcely more than 25,000 Catholics. Catholics were lost to the faith during these years by reason of the lack of facilities for the practice of their religion in many areas, but for the most part the colonial Catholics held tenaciously to their faith amid the most trying circumstances. There were even some conversions among the Protestants, as, for example, the Brooke and Taney families of Maryland from whom the later Chief Justice of the United States was descended.

Why did Catholics come to America in the first place? The predominant motive was the same as that which had prompted the Puritans to settle in Massachusetts and the Quakers in Pennsylvania, namely, the hope that they might worship God according to their consciences, free from the hampering restrictions of England's penal laws. As the penal code tightened its hold about the lives of the English Catholics in the last years of Elizabeth, several furtive projects were set on foot to find a haven for the Catholics abroad. After several abortive attempts by others, a convert member of the gentry offered the first viable plan to the oppressed Catholics for a home in the New World. That man was George Calvert, the first Baron of Baltimore, to whom Maryland owed its origins. Calvert was a man of real although not striking abilities. He was honorable and benevolent by nature, had a good eye for business, and the strength of his character may be measured by the fact that, when he became convinced in 1624 of the truth of the Catholic faith, he did not hesitate to resign his state office and surrender his seat in Parliament to follow his religious convictions. Calvert had enjoyed high favor with King James I, and even his change of religion did not cause him to lose entirely the advantageous position which his winning personality and social standing had earned him. His conversion to Catholicism had, however, focused his attention on the meanness of life to which the penal laws had reduced the Catholics, and he determined to employ his wealth and prestige in their behalf. Calvert's first attempt of 1627 to establish a colony in Newfoundland was wrecked by attacks from the French and the severity of the climate. In 1629 he turned to Virginia, of whose founding company he was a member, in the hope of better fortune. But on his visit to Virginia he was quickly disabused of the notion after being informed that Catholics were not welcome there. It was then that he decided to ask Charles I, the son and successor of his old patron, to grant a charter for a colony north of Virginia.

The first Baron Baltimore was an enterprising man, and the commercial aspects of his American colony were never absent from his thoughts. But as Charles Andrews remarks, "He was under the impelling influence of motives and obligations that were more imperative than those of a mere colonizer—among which was the sacred duty of finding a refuge for his Roman Catholic brethren." George Calvert himself died on April 15, 1632, just two months before the charter of Maryland was issued. The project then devolved upon his son, Cecilius, who like his father was anxious to draw the support of Protestants as well as Catholics. Loyal Catholic that he was, the second Baron Baltimore nonetheless saw no reason why men of different religious faiths could not join in a business of this kind if all practiced moderation and good will. Even if he had not been sincerely of this belief, and there is no evidence to doubt it, he was too much of a realist to think in terms of an exclusively Catholic colony. For that reason he raised no theological questions when the charter empowered him as proprietor to erect churches "to be dedicated and consecrated according to the Ecclesiastical Laws of our Kingdom of England."

It was clear from the outset that Maryland was intended to be a colony where all Christians would find peace of conscience. Ten days before the colonist sailed in late November, 1633, the proprietor wrote out for his deputies a set of instructions by which he hoped to establish that as a permanent policy. He urged the leaders of the expedition to have all Catholic religious services conducted as privately as possible, both on board ship and on land, and to instruct the Catholics to be silent on occasions when religion was discussed, to which he added the wish "that the said Governor and Commissioners treat the Protestants with as much mildness and favor as Justice will permit." It was an act of expediency, true, but it was just as obviously an act of fairness and tolerance altogether unique at the time. Thus two years before Roger Williams fled the Puritan wrath of Massachusetts Bay to establish religious tolerance in Rhode Island, Baltimore had laid the groundwork for such a policy in Maryland. For the first time in history there was a real prospect for a duly constituted government under which all Christians would possess equal rights, where all churches would be tolerated, and where none would be the agent of government. Such, in fact, Maryland did become, for to the "land of sanctuary" came Puritans fleeing persecution in Virginia and Anglicans escaping from the same threat in Massachusetts. This policy of religious tolerance has rightly been characterized as "the imperishable glory of Lord Baltimore and of the State."

After some delays caused by minor mishaps, the "Ark" finally put to sea on November 22, 1633, and was later joined at Barbados by the "Dove." On board the "Ark" were Fathers Andrew White and John Altham, two English Jesuits who managed somehow, like the Catholic laymen in the party, to set off without taking the customary oath that would have involved the denial of their religious faith. In all there were between two and three hundred persons, the Catholics among them including Leonard Calvert, brother of the proprietor, the two priests and two Jesuit lay brothers, sixteen gentlemen adventurers with their wives, children, and servants, and a number of Catholic yeoman farmers and laborers. The remainder of the passengers on the "Ark" and the "Dove," a numerical majority, were members of the Church of England. On March 24, 1634, the colonists landed on an island in Chesapeake Bay which they called St. Clement's, and here Father White offered the first Mass for the Catholics. After the celebration of Mass they held a procession in which they carried a cross that had been hewn out of a tree, and at the appointed place, as White described it some weeks later, "we erected a trophy to Christ the Saviour, humbly reciting, on our bended knees, the Litanies of the Sacred Cross, with great emotion." Meanwhile the Protestants held their own religious service.

The experiment in Maryland put Catholics and Protestants side by side on terms of equality and toleration unknown in the mother country. "In that respect," says one historian, "the settlement of Maryland holds a unique place in the history of English colonization."

During the early years religious differences were regarded peacefully as the colonists went about the business of laying out their plantations and building their homes. But the favorable auspices under which the colony had begun were not to endure. The chief source of trouble arose from William Claiborne of Virginia, whose deep hatred of Catholics made him resentful of their proximity in Maryland, and who likewise harbored a personal grudge against the Calverts for their claim to Kent Island on which he had a plantation. As the Puritans became stronger in England and the shadow of civil war between Charles I and the Roundheads loomed, Claiborne and his kind grew bolder. The fact that Baron Baltimore had permitted several hundred Puritans, unwelcome in Virginia, to cross over into Maryland in 1648 added a further complication, since the newcomers soon showed how little they appreciated the proprietor's hospitality by making common cause with Claiborne.

The English civil war had begun at Nottingham in August, 1642, and the suspicions concerning the Catholic sympathies of Charles I led to renewed persecution in England, where in 1641-42 eleven priests were put to death. The smoldering resentment of some of the Protestants in Maryland against the Catholics for holding most of the leading offices and against the freedom with which the Jesuits evangelized the Indians and ministered openly to the white settlers was now sharpened by the developments in the homeland. Where facts were missing to back up their grievances, rumor often supplied. In these years arose a campaign of suspicion against the Catholics that at intervals was to bedevil their lives up to the time of the Revolution. Waves of rumor and suspicion were a constantly recurring phenomenon of American colonial life, and in that respect "few colonies suffered more from innuendo and whispering manoeuvres than did Maryland."

It was against a background of this kind that Baron Baltimore sought to save the internal peace of his colony by drafting

John Tracy Ellis

and sending out to his assembly in America the famous Act of Toleration of April, 1649. In that measure, passed by a body composed of both Protestants and Catholics, blasphemy and the calling of opprobrious religious names were made punishable offenses. But the most important clause of the act read as follows:

> And whereas the inforceing of the conscience in matters of Religion hath frequently fallen out to be of dangerous Consequence in those commonwealthes where it hath been practised. . . . Be it Therefore . . . enacted . . . that noe person or psons whatsoever within this Province . . . professing to believe in Jesus Christ, shall from henceforth bee any waies troubled, Molested or discountenanced for or in respect of his or her religion nor in the free exercise thereof.

This law, liberal for so early a date, introduced nothing essentially new into Maryland, for there had been toleration for all Christians since Cecilius Calvert had incorporated that principle into his instructions of 1633, a principle that was confirmed in 1648 when William Stone, the first Protestant governor, took his oath of office. The religious strife had, indeed, called the measure forth, but that fact in no way lessens the significance or value of the act, coming as it did at a time when the religious enactments of Maryland's sister colonies were showing an increasingly intolerant spirit.

In spite of this memorable action of Baron Baltimore's government, the effort proved vain; for in the ensuing struggle the Puritan element overthrew the proprietor's regime, and thereupon the assembly of October, 1654, repealed the Act of Toleration and outlawed the Catholics. Once in power, the Puritans wreaked a terrible vengeance on the Catholics by condemning ten of them to death, four of whom were executed, plundering the houses and estates of the Jesuits, and forcing the priests to flee in disguise into Virginia. It is true that Baltimore regained control for a few years, but the sequel to the "Glorious Revolution" of 1688 which had encompassed the downfall of King James II also deposed the Catholic Calverts. In June, 1691, Maryland became a royal colony, and with the accession of

229

William and Mary the penal legislation of the mother country soon found a counterpart in Maryland. The Church of England was established by law in 1692, and the Catholics were compelled to pay taxes for its support. From the time that they were completely disfranchised in 1718 down to the outbreak of the Revolution, the Catholics of Maryland were cut off from all participation in public life, to say nothing of the enactments against their religious services and the law that forbade them to have schools for the Catholic instruction of their children. Remarking the very small number of Catholics against whom these laws were directed, and the fact that during the half-century the Catholics had governed Maryland they had not been guilty of a single act of religious oppression, it is not surprising that Cobb should have characterized this legislation as "specially unwarranted and base."

A decade before the exclusion of the proprietor had ushered in the darkest years for the Maryland Catholics, a new colony had begun to form immediately to the north. The persecution that William Penn had already undergone for his Quaker faith prompted him in 1681 to launch his "holy experiment" with a broad grant of freedom of worship and civil rights to all who believed in God. Even though this policy was found much too liberal for the taste of the English government which forced restrictions upon Pennsylvania in 1705, the mild character of the Quaker regime attracted a number of Maryland Catholic families northward. In 1706 the Jesuits likewise acquired land in Cecil County near the Pennsylvania border, where they opened St. Xavier Mission and for a few years conducted a school. In fact, so tolerant was the government of the Quakers on religious matters that about 1734 Father Joseph Greaton, S.J. appeared in Philadelphia and opened a chapel, thus becoming the first resident priest in the colony. Soon other missionaries followed, and after Father Henry Neale had been there for some months he told the English provincial in the spring of 1741, "We have at present all liberty imaginable in the exercise of our business, and are not only esteemed, but reverenced, as I may say, by the better sort of people." In the same year several German Jesuits arrived in Pennsylvania to minister to the German Catholic immigrants from the Palatinate who had settled in fairly large numbers in thriving rural communities around Goshenhoppen, Conewago, and Lancaster.

Only once in the history of colonial Pennsylvania did the Catholics experience a period of serious tension, and that was related to the renewal of war between England and France. Long before the outbreak of war the two powers had been preparing for battle. As a move in the game, England drastically fore-stalled possible trouble in one quarter by herding over 6,000 Catholic Acadians on board British ships and distributing them in the colonies from Massachusetts to Georgia. In November, 1755, Pennsylvania received 454 of these unfortunate people. Their arrival, coming as it did four months after the humiliating defeat which the French had inflicted on Braddock's army near Fort Duquesne, heightened suspicion and fear. Pennsylvanians in 1756 heard wild rumors of a "popish plot" in which the Acadians figured. A census of the population to determine the number of men capable of bearing arms revealed that there were in the entire colony only 1,365 Catholics out of a total of about 200,000 residents. Extremists were eager for proscriptive legis-lation against the Catholics, but the Quaker officials refused to be stampeded into any violation of their traditional policy. Gradually, therefore, the Catholics had resumed an unharried life when in July, 1765, Father George Hunter, S.J., reported to his provincial in England that there were about 10,000 "adult customers" in Maryland, with nearly as many children who had not yet been admitted to the sacraments, while in Pennsylvania he counted around 3,000 adults, with approximately an equal number of children.

Catholics in the other eleven colonies went uncounted and little known by the Jesuit missionaries for the very good reason that there were few if any living in those regions. Now and then, it is true, a Catholic name appeared in other colonies, but aside from a few Catholics in northern Virginia, the Abenaki Indians in Maine, and the special case of Father Gabriel Druillettes, S.J., who came to Massachusetts Bay in 1650 on a diplomatic mission for New France, the only other colony that saw them in any numbers—and that only for a few years—was New York.

During the period from 1609, when Henry Hudson took possession of the area in the name of the Dutch, to 1664, when the colony of New Netherland was conquered by the English, about the only Catholic appearance of which we know anything was Father Isaac Jogues' visit to New Amsterdam in the fall of 1643 on his way to Europe after the Dutch had rescued him from the Iroquois. The English occupation, however, brought the proprietorship of James, Duke of York, whose conversion to Catholicism in 1672 soon reflected itself in his American domain. In 1682 James appointed Colonel Thomas Dongan, a Catholic, as governor, and the colonel arrived in August, 1683, with an English Jesuit in his party, Father Thomas Harvey, who was later joined by two other priests and two lay brothers of his order. For some years there had been serious agitation in New York for a more representative government, and in an assembly which he had summoned in September, 1683, Dongan stood sponsor for a bill of rights which was adopted in late October. This document contained a guarantee of religious freedom which read in part:

> . . . that no person or persons, which profess faith in God by Jesus Christ, shall at any time, be any ways molested, punished, disquieted, or called in question for any difference in opinion or matter of religious concernment, who do not actually disturb the civill peace of the Province, but that all and every such person or persons may, from time, and at all times freely have and fully enjoy his or their judgments or consciences in matters of religion throughout all the Province, they behaving themselves peaceably and quietly and not using this liberty to Licentiousnesse nor to the civill injury or outward disturbance of others. . . .

Thus did New York's Catholic governor join the honorable company of Roger Williams, Lord Baltimore, and William Penn as the chief promoters of religious freedom in colonial America. The significance of Dongan's action is not in any way lessened by the fact that the events of 1688 brought reaction to New York in the form of rebellion which quickly blotted out his generous policy in religious affairs. In May, 1689, a German-born Calvinist, Jacob Leisler, overthrew the government and inaugurated a reign of terror against the Catholics. Dongan himself was hunted like a criminal, the Jesuits were forced to flee, and in September, 1693, the Church of England was established by law in the four leading counties of New York. In due course followed all the familiar English penal legislation against Catholics, a series of laws from which they were not entirely freed until 1806.

Here, then, was a minority second to none but Roger Williams in the broad toleration granted to men of other religious beliefs. Had the Catholics never held power in colonial America, it would remain a matter of speculation what they would have done on matters of religious policy. The half-century, however, of Baltimore's regime in Maryland and the five years when there was a Catholic governor in New York afford us two instances by which to judge them extraordinarily tolerant for the seventeenth century. Baltimore, Dongan, and their Catholic assemblymen were not philosophers or theologians, and they wrote no treatises on the theories of religious tolerance or intolerance. They were intensely practical men who found themselves confronted with the real problem of differing religious beliefs among those whom they governed. To that problem they applied a practical solution based upon experience, an experience reflected in the words of the Maryland act of 1649 which spoke of how "inforceing of the conscience in matters of Religion hath frequently fallen out to be of dangerous Consequence in those commonwealthes where it hath been practised." Their settlement of the question resembled the final solution of the Founding Fathers of the Republic. They were, of course, painfully aware of the disadvantages under which they labored by being Catholics, and both Baltimore and Dongan had seen in their native England and Ireland how their coreligionists had been made to suffer on this score. The memory of it made them all the more anxious, therefore, that this sort of oppression should not be visited upon others by the governments over which they presided in the New World.

By reason of the penal status in which the colonial Catholics were compelled to live until the American Revolution, there was obviously no hope of a normal government for their Church. The English Catholic hierarchy had become extinct in 1585, and not until 1688 was there a bishop at London who could even make pretensions to any jurisdiction over the Catholics in America. Consequently, Catholic affairs were almost entirely in the hands of the 186 Jesuit priests who worked in the colonies as missionaries between 1634 and the suppression of their order in 1773. These priests got their faculties for administering the sacraments either through the General of the Jesuits at Rome, who dealt directly with the Congregation de Propaganda Fide, or through the missionary bishop who functioned under the title of Vicar Apostolic of the London District after 1688. In neither case was it a satisfactory arrangement, but the general anti-Catholic bias—especially the bitter prejudice against bishops —made it unthinkable for a bishop to be appointed for the colonies by the Holy See. Some 156 years passed between the coming of the first missionaries to Maryland and the appointment in 1790 of a bishop for the American Catholics. This long period of abnormal rule not only deprived them of the sacraments of confirmation and holy orders but likewise left them with little or no knowledge of the traditional form of church government, an ignorance that caused some very strange notions among both priests and laity concerning the episcopal office and its functions.

In the political realm the friendliness which colonial Catholics had shown toward the principle of religious freedom during their tenure of power in Maryland and New York was, as might be expected, only strengthened by the long dark night of penal legislation which descended upon them during the eighteenth century. It was not until the 1770's that one hears prominent mention of a Catholic name in colonial America, since for the better part of a century they had been entirely excluded from public affairs. But as the tension mounted between the colonies and the mother country, life in America began to change in many ways. When Charles Carroll of Carrollton in February, 1773, launched a series of remarkable letters in the *Maryland Gazette* against the arbitrary actions of the royal governor, Robert Eden, he was not only listened to but won general acclaim. Carroll wrote under the pen name of "First Citizen" against the governor's protagonist, Daniel Dulany, who used the name of "Antillon." Realizing that he was losing the debate, Dulany resorted to an attack on his opponent's religion. Carroll put the issue straight when he replied:

> What my speculative notions of religion may be, this is neither the place nor time to declare; my political principles ought only to be questioned on the present occasion; surely they are constitutional, and have met, I hope, with the approbation of my countrymen; if so Antillon's aspersions will give me no uneasiness. He asks, who is this Citizen? A man, Antillon, of an independent fortune, one deeply interested in the prosperity of his country; a friend to liberty, a settled enemy to lawless prerogative.

It was the kind of talking Marylanders were prepared to hear in that exciting spring of 1773, and in the end Carroll's effective polemics not only vanquished Dulany but played a major role in swinging the Maryland election in May of that year in favor of the patriot party that opposed the royal governor. Moreover, the forthright manner in which he had met the attack on his religion gave heart to many of this coreligionists who for the first time had witnessed a Catholic defend his faith and win the respect of many non-Catholics for doing so. Even so prejudiced a spectator as Jonathan Boucher, one of the leading Anglican ministers of Maryland, and himself a loyalist, credited Carroll with settling the doubts of the Catholics who, he said, soon "became good Whigs, and concurred with their fellow-revolutionists in declaiming against the misgovernment of Great Britain." Twenty years before, Dulany's appeal to religious prejudice would have clinched the argument, but by 1773 Americans were beginning to realize interests broader than that of nursing the traditional bias against Catholics. In the changing climate of opinion that permitted a Catholic patriot to speak in the name of his fellow countrymen, one detects the first break in the isolation that had sealed them off from other Americans. It was an initial step toward the dawn of religious liberty for Catholics, a step that would lead the same Charles Carroll three years later to Philadelphia where he would proudly affix his signature to the Declaration of Independence of his country.

Yet before the American Catholics were permitted finally to emerge from the catacombs in which the penal codes had buried them, they were destined to suffer further ignominy over the grant of religious freedom to their Canadian brethren. To counter the rising temper of the colonists, the English government was naturally anxious to assure the loyalty of the French Canadians to the crown. They accomplished this purpose by the Quebec Act of June, 1774, which extended the boundaries of the province to the west, restored French law, and, most important of all, guaranteed freedom to the Catholic Church. The measure raised a frightful tempest throughout the colonies. Protests from all sides influenced the Continental Congress to adopt on September 17, 1774, the Suffolk Resolves, which highlighted that body's dislike of the Church. A month later the congress addressed letters to King George III and to the people of Great Britain in which the Americans declared themselves to be astonished that Parliament should have established a religion "that has deluged your island in blood, and dispersed impiety, bigotry, murder and rebellion through every part of the world." What made the tone of these words all the more extraordinary was the fact that five days later the same congress sent a letter to the Canadians in an effort to enlist their aid. The congressional penmen mentioned Switzerland as a country where Protestants and Catholics lived together in peace, held out the promise of religious freedom if the Canadian Catholics would join the American cause, and piously signed themselves "your sincere and affectionate friends and fellow-subjects." The Quebec Act, however, had done its work well enough that the Canadians were not beguiled by the blandishments from Philadelphia.

If in times of stress it is often difficult to maintain sincerity, as the actions of the Continental Congress demonstrated, it is then just as difficult to adhere to old prejudices and principals. General Washington—who was personally free from religious prejudice—made that evident to his troops encamped at Cambridge in November, 1775, when he discovered that they were once more preparing to burn the pope in effigy and insult the Catholics in the annual celebration of Guy Fawkes Day. He put an end to the nonsense at once, and in rebuking those who were planning the affair at a moment when the Americans still hoped to gain Canada, he remarked, "To be insulting their Religion, is so monstrous, as not to be suffered or excused." That very month Congress had appointed a committee and appropriated funds for initial diplomatic and trade relations with foreign powers. It would ill become the Americans, then, to indulge their prejudices lest word of it reach Catholic countries like France and Spain which, it was hoped, might be of service to the revolutionary cause.

Congress decided in February, 1776, to send a commission to Canada in another attempt to win its support. Not only did Charles Carroll of Carrollton accompany Benjamin Franklin and Samuel Chase to Canada, but Father John Carroll, distant cousin of Charles, was also asked to go. Neither of the Carrolls had sought the appointment, and it took a great deal of persuasion on the part of Charles to secure that consent of his priestly cousin. John Carroll deeply feared the effect that the Canadian mission might have on his standing as a priest; for as he confided to a private memorandum on the subject, "I have observed that when the ministers of religion, leave the duties of their profession to take a busy part in political matters, they generally fall into contempt, and sometimes even bring discredit to the cause in whose service they are engaged." It was an eminently sound view, and only the urging of his distinguished cousin and his own sincere patriotism overcame his reluctance. The mission to Canada failed, but it offered one more chance for the Catholics to escape isolation and serve honorably in the public affairs of their country.

By the time that the delegates returned from Canada, Virginians were in the process of passing their act of religious toleration of June, 1776, and Pennsylvania and Maryland followed suit before the year was out. The Catholics, sharing in the revolutionary struggle as equals once the legal barriers were removed, responded generously to the national crisis. Charles Carroll took his seat in Congress at Philadelphia as a delegate from Maryland, John Barry came forward to win fame as one of the chief founders of the American navy, Stephen Moylan joined Washington's staff as muster mastergeneral, Daniel Carroll was named a member of Congress from Maryland, and

Thomas FitzSimons represented Pennsylvania. Moreover, after the alliance with France was signed in February, 1778, units of the French fleet began to dock at Philadelphia, each with its Catholic chaplain. Soon, too, the first French minister, Conrad Alexandre Gérard, became one of the leading personalities in the capital city, and when he sent out invitations in 1779 to a *Te Deum* in St. Mary's Church to mark the third anniversary of American independence and two years later to commemorate the victory of Yorktown, members of Congress found it expedient to be present. It had now become unthinkable to offer public or official slights to Catholics with France so close and powerful an ally.

The patriotic part played by the Catholics during the war, the influence of the French alliance, and the growing consciousness of the extreme complexity of the American religious pattern—all helped to dilute the anti-Catholic bias. In fact, after the war was over and a number of states had acted on their own in granting full religious liberty, it became evident that toleration necessarily would be the ultimate policy of the national government. In the Constitutional Convention the two Catholic delegates, Daniel Carroll of Maryland and FitzSimons of Pennsylvania, were heartily in favor of the principle, as they were likewise outspokenly in favor of a strong national government in opposition to those who would restrict its powers. In 1784, Father John Carroll had been named by the Holy See as superior of the American Catholic missions, then staffed by about twenty-five priests. Carroll, too, shared the belief that the fairest settlement of the religious issue would be to declare all churches equal before the law and to have no ecclesiastical establishment of any kind. A brochure which he wrote that same year in answer to an attack upon the Church revealed his reluctance to engage in religious controversy lest it should disturb the harmony then existing between the various Christian churches. That Carroll wholeheartedly accepted the pattern of Church-State relations then emerging in the United States, and which in less than a decade would be incorporated into the Constitution, was clear when he alluded to the promise which civil and religious liberty held out, a promise which, he said, "if we have the wisdom and temper to preserve, America may come to exhibit a proof to the world, that general and equal toleration, by giving a free circulation to fair argument, is the most effectual method to bring all denominations of Christians to a unity of faith."

The final solution to the perplexing problem of religion as embodied in the Constitution and Bill of Rights was received by no American religious group with more genuine satisfaction than by the Catholics. It was a boon appreciated by their oppressed coreligionists in England and Ireland as well, and as at the consecration of Carroll in August, 1790, in England as the first Catholic bishop of the United States, the preacher of the occasion, Carroll's old friend Father Charles Plowden, testified when he remarked of the American Revolution: "Although this great event may appear to us to have been the work, the sport of human passion, yet the earliest and most precious fruit of it has been the extension of the kingdom of Christ, the propagation of the Catholic religion, which heretofore fettered by restraining laws, is now enlarged from bondage and it is left at liberty to exert the full energy of divine truth." It was a sentiment which Bishop Carroll fully shared with his priests and Catholic people in the new United States. They and their ancestors had experienced the humiliation of practical outlawry for a century or more, and the prospect of freedom to worship God according to their consciences was the most singular blessing which the new Republic had brought to them.

Some months before Bishop Carroll went abroad for his consecration, a group of the leading American Catholics had expressed their esteem for President Washington in a formal address. Washington replied that he believed that as men became more liberal they would be more likely to allow equal rights to all worthy members of the community, and in this respect he hoped to see America among the foremost nations of the world. He then stated: "And I presume that your fellow-citizens will not forget the patriotic part which you took in the accomplishment of their Revolution, and the establishment of their government; nor the important assistance which they received from a nation in which the Roman Catholic religion is professed." The exchange of compliments between the chief executive and his Catholic citizens had been a pleasant and heartening experience, and the latter could thank God that their interests in Church and State were now in the hands of two such leaders as President Washington and Bishop Carroll.

Yves Marie Joseph Congar
1904-

Yves Congar was born in France in 1904 and went to school in Sedan and Rheims, then studied philosophy for three years at the Institut Catholique under Jacques Maritain. He entered the Dominican novitiate in 1925 and Père Chenu was one of his teachers who made a lasting impact on him. After ordination he taught fundamental theology in Le Saulchoir, Belgium, from 1931 to 1939, when he was drafted into the army. In November, 1940, he was captured by the Germans and remained a prisoner until the end of the war in 1945. From 1945 to 1954 he taught again at Le Saulchoir, which had been moved to the environs of Paris. At that time he was the victim of the "witch-hunt" that required him to give up his teaching for two years. In 1956 he went to the Dominican house in Strasbourg.

The suspicions raised in ultraconservative quarters by Congar's pioneering efforts to revitalize the theology of the church were finally put to rest when his chief insights were embraced and incorporated by Vatican II. No one was better equipped than he for that Council. While others who thought they were more loyal were repeating the formulas of the past, Congar was laboring mightily to discover the roots of renewal. In 1950 he published True and False Reform in the Church, *showing that reform must be a permanent fact in the life of the Church.*

For true reform Congar found four conditions necessary: 1) love and service must hold primacy over concerns about the system; 2) continued membership in the community must be maintained; 3) patience that avoids making unconditional demands must prevail; and 4) the reform must be a recurrence to principle and tradition.

The selection that follows is from his famous Lay People in the Church, *published in 1952. In French the title is actually "Signposts for a Theology of the Laity." The work was absolutely without parallel at the time. Numerous circumstances, including the interruption of Vatican I in 1870, resulted in a view of the Church dominated by the clergy. What was needed was a vision of the Church as "structured communion."*

Having no models to go by, Congar explains how he finally organized the amazing wealth of material in this book: "After a preliminary chapter giving an elementary idea of what a lay person is, the subject is treated in two parts. The first gives the general position of things. . . .We first consider the place of a theology of laity, and then the place of the laity itself in God's purpose. In the second part we study the laity in action in the Church's life. This we do first in the framework of those three functions among which it is more and more agreed to assign the Church's acts as those of Christ: the priestly, the kingly and the prophetic functions. . . . We have given a special chapter respectively to lay people in the life of the Church as community and to lay people in regard to the Church's apostolic mission . . . a chapter has been added on a subject of much interest at present, "spirituality" and the sanctification of lay people amid the distractions of "the world." A final section endeavors to summarize the results of investigations which will have been sometimes rather hard going, even if not far too technical."

LAY PEOPLE IN THE CHURCH

T he word κλῆρος, from which the English words 'cleric' and 'clerk' are ultimately derived, is of frequent occurrence in the Bible, especially in the Old Testament. Its primary meaning is 'lot', and then 'portion' or 'heritage'. In I Peter v, 3 the word in the plural designates the community allotted to each of the presbyters. The word λαϊκός, whence our 'lay', is not found anywhere in the Bible, but the use of λαός, of which λαϊκός is the adjective, is frequent. A meaning given to this word is 'people', especially in the Bible: in the Old Testament λαός is often opposed to τὰ ἔθνη, and expressly designates the people *of God*, distinct from the gentiles (the *goim*). Our word 'lay', then, is connected with a word that for Jews, and then for Christians, properly meant the sacred people in opposition to the peoples who were not consecrated, a nuance of meaning that was familiar, at any rate to those who speak Greek, for the first four centuries and more.

We see then that there is no distinction between 'lay people' and 'clerics' in the vocabulary of the New Testament. Nineteenth-century Protestant historians—Hase, Hatch, Achelis, Harnack—have dogmatised a lot about this as a fact that supports their theory of an undifferentiated primitive community living under a charismatic regime. But another fact does not favour their interpretation of history, namely that the first use of the word 'layman' as opposed to 'priest' is found in a Roman document, the letter to the community at Corinth, written by Clement. An examination of the views of the historians just named would involve a full consideration of the constitution and nature of the apostolic Church, its ministries, its relations with the Synagogue, a field where history and theology must come together and talk if sound conclusions are to be reached; a field too wherein questions of method are involved, themselves subject to doctrinal choices. A particular point in mind here, which the writer has touched on elsewhere, is this: in what degree does the analysis of terms used authorise the making of a judgment about a reality? Concretely, in what degree does the absence of our words 'cleric' and 'lay', and of the word 'priest' (*hiereus*), from her vocabulary allow us to affirm that the Church in apostolic times was an undifferentiated community with a charismatic regime, a stranger to what we express, and what Clement, contemporary with the Apostles, expresses, by the words 'cleric', 'layman' and 'priest'?

We cannot go into such questions here. For our purpose it is sufficient to grasp the difference between clerics and lay people when it occurs in the vocabulary. We have seen Clement of Rome's text; and it is the first of many. Evidence abounds at the beginning and middle of the third century and, expressed in various terms, the distinction is quite clear: in the East, for example, in Clement of Alexandria and Origen, in the West in Tertullian and St. Cyprian. With Cyprian, moreover, we have for the first time the broad lines of an ecclesiology properly so called, that is, of a theory not concerned solely with Christ and the relation of the faithful with him by salvation and grace, but with the ecclesial institution in the order of means of the calling to salvation.

We have got our landmarks. From vocabulary we can go on to an interpretation. This, directly it begins to be formulated a little systematically, confronts us, not with two terms only, but with three. We find between clerics and lay people a third category, that of monks. From the time of Clement of Rome, doubtless from that of the Apostles, there were ascetics, 'continent ones' and virgins in the Christian community. Monachism properly so called began about the middle of the third century, while Origen and Cyprian were still alive, for we find that when St. Antony wanted to go into the wilderness, around 250-275, he met a man who had already led the solitary life for several years.

So from the middle of the third century three states could be distinguished in the Church, which were obviously there in fact before they were subjected to formula and code, but which did not have to wait long for formulation and, in the most exact sense, canonical existence. From then on the Church not only lives—she has done that since she received the breath of the Spirit at Pentecost; she not only has her essential structure—the Lord gave her that at different times during his earthly life: but she has her permanent pattern. If the distinction between clergy and laity is essential in the Church's structure and life, her permanent pattern includes a distinction between three states or conditions, lay, clerical, monastic.

The Lay condition is not so much a matter of definition as of something immediately given as a basis, the condition of Christians who are working out their salvation in the everyday life of the world. The clerical condition is defined by the service of the altar and the religious service of the Christian people. Clericature itself then is an office, a function, not a state of life. It is brought about by entry into the ministry, the 'diaconia', the service of sacred things; and the entry is made by being 'ordained' to this service, that is, in all strictness, by ordinations properly so called. The monastic condition is not defined by service of sacred things, not even by service of the altar: the first monks in the East had hardly any 'liturgical' life (the 'liturgy' is by definition a public service, and therefore the business of clerics), and in some medieval Western monasteries the part of the monastic church used by the laity was put in charge of clerics who were not monks. The monk as such is not a cleric, though of course he can become one by ordination. His condition is not defined by an office or function but as a state or way of life: in order that he shall not live for the world and in the world's way but rather so much as possible for God and in God's way, this consists in living apart from the world, leading so far as may be a heavenly or angelic life, the life of the Kingdom that is not of this world.

In principle, then, clerics and monks were sharply differentiated: 'cleric' indicates a function, 'monk' a state or way of life. A man is a cleric by ordination to the sacred ministry, a monk by personal renouncement of the world. The two things are not unrelated, however, and in the West the relationships have been understood in such a way that the two conditions reinforce one another. The reasons for this can be brought under three heads.

(1) Monastic life being, in its widest connotation, a life of holiness and total personal consecration to God, it was fitting that clerics dedicated to the service of the altar and the sacred ministry should have the spirit and virtues of monks. This fittingness was very soon seen and formulated in the West. On the one hand, communities of clerics living monastically, in the wide sense, were formed around their bishop, as in the case of St. Eusebius of Vercelli, of St. Ambrose, of St. Martin and especially of St. Augustine (his *De vita et moribus clericorum* and certain texts, under the title of *Regula*, came to exercise a very strong influence that subsists to our day). On the other hand, a whole body of ideas—we could say a whole 'spirituality' —was developed in connexion with the idea of clerical life, starting from the etymology of the word. Here it was not St. Augustine who was decisive: his explanation of the word *clerus*, given in passing, as deriving from the idea of the choice and election of Matthias by drawing lots, did not catch on. But the following text of St. Jerome became immensely popular: 'The cleric who serves the Church of Christ should in the first place construe and ponder his name and, when he has explained it, try to be what the title means. The Greek word *kleros* signifies 'portion', a part drawn by lot; and he bears the name of cleric either because he is the Lord's portion, or because he has the Lord for his portion. The man who professes the one or the other should show by his behaviour that he possesses the Lord or that he is possessed by the Lord. But he who possesses the Lord, and says with the Prophet 'the Lord is the portion of my inheritance' (Ps. xv, 5, lxxii, 26), can have nothing outside the Lord . . .' The idea of being the Lord's portion and of having a portion in him has been as it were the soul of the clerical state through an age-long tradition that is impressive in its unchangingness. Psalm xv is the 'tonsure psalm', and for centuries consecration to the service of the altar and the faithful of Christ has been expressed in the words, 'Dominus pars haereditatis meae et calicis mei. Tu es qui restitues haereditatem meam mihi.'

Indeed, the very fact of the tonsure, with the spiritual significance attached to it, was calculated to soften any too sharp distinction between cleric and monk. From the fourth century the tonsure, whatever form it took, was the token of monks *and* of clerics. It was materially the same for both even if it did not have exactly the same meaning for both—it is sometimes said that the monastic tonsure is not *signum clericale, sed poenitentiale*. From the point of view of collation to the tonsure, *clericum facere* and *monachum facere* were the same thing. So it is not surprising that their 'crowns', sign of their institution and their condition, were confused.

(2) In the West still more than in the East monks, who have been very generally cenobites, have been given a thoroughly liturgical rule of life. Doubtless Cluny went further than the Rule of St. Benedict and the regulations given to monks by the synod of Aachen in 817, but it cannot be said that she was not developing an authentic element of Benedictinism. One is inclined to say that in the West there were scarcely any monks who were not, if not clerics, at least in line with the clericature. We have seen that the cleric is specified by service of the altar, the ministry of sacred things; and certainly, strictly and canonically speaking, monks became clerics only by subsequent ordination, whether properly sacramental ordination to the diaconate and priesthood or lesser consecration for some office in public worship. But as soon as the religious life, monastic life in the wide sense, has a marked liturgical orientation, the monk becomes a man in the service of the altar. The canons regular and clerks regular not only developed extensively in the West, they influenced monastic institutions as well, contributing to their taking on a complexion of cleric-monks, dedicated to the liturgical office and sometimes even to the ministry. And we often see monks assimilated to clerics when they actually and habitually exercise liturgical functions.

(3) This assimilation has often been made on account of circumstances or to meet the requirements of controversy. Thus importance has been given to one category of texts, which originally had in view the other category; faced by the canons regular of the twelfth century the monks claimed the title of cleric, with the help of certain distinctions; or, taking this last

claim as a starting-point, it was acknowledged that at bottom monks were clerics who added a form of life under a rule to the clericature. In any case *clericus* and *monachus* are sometimes taken purely and simply one for the other.

The details of all this are of no concern for our purpose here. What matters to us is that the triple division into lay people, clerics and monks became, by a process of assimilation of clerics to monks and of monks to clerics, a double division into men of religion and men of the world. 'Duo sunt genera christianorum', says Gratian in a canon of which he makes St. Jerome the father; and in the first category he puts both those who are dedicated to divine worship, clerics, and those who simply seek the improvement of their own lives, monks.

Although, in distinction from the lay state understood as a secular condition, that of clerics and that of monks tend sometimes to be fused into a single condition of men of religion, the duality of clericature and monasticism nevertheless remains in the nature of things and in canonical definition. The monastic condition has reference to a manner of life having evangelical perfection in view; the clerical condition has reference to function, a ministry or service. From the canonical point of view, and speaking exactly, neither 'lay' nor 'cleric' is inconsistent with 'monk', for one can be a monk (form of life) and at the same time a cleric (ordained for liturgical service) or a lay person. Canonically, the layman can be defined only by distinction from the cleric: Fathers Vermeersch and Creusen can define him in no other way than they do because they are concerned only for a canonical definition. But this point of view cannot supply a complete positive notion of the lay condition; and we, with a comprehensive grasp of it, need to find a more detailed and accurate conception of that condition.

The fact is that the Church's tradition offers us three notions which, without being all on the same level or being opposed to one another in strict logic, are distinct. During the course of history the lay condition has sometimes been defined from the point of view of way of life, in opposition to the condition of monks and of churchmen, monks and clerics being grouped together indiscriminately; and sometimes it has been defined from the point of view of function or, more exactly, of competence [A] in opposition to the condition of clerks. These are two different approaches, leading to two notions of the laity that are complementary: what may be called the monastic notion, defined by way of life, and the canonical notion, defined by function and competence.

The Monastic Notion. — Here the distinction is made in terms of state of life, of the manner or means of sanctification. Clerics and monks are men given over to the holy, so far as may be they live in the divine world. The laity lives among earthly things. At the same time not only holy people but true contemplatives may be found among them: this has always been recognised, even by upholders of the solitary life. God has often made known to some hermit or other distinguished for his austere life, that this married woman, that confirmed thief who helps his neighbour in distress, equal him in holiness in God's sight. Inversely, there are always clerics and monks to be found who are full of worldly preoccupations, and sometimes corrupted by vice. But these are personal situations; they do not affect the difference between states of life that Christian tradition, up to the Protestant criticism of the sixteenth century, has looked on as in themselves representing different conditions of holiness. It still remains true that the cleric (and the monk) is *by his very state* dedicated to divine things, and the layman, by *his* state, to human things—*et divisus est* (I Corinthians vii, 33). This is not the place to show that these great convictions of the Christian consciousness, if properly understood, are neither a transposition of philosophical attitudes nor a self-interested invention of churchmen, but a conclusion from a literal observance of the deepest imperatives of the Gospel. This will be referred to later.

In defining the layman by state of life obviously we must range alongside the clerics certain people who are not clerics strictly speaking, in the sense that they have no hierarchical grade—unordained monks, lay-brothers (*conversi*) and lay religious, nuns.

This way of regarding the lay condition seems to have been specially in favour during the twelfth century. There had been a great religious renewal in the previous century: even before the

Gregorian reform, and still more in consequence of it, a wide-ranging movement impelled souls towards an evangelical, 'apostolic', life of poverty, charity and apostleship. There were 'Apostolic' lay movements; especially were there many movements of renewal of clerical life, modelled on the early Church, through the observance of poverty and chastity within a framework of common life under a rule. Then there was the action of the papacy, aimed at enforcing the celibacy of clerics. Thus clerical life was renewed in a monastic sense; and it certainly seems that this fact encouraged a twofold division of Christians into lay people on one side, monks and clerics on the other.

We have already met Gratian's text 'Duo sunt genera christianorum'. Here is the continuation of the quotation given above: 'There is another sort of Christians, who are called lay folk. Λαός means "people". These are allowed to possess temporal goods, but only what they need for use. For nothing is more wretched than to set God at naught for the sake of money. They are allowed to marry, to till the earth, to pronounce judgment on men's disputes and plead in court, to lay their offerings on the altar, to pay their tithes: and so they can be saved, if they do good and avoid evil.' From our angle of interest here two things are particularly noticeable in this passage: the lay position is presented as a concession, and its general tendency is to deny that the laity, concerned in temporal affairs, have any active part in the sphere of sacred things.

(1) The lay condition is presented as a concession to human weakness. 'His licet . . ., his concessum est', says Gratian. Other texts of about the same time reflect the same idea. There is, for instance, Urban II's bull of 1092 confirming the foundation of the canons of Raitenbach, a document which, Canon Petit tells us, was afterwards often reproduced or invoked, as when Honorius II confirmed the Order of Prémontré: 'From her beginning the Church has offered two kinds of life to her children: one to help the insufficiency of the weak, another to perfect the goodness of the strong . . .'. Or again the words of Gerhoh of Reichersberg (d. 1169), with their echo of the boundless desire to be remade in the spirit and letter of the primitive Church which was moving western Christendom from the middle of the eleventh to the middle of the thirteenth

centuries: in the primitive Church, he says, those who were perfectly converted pooled their property for the benefit of the poor. And he goes on: 'So, excepting those who, being married, used this world as if they did not use it, bought as not owning, rejoiced as not making merry, people whose place was among the imperfect . . ., excepting them, I say, who are numbered among the women who followed the Lord from afar, the people who entirely cleaved to Christ with his disciples, and deserved that name by excellence, were those only who put themselves under the yoke of continence and at one stroke left all they had for the Lord's sake'. Gerhoh's style is clumsy, even in Latin, but his meaning is clear: from the Christian point of view life in the world is a compromise. A Christian who is completely consistent with the gospel principles that he professes ought normally to leave the world that he may lead the 'apostolic life', a life according to the gospel ideal and in accord with the laws of the kingdom of God.

Only at the expense of ignoring the whole of history can it be denied that this idea is in conformity with Christian tradition and, in the last resort, with the nature of things. Christian life led integrally and without compromise in accordance with its proper requirements is what is traditionally called the angelic or apostolic life, that is, the monastic life (in the wide sense). But one cannot but feel a certain unsatisfactoriness about an estimate of Christian life so exclusively dominated by the ideas of renunciation and the wickedness of the world. One may well ask whether all the aspects of New Testament teaching have been given their weight; from the point of view of a theology of laity its pages have been turned rather too quickly.

(2) The idea that the laity, concerned in temporal affairs, have no part in the sphere of sacred things. *Duo genera christianorum.* Certainly it was well understood that clergy and laity are both part of the one Church. Master Vacarius replied to his former fellow-pupil Speroni (who gave to the twelfth-century so many of the theses of the sixteenth-century Reformers with surprising closeness) that laity and clergy are united in the faith and that the distinction between them in no way compromises the unity of the Church. But for the mind of the middle ages this unity in the faith had a depth and realism that we can no

longer easily appreciate. Towards the end of the century Stephen of Tournai joined affirmations of unity and duality in the same passage: 'In one city and under one king there are two peoples whose difference corresponds to two sorts of life; and to them correspond two sovereignties, a double order of jurisdiction. The city is the Church; her king is Christ; the two peoples are the two orders of clergy and laity; the two sorts of life are the spiritual and the fleshly; the two sovereignties are the priesthood and the kingship; the two jurisdictions the divine and the human.' Hugh of Saint-Victor expressed this idea by an image which came to be widely used, that of the two sides of a human body. Hugh and his followers understood the unity of the Church, or more exactly of the *respublica christiana* (*corpus christianum, christianitas* was used more rarely), in this way: Church and society form one single body, in which two powers are operative and two lives are led, somewhat as a man's body has a right side and a left side. All right; but one may be allowed to point out some objections against this way of looking at things. What are they?

Essentially, what has already been said, that it does not show the laity's place in the building together of the Church, in the specifically Christian achievement worked out in human history (and not above it, in some vague Platonic universe). That call and those problems felt so acutely today, which are referred to in our introduction and to which this book seeks to give some elements of a reply where theology is concerned, these hardly have a place in that calm distribution of roles between the spiritual and the temporal—or what Stephen of Tournai calls 'the fleshly'.

Already in the eleventh century (in the *Exultet*-rolls in the British Museum and among the Barberini MSS. of the Vatican Library), and more frequently in the fifteenth and sixteenth, the Church is represented according to Hugh of Saint-Victor's scheme, under the form of two peoples. One, behind the pope, is made up of bishops, priests and monks; the other, behind the emperor, of princes, knights, peasants, men and women. It is true that the middle ages looked on the emperor (or king) as a church person, at any rate when the Church was considered also as *respublica christiana*. In accordance with the mind of Hugh and of Boniface VIII the diagram of the two sides was meant to affirm unity. But in the critical and antihierarchical currents of the fourteenth and fifteenth centuries, which prepared the way for state laicism and the ecclesiology of the Reformers, it lent itself to quite another interpretation. Instead of two sides, a figure of unity, the fourteenth-century critics spoke of two bodies, each with its own head, of one side the emperor or king, of the other the pope, and later on a head for each country. Two bodies, two heads. . . . The mind loves unity, and will perforce restore it. Starting with this untoward dualism, there was plenty to draw the Church towards one extreme or the other. In one direction, we shall see in the next chapter how some arrived at conceiving the Church theologically as a church of clergy, consisting in the hierarchy alone; we shall produce texts which clearly insinuate this idea. In the other direction one-sidedness became more catastrophic still—we shall see why. Princes will lay claim to the headship of the Christian body, and so of the Church; they will find theologians ready to recognise their claim, even to offer it to them, as Nicholas of Dinkelsbuhl did to King Sigismund at the council of Constance in 1414. Or a theology of the Church will develop, in line with certain elements of medieval ecclesiology, which conceives her purely as the congregation of the faithful; that is the path the Reformers will take. 'Christ has not got two bodies, nor two kinds of body, one temporal and the other spiritual', wrote Luther. So while some tended to see the Church actualised in a priesthood without people, others came to see it as a people without a priesthood. For the sixteenth-century Reformers the Church tended to be simply lay society as submitted to the law of God. The reaction against a too overpowering development of the aspect of hierarchical mediation and the clergy's part took the form of elimination of this order of things. We may well think that the remedy was worse than the disease. But for Protestants the glory of the Reformers is that they brought into lay life, into everyday life, the holiness which had formerly been kept in the cloister; that they denounced the distinction between an ordinary goodness and morality, just sufficient for salvation, and a higher morality available only to churchmen; that they restored dignity and Christian value to the various activities of secular life, and particularly to man's trades and professions. There is no need to give references; they would be endless, for these ideas were found everywhere.

Neither shall we undertake an apology for the Catholic middle ages or an account of holiness attained in secular life: this will be the concern of several chapters later on and of a special treatment of the medieval idea of 'estates' or 'orders' and of the Christian conception of occupational calling.

The Canonical Notion. – This rubric does not imply that the conception just dealt with is not canonical, but it is dominated by moral considerations. The view to be set out now is more juridical.

We start with some words of St. Bonaventure, who is giving an account of the sacramental characters [B] conferred by baptism, confirmation and holy order. 'Character', he says, 'is a sign distinguishing the faithful in the spiritual people of the New Covenant: he discriminates between different states in respect of faith, and includes in the same state those who are marked with the same character. There are three states in respect of faith, according as that faith is simple, forceful or fruitful. Baptism distinguished the faithful from the non-faithful; among the faithful, confirmation denotes the strong; by holy order 'homo ut sanctus ad ministerium templi a laicis separatur'.—So the cleric is distinguished from the layman as having the charge, not only of living by faith and upholding it, but of imparting it. That the emphasis is put more on the prophetical than on the properly liturgical aspect of the clerical function follows from the point of view from which Bonaventure was writing, a point of view normal in a mendicant teacher. The fact remains, and it is the point here, that the layman's condition is defined by function and not by way of life.

Elsewhere St. Bonaventure says: 'For him who is engaged in the Church's service or who becomes a cleric, renunciation of temporal things belongs to perfection and not to necessity. We see it done in the early Church . . . and we still see it done today in religious perfection, but neither divine nor human law imposes it on a cleric. All the same, it is right and proper that clerics should not bother so much about temporal things as do lay people, who have got to think about their children. . . .

Moreover, temporal preoccupations are bad for spiritual ones. That is why the texts appealed to speak as if the clergy ought to give up all earthly things. They don't mean that with respect to ownership but only with respect to attachment. This last comment shows a shift of emphasis. The point of view is no longer that of clericature as a form of life in which clergy approximate to monks, but that of active duties, of an office, of a competence: we have moved from a monastic world to one which is sociologically and culturally much nearer our own.

For it is this writer's conviction that the deep change that took place between the end of the eleventh century and the beginning of the thirteenth had consequences that persist down to our own time. The synthetical and symbolical intellectuality of the patristic age and monastic culture became analytical and dialectical. Predominantly moral considerations gave way to those that are predominantly juridical. The idea of *forum externum* was disentangled from that of *forum internum*, with all that that involves for a theology of excommunication and for an ecclesiology. In considering the Church, jurisdictional and sociological elements were developed and, *vis-a-vis* the more mystical and sacramental views of the preceding age, were on the way to becoming pretty well preponderant. So it can be said that, if 'in the eleventh century the accent was put on the monk, not on the priest, in the thirteenth it threatened to be put on the prelate and on ecclesiastical power. All this is of no great importance for our present purpose, however. All we need do is to grasp a notion of the lay condition different from (and complementary to) the previous one: one no longer looking at way of life but at function or competence.

From the canonical point of view it is this second notion that is formal and exact. Where conditions of life are concerned, the layman is he who lives 'in the world', as opposed to the monk. But canonically a layman can be a monk, for he is defined as 'one who has no part in the power of jurisdiction and, especially, of holy order', as opposed to the cleric. The principal canons of the Code that speak of lay people in a general way show them as having to receive, as having the right to receive, spiritual goods from the clergy, especially the helps necessary for salvation. This will be shown to be normal when we come to define the laity's position theologically. It could also be demonstrated from the very nature of canon law, which in the first place is a law of the sacraments. This last is an historical truth which, it seems to us, may be taken as established by Sohn and his school (without, however, adopting their systematic construction), and a theological analysis of the content of canon law leads to a similar conclusion. It would be easy enough to find a basis for it in ecclesiology, but this is not the place to do it.

Obviously if we stop there our idea of laity will be rather negative; going from one definition to another has not helped us much in that respect. According to the monastic view, lay people only exist by favour of a concession; according to the canonical view, they are negative creatures. . . . It is always the same old stumbling-block, which this book is trying to do something to remove.

However, there is no need to suppose that the distinction between laymen and clerics (canonical view), coincides with a distinction between people who have only a secular field of action and people who have a sacred or holy field of action. Lay people too exercise sacred activities. Not for a moment may we entertain any idea of them that is inconsistent with their membership in the people of God to which the very etymology of their name bears witness. Once again, the purpose of this book is precisely to study the sacred state of Christian laity, first in its constitution (*statut*) as a whole and then in the detail of its substance.

When we attempt, if not to define, at any rate to outline the characteristics of the lay condition, we see that our two notions of it eventually reach down to one same point, which we will try to indicate by two successive approximations.

First approximation.—As members of the people of God, lay persons are, like clerics and monks, by their state and directly, ordered to heavenly things. All of them have been made fit 'for our portion of the inheritance of the saints in light' (Colossians i, 12). But they are not all ordered in exactly the same way. It would be biblically, dogmatically and in fact inaccurate to say: Clerics and monks are, by their state and directly, ordered to heavenly things; lay people are, by their state and directly (though not exclusively), ordered to earthly things. But it is true to say that: (1) Lay people do not live exclusively for heavenly things; that is, so far as present circumstances allow, the condition of monks; (2) Lay people are Christians to the fullest extent as touching life in Christ, but they have no competence, or only a limited competence, touching the properly ecclesial means to life in Christ; these means belong to the competence of clerics.

Lay people are called to the same end as clergy or monks—to the enjoyment of our inheritance as sons of God; but they have to pursue and attain this end without cutting down their involvement in the activities of the world, in the realities of the primal creation, in the disappointments, the achievements, the stuff of history. The laity is called to do God's work in the world; not merely in the sense that its members should move heaven and earth to introduce into lay life what monks and nuns do in the cloister; or not again in the sense that, having to do the works and adopt the form of holiness of the religious life, they *in addition* do the work of the world, which religious don't have to do. There is a certain type of hagiography, not unknown in the *legendae* of the Divine Office, that perhaps turns the mind in this direction; and moreover there is too much truth and depth in it for it to be lightly dismissed. But there are indications that God wills something quite different. Lay people are Christians in the world, there to do God's work *in so far is it must be done in and through the work of the world*. We believe that this is necessary, in accordance with God's purpose, and that his work can be actualised as he wills it should be only through a full, real participation in the world's travail. This is what we shall seek to establish in our third chapter. For the fullness of her work in accordance with the purpose of the living God, the Church has to have laity, faithful who do the work of the world and reach their last end in dedication to that work. This is essential to the Church. She has to have some members who are directly and exclusively dedicated to the work of God's kingdom, and for that purpose are dispensed from the world's work: such are monks and priests. So, too, in Israel the levites were given no allotment when the land was shared out. But the total mission of the Church, corresponding to God's design, requires that the Lord's reign be prepared in and through that creation in the perfecting of which man must co-operate. Therefore do God's design and the Church's mission call for the existence of lay faithful; they need a laity which, in its wholeness, is called to glorify God without lessening its engagement in the work of the world. The laity's relation to the one last end is perhaps less immediate, certainly less exclusive, than that of clergy and monks; but it partakes of theirs in a secondary sense, with reference to the decisive fact that the *whole* of God's people is advancing towards its Promised Land.

Second approximation.—The layman then is one for whom, through the very work which God has entrusted to him, the substance of things in themselves is real and interesting. The cleric, still more the monk, is a man for whom things are not really interesting *in themselves*, but for something other than themselves, namely, their relation to God, whereby he may be better known and which can help towards his service. This parallel could be prolonged with the aid of those passages wherein St. Thomas Aquinas contrasts the points of view of the philosopher and the *fidelis*. The philosopher, that is, the man of learning, is interested in a thing's own nature, the *fidelis* in its transcendent reference; the philosopher seeks the explanation of things, the *fidelis* their meaning. The subject could be carried further by looking in history for types and movements representative respectively of the attitude of the *fidelis* and that of the learned man, in other words, of the cleric and of the layman. Our attention would probably be caught particularly by two great movements: firstly, what has been called the 'Albertino-Thomist revolution'; then, by the upsurge of modern 'laicism' (in the sense that will be explained in a moment), the reconquest by reason of fields in which she had been unduly held in tutelage by the authority of clerics.

The clerical condition as we have described it is full of danger. First of all, so uninterested an attitude towards earthly things as such commands respect only when it is genuine and uncontaminated, especially in a world so concerned with sincerity as ours. Everybody respects Father de Foucauld. But there is great danger that an attitude adopted in the name of one's state, one's calling, should be too theoretical; that one should lay claim to its honour and benefits without having its spirit or taking up its burdens. And the scandal becomes glaring if a man claims to be disinterested towards the process of history and of the world, when he is really seeking power, wealth (in any of its forms, which are many), advantageous influence in secular things.

That, however, is not the biggest danger. That lies in a loss of respect for the true inwardness of things. The man concerned with the transcendent relationship of things with their principle and end, the *fidelis* and more especially the cleric through his profession, runs the risk of forgetting that things exist in themselves, with their own proper nature and needs. The temptation is to make these things simply occasions or starting-points for an affirmation of the sovereignty of the Principle, or as mere means towards the carrying-out of some religious programme. When earthly disinterestedness is total, when it is truly a matter of pure religious relation, such attitudes, though perhaps still irritating, have something about them that is not only religious but unexceptionable. In the concrete, however, the religious relationship is actualised in a Church, through the ministry of churchmen. Church and churchmen have an historical, sociological existence, and for religious ends they make use of means borrowed from historical and sociological life. The danger, then, is of withholding full respect for earthly human things on the ground that they are being given a transcendent reference, whereas concretely they are simply being used among the sociological and historical means of the Church—as when they are referred and made subservient to 'accepted ideas' more than to the faith, to the conventions of 'the Christian world' more than to the requirements of Christianity, to the 'politics' of Catholicism more than to its mystery. From the minute the (historical) Church is thought of in this way we go from one thing to the other on the temporal place without hesitation or discrimination. Perhaps, even certainly, this is a sign of the Church's transcendence; but there is also unquestionably a danger that the temporal engagement should not be treated seriously, and that the nature and truth of the earthly things that compose it are not fully respected. This is particularly serious when it is a question, not of practical action, whose truth is less objectively determined, but of objective truth: in that case any sharp practice 'in the good cause' is a betrayal that no apologetic or allegedly apostolic advantage can excuse.

Historically, the Christian regime of the West after the dissolution of the Roman empire, and especially from Charlemagne till the coming of the modern world—which began during the last third of the twelfth century, had its age of power, spiritually, at the Renaissance, politically, after the French Revolution and is not yet over—this Christian regime, 'Christendom', was marked by the organisation of the whole of temporal life under the supreme regulation of the Church and in her setting; and this meant that all relative realities were brought under tutelage. It is no part of our present purpose to set forth the benefits that accrued to human society from this state of affairs, nor to examine the theoretical question of relations between the temporal and the spiritual. We will simply note two points. (1) In this regulation of earthly matters—the sciences as well as civil affairs—by religious authority, interpreter of the absolute, there was an element of confiscation or, to use a Marxist word, alienation. This alienation was never complete, these earthly matters always had a relative autonomy; but, having been taken into the service of the faith, they were never considered and developed for their own sakes. (2) Guardianship is good for children; but it was unduly prolonged in fields wherein men had, as we now say, come of age. The most typical example—which the clergy can never think about too much—is clearly that of Galileo, threatened with torture when he was seventy years old and made to retract in a scientific matter, and when he was right: this in the name of Revelation—but actually in the name of certain 'accepted ideas' which were taken for revealed truth and sound philosophy.

It is against the confiscation of the internal truth of second causes by the First Cause that modern laicism rebelled; fundamentally it was a movement to recapture rights in second causes, that is, in earthly things. The various priesthoods of second causes rose against the alienation of their domain into the hands of the priesthood of the First Cause. A superabundance of proofs could be adduced that this is the true, profound meaning of the lay movement—and of the modern world too. But are any proofs needed when the evidence is so clear? It would be embarrassing to have to choose among all the statements of leaders in the priesthoods of second causes—statesmen, philosophers, scholars, medical men, philanthropists. The following passage from Lavisse has often been quoted: 'To be secular (*laique*) . . . is not to make the best of ignorance about anything. It is to believe that life is worth the trouble of being lived, to love life, to refuse to look on the world as a 'vale of tears', to deny that tears are necessary and beneficial, that suffering may be providential; it is not to make the best of any unhappiness. It is not to leave feeding the hungry, giving drink to the thirsty, righting injustice, consoling the sorrowful, to a judge seated outside of this life: it is to join battle with evil in the name of justice.' Forget the mockery and the irreverence: it is accidental and peripheral to the meaning and essential intention of the words. The real affirmation is this: To be secular is to use all the resources within us in that pursuit of justice and truth for which we hunger, the very stuff of human history.

Have we then been asking 'What is a layman?' only to end up with a definition of 'lay' in the sense of laicism? Of course the answer is No. But in a sense the answer could be Yes. Because there is laicism (*laicisme*) and there is laicity (*laicite*), a distinction made classical by a declaration of the cardinals and archbishops of France; it is something like 'scientism' and science, the 'modern world' in the sense of Pius XI's Syllabus of Errors and the modern world to which we belong; or somewhat as there is clericalism and there is the Church. There has been, and there still is, a laicism whose foundation-stone is a doctrinal, metaphysical affirmation that there is no God in the sense of the positive Judaeo-Christian revelation; or at all events, no 'supernatural' according to the Church's meaning. But there is also a lay affirmation which does not exclude the supernatural: it simply requires the relative not to be absorbed by the absolute to the point of evaporation; it says that reference to the First Cause should not do away with the reality of second causes and the internal truth of all that fashions the world and the history of men. This 'laicality' (if so barbarous a word may be allowed) does not refuse to believe in God; it simply asks for belief in things as well. It wants to respect their nature, their laws, their needs; it thinks that, given the unique Absolute, the one thing necessary, men as a whole ought to make their way to God without taking short cuts or minimising their passage through history and the things of the world.

Believers are often reproached for not interesting themselves in things, for being content with purifying their intentions in view of God's law, and for not believing in good or evil *in things*: people today, since they belong to the world and to their age, have become hypersensitive to this reproach. Many Christians—in France, at any rate, Christians as a whole—are conscious of this peremptory problem, and it has often found expression in the self-criticisms that have been so common since the war. They see it as one of the bigger questions they have to answer, and perhaps the most important element in their insistent need to know the function of Christian lay people—or of lay Christians.

A few pages back St. Thomas Aquinas was invoked. This Christian genius was providentially set at the junction of the ancient world, sacral and monastic (but also feudal), with the modern world, scientific and positive, to help educate the second in respect for what was of everlasting worth in the first. He himself began as an oblate of the great family of Monte Cassino; but his own intellectual beginnings were philosophical and naturalist and, the 'arts-men' [C] of Paris looked on him so much as one of themselves that when he died they wanted his body, as well as the treatises he had promised them. At one and the same time Aquinas appreciated the ordered unity of things— the most fundamental and universal idea of the middle ages—and the particularity of their nature, each one having its specific note and its content of truth. He is a model and a peerless guide for a world given over to technique and particular explanations without any unifying references, and suffering accordingly. He may be said to have been authentically lay, even though a cleric.

Can the same be said of St. Thomas's spiritual children? That fine man Theophile Foisset remarks several times that there was something of the layman about Lacordaire (whose friend and biographer Foisset was). For example, when his lectures at the College Stanislas were interrupted Lacordaire wrote to the archbishop of Paris, Mgr. de Quelen: 'I ask the Church, in the person of my bishop, to trust me and to honour my priesthood. . . . I claim what is the priest's sole good and sole honour, freedom to preach Jesus Christ. . . .' On which Foisset comments: 'There was something manly, something of the layman, in these words.' That reflexion is significant. It looks as if people think one is 'lay' when one asks respect for what is human and natural, but that the priestly office is bound entirely to absorb the human man: that office not only in its spiritual and divine aspect but also in the aspect which involves submissiveness to a system whose pattern is one of authority and submission. That that is an altogether happy view may be questioned, but this is not the place to discuss it. The point, however, brings us round once more to this idea: a lay person is one for whom things exist, for whom their truth is not as it were swallowed up and destroyed by a higher reference. For to him or her, Christianly speaking, what is to be referred to the Absolute is the very reality of the elements of this world whose outward form passes away.

* * * * *

CONCLUSION

Let us summarize the principal conclusion of our laborious inquiry into the position and proper role of the laity in the Church. That the end may correspond with the beginning, we will recall how priests, monks and laity are and make the Church, or, in technically more exact terms, how they are the subject of the operations by which the Church is constructed, and by what title they are necessary to her.

The laity (and monks as such) are not the subject of the acts by which the Church receives her structure as institution of salvation, which involve the exercise of apostolical powers; they are not the subject of the juridical mission constitutive of apostleship, which is carried out in various organs of apostolicity. In the gospels and Acts we see that the Apostles, and those joined with them or appointed afterwards to exercise part of their ministry, partake of competences that the other faithful do not share, competences that enable them to play the part in the building up of the Church that St. Paul calls that of master-builders (I Corinthians iii, 9-17) and of foundations (Ephesians ii, 20). The faithful are indeed living stones and are all part of the temple (I Corinthians iii, 16-17; Ephesians ii, 21-22; I Peter ii, 5; etc.); they are neither master-builders nor foundation, but rather are themselves built and based. There are gifts of authority and mediation in the Church, and they are accorded to some members only. This is the hierarchical principle.

But apostolicity is an organic function, a service, a ministry. It is not an end in itself. It exists for the body and in the body; for the body, in somewhat the same way as the master-builder exists for the house; in the body in somewhat the same way as the foundations exist for the house once it is built. Foundations that are not organically part of the building do not make a house—they belong to an unfinished plan, or a ruin. All the stones are the house, and each one for itself makes the 'act of the house', so to speak; some of them do this as foundation, but in order that all the others may be a house and not simply a formless mass of materials. The Church's hierarchical principle is of necessity accompanied by a communal principle.

These two principles are in no wise opposed, since the first is expressed in an organic function of a body wholly living throughout. Nothing is more noticeable than the persistence with which the Bible joins in the same passages mention of the functions or competences proper to the apostolic ministry with affirmation of a life and spiritual quality in which all share. The Scriptures and tradition speak of the Church essentially as a living organism. She is the Body of Christ; she is a city or a family all of whose members are active, though not all equal; if she is called a temple, it is a temple whose stones have life. All do not take part in the laying of the foundations and in directing the building, but all share in the dignity of the whole, in the functions that compose it and in the activities of its life.

In the Church's *dignity*. We are inclined to overlook this aspect, but the Fathers were very conscious of it. As members of the Body of Christ, the faithful share in his kingly and priestly dignity. There is in the world an order of inert existence, then an order of sensitive and perishable life, then an order of spiritual life; but beyond that there is an order of properly divine life, in and through the Son of God made man, Jesus Christ. The name of Christian that every baptized person bears raises us to *that* height of dignity.

In the Body each one fills a part determined by his vocation, by the gifts accorded him, and by his state and *function*. We have seen with what vigour this teaching of St. Paul and the Fathers was taken up in the encyclical letter *'Mystici Corporis'*. Hierarchical functions alone assure the Church's structure as institution of salvation and, in that sense, they alone are essential to her existence pure and simple; but other functions enter into the concrete morphology of the Church and form part of her internal organization. The encyclical mentions charismatics (apparently in the modern sense of the word, which implies exceptional gifts); religious who make public profession of the evangelical counsels, whether in contemplative life or in the doing of works of spiritual or corporal mercy; married people, fathers and mothers, godparents; all the members of the 'order' of laity, and especially those who strive in Catholic Action. Here we see, with the addition of a new category, the classic list of 'ministries, grades, professions, states, orders and functions' (these words occur in the encyclical), of which tradition has always seen the Body of Christ, the Church, to be made up (sometimes with the addition of preachers, widows and deaconesses). The Church is, then, presented to us as an organism in which certain functions ensure the existence of the institution and others ensure its perfection, in accordance with the will of God who bestows his gifts and his vocations as he pleases. So far as concerns its essential structure, the Church existed in the Apostles, whose heirs and successors are the bishops: their priesthood is necessary to the institutional structure. But from the beginning Jesus willed that, side by side with the Apostles, there should be the seventy (or seventy-two) disciples, the holy women, and others. The list of the different 'orders' of which mention has been made could be increased, or all could be reduced to two, religious life and life in the world; but in any case they too are necessary, not that the Church as institution may exist, but that she may fulfil her mission to the uttermost and fully carry out her work as the Body of Christ.

The lay function is necessary for the carrying out of this mission and work. Were it only a question of a receiving subject, a beneficiary, of the work of grace carried out by the priesthood, the monastic function would be enough. Monks are, one might say, mankind passing into a pure state in the Church, so offering themselves that Christ's life may inform them directly and wholly. But God's purpose is not that there should be only a Church here below, but rather a Church *and* a world, a Church with a mission to the world and making use of its resources; and at the last a Kingdom, which each after its fashion will have prepared. The work of the mystical Body involves the bringing together under Christ of all that the wealth of creation and the virtualities of mankind can achieve: the first Adam needs the Second Adam that he may be saved, but the Second Adam supposes the first, that he may save him and have something to reign over. As for the Church's mission, it is fulfilled only if the gospel be declared to every creature, if creation with all its growth and increase be offered in Christ; it is not fulfilled in all its requirements and consequences unless there be a Christian influence opening the way to faith at the level of human structures, at work throughout civilization to turn it Christward.

These things can be done only by lay people, for they belong both to the world and to the Church in a way that is true neither of the clergy nor of monks. And so the lay function as such is necessary to the Church's mission and to the economy of grace. Lay people are the proper and irreplaceable subject of some of the activities through which this mission and this work are accomplished in their fullness. We have seen how this, their own, mandate is determined by the providential circumstances of their mundane engagement; how it corresponds to the part of the Church's mission in which she acts through her spiritual 'powers'; and how this mandate *ex spiritu, ex circumstantiis*, is confirmed by the hierarchical apostleship, which joins that of the laity to itself and therein finds its complement. We asked by what title lay people are the subject of functions by which the Church is constructed and how far they are necessary to her, and we find the answer is to a considerable degree positive. But that is not all. The laity also share, and fully, *in the acts of the Church's life*.

Yves Marie Joseph Congar

So far as its final determinations are concerned, that life reaches the body through the channel of apostolicity; but this is an organic function ordered by the Holy Spirit to the quickening of the whole body with the life of its Head. Thus animated, the entire body is, in the strongest sense of the word, concerned in the prophetical, priestly, apostolic, saving activity in which Christ takes those who are his as partners; the Body is the true subject of all life in Christ, and is alone its adequate subject. This life is actualized in its fullness only in the totality of the body. And therefore, on the one hand, the Lord can be wholly found and truth fully known only in the fellowship of the whole; on the other, the hierarchical instances of apostolicity themselves, being what they are only in view of the Body, can be exerted only in and with it.

That is a truth that we came upon at the end of all our inquiries, and principally under two forms, namely, the idea that the faithful are the *pleroma* of the hierarchy, and the idea of an association of communal principle with hierarchical principle. This is more particularly noticeable in the spheres of liturgical worship, of the life of faith, and of apostleship. There we find both duality and unity of subject. Duality, since the hierarchical priesthood and the magisterium are not at all a delegation by the people; the apostolic mission of the Twelve, continued in the episcopal hierarchy, is complete and whole in itself; and yet there is a priesthood of the faithful, an infallibility of the believing Church, and an apostolic mission of all. Unity, since we have recognized that there is a sense in which the faithful with their clergy form one single subject of worship, of infallible faith and witness, and of apostleship. There is but one Lord, one Spirit, one Body (Ephesians iv, 4-6); the Holy Spirit that quickens the hierarchical organs in order that the body may have life, and the Holy Spirit that quickens the whole body in order that it may do the works of that life, can only go together, if we may venture to put it so, for they are the same. As in the whole of creation, so in the Church, God goes from unit to unity through the many; he distributes his grace by communicating it to many individuals and he brings that many to unity in communion, in a kind of concelebration of the mystery of the same life. In so doing, God is only reflecting his own mystery in the Church, for everything in him is a proceeding from one Principle, a communication to several, and a perfect communion in unity. *O beata Trinitas!*

The association of the laity with the hierarchy extends to a certain co-operation with it, at any rate at the level of execution, in the order of the juridical mission of which the hierarchy is the proper subject. We remember what we have found in the liturgy of worship, in teaching, in the apostolate and even in the regulation of God's household. There were the hierarchical power and acts coming from above, and the acts of life of the whole body from below: but also a sort of taking over of the second by the first which leads to, for instance, a liturgical worship of the Church as such, coming between properly sacramental acts and private personal prayer; or again, between apostleship of purely personal inspiration and the hierarchical apostleship, a certain 'sharing' of the latter, and the instituted apostolate of Catholic Action. There were, too, the participations—however tenuous—in teaching authority and the functions of regulation. Thus the principle of association is found even in institutions and is expressed canonically. But it is most fruitfully at work in the wider sphere of life, in an association of clergy with laity, wherein the priest energizes most effectively as spiritual man, as thoughtful and cultivated man, as apostolic man, his people's guide, joined with the faithful in seeking ways and means for the Church's well-being in the actual circumstances and events of history.

It is true that the development of ideas has worked rather against the combination of the communal principle with the hierarchical principle, and for an elaboration of the latter alone, especially in the West. For a long time the idea prevailed that hierarchical acts, sacramental celebrations in particular, were acts of the mystical Body and that they could be accomplished only in the fellowship of the body. It became necessary to make it clear that their validity does not come from the body as such, but from on high. This necessary precision was secured at the beginning of a whole movement which developed the theology of hierarchical powers and means of grace—and therefore of the Church as institution—and it certainly contributed to the isolation of the hierarchical principle. During the same era (eleventh and twelfth centuries), the old discipline that connected it clearly and effectively with the communal principle gave place to other usages. There was a change from priestly ordinations made for the service of a given church to ordinations 'without title'; from episcopal elections with a lower clergy and people's element to elections reserved to the cathedral chapter; from canonizations made in various ways from below to canonizations reserved to the pope; from the idea of authority as guardian of tradition to that of authority as source of law; from communion bound up with the eucharistic celebration to communion out of Mass, from reserved hosts. These points could be illustrated by many references and the list could be easily lengthened: they all represent an impulse in the same direction, namely, towards isolated affirmation and exercise of the hierarchical principle.

In this matter there is considerable difference between the West and the East, which became so unhappily separated from one another at the time to which we have just referred. The West has tended to emphasize the hierarchical principle, the East the communal principle. The West looks at and stresses above all that there is only one principle and that the body receives from it: this can be seen in the idea of priesthood, in the theology of papal power, even in Mariology, wherein one can easily tend to make God's gifts a personally held privilege; it can readily be seen in the liturgy, in the eucharistic celebration, for example, where it looks as if nothing can be said or done unless the priest says or does it, to the length of his saying, 'Domine, non sum dignus . . .' and 'Amen' at communion instead of the people doing so. The East, however, looks at and puts more stress on how all share that in which the hierarchical principle resides. But she does not deny the hierarchical principle, any more than the West entirely disregards the communal principle. The two are complementary, just as, fundamentally, the East and West are themselves complementary, having been providentially willed by God to be thus *without separation*, in a duality and fellowship which themselves form part of the concrete pattern of the Church.

Every idea ought to be both expressed and safeguarded in outward signs. For its proper expression in the Church, the union of our two principles has to have its significant signs, and there are no finer and better ones than those of the liturgy. As Pope Pius XI said to Dom Bernard Capelle, the liturgy is not simply 'the Church's *didascalia*'; beyond its defined ideas, it is the sacred ark wherein the spirit of the Church is kept and expressed. We have seen how at Mass all the forms of priesthood are operative in their mutual organic relationships and connexions. When priest and people assure one another that the Lord is with them and, thus assured, the priest says 'Let us pray', the hierarchical principle is effectually completed in the communal principle and the true nature of the mystical Body is made manifest. The whole Mass is a wonderful expression and making real of the Church's symphonic unity, different members filling diverse roles in the oneness of the whole: one percents, another picks up the chant from his lips and continues it; one reads, another blesses; one consecrates, the others communicate; the priest, the deacon, the acolyte have their various offices and the service is made a whole only through their respective actions. In this connexion, what a matter for rejoicing it is that in the paschal vigil service, as restored in 1951, the celebrant listens to the prophecies read by another minister, without reading them privately himself. It is very regrettable that circumstances which no longer exist should have led to the prescription that the priest at high Mass should himself read inaudibly those things that the various ministers or the people sing. It is a liturgical anomaly; it is also a sort of symbol of the fact that the hierarchical priesthood has as it were taken over everything. It makes it look as if nothing can be done in the Church unless the priest does it and, from the point of view of apostleship, expression of thought and so on, as if the Church is not present there in any place if there is no cassock about. Personally, we attach great importance to significant signs. They are guardians of the spirit. Not to raise one's hat shows that respect is waning. The laity will not be reestablished in the fullness of its quality as the Church's laity until the spirit of that small Easter reform of 1951 shall have been extended to all the spheres where it is relevant.

I am happy to finish this big volume with the evocation of the Easter vigil, between the tomb and life renewed: it is the dawn of spring, too!

Thomas Francis O'Dea
1915-1974

Thomas O'Dea was born and grew up in Amesbury, Massachusetts. When World War II began he enlisted in the Air Force and served in the South Pacific, India, and China. After the war he took advantage of the GI Bill to go to Harvard. After graduating summa cum laude *in 1949, he stayed on to do his M.A. (1951) and Ph.D. (1953). He was assistant professor of sociology at M.I.T. from 1953 to 1956, associate professor at Fordham from 1956 to 1959, professor at the University of Utah from 1959 to 1964, then professor at Columbia University from 1964 to 1966. In 1967 he became professor of sociology and religious studies at the University of California, Santa Barbara. He died in Santa Barbara, three weeks short of his 59th birthday.*

O'Dea's unusual ability to employ sociological analysis to derive consistent insight in things religious was first demonstrated in his work on Mormonism. The Mormons *(1957) is still a model of such studies. But it was in the following year that he published his first challenge to his fellow Catholics,* American Catholic Dilemma: An Inquiry into the Intellectual Life. *His was one of those early (pre-Vatican II) voices, along with John Tracy Ellis and Gustave Weigel, that insisted that criticism and commitment were not only not opposed but actually ought to go hand in hand.*

THE CATHOLIC TRADITION: The Church

In The Sociology of Religion *(1966) O'Dea showed that he was at his most creative when dealing with the "dilemmas of institutionalization" in religion. He was a dialectical thinker who always avoided the simplistic solution. From his days at Harvard and M.I.T. he had come to the conviction that it was the modern scientific mentality that represented the real challenge to religious faith today. In* Alienation, Atheism, and the Religious Crisis *(1969), in typical fashion, he analyses the dilemma of contemporary confused consciousness: most people cannot believe with the depth and fervor that would give direction to their lives, nor can they disbelieve with the vigor and conviction that might produce creative negation that could lead to a more positive human orientation.*

In The Catholic Crisis, *which appeared in 1968, the year of Pope Paul VI's controversial encyclical* Humanae Vitae *on birth control, O'Dea gave a penetrating sociological analysis of Vatican II. In his eyes the questions faced by that Council were of burning concern not only to Catholics but to the entire Western world. If Christianity had largely failed in grappling with modernity since the 18th century, so had its would-be substitutes: Humanism, Marxism, Scientism. If Vatican II could succeed in the attempt to resolve the crisis over modernity, this could provide a sense of direction in a worldwide intellectual and moral stalemate.*

The selection that follows consists of chapters four and five from O'Dea's early work, American Catholic Dilemma. *Appearing in the very year that Pius XII died and John XXIII was elected, it was a remarkable achievement for the time. Few Catholics of the time combined his deep love and his sharp perception of the shortcomings of American Catholicism. He succeeded in not letting the strengths blind him to the weaknesses, and no one could seriously question his motives in wanting to see problems discussed openly. He was the right man in the right place at the right time to help a generation of American Catholics gain a better awareness of their past, appreciation of their present, and orientation for their future.*

AMERICAN CATHOLIC DILEMMA

CHAPTER IV

THE AMERICAN CATHOLIC HERITAGE

S o far in our analysis two elementary points have been made, and they provide the basis for the whole of our future discussion. First, the relation of reason to life is characterized by a fundamental ambiguity, and this ambiguity will be reflected in the role of the intellectual in any society which accords reason a place among its central values. Secondly, because of its altogether unique solution to that fundamental ambiguity and its defense at the same time of the role of reason, the basic tension between thought and living will, for Christianity, often take the form of a tension between reason and faith. Yet, vital though these two starting points are for our analysis, it is not sufficient to see these major aspects of the problem in the abstract. Consideration must also be given to their concerte manifestations in the context of American Catholic history. All that we have already said has implied that past experiences have an important effect in conditioning present actions. Hence it is necessary at this point to examine some of the salient aspects of our past which bear directly on our present concerns. We cannot hope to do anything like justice to this immense and important topic, but we can at least indicate the broader lines of influence which are involved.

Let us proceed directly to the basic historical problem. It must be recognized that in the task of developing a native intellectual tradition the Catholic community in this country has been faced with two problems, whereas for our fellow citizens of Protestant background there has been but one. Both they and we have to relate the basic ideas 'and values of our respective heritages to the unfolding events of the American adventure. But we have had, in addition, the difficulties arising from the fact that we have been a minority group endeavoring to relate our distinct religious and cultural traditions to the changing patterns of a dominant non-Catholic culture. Under any conditions the difficulties which faced us would have been twice as great as those which faced the Protestant majority. But the fact that we were for so long an immigrant group, or a group not far removed from immigrant status, and were consequently to such a great extent the hewers of wood and the drawers of water, made the problem still more acute. These conditions caused us to remain much longer than might otherwise have been the case in a state of intellectual dependency upon the Catholic culture of Europe, from which we were moreover cut off to some extent, owing to our economic circumstances.

Although Catholics were not at first well received in this country, and our history is marked by the intolerance and prejudice which we met upon arrival on these shores, the assimilation of the successive streams of Catholic immigration was nevertheless genuine. Catholics came to consider themselves true Americans, and eventually to be accepted as such by the majority of their non-Catholic neighbors. Yet in a real sense we differed from the immigrants of other religious backgrounds in our ability to assimilate ourselves to American culture in the various realms of social life. In the political and economic spheres, Catholics, like the descendants of other immigrants, came to participate wholeheartedly in the common life of America. Loyalty to American institutions and identification with them became deeply imbedded in the American Catholic consciousness.

But in the intellectual sphere, in the area of values and ideas, the Catholics had to stand somewhat apart from the general run of their fellows; the distinct character of the Catholic cultural heritage had the effect of preventing the Catholic community from participating fully in the general American developments. Much of American intellectual history represents the transformation of Protestantism—especially of Calvinism—under the impact of American conditions and liberal ideas derived from the eighteenth century European Enlightenment. Typical of the processes involved are: the revivalism of the eighteenth and nineteenth centuries; the long-term revolt of American Protestants against Calvinist pessimism, culminating in the recognition of the freedom of the will and the efficacy of human action; and the

274

intensive secularization of American culture during the second half of the nineteenth century. All these processes started from the older Protestant positions, and all represented great collective experiences of the American Protestant population. While these transformations were taking place, Catholics were generally engaged in the basic processes of assimilation to the new society and its culture. Their separate heritage as well as their specific contemporary problems served to detach them from these processes. But while it was the nature of the case that the Catholic community could not participate directly in these developments, it could not avoid experiencing their effects.

Part I: The Divided Man

One result of this experience—one that deserves very careful analysis and evaluation by Catholic writers—has been our simultaneous incorporation into and alienation from American culture. Our minds are in a sense compartmentalized in relation to American society as a whole. On the one hand we have formed a firm identification with certain aspects of the national culture—notably in the fields of politics, constitutional law, and economics. On the other, we have developed in certain areas an aloofness amounting at times to alienation. This is especially true with respect to the development of native thought in spheres involving basic world views and values, where our past has made homogenity with the Protestant-derived tradition difficult or even impossible.

This subtle marginality of ours has been the cause of inner conflict as well as of external difficulties. It has resulted in a subtle division of the American Catholic mind. On the one side is a firm identification with American society and strong loyalty to and love for its basic institutions. On the other is an alienation from the intellectual and spiritual experiences which, as we have seen, were central for those of Protestant background. Sometimes this cleavage manifests itself in a superficial over-identification which disguises a profound alienation. Our past difficulties increase our present tendency toward such over-identification.

It is this problem, almost more than the obvious reasons, which justifies the existence of Catholic institutions of higher learning in this country. An institutional context is necessary for the correlation of the Catholic- and Protestant-derived elements of the continuous American tradition if the dilemma arising from our history is to be resolved. Moreover, in serving the Catholic community of America by performing this function, the Catholic university is also of service to the American culture in general, for it thus provides another voice in the great cultural exchange without which national intellectual development might be deprived of a whole range of contributions.

It cannot be repeated too often, to cite but one example, that in part the role of the Catholic intellectual in America must be "prophetic"—endlessly championing points of view which are counter to those prevailing in his society. Divorce is now part of the American way of life; euthanasia may become so. The Catholic intellect, rightly used in the secular order, not only can profit by the positive results of the best modern thinking but can also serve to correct some of its unfortunate elements, but only on condition that Catholic thinkers be regarded as collaborators and not as deadly enemies.

Hence it is necessary first that a genuinely creative intellectual tradition should be developed among American Catholics. At the present time, unfortunately, the means taken to resolve this inner conflict—one from which no literate Catholic can be wholly immune—are often inappropriate. For some Catholics this division and compartmentalization has resulted in an over-anxious desire to identify themselves with America in those areas where their history has made such identification possible, and to proclaim these areas of life, and the views derived from them, as the very essence, the "badge" of true "Americanism." Such people tend to see certain liberal ideas and ideals—in fact quite genuinely American in origin and descent although different from, and at times in opposition to, Catholic values—as "un-American," and to join in strictly partisan conflicts to exorcise them. There are indeed those for whom the whole Enlightenment tradition, long since transplanted and developed in its American setting, becomes a subversive foreign import of the latter days. Such behavior tends merely to increase and make more rigid the Catholic alienation and to make a positive solution to the underlying problem much more difficult.

Thomas Francis O'Dea

Part 2: Catholic Defensiveness

To this major structure of our problem must be added another dimension, already alluded to above and to be discussed in further detail below. The fact is that Catholicism has been thrown on the defensive by the secularization of culture which has marked the last four centuries of European and American development. These centuries have seen until quite recently a steady retreat—a defensive rear guard action—on our part (and in fact on the part of all believing Christians) before an advancing, and at times a militant, secularism.

A little less than a hundred years ago, educated non-Catholics considered that the Catholic Church had been vanquished, and many had written it off as defunct. "Popery can build new chapels," said Carlyle a little over a century ago; "welcome to do so, to all lengths. Popery cannot come back any more than paganism can—which still also lingers in some countries. But, indeed, it is with these things as with the ebbing of the sea: for minutes you cannot tell how it is going; look in half an hour where it is—look in half a century where your popehood is!" Carlyle has proved to be a bad prophet, but the extremities to which the Church was reduced in the mid-nineteenth century were real enough. As Paul Tillich said some twenty years ago: "Since the Counter-Reformation Catholicism has been fighting a defensive war directed equally against Protestantism on the one hand and autonomous civilization on the other." By "autonomous civilization" Tillich refers to a self-sufficient secularism.

This defensiveness affected many aspects of the Catholic outlook and militated against a more flexible engagement with the modern world. But it was primarily a defensiveness dictated by harsh necessity and not one deriving from any basic ridigity of the Catholic faith in terms of meeting new situations and diverse cultures. Moreover, it was a defensiveness which, however heavy the cost—and the cost was heavy—accomplished its object. It has preserved the deposit of faith and remained true to the Church's divine commission.

For the last several decades in Europe there has been evidence that the state of siege has passed. A new flowering of Catholic thought and culture seems imminent and has indeed

277

already come. A period of cultural advance appears to be opening up for the ancient Catholic tradition. In fact, Catholicism today stands foremost in the defense of the whole of European civilization, while it reaches out creatively to meet new problems and to bring its eternally new message to the continents struggling for maturity.

But this state of siege of the Universal Church in the last century deprived American Catholics, pioneering in the new country, of the stimulus they might otherwise have received from their European brethren. Had the present Catholic renaissance come earlier in France, perhaps the intellectuals of that country might have given more significant aid, instead of at times almost interpreting our national attitudes as a new heresy. Yet in America the Church accomplished the basic tasks under conditions often difficult and trying. The Americanization of the immigrant, the building of churches and of schools, the development of colleges and universities, and the contribution of able men, lay and clerical, to American life bear testimony to this. We have not done as well in some of these respects as we should have, but even here the judgment is our own, and our present discussion of these problems, to which this book is but one modest contribution, bears testimony to our growing ability for mature self-criticism. It is on the basis of the accomplishments of the past that the present discussion is possible, and it is those very accomplishments which give us so many reasons to anticipate its success.

Within this larger historical context we must now examine some of the more detailed processes of our historical experience and their effects upon us. A number of works by Catholic writers in America have dealt with the various aspects of these problems, and from these we shall try to extract the elements most pertinent to the present problem. Catholic writers have generally ascribed the lack of a vital intellectual tradition among American Catholics to a cluster of past difficulties and their present derivatives which can be summarized under six heads.

1. The lack of a Catholic intellectual heritage in this country related both to the lower-class origins and the present dominantly lower- and lower-middle class composition of the American Catholic population.

278

2. The lack of scholarly motivation among American Catholics related to such lower social positions and origins on the one hand, and, on the other, to the expectation that the priests will do the scholarly work while the laity concentrate on other things.

3. The inferior economic position of Catholic groups.

4. The difficulties involved in the process of assimilating millions of immigrants and the problems related to immigrant and post-immigrant status.

5. The defensive, martial, and even ghetto mentality brought about by partial alienation and the specific minority experience of American Catholics.

6. Prejudice, hostility, and discrimination.

To the difficulties inevitable for a Catholic community adjusting itself to a dominantly non-Catholic culture, which we have already described, must be added the positive disabilities imposed upon Catholics, the intolerance with which they were often treated and the problems of immigration and assimilation. All these factors have tended to segregate the American Catholic population, to hinder the participation of Catholics in the national life, and to make the development of a creative relationship between Catholicism and the national culture more complicated and difficult. These difficulties no longer exist in quite the same form as they once did but they have not passed away. Rather they live on in the attitudes of voluntary segregation and defensiveness which form part of the present American Catholic outlook and erect intangible barriers across the path of our progress.

Moreover, there has developed a considerable lack of awareness among American Catholics, laity and clergy alike, as to the degree to which such attitudes are not the result of our free choices, intellectually considered and rationally concluded, but are merely an automatic response produced by an earlier process of social conditioning. The widespread persistence of such attitudes and their inaccessibility to rational analysis and criticism constitute an important aspect of our problem and will be the object of later consideration.

279

It is most important that the six factors we have listed should not be understood simply as elements of the past which time alone will cause to disappear. The writers who have suggested them have not put them forward as excuses, but rather as contributions to a diagnosis of the contemporary situation. That these disabilities are far from correcting themselves with the passage of time but instead remain entrenched in our present-day psychology is suggested by a number of further considerations. Our defensiveness, for example, forced upon us as it has been by circumstances, is a *present barrier* and not merely a remnant of our past. The fact is that although Catholics elsewhere—and not Catholics alone but all believing Christians—have been placed on the defensive by the alienation of the Christian spirit from the modern world, they have produced important intellectual contributions. Yet in America, a country that ranks third among the nations of the world in Catholic population and first in Catholic financial assets, the problem of the lack of an adequate intellectual development has been most acute in its manifestations. That is to say that while the American problem is indeed a part of a worldwide problem—the loss of Catholic initiative over a whole range of vital intellectual fields—it is a much more severe and serious variation of it, complicated by native American Catholic elements.

Sometimes attempts are made to explain the present situation by putting the blame, as it were, on the specifically American quality of American Catholics and of American Catholic life. America as a whole, so this argument runs, has preferred action to thought. It has tended to play down and belittle things of the mind.

There is no denying that this characterization contains an element of truth and that American life has from the beginning placed a premium upon action. But there is another side to the picture. America's early desire to produce an educated Protestant clergy gave rise to great universities on the east coast—Harvard, Princeton, and Yale—which have produced Presidents, statesmen, scientists, and thinkers, in no small numbers. Around them a host of other institutions of learning grew up, each producing men of genuine capacity. The history of American thought, of American science, of American literature, and of American art in the brief 182 years since the colonies won their independence shows clearly that thinking has been an American vocation. The American developments and experiments in education, the pioneer foundation of schools and the establishment of land-grant colleges—in short, the whole American past—prove that in spite of her orientation toward practical activity, America has both produced and honored men of considerable intellectual stature, as the range of names from Jefferson through Peirce, Mann, Dewey, and our growing list of Nobel Prize winners attests.

This attempt to place the responsibility for our difficulties upon the supposedly unintellectual nature of our national life may appeal to some European intellectuals who, uninformed about America and American things, repeat stereotypes of their own concoction in order to find a scapegoat for their present native frustrations and aggressions; but no American, Protestant or Catholic, can take it quite seriously. In fact the European myth of America's "Materialism" collapses with a very cursory examination of the realities, and today few informed Europeans would give it much attention.

Intolerance is, however, another matter, for the reality of such intolerance in the past and even its subtle persistence in some forms in the present cannot be denied. But here matters have certainly improved in terms of the objective American situation. Moreover, we must not make the easy assumption that the experience of intolerance is incompatible with intellectual growth and development, for were this the case how could one possibly explain the tremendous intellectual development shown by American Jewry?

Poverty has certainly been an important factor, but here comparison with this same group gives food for thought. It is doubtful if even the Irish immigrants, perhaps the poorest of the nineteenth-century arrivals to these shores, were much poorer than the eastern European and Russian Jews who came after 1890, except possibly in the worst years of the Irish potato failure of the 1840's. Yet these eastern European Jews would, upon an empirical count, be found to have contributed a larger proportion of their children and grandchildren to academic and scholarly life than have Catholic immigrants as a whole.

281

It may be seriously questioned whether an examination of Catholic and non-Catholic immigrants would reveal conditions so disproportionately unfavorable to Catholic immigrants as one might conclude from certain explanations that have been given in connection with the present problem. It must be conceded, however, that the development of American Catholic life from immigrant origins has been complicated by the partial segregation of the Catholic community and the partial alienation of American Catholicism from important aspects of American secular culture. At this point the question might be raised as to what extent intellectuals were actually produced from immigrant Catholic origins but were lost to the Church by apostasy. Certainly the objective segregation and disarticulation we have examined would suggest that this may have been so. It is doubtful if such cases are numerous, but numbers would not be the most important criterion for judging the problem, since intellectual groups are always a minority in any population.

Two further aspects of this situation have at times been suggested. The first is that a great majority of Catholic immigrants not only had to enter the American social system with lower-class status, but they also came from peasant backgrounds in Europe. Hence the problems inherent in the assimilation of a lower-class Catholic group to a Protestant-derived culture were complicated by the problems of a peasant group adapting itself to urban life. This has certainly been involved in our difficulties in the past century. But this, as well as the other factors we have considered, must be kept in perspective. It must be stressed that immigration, with the exception of newcomers from Puerto Rico and from the ranks of displaced persons, has not been an important aspect of American life for more than a generation. The year 1924 saw important legal changes which put an end to more than a century of relatively free immigration to this country. In fact, for large members of American Catholics, immigration has become sufficiently a thing of the past for them to oppose liberalization of the immigration laws.

Let us further note that in the 124 years from 1820 to 1943, some 6,000,000 Germans and 4,600,000 Irish came to this country. The Germans were Protestant in a majority of cases, although the Catholic minority was of considerable proportions. The Irish were overwhelmingly Catholic. In the same period 4,700,000 Italians came who were, at least nominally, Catholic almost to a man. The peak year of German immigration was 1882, that of Irish immigration 1851, and that of Italian immigration 1907. In other words, the peak year for the most recent of the three most important Catholic groups of immigrants was half a century ago.

The Poles comprise another important Catholic ethnic group. Their peak year for immigration was 1921, when 415,000 Polish immigrants arrived. Thus even in the case of the Poles, the peak year was over a generation ago. Moreover, this figure is deceptive. It must be recalled that Poland had been deprived of independent national existence for a long time prior to the First World War. That means that Polish immigrants came to the United States before that time as Russians, Germans, and Austrians. The peak year for Austria-Hungary was 1907, for Russia, 1913.

Thus, the peak decade for Catholic immigration as a whole to this country was that of 1900-1910, almost half a century ago. It certainly seems rather late in the day to attribute to immigration and the immediate problems of assimilation the chief influence upon the evident problem.

The decline of intolerance and nativism is too evident to need any documentation, despite the regrettable rise of new Catholic-Protestant tensions recently and the anxieties of those non-Catholics who imagine they see "Catholic aggression" in this country today. There is evidence from recent studies which indicates that in business leadership and economic status Catholics have improved their condition considerably in the recent past. Plainly, therefore, both the factor of intolerance and that of economic hardship must receive reduced emphasis as present causes contributing to our problems.

What these considerations suggest is that the present problems of developing an adequate intellectual life among Catholics in America are not to be identified to any significant degree with those that characterized our history up to now. They are rather the products of that past. That past lives on, not in the forms that it displayed fifty or one hundred years ago, but rather in what we have inherited from that past experience and development. It is in present-day attitudes, in contemporary values, in current definitions of the situation, that the past history of American Catholicism persists in the present.

The partial segregation of Catholicism from basic elements of the general American culture, the over-identification with other elements, the defensiveness, the definition of life in terms of getting ahead in the new world, the odd divisions of labor between clergy and laity, the lack of a continuing tradition that gave a place of honor to intellectual pursuits—these are some aspects of our past history which affect our present. The past affects the present in those forms in which it exists in the present. It exists in the present, objectively, in terms of contemporary social and cultural patterns and, subjectively, in terms of attitudes operative in the here and now although formed in the past.

Thus, we cannot blame too much of our present upon the difficulties which Catholic immigrants found in assimilating themselves to America. Experience of living among American Catholics, as well as the general level of American Catholic life as it meets the eye of the casual observer, suggests that in *non-intellectual* areas American Catholics have not been late in assimilating themselves to the national milieu. The taste for automobiles, the styles of clothing and hair-dressing and use of cosmetics, the felt necessity for radio and television, the interest in movies and sports—in short, all the other indices of superficial conformity—seem to be quite visible in the American Catholic sense. Catholics have not been slow to accept what are often called—especially by our Catholic intellectual brethren in Europe —the more materialistic aspects of American life. Catholics, laity and clergy alike, have been able to come to terms with these aspects of modern America, although it seems possible that on a deeper level some of them deserve more critical examination by the Christian conscience.

A casual observer might further note that a considerable proportion of the diocesan press reveals at times serious hostility toward certain aspects of non-Catholic culture in this country. Yet such hostile treatment—often rather belligerent, let us add— of aspects of American culture that create difficulties for Catholics often conveys at the same time the impression that only Catholics—in fact, only Catholics who share the writers' opinions, plus one or two prominent non-Catholic spokesmen who agree with them—are true Americans. Such journalistic examples are evidence of the over-identification with America in a formal sense while evincing the signs of alienation from other aspects of American culture.

The important point to be stressed here is that the problem we face is a contemporary problem and calls for analysis of those contemporary factors which today inhibit the development of a native Catholic intellectual life proportionate to the numbers and resources of the American Catholics. These factors and their operation at the present time will occupy our attention in the chapters to follow. In that analysis we shall refer to the American past only to the extent that may be necessary to throw light upon the origin and evolution of these contemporary factors.

CHAPTER V

LATENT CULTURE PATTERNS OF AMERICAN CATHOLICISM

In our discussion of manifest Catholic culture-patterns (Chapter II, Part 4) we considered, along with the explicit teachings of the Church, explicit Catholic attitudes which might possibly qualify or even distort and subvert the teachings themselves. We found in addition that many times we were dealing with attitudes which might not be entirely explicit but nevertheless produced their effects in the general atmosphere surrounding the more clearly defined attitudes. In the present chapter we shall develop this line of investigation further and consider the latent content of Catholic culture patterns in America in their relation to the intellectual life.

These are more obscure orientations which grow out of the American Catholic situation and which can pervade the general approach we have to the problems of life. Despite their subtle and implicit character, they are of first importance. In fact, precisely because they are less accessible to examination and are often communicated indirectly by cues, by example, and by unconscious implication, they may speak more loudly and more effectively than our words. The subtlety of this area of cultural analysis is such that only careful research could uncover all the problems involved. The best we can do here is to suggest the historical background out of which such latent culture patterns really develop. This we shall attempt to do by asking certain questions and trying to determine how our answers to them have been dictated by historical circumstances rather than by a full examination of problems as they exist today.

Part I: How Important Is the "World"? Is It "Dangerous"?

One important aspect of the tension between Christianity and the world reveals itself in the problem of maintaining a proper hierarchy of ends. Catholic philosophy sometimes rest content with an architectonic solution to the problem, affirming the value of nature and its subordination to and fulfillment by grace. Such solutions are helpful so far as they go, but what is actually needed by the person who acts in a real-life situation is a working solution—or equilibrium—for the tensions produced by demands and calls directed to him by values and ends whose significance must be weighed by the Christian in the light of his religion. Ultimately, of course, such problems are solved by the development in the individual of prudence, a virtue of the practical reason.

Problems of this kind are many and highly ramified; here we are concerned wth recording the fact that the lay American Catholic who must make a concrete Christian way of life for himself often finds himself on a veritable frontier when he attempts to relate his worldly occupation to the inner meaning of the Christian life. The work to be done in society is not in any practical, realistic sense perceived by most Catholics as a structure of potential vocations, and it is not always easy to see it as such. The priest and the religious are called through their professions. The layman is called, it sometimes seems, in spite of his.

Such a definition of the layman's lot and of life in the world is often only implicit in the great body of Catholic writing; at least it is not part of explicit teaching on a high level, although it may be conveyed in certain kinds of sermons, devotional tracts, etc. The absence of a developed theology of work, or of a theology of the lay life in the world, is however, an eloquent if silent testimonial to the nature of the situation. Throughout its career the Church has been under both obvious and subtle pressures to reject the world and the flesh. Throughout, it has stood fast, and in terms of the enunciation of Christian doctrine it has always refused to yield to these pressures. Yet on the practical level these pressures have had their effects. The concrete conditions of Christian life over the centuries have inhibited the development of lay spirituality; they have also, at some times and some places, created a breach between clergy and laity and thus have been the cause of apostasy.

In the early Middle Ages the life of the monk became the concrete embodiment and the model of the Christian life. Alongside this ideal the Church accepted a norm—regarded as a lesser good and a compromise—for the Christian who did not leave the world to live under a monastic rule. This "compromise" governed the Christian lives not only of the laity but in most instances of the secular clergy as well. Later on, with the growth of trade and the rise of the cities, the Middle Ages saw the emergence of a lay culture and with it the establishment of political liberty. The layman was coming of age. This development in the medieval commune produced in many instances something that looked more like a Christian lay society than anything Christian antiquity had known.

Although this culture, which "from the beginning showed that characteristic of being an exclusively lay culture," gave impetus to education and created the basis for a great civilization, the higher learning remained to a certain extent a clerical prerogative, and no adequate practical theology was developed to convey the message of the Church to this new lay society. Often the clergy were not aware of the tremendous processes of social change that were at work; or rather, they were not aware of their significance.

Henri Pirenne has commented on this blindness. "Written exclusively by clerics or by monks," he says, the history written in the Middle Ages "naturally measured the importance and the value of events according to how they affected the Church. Lay society did not claim their attention save in so far as it related to religious society. They could not neglect the recital of the wars and political conflicts which reacted on the Church, but there was no reason for them to have taken pains to note the beginnings of city life, for which they were lacking in comprehension no less than in sympathy."

The opportunities for developing a lay spirituality at this time were not absent, had an effective group been in existence to undertake it. For the new lay spirit was, as Pirenne has pointed out, "allied with the most intense religious fervor." The proof of this may be seen in the "innumerable religious foundations with which the cities abounded, the pious and charitable confraternities which were so numerous there." Yet this new class found itself in conflict with ecclesiastical authority that was often too closely identified with the older conservative political and economic elements of the society and opposed the new cities in their bid for political liberty and constitutional government. And as Pirenne has noted, "If the bishops thundered against them with sentences of excommunication, and if, by way of counterattack, they sometimes gave way to pronounced anti-clerical tendencies, they were, for all of that, none the less animated by a profound and ardent faith." Here we see the beginning of the alienation of the new lay classes from the Church which will become the terrible "normal" condition in our contemporary world.

Since higher theological learning was the property of the educated and since these were largely clerics, this ardent faith was not given the benefit of long and fruitful contact with intellectual developments. Small wonder that the piety of laymen "showed itself with a naiveté, a sincerity and a fearlessness which easily led it beyond the bounds of orthodoxy. At all times, they were distinguished above everything else by the exuberance of their mysticism. It was this which, in the eleventh century, led them to side passionately with the religious reformers who were fighting simony and the marriage of priests; which, in the twelfth century, spread the contemplative asceticism of the Beguines and Beghards; which, in the thirteenth century, explained the enthusiastic reception which the Franciscans and Dominicans received. But it was this also which assured the success of all the novelties, all the exaggerations, and all the deformations of religious thought. After the twelfth century no heresy cropped out which did not immediately find some followers. It is enough to recall here the rapidity and the energy with which the sect of the Albigenses spread." Lay piety developed outside genuine contact with clerical learning in general until the coming of the mendicant orders of the thirteenth century. The often-related dream of the Pope who saw the Lateran tottering, held up by St. Francis and his little brothers alone, was a reflection of that situation.

In thus failing to understand the developing situation and the need it presented for a mature Christian lay population, Church leaders were, quite unwittingly, preparing to lose much of the future. The burghers of the Middle Ages, laymen yet deeply religious, "were thus singularly well prepared for the role which they were to play in the two great future movements of ideas: the Renaissance, the child of the lay mind, and the Reformation, toward which religious mysticism was leading."

In any society the strategically influential elites will shape the formation of those values and definitions of the human situation in terms of which policies and decisions are made. In medieval society, the ecclesiastic and monastic groups were the effective elites, and they failed to grasp the significance of the new developments taking place among the laity. This difficulty which persons in certain statuses and roles have in perceiving the problems of those in other strata of society is a persistent problem in sociology. As it affected the clergy of the Middle Ages it placed the Church in a position which was later to cause severe difficulties.

As Père Congar had said, "The fact that (in principle) the Church absorbed the world and imposed on it regulations proper to herself eventually meant the ignoring of the secularity of what is secular; preoccupation solely with the last end—the normal point of view of the clergy—led to the disregarding of secondary causes, the proper and immediate causes of things. . . . Medieval Christendom was, very generally speaking, a sacral regime, and by its hold of the spiritual over the temporal it brought about a union of the two that was in some ways premature and bought too cheaply. Earthly things were hardly considered except for their use in the Church's sacred work, hardly at all in their own reality and causalities, and so they were not taken really seriously and received neither the attention they deserve nor the development they call for. . . . Only since the end of sacral Christendom, with its monastic and clerical set-up, have we been able to get the full measure of the extent and requirements of the secularity of things and of the fidelity we owe them."

THE CATHOLIC TRADITION: The Church

We all know what happened. Laymen revolted against the Church in two directions. In the north of Europe, they often revolted in order to remain Christian in the face of what looked to them like ecclesiastical secularization and even exploitation. In the south they often revolted in order to assert a confident humanism. Between the two they built most of that civilization of modern Europe and America which has changed the whole world, and in which the Church has remained in the status half of an alien and half of a progenitor. The currents of Protestantism and the Enlightenment which were brought to America, and from which American Catholics have felt so strongly alienated in some respects, derived ultimately from these sources.

Moreover, it can hardly be said that Scholastic philosophy in its treatment of social problems prepared the Church to meet the new and important development of capitalism. Most theological writers—with a few exceptions, such as St. Antoninus of Florence—saw in the new world of commerce and trade not the accumulation of the necessary wealth for the development of a high civilization but simply the attendant social evils. The Church's stand against the outrages of greed and exploitation that accompanied these developments is greatly to its credit. Yet the battle was lost. The result of the failure of churchmen to understand what was actually happening and to relate it to the Christian life was that a secularized modern world evolved in which the sphere of religion was ever more narrowly restricted. The new social classes and strata that emerged were in many instances lost to Christianity or alienated from the Catholic Church.

The process of alienation was complicated by other aspects of contemporary life, lay and ecclesiastical, such as the rise of the sense of nationality; corruption in the Church, and the decline of fervor among the clergy. The result was, broadly speaking, the loss of a devout group which became Protestant and of a humanist group which later became Deist, and still later completely secularized. Protestantism and Liberalism (in its European philosophical sense) thus resulted in part at least from the failure of the Church's leaders to relate the Christian way of life to the dynamic changes that were in the process of transforming medieval and early modern society. In the event, Church leadership was replaced by a world outlook which secularized all values, since it was based on the experience and the values of lay classes which had developed outside of and away from Catholicism.

These remarks, the purpose of which is analytical rather than descriptive, must not be taken to imply that no lay Catholic culture developed in the Middle Ages, for nothing could be farther from the truth. The statement we have quoted from Pirenne bears testimony to such a development alongside the unfortunate incompleteness to which we call attention. Figures such as Dante, Chaucer, the author of *Piers Plowman* and later St. Thomas More and Erasmus (who although a priest certainly was imbued with much of the lay spirit) bear testimony to the richness of that lay Catholic culture. And in fact English universities not only had laymen within their confines in the later Middle Ages, but in the fourteenth century even offered business courses.

Moreover, the partial clerical monopoly of the higher learning, with its semimonastic approach to the world, was not the only factor involved in the loss of the layman. It was one among several such factors, but it was—and this is important for our present purposes—one that was not completely resolved, with the result that many of the problems it produced persisted. Furthermore, it is to be suspected that certain of the Tridentine reforms, in a not surprising reaction to Luther's thesis of the "priesthood of all believers," increased this tendency to set the cleric apart and to give him a monopoly of certain aspects of the religious life.

We have considered these developments because they are the background from which many contemporary attitudes have emerged. To what extent is our attitude toward the world still influenced by those earlier attitudes? To what extent are we still relegating lay groups to relative unimportance in terms of the Christian life? How much better prepared are Church leaders today to face the new problems that are upon us? Many clerics, especially in America, do not seem to have any deeper understanding of social and historical processes than did their predecessors. The social sciences, history, and the humanities—the intellectual products of the very developments we have been discussing—do not seem to have entered to any great extent into their intellectual formation or brought them into meaningful contact with the world of the educated layman.

We have seen that the failure of her leaders to understand the development of lay classes was most costly to the Church in the past, especially with respect to the emergence of a lay intelligentsia and the origins of modern science. Certainly science and humanism grew in soil that centuries of Christian culture had prepared. A. N. Whitehead has shown how the starting-points of modern science took for granted the basic Christian view of the world. But it is just as certain that despite their Christian foundation and the support which was originally given to them by the Church, science and humanism were in large part developed by lay classes increasingly alien to the Christian view as it was held and propagated by churchmen, and often in face of ecclesiastical opposition. Science proved to hold important keys to the future. Hence Catholic thought not only failed fully to meet the development of the modern world—the world of the layman—with an appropriate presentation of its basic message; it quite unintentionally and unknowlingly guaranteed that Catholic thought should enter the modern world on the defensive, and suspecting evil of much that was new, healthy, and great with promise for the future.

This is not made as an easy or hasty judgment. It is far easier to criticize with hindsight than to achieve a policy based upon genuine foresight. But foresight is what our present analysis is attempting to achieve. To what degree do we still see the intellectual world in a way analogous to the costly misapprehensions of our predecessors?

We have been urged by the Popes—especially the present Supreme Pontiff—to overhaul our thinking in this regard. But to what extent have any large numbers of us done so? In an earlier chapter we found that many teachers of religion had not even thought to scrutinize their attitudes and teaching in the light of these Papal pronouncements. If on the manifest and explicit level we find such situations, what is the situation on the deeper, more implicit level?

The over-cautiousness, the negative moral attitudes, the desire for conformity, the hedges placed about students' reading which we found on the manifest level of Catholic culture patterns

292

all point to the fact that some Catholic thinking is still being done in the historical framework from which modern society has long since emerged. It is obvious how detrimental this is to the development of a lay Catholic culture of richness and profundity. Moreover, such an attitude of defensiveness inhibits spontaneity and threatens originality, both necessary for the development of the intellectual life.

A recent example should be mentioned in this connection. It is well established that Catholics were among the first to explore the possibilities of modern Biblical scholarship. But since pioneering in thought and in knowledge means saying something new and involves the possibility of grave error, such Catholic efforts were not well received in some ecclesiastical quarters. Moreover, when the Modernists came forward with what was actually one of the most dangerous heresies to be presented for many centuries, Church leaders, although acting quite justifiably in the defense of the revealed deposit of faith, nevertheless did so in a manner that caused Catholic Biblical scholarship to lose ground for at least a generation—a setback from which it has succeeded in recovering only in the last two decades. The atmosphere—the informal, implicit expectations—in the Catholic milieu was such that creative scholarship was made difficult. This sort of defensiveness has militated in similar ways against creativity in other fields in our own times.

Even a cursory knowledge of history and sociology reveals that institutional systems tend to be conservative. The men who occupy positions in such systems come to define the basic purposes of the institution in the narrow status-perspectives of their own particular roles. Moreover, careerism—often of a subtle and not necessarily reprehensible kind—dictates that many who are not really interested or do not actually understand the issues involved will rally to the narrow definitions of the conservatives. Thus the innovator is seen as a kind of traitor.

Examples can be seen in many institutional systems of a quite various nature. General Billy Mitchell, an early advocate of air power, had difficulties with the army leadership and was court-martialed. Moreover, a rational, philosophical, or even a scientific base for the institution does not rule out such developments. In fact there have been several examples in the history of medicine and also of scientific research. The innovations of Pasteur, Ehrlich and Semmelweiss were resisted, and those of Mendel were neglected to the extent that they had to be rediscovered. It is one of the ever-present paradoxes of human life that progressing human activity demands, and actually always tends to establish, institutional structures as a stable context for itself. Yet such structures tend to become rigid and to inhibit creativity, and new advances can at times be made only in resistance to them.

This paradox cannot but affect the Church, since it is on one level a human organization. In fact, since the basic function of the Church cannot be other than a conservative one—to guard the deposit of faith—the problem is further complicated for churchmen. To the essential conservatism of the Church as an institution there is added the socially conditioned conservatism of the office-holder, whose views, as we have already observed, tend to be molded and circumscribed by his status.

From the point of view of the sociologist there are important analogies between the case of Galileo and that of Mitchell. The defensiveness which the conditions of modern times have forced upon the Church only circumscribes further the views of many Catholics toward the problems that arise. Many Catholics are aware of the analogies between what has at times happened in the Church in face of new situations and similar developments in other institutional contexts—governmental, scientific, and the like. But often they see them only as material for apologetics. The point they make is that the Church in history is on the natural level a human institution, and that therefore we must not condemn it for the blunders characteristic of human institutions. Such misadventures leave the supernatural nature of the Church unimpaired.

While such statements are perfectly true, they represent a completely inadequate response to the issue. For if such confusions and their unhealthy consequences for the Church are to be expected from the nature of the Church, then the rational and intelligent thing to do is to study their causes and attempt to restrict them and their injurious effects. To take any constructive course is to transform apologetics into a mere apology for our stupidities and shortsightedness, a serious distortion indeed.

The analysis of these latent culture patterns and the role they play in our lives becomes one of the important tasks of Catholic education. But all too often the extreme formalism of that education—the failure of the instructor to disclose the full implications of principles and definitions in terms of the student's experience—not only militates against understanding of the principles themselves but sets up a block to the perception of factual situations. Many Catholics, lay and clerical, in practice often confuse the rational motives for faith and the implications of Christian doctrine with an uncritical conformity to the prejudices of their own concrete social settings. How often, for example, editorials and statements by prominent Catholics on such subjects as psychoanalysis, the arts, international, co-operation or technology show less acquaintance with Catholic thought than with lower-middle-class prejudices. In this way is the Universal Church made to look and to act in a provincial manner, and this distorted point of view is presented to the world as Catholicity. Such distortions derive not from bad intentions, but from normal sociological processes. However, these processes can be understood, and to some extent safeguards against them can be developed which will obviate their most unfortunate consequences.

These elements in our latent culture patterns and social structures militate against the development of a vigorous intellectual life among us. On the other hand, only such an intellectual life can provide some measure of the larger view by means of which such unfortunate developments can, in part at least, be avoided.

Part 2: Have We Lost the Sense of Quest and the Sense of Mystery?

Related to our general defensiveness and a further aspect of the formalism to which we have already referred is a peculiar kind of Catholic rationalism inherited from the seventeenth century. Ironically enough, this rationalism outside the Church has definite anti-Christian implications; inside the Church it has—at least in our own day—anti-intellectual effects. Yet these consequences have not been recognized by many Catholics, who perceive concrete, existential problems only in their technical aspects, which require the attention of the expert in the practical sphere. They tend to think of some of the gravest difficulties affecting the life of society as "merely problems in the concrete order," not affecting "the essential order." They seem to think that no matter what happens in the "concrete order" (where, of course, everything happens that does happen), so long as the abstract philosophical heaven of essences is untouched and uncorrupted, there is no great problem for the Catholic. So long as the Church preserves and enunciates the principles governing right social order, the role of the Catholic is fulfilled. Such is the strange idealism which lurks behind this point of view! In its effects it is indistinguishable from anti-intellectualism, and it accounts, in part at least, for the relative paucity of Catholic writing on and participation in such areas as community relations, urban planning, religious pluralism, the ethics of mass communication, and civil liberties.

This philosophical approach seems characterized by a positive addiction to formulae. Correctness of formula often threatens to replace understanding, while rote memorization is held to be the essence of learning. The results are often lamentable. Words replace reality. The effect is often to make it appear to ourselves that we have all worthwhile knowledge and that any further quest is unnecessary. Or that we have explained and shown the rational transparency of all existence and that as a result there are no mysteries to challenge the mind to a cognitive quest. Everything profound is thus rendered superficial and everything that eludes the net of a formula is almost considered nonexistent.

Many teachers of religion seem to see their jobs as providing a lifetime supply of answers to "difficulties" to be memorized and "filed" away for future reference, and often the role of the laity is conceived as that of having in readiness the "Catholic answer" to give to non-Catholic friends. There seems to be an implicit notion abroad in some quarters that the Catholic mind will be the product of the catechism, the scholastic manual, and finally of the pamphlet rack. Too often Catholic college students memorize formulae from philosophical textbooks, formulae which condense the subtle thought of generations of creative effort. It does not occur to some Catholics that profound knowledge cannot really be transmitted in this way.

Knowledge and knowing mean seeing something new, seeing it in a new way, seeing another aspect to reality that one did not see before. Thus, while the modern world has been engaged upon the great adventure of science, Catholic thought has often tended to regard such developments as a series of "problems" and "difficulties" to be withstood and met with cautious, apologetic compromise. Since in the view of some teachers every Catholic college senior must be equipped to handle all important questions in the field of apologetics, the emphasis must be placed on "covering the ground." A student mentality must be developed in which there are no lacunae challenging original investigation.

One may summarize the issue here briefly as follows: Unless it is possible for a Catholic youth to understand his faith, to know what faith really is, and maintain his faith, without having on the one hand to be spoon-fed when genuine difficulties are involved, and, on the other, having his head jammed with ready-made formulae memorized in religion and philosophy classes, there is really no hope for the development of an intellectual life among Catholics. For to be an intellectual means to be engaged in a quest. As Aristotle long ago noted, knowledge begins with wonder. Many Catholic students get an impression that there is really very little wonderful about their faith—that it is so close to the rationally obvious that the real wonder is that outsiders do not see it as such. Such Catholics often seem to be puzzled by the existence of a long, honorable, and honestly searching philosophical tradition outside their own semisectarian world. They even express impatience with it, and feel superior to the "confusions" of modern thinkers over issues which they themselves have failed to recognize and too frequently fear when they recognize them even partially.

Such a frame of mind is based upon quite erroneous implicit assumptions, and such assumptions militate against genuine and profound Catholic contact with the non-Catholic tradition. The great Protestant and secular thinkers of America are not just men who make mistakes, like the "adversaries" of the scholastic manual. They have positive things to say to those American Catholics who have neglected the search itself. The partial segregation of

Catholic life from that of the general community adds difficulties in that respect, but further defensiveness concealed under lethargic self-satisfaction is hardly an adequate response to the situation. We repeat: to be an intellectual means to be engaged in a quest, and if to be a Christian has come to mean to have the whole of truth that matters—albeit in capsule form—in advance (to know, for example, that "Plato had an erroneous theory of human nature," that "Comte held God knows what, which is absurd") without ever having been introduced to a genuine philosophical experience, then we are hopelessly lost.

If the Christian faith cannot enable a man to face the unknown without blinding himself to the fact that the mystery is there; to follow, in the unknown, the traces of meaning accessible to his mind; to live with his face to the existential winds that blow across the great void which modern science has opened up before us in many spheres: then it cannot really be Christian faith. To attempt to substitute for such a faith a worldly human consensus of cultural attitudes is a dishonest—and an unworkable—procedure.

It is quite true, as we have said, that a naive youth cannot be thrown into the depths of modern secular thought to sink or swim. But he can be taught to swim.

These matters need much more empirical investigation than a study of this length can provide, but attempts to study them will meet considerable opposition based upon a fear of frankness and a false reticence in face of reality. The implicit attitudes which constitute the latent culture patterns are an important aspect of the social milieu; they can be the most influential so far as what we are actually doing in respect to the problem under discussion is concerned.

We must ask: Is it true that many Catholics are not moved by the intellectual challenge of the modern scientific and scholarly world because they are told—implicitly—that they already know everything important—or can know it in capsule form—and that there is nothing further to look for? Are they also allowed to infer that a genuine intellectual quest is incompatible with faith? Are they taught to accept their faith not as a stimulus to a Christian adventure but as a soporific? Does Christianity, which should act as a Socratic gadfly upon them, actually serve as a kind of intellectual tsetse fly?

Part 3: Lay Christianity and American Social Mobility

The failure of Church leadership to meet the needs of lay classes created by modern developments is seen in a peculiar form in the United States. The history of this country involves a continuation of that process of social mobility and democratization which de Tocqueville characterized as a "providential drift" of several centuries' duration. Social progress in America has been marked not only by an increase in material means and in leisure for the whole population but also by a progressively higher attainment in terms of formal education and other cultural benefits, such as art, music, literature, etc. As is well known, among the factors which medieval Christianity was not prepared to meet and to understand in the emerging urban civilization of the layman was the factor of social mobility. Medieval Christian thought as a whole conceived the social order as a hierarchic structure in equilibrium, more or less static. The instability which had posed a constant threat to Europe for many centuries after the fall of the Roman Empire had had the effect of concentrating the attention of Christians on the need for order. Order and stability became almost ends in themselves, and change and development were not sufficiently understood. The Christian sense of history to be found in the Greek and Latin Fathers and in the epistles of St. Paul was not related by most medieval thought to the concrete processes of social development. We have seen how the status-conditioned outlook of the medieval cleric had the effect of obscuring these aspects of reality. Catholic thought emphasized ontology rather than history, an emphasis which may have led to an excessive concern with essence at the expense of existence. One important consequence was that the Catholic mind often failed to recognize in the intensified social mobility of the rising civilization a factor full of potentialities for the future; failed to foresee it as the great historic process which, beginning in the early Middle Ages with the development of cities and the manumission of serfs, was to continue into revolutionary modern times and to reach a kind of high point in the prosperous urban American society of our own day.

THE CATHOLIC TRADITION: The Church

There are some conservatives today who pretend to see in this process only the vulgarization of culture and the leveling of all values. Such leveling tendencies are undeniably involved, but a sober sociological analysis reveals other, more positive, elements. Man's conquest of nature and his creation of the conditions for a prosperous society can scarcely be said to be without spiritual significance. No one proposes that we return to the unheated churches of the Middle Ages, that we give up modern medical advances, that we substitute for the comfortable home of the common man in America the hovel of the thirteenth-century peasant. Can the mortality rate of the Middle Ages before scientific control had been established over epidemics be considered a positive value? Here again we must not take refuge in verbalism. While we must not be unaware of the corrupting and corroding factors in modern developments, we must also realize that in this country capitalism, democracy, science, and a faith in the common man have laid the foundation for a social order which goes further toward meeting the standards of Christian humanism than that of any era in the history of the world. Yet the basic processes of social mobility which have issued in these developments were not recognized for what they were even by some of the greatest Christian thinkers of past centuries. They counseled instead contentment in one's station here below; many of the scholastics conceived the desire to rise in status as an evil.

In this country the Church did implicitly encourage social mobility. It was closely associated with, and affected by, the aspirations of Catholic immigrants, and even in their status-conditioned perspective the clergy recognized that the Americanization of the Church depended upon the upward social mobility of its members. But the fact remains that this recognition was more a matter of practice than of precept. Explicitly and in theory the Church in America came no closer to a confrontation of the great "providential drift" than had the Church in Europe. It never faced the theological problem posed for the Christian life of the laity by this factor of social mobility. The clergy, which continued to do most of the thinking for the Catholic community, did not see this problem as one of those demanding its attention. And since social mobility was among the most significant processes at work in American culture, failure at this point meant in large part a failure to come to grips with America and its spiritual significance. The result has been that a concrete Christian way of life built around this basic American process has not appeared. There has not been developed, for example, a "spirituality of the suburbs," if we may use that term. One of the consequences is that there has been produced and maintained in the American Catholic mind a cleavage between the sacred and secular spheres.

This divided Catholic mind has not been able to seize in its wholeness the problem presented by life in American society. It has been intent on a cautious morality confined to certain areas, while aspects of American life which superficially are morally neutral but are in fact full of possibilities for spiritual damage in the long run are left unevaluated. Outside the narrow moral sphere which American Catholicism has taken as its central province, the American Catholic is assimilated to the materialistic society, about him in some of its most pernicious aspects. It is for this reason that middle-class Catholic ideals so often appear to be false, shallow, and derivative. Catholics tend to be imitators of non-Catholics in everything from educational procedures to tastes in house furnishings, but they do not always show much understanding of what is best and most worthy of imitation in the culture of non-Catholics. Catholics in sermons and editorials often decry the "materialism" of our age, but it is not always clear what they consider that "materialism" to be. Indeed, the hypothesis proposed here is that outside a specifically religious, and often quite closed-off, sphere of consciousness which we may designate as "sacred," American Catholic middle-class life often tends to be more materialistic than is that of many Protestant and secularist groups. That is one reason why learning, which does not receive great material rewards in this country, and the learned professions, which often demand material sacrifices, make a considerably weaker appeal to Catholics in comparison with many other groups, while a very high proportion of Catholics enter the comparatively lucrative professions of law and medicine. It is not the only reason. But it is one that deserves attention from us. There is evidence to suggest that large numbers of American Catholics do not understand the possibility of any kind of genuine vocation outside that strictly segregated "sacred" sphere. Learning, the arts, literature—these fields offer little attraction in terms of Christian vocation to these people. This naturally intensifies the tendency to see the clergy as the thinkers, while the laity devote themselves to worldly tasks which they try to keep as morally innocuous as circumstances permit.

Part 4: Do We Avoid the Problems of Maturation?

Certain aspects of Catholic culture patterns in this country, both on manifest and on latent levels, have been examined in order to reveal the motives and ideals which are operative in the American Catholic community. We have endeavored to uncover what is expected and acceptable, what lies at the bottom of certain Catholic attitudes, what the actual context of Catholic behavior is beneath the words and expressions which play the double role of expressing and concealing the deeper latent level. These basic attitudes, despite their indirect expression in most cases, will have the most important influence upon the socialization process and the formation of character.

Thus, from one angle our study of American Catholic culture patterns is a study of the factors which shape the personality structures of our young people in the course of their development. Here we shall be concerned with the effect of these patterns —especially their latent content—on one aspect of personality development. What is the effect of these factors upon the growth to maturity?

Contemporary American society is based upon education, science, and the exploitation of technology, and made up of diverse groups and values. In such a society adult attitudes and behavior require clamness in face of confusion, patience with one's own ignorance, reasonable attitudes toward differences, and flexible action in meeting the unexpected. Balance and levelheadedness in face of new situations, and moral integrity, together with tolerance for honest differences, are most important. To these must be added the ability to sympathize with those whose background and experiences may be quite different from one's own.

The achievement of maturity requires successful mastery of the concrete problems which life presents to the growing person. Maturation is a process marked not only by continuity but also by radical discontinuities, which are often experienced subjectively as crises. Such crises mark transition points, and the way in which they are met is of vital importance to the future psychological, intellectual, and moral health of the person. Yet American Catholic culture often seems implicitly to encourage an evasion of these necessary crises so far as is possible. What is suggested here is that the verbalism and the defensiveness so characteristic of much of American Catholic life result in a refusal on the part of many to face frankly and honestly the risk of growth in the psychological and intellectual sense.

Just as the great adventure of modern man, the scientific exploration of the unknown, is too often seen by American Catholics as a vain quest since they already have the whole of essential truth, or as a source of "difficulties" to the faith which must be counteracted by nice formulae, so, it is suggested here, the great adventure of the adolescent, the exploration of the new world of adulthood opening out before him, is often treated as one in which a cautious resistance to change is best, or in which challenges are seen as difficulties to be got around with as little risk to the ideas of childhood as possible.

To be an adult Christian means the growth to maturity of one's Christian outlook as well as of other aspects of the personality. To make the transition from the faith of childhood to that of manhood involves drastic discontinuities: when the stage of childhood has come to an end, there is often a hiatus, marked by intense emotional and intellectual tension, before the stage of manhood can be entered by the re-integrated personality. But it seems as if American Catholic culture patterns and practices often encourage the avoidance of such normal crises of personal growth. One is led to suspect that the improper handling of these crises may be a prime source of leakage to the Church, and such leakage is terrible damaging because often it is people of genuine intellectual caliber who are lost.

Sometimes one is told by priests that youths are lost at this time because of moral and not because of intellectual difficulties. A diagnosis in terms of such a facile "either/or" often seems completely unrealistic. These crises are of a mental-emotional-moral nature, as in fact are all crises, and they are part of the normal growth process. They must be understood and dealt with as such. To see them merely as the result of moral problems is the survival of that medieval mentality which looked on the heretic as always in bad faith, combined with seventeenth-century rationalistic psychology.

Msgr. Romano Guardini has written an article that contains a great deal of insight concerning "Faith and Doubt in the Stages of Life." He has shown how each stage involves its own peculiar religious and moral problems and how each at the same time presents a challenge and an opportunity for spiritual growth and development. Calling our attention to the important discontinuities involved in growth, Msgr. Guardini writes: "Human development runs along not evenly but in segments. The child's condition of soul does not merge gradually into that of the youth, or the youth's faith into that of the mature person; each stage is characterized by its distinctive form. These forms do not slip easily from one into the other; the new form supersedes the earlier one. To be more explicit, it is rather like this: the first form develops, finds expression in the ways of thinking and feeling and in dealing with things and people. Meanwhile, the new form is in the process of taking shape below the first. Then the new form breaks through more or less suddenly, and affects the person's whole nature. In every case a reconstruction is involved—often even a violent shattering of the old form. On the other hand, it is the same life fulfilling itself. All that one had experienced, learned, and appropriated remains, and bears the stamp of the preceding period. Thus arise tensions, complications, ambiguities and contradictions—crises of development. Since it is not an abstraction who believes, but a real, living person, these changes affect faith itself, and become religious crises."

The hypothesis proposed here is that American Catholicism —except in the individual work of certain thoughtful priests and sisters—does not meet these crises with anything like adequacy. It fails to recognize them as normal, and by its defensiveness and its verbalism it inhibits a fruitful working through of them. It is oriented to smoothing out difficulties instead of meeting and overcoming challenges, and as a result it fails to integrate such crises into a pattern of spiritual and intellectual growth for its youth.

Thomas Francis O'Dea

Why is it that converts seem to be more creative in intellectual activities than so-called "born Catholics"? Is it because they have gone through the necessary crises of growth? Is it that such crises have often been evaded by "born Catholics" and therefore a comparable maturity is not reached and comparable creativity is not produced? Some Catholics respond to a discussion of this kind by saying, "Yes, that is all well and good, but won't a lot of people lose their faith?" What strange half-conscious attitudes such fears reveal! The latent culture patterns involved imply that faith cannot stand growth. The risks are real, and no attempt should be made to minimize that fact; but the potential for growth is no less real, and it too should not be minimized.

It is suggested here as a working hypothesis that as a result of the failure to relate social mobility to the spiritual life in any but an extrinsic way, and the failure to develop institutionalized culture patterns to enable Catholic youth to meet the crises of growth openly and with beneficial consequences, immaturity in the cultural and intellectual sense is one of the striking characteristics of American Catholicism as a whole. Hence the American Catholic community not only fails to produce an intellectual elite, but even tends to suspect intellectuals because American Catholics sense the relation of the intellectual to these two partially repressed American problems. The intellectual symbolizes in some way the facing of crises and the challenges of uncertainty, as well as a critical attitude toward the accepted values of middle-class life, especially those which are most crassly materialistic. Catholics, who pride themselves on their spirituality, are more prone to support anti-intellectualism than are many other of their countrymen. They see the intellectuals as those who seek to reveal the basic existential ambiguities that they themselves wish to evade. They often project this dilemma onto current politics and see such intellectuals—who are in our culture, for all the reasons we have examined above, often liberals—as "disloyal." One sometimes feels that for some Catholics "loyalty" is so supreme a virtue that it would be disloyal and almost sacrilegious to ask, "Loyalty to what?"

For such Catholics this too is an intellectual-emotional-moral problem. To the extent that faith—not the verbal arguments for it but the real intellectual hold on it—is weak, to that extent the intellectual is seen as an enemy. If one's life is projected upon the fragile bridge of a superficial faith, then any criticism becomes a severe threat. Any atmosphere in which Catholic values are not taken for granted—not simply not violated in practice but never challenged—becomes dangerous. But in our society, in view of the last four hundred years of Western history, Catholic values are bound to be challenged in most intellectual circles. If the Catholic is not prepared for this, he is simply not prepared for life.

If the Catholic has an immature faith and many unsolved, partially repressed problems in his own mind, then the intellectual critic becomes the external surrogate of the repressed interior questionings, and the well-known psychological mechanism of displacing aggression and guilt ensues. One sees a good deal of what looks like this—the rigidity and hardly disguised panic are telltale signs—in American Catholic life, but such Catholics, often the victims of their facile and superficial rationalism and verbalism, do not seem to see what is going on. If one has repressed the unsolved problems at one of the crises of transition to which modern psychology has called our attention, one will of course have one's intellectual difficulties compounded with psychological ones, and often with moral ones.

From these problems the Church suffers two important kinds of loss. First, there is the positive secession of potential intellectuals among our youth. Some of them go on to become important in the cultural scene. Every sensitive parish priest can tell you of this kind of problem. Secondly, others, who do not revolt, sink into a kind of stultified intellectual lethargy, avoiding dangerous areas of thought or life; or they may fail ever to have had their intellects vitally engaged in living at all. This last category is not necessarily confined to laymen. Such persons may channel their energies into other areas, but it is to be suspected that their activities in those areas are often unrelated in anything except the most residual way to the life of faith which they continue in terms of the performance of the required practices.

Certain aspects of this problem may be seen again in many Catholic utterances and even in Sunday sermons in some parts of the country. What is most noticeable is the relative absence of the presentation of the great dogmas of the Catholic religion in preaching and writing, combined with a great deal of unwarranted dogmatizing on all sorts of unessential questions, precisely in fact in the areas where the Universal Church leaves the Catholic explicitly unbound and urges him to use his own judgment. Persons in this category dogmatize about everything from the Fifth Amendment to psychoanalysis, although their knowledge is usually not proportionate to their misdirected zeal. Such behavior is found unfortunately among clerics as well as laymen. It deserves to become the object of serious study. If such attitudes are in fact widespread in the Catholic milieu, and if they make up a considerable part of the latent content of Catholic culture patterns in certain areas of this country, then it is small wonder that no intellectual stratum of sizable proportions has emerged.

Hans Küng
1928-

Hans Küng was born in Lucerne, Switzerland, in 1928. He received licentiates in philosophy (1951) and theology (1955) from the Gregorian University in Rome, then in 1957 was granted the doctorate in theology by the Institut Catholique, Sorbonne, University of Paris. He had been ordained in 1954 and spent the years 1957 to 1959 in pastoral work in Lucerne. After a year as assistant in dogmatic theology at the University of Muenster, Germany, he received an appointment as ordinary professor at the University of Tübingen in 1960 and has been there since. In 1962 Pope John XXIII appointed him a "peritus" to the Second Vatican Council.

Küng has demonstrated an extraordinary capacity for work. His doctoral dissertation on Karl Barth's doctrine of justification began a stream of publications that continues in a most impressive way. In 1960 came the first German edition of The Council, Reform, and Reunion, *introducing many people to the themes that would soon prevail as Vatican II got under-way. His ability to simplify and popularize was demonstrated in 1962 by* That the World May Believe: Letters to Young People. *The same year his special studies in the doctrine of the Church were set forth in* Structures of the Church. *Cardinal Cushing of Boston wrote a preface for the English edition. In 1963 he published his theological reflections on Vatican II up to that point as* The Council in Action, *and edited with Yves Congar and Daniel O'Hanlon the best* Council Speeches of Vatican II.

The selection given here is the first chapter of his 1967 work, The Church, *which represented Küng's most ambitious project up to then. In the footsteps of Moehler and Adam before him, he continued the Tübingen tradition of critical biblical and historical investigation. In 1968 came* Truthfulness: The Future of the Church, *in 1970* Infallible? An Inquiry, *in 1971* Why Priests?, *and in 1974 his comprehensive* On Being a Christian, *a runaway best-seller in Germany.*

Küng is easily the most controversial Catholic theologian of renewal on the scene today. Many, including some in high places in Rome, would like to see him silenced, feeling that his criticism goes too far. His restless spirit disturbs many. As he himself put it: "I have an infinite intellectual curiosity. I am never satisfied. I must always know more about everything so I can detect just what are the problems. I do not have many prejudices before starting, because I do not fear the outcome." But to belittle his contribution because of questionable aspects or shortcomings in his theology is the essence of myopia. As Avery Dulles expressed it in 1977: "I strongly believe that Küng should continue to have his say in the Catholic church. Like any theologian who moves out ahead of the pack, he has become an object of vilification for theological vigilante groups. Against such malicious attacks he deserves to be defended. He merits our respect, for he has few equals in the church of our day for theological talent, courage and sincere devotion to the truth."

As for Küng's book The Church, *Dulles did not hesitate to describe it as "perhaps the most useful synthesis of ecclesiology by any Christian in the past generation. . . . (It) is erudite, comprehensive, ecumenical and eminently readable. No contemporary ecclesiologist, Protestant or Catholic, can afford to ignore this book."*

THE CHURCH

CHAPTER I

HISTORICITY AND THE IMAGE OF THE CHURCH

1. ESSENCE AND HISTORICAL FORMS

T he Church is rapidly approaching its third millennium. For the world in which the Church lives, the future has already begun. Science has begun to investigate both microcosm and macrocosm, both the atom and the universe; there are increasingly rapid and more efficient means of communication and transport; there is a wealth of new instruments, synthetic materials, methods of productions are being rationalized; the expectation of human life has been increased by a decade or more; tremendous achievements have been made in physics, chemistry, biology, medicine, psychology, sociology, economics, historical research. All in all, despite those worldwide catastrophes and perils which have been the particular fate of our century, the story has been one of breathtaking progress. The highly industrialized nations of Europe and America have spread their knowledge throughout the world, the peoples of Asia and Africa have come to life; the world is becoming one and a single economic unit, a single civilization, perhaps even a single culture is emerging.

And what of the Church? Has the future begun for it too? In some respect perhaps, but in many others it has not. At all events we have surely come to realize that the Church cannot, even if it wants to, stand aside from this world-wide reorientation which heralds a new era; for the Church lives in this, not in another world. Our age, like all times of transition, is one of unrest. For all the triumphs of science and technology, there is a feeling of disquiet which finds expression in art, in films and in the theatre, in literature and in philosophy: it is an experience of individuals and nations alike. The Church too, behind its facade of seemingly timeless self-confidence, is affected by this unrest, since it affects the people who make up the Church. It is a healthy, even salutary, unrest and it should give us cause for hope, not anxiety. What looks like a serious crisis may mark the moment of new life; what looks like a sinister threat may in reality be a great opportunity.

Enormous tasks, both familiar and unfamiliar, confront a Church which sees itself as a part of this changed and changing world and claims to exist for the world. It must renew, reassemble and revitalize its people, who have often become stale and rigid because of traditional forms and formulas. It must preach the Gospel in countries which were once Christian but are now largely pagan, to educated and uneducated people who are today estranged from the Church and its message. It must achieve an ecumenical encounter and a reunion of separated Christians and Christian Churches. It must establish sympathetic dialogue with the great non-Christian religions, Islam, Buddhism, and Hinduism, in the context of a unified world. It must play its proper part in solving the world's enormous problems, helping to prevent wars and promote peace, to fight against famine and poverty, to educate the masses. There are many problems; there are many opportunities.

The Church cannot face these problems and use these opportunities if it is a prisoner of its own theories and prejudices, its own forms and laws, rather than being a prisoner of its Lord. As the prisoner of the Lord it is truly free, ready and willing to serve the constantly new requirements, needs and aspiration of mankind.

Our concept of the Church is basically influenced by the form of the Church at any given time. All too easily the Church can become a prisoner of the image it has made for itself at one particular period in history. Every age has its own image of the Church, arising out of a particular historical situation; in every age a particular view of the Church is expressed by the Church in practice, and given conceptual form, *post hoc* or *ante hoc*, by the theologians of the age. At the same time, there is a constant factor in the various changing historical images of the Church, something which survives however much the history of mankind, of the Church and of theology may vary, and it is on this that we must concentrate. There are fundamental elements and perspectives in the Church which are not derived from the Church itself; there is an "essence" which is drawn from the permanently decisive origins of the Church. This constant factor in the history of the Church and of its understanding of itself is only revealed in change; its identity exists only in variability, its continuity only in changing circumstances, its permanence only in varying outward appearances. In short, the "essence" of the Church is not a matter of metaphysical stasis, but exists only in constantly changing historical "forms". If we want to discover this original and permanent "essence", given that it is something dynamic rather than something static and rigid, we must look at the constantly changing historical "forms" of the Church. It is vital to distinguish permanent and continuing elements from changing and transient features, and to make this distinction we must take into account right from the start the fact that the Church's image contains impermanent features, conditioned by time.

The starting-point of the following discussion is the fact that the "essence" of the Church is expressed in changing historical forms. Rather than talking about an ideal Church situated in the abstract celestial spheres of theological theory, we shall consider the *real* Church as it exists in our world, and in human history. The New Testament itself does not begin by laying down a doctrine of the Church which has then to be worked out in practice; it starts with the Church as *reality*, and reflection upon it comes later. The real Church is first and foremost a happening, a fact, an historical event. *The real essence of the real Church is expressed in historical form.* There are two important points here:

1. Essence and form *cannot be separated.* The essence and the form of the Church should not be divorced from one another, but must be seen as a whole. The distinction between essence and form is a conceptual, not a real, distinction. There is not and never was, in fact, an essence of the Church by itself, separate, chemically pure, distilled from the stream of historical forms. What is changing and what is unchanging cannot be neatly divided up; while there are permanent factors, there are no absolutely irreformable areas. The relationship between essence and form is not simply that between core and skin. An essence

without form is formless and hence unreal; a form without essence is insubstantial and hence equally unreal. For all its relativity, historical form should not be seen as totally irrelevant and contrasted with an essence existing somewhere "beyond" or "above" it. It is all too easy for us to retreat into harmless theologumena, remote from real life, about the "essence" of the Church, and so try to avoid having to make historical judgments and distinctions. At the same time it is equally easy for us to disregard the essence of the Church which is dictated by its origins, to be mentally lazy and uncritical and concern ourselves simply with the present form of the Church, becoming absorbed with ecclesiastical activity or even resigning ourselves to a totally passive role. We can only glimpse the real Church if we see the essence of the Church as existing in its historical form, rather than as existing beyond and above it.

2. Essence and form *are not identical*. The essence and the form of the Church should be not equated, but must be recognized and distinguished. Even if the distinction between essence and form is a conceptual one, it is none the less necessary. How else can we decide what is permanent in the changing form of the Church? How else can we judge its actual historical form? How else can we establish a criterion, a norm, which will enable us to decide what is legitimate in any historical and empirical manifestation of the Church? No form of the Church, not even that in the New Testament, embraces its essence in such a way that it is simply part and parcel of it. And no form of the Church, not even that in the New Testament, mirrors the Church's essence perfectly and exhaustively. Only when we distinguish in the changing forms of the Church its permanent but not immutable essence, do we glimpse the real Church.

The essence of the Church is therefore always to be found in its historical form, and the historical form must always be understood in the light of and with reference to the essence.

2. THE DEVELOPMENT OF THE IMAGE OF THE CHURCH IN CHURCH HISTORY

Ecclesiology, the theological expression of the Church's image, varies, consciously, with the varying forms of the real ecclesia. A few historical examples will suffice to illustrate this point.

Even in the *ecclesiology of the primitive Church* there are significant distinctions and variations, as can be seen from the following simplified account. While the second-century apologists, with the exception of a few passages of Justin, scarcely use the word "ecclesia"—their apologetics were concerned with the one God and with Christ, not with the Church—the idea of the Church becomes important in the writings of the later Fathers. It is one of the main themes of their theological treatises and of their exegesis both of Old and New Testaments. The image of the Church in the first three centuries was determined by the opposition between a hostile pagan State and a Church which, under various kinds of persecution, knew both victory and defeat. In the following centuries, however, the image was determined by the harmony between an established Church, reaping the fruits of victory, and the Christian empire. Hippolytus of Rome, for example, saw the empire as a satanic imitation of Christ's kingdom, in complete contrast to the later imperialistic theology of Eusebius, the Church historian and court bishop. For him the empire was divinely ordained to prepare the way for Christianity, since both had arisen about the same time; he saw the Christian emperor as the Church's defender and protector against irreligion and false gods.

Ecclesiology varies according to whether, as is often the case in the writings of the apostolic Fathers, it is a means for the leaders of the community to edify their people, or, as is variously the case in Irenaeus, Cyprian and Augustine, it is a weapon for a frontal assault on heresy. A theologian who prefers to believe in the unobtrusive inner development of truth and its gradual victory and who, living in the subtle intellectual atmosphere of the hellenistic world, regards refined dogmatic formulas as the most effective, will produce a particular brand of ecclesiology, even if he is principally concerned with christology and trinitarian doctrine. A totally different kind of ecclesiology will be produced by his Latin contemporary, who belongs to a Church which sees itself as *acies ordinata*, who interprets Christ and the Church in terms of battles and victories, rewards and punishments, and who erects his theology on the basis of strong ecclesiastical institutions, clearly defined rights and a smoothly running organization. A particular form of ecclesiology will be created if, in the wake of Greek Neo-Platonism, the Church is seen principally as the school of truth and a fellowship of adepts; if the pure apprehension of teaching of truth and the symbolic and saving power of sacred rituals are seen to be all-important; and if the Church's aim is seen as the establishing of a universal, all-embracing philosophy and the setting up of a culture community on a religious basis. A very different form of ecclesiology will result if, more on the basis of the pragmatic popular philosophy of Roman stoicism, the Church is principally seen as a well-ordered community governed by laws; if the holiness and obedience of Church members and an ecclesiastical order which imposes strict penitentiary discipline and precise norms for daily life are seen as all-important; if the Gospel is regarded as the "new law", preparing the way for a holy State as part of God's kingdom on earth. In the former case there is the danger that the Church will be platonically hypostatized and made purely abstract; there is the risk of interpreting Scripture ecclesiologically in an arbitrary and allegorical way, and a risk of ecclesiological triumphalism of a purely intellectual kind. In the latter case there is the danger of a juridical approach in theory and practice, of an ecclesiastical legalism which is purely formalistic; there is the risk of clericalism and of ecclesiological triumphalism of an authoritarian and traditionalistic kind.

Other differences in ecclesiology can be noted. Some ecclesiologies, as in Alexandrian theology of the third century, and Origen in particular, will stress the priesthood of all believers, and draw a more important distinction between imperfect unthinking believers and perfect conscious gnostics than between laity and clergy; for them the holy doctors of the Church will basically hold the highest rank in the Church (ecclesiastical office is seen here primarily as a teaching office). Other ecclesiologies, as in the African and especially the Roman theology of the same time, will emphasize the idea of office and its legal character; they will ascribe the highest authority in the Church to the bishops (ecclesiastical office is seen here primarily as a governing office), and will minimize the importance of the priesthood of all believers and the charismatic element in the Church. The stress on ecclesiastical office can itself take different forms. In Roman theology, for example, the authority of the bishop is seen as derived solely from his official position, and as quite independent of his personal sanctity. The apostolic succession is primarily interpreted in an historica-canonical way and the achievements of a bishop are measured in terms of laws and correct formulations. An alternative view, taken by Cyprian, following Tertullian, is that the authority of the bishop depends essentially on the charismatic gift of the Spirit and hence on his personal sanctity. In this view the apostolic succession must also be a pneumatic succession, and the personal qualities of the bishop are taken fundamentally into account in measuring his success. There are also differences in the theologies of office. For some theologians it is the *episcopate* which is first and foremost the guarantee of unity; the person of Peter is regarded simply as a *sign* of Church unity and his successors are only accorded a kind of honorary primacy; this was the view of Cyprian and many other, especially Eastern, theologians. Other theologians see the *Roman bishop* as the primary guarantor of unity; the person of Peter is regarded as the *repository* of Church unity and his successors have a specific canonical primacy; Stephen I was the first pope to cite Jesus' words about the rock in Matthew 16:18 in this connection and these views were later held even more clearly by Siricius, Innocent I, Celestine I, and Leo I.

The image of the Church in the first centuries shows enormous variations; see the writings of Hermas, Clement of Rome, Ignatius of Antioch, Irenaeus of Lyons and Hippolytus of Rome; Victor I, Stephen I, Leo I, Gelasius I and Gregory I; Clement of Alexandria, Origen and the Cappadocians; Tertullian, Cyprian and Augustine; Pachomius, the Egyptian monks, Benedict of Nursia and Western monasticism.

Changes and variations are equally striking in medieval ecclesiology. At some periods, as in the first millennium, ecclesiology arises unsystematically from the life of the Church, is not particularly emphasized, and is dealt with in conjunction with the doctrine of redemption. At other times, it becomes a special part of the Church's teaching, is dealt with consciously and systematically, and may even appear in the form of a separate and detailed tractatus, as became customary after

Boniface VIII's quarrel with Philip the Fair, beginning with those theologians involved in the quarrel, James of Viterbo, Giles of Rome and John of Paris. There is an important difference between ecclesiologies which regard the legal constitution of the Church as relatively unimportant (cf. Rupert of Deutz, Joachim of Flora and others), and those which stress the legal and institutional aspects of the Church and the power and authority of the clergy, ideas which are especially expressed in systematic theology (cf., in addition to the medieval canonists, Thomas Aquinas in particular; for him submission to papal authority is necessary for salvation).

It is by no means unimportant whether an ecclesiology attributes to canon law a subordinate and serving function or whether it sees canon law as having a superior and dominating role, as something which provides ecclesiology with its materials and limits it with fixed concepts and formulas, as something which takes Church laws, laid down by men, as setting compulsory limitations on theological speculation. This latter view held sway particularly after the establishing of the faculty of canon law at Bologna in the twelfth century. Again, there are two completely different ways in which the power of the bishops can be strengthened. One, the method of the sixth-century Neo-Platonist who assumed the mask of Dionysius the Areopagite, disciple of Paul, was based on verbose mystical interpretations of the Church's cult; the bishop was held up as the bearer of mystical powers and the community was seen as bound to him above all by the cultic mysteries; the earthly ecclesiastical organization was depicted as reflecting the heavenly hierarchy. A different method, as followed by the Frankish jurist at the beginning of the Middle Ages, who was believed to be Isidore of Seville, was based on ingenious forgeries of ecclesiastical laws; the bishop was seen as the bearer of all legal powers and the community as bound to him by the power of the keys. This latter view, in order to guarantee the Church's independence of the State, decisively strengthened papal primacy and decisively weakened the metropolitans and provincial councils. Under Charlemagne the actual leadership of the whole Church is ascribed to the *emperor*, whom the Carolingian theologians called the defender and guide of the Church; it is through him that the bishops hold their sacred rights, can call councils and choose popes. At a later point this leadership is ascribed to the *pope*, a view presented with renewed vigour by Nicholas I, who referred to the popes as princes of the whole earth. A different ecclesiology is implied in each case. A similar contrast in ecclesiologies is implied when on the one hand the Saxon and Salic emperors of the pre-Gregorian period defend and develop the idea of a harmony between *regnum* and *sacerdotium* and a sacral-priestly overlordship by a ruler ("the Lord's anointed" and "the vicar of Christ"!) who appoints bishops and can appoint and dethrone popes; and on the other hand Gregory VII and the Gregorians in the so-called Investiture contest put up the opposing view, confronting the traditional rights of monarchy and nobility with a renewed and centralized canon law, defending an hierarchical Church which claims to be independent of the regnum and a pope who is "prince of the kingdoms of the world", maintaining that the pope has priestly sovereignty over political authorities and can dismiss kings and emperors without being answerable to anyone. Again an ecclesiology like that of the primitive Church which comes "from below", from the Church as the people of God, the Church which all ecclesiastical office is designed to subserve, will be very different from an ecclesiology imposed "from above", beginning with the pope. In the latter view, dating from about the time of Gregory VII, and partly based on pseudo-Isidore, the pope is regarded as the head, foundation, root, source and origin of all power and authority in the Church.

The conciliar idea is another important expression of ecclesiology, and here again we can trace remarkable variations. We have only to compare the writings of the decretists, the commentators of the *Decretum Gratiani* in the twelfth century (e.g., Huguccio, Johannes Teutonicus, etc.), with those of the decretalists in the thirteenth century, who applied company law concepts to the Church (especially Hostiensis, also Tancred, Bernard Parmensis, etc.), and finally with the actual conciliarists in the fourteenth century and at the time of the Council of Constance (Conrad von Gelnhausen, Heinrich von Langenstein, Dietrich von Niem, Jean Gerson, Cardinal Pierre d'Ailly, Andreas of Randuf, Cardinal Francesco Zabarella).

The medieval Church also presents a great variety of images of the Church; how different are pseudo-Isidore and John Erigena; Abelard and the Victorins; Peter Lombard and Bernard of Clairvaux; Gerhoh and Arno von Reichersberg and the great scholastics; Leo IX, Gregor VII, Innocent III, Innocent IV, Boniface VIII and Joachim of Flora and Francis of Assisi; William of Ockham and the German mystics; Nicholas of Cusa and Torquemada!

Finally, there have also been great changes and variations in the Catholic ecclesiology of recent times. Whereas in patristic and medieval times ecclesiology was marked by a considerable wealth of viewpoints and a breadth of perspective, many controversial theologians of the Counter-Reformation turned the theology of the Church into treatises on the various points of controversy.

The doctrinal statements of the Council of Trent consciously avoided the central controversial issue, that of the papacy. After some initial hesitation, the First Vatican Council then grasped this nettle; it was the only one of all the outstanding ecclesiological questions that was the subject of a declaration of dogma. Again, there are two different kinds of ecclesiology in the background. That of the Gallicans was largely determined by political considerations; it begins with Philip IV's lawyers and pre-Reformation Gallicanism, is continued by Pithou, E. Richter and Bossuet under Louis XIV, and survives into nineteenth-century Gallicanism. Its basic inspiration, following seventeenth- and eighteenth-century researches into Church history, is the image of the primitive Church; it takes a stand on the autonomy of the national Church with its traditions, customs and usages, and hence on the autonomy of the national episcopate and local synods. The ecclesiology of the Ultramontanes on the other hand, which was equally conditioned by politics, was increasingly reduced to apologetic disquisitions on papal authority, in opposition to Protestants, Gallicans and Jansenists, as well as the various forms of episcopalism existing in Germany and Austria.

There is a world of difference between the ecclesiology of the Enlightenment which, basing itself on natural law, saw the Church from a juridical viewpoint as a *societas* having specific rights and obligations, and the later ecclesiology of Johann Michael Sailer which, under the influence of revivalist movements, mysticism and romanticism, concentrated above all on the religious and also the ethical side of the Church: the Church as the living mediatrix of a living spirituality. Similarly, there is a vast gulf in the nineteenth century between the reactionary ecclesiology of the Restoration period in France, as exemplified by de Maistre, and the new and influential ecclesiology of the Catholic Tübingen school, as exemplified by the young Möhler. De Maistre defended the idea of the absolute monarchy as the foundation of Christian Europe, in opposition to current democratic trends, and transferred his concept of the sovereignty of the absolute monarchy to the position of the pope in the Church. Möhler, on the other hand, rejected the alienated clericalistic ecclesiology of an official and institutionalized Church and saw the Church as a community of believers brought together in love by the Holy Spirit, a community which all ecclesiastical office was designed to subserve.

Again, what a contrast there is between the attitude of the First Vatican Council, when several of the fathers refused to take the "obscure" concept of the body of Christ as the starting-point for the schema on the Church, and that of the encyclical *Mystici Corporis*, which precisely tried to present the whole of ecclesiology in terms of the mystical body. What a contrast there is, finally, between the encyclical, which at several points is explicitly or implicitly polemical, and the more ecumenically orientated constitution of the Second Vatican Council, *De Ecclesia*, which has corrected a number of biases in previous ecclesiology. This constitution has given the oldest definition of the Church, the people of God, its rightful place at the beginning and the heart of ecclesiology, and by doing so has clarified the position of the laity as the Church and the clergy as its servants, as well as establishing the position of bishops in their relationship to the Petrine office.

Even in the post-medieval Church, then, there are many different images of the Church, as we can see if we compare Erasmus, Johannes Eck and Bellarmine; the *Imitation of Christ* and Ignatius of Loyola; the Spanish inquisitors and the mystics they persecuted; Suarez, the baroque scholastics and the German theologians of the Enlightenment; the French crown jurists, the theologians of the Sorbonne, Bossuet and Pascal; Drey, Möhler, Hirsch, Kuhn, Staudenmaier from Tubingen and Perrone, Schrader, Passaglia, Franzelin and Scheeben from Rome; Lamennais, Veuillot and Maret; Karl Adam, Emil Mersch and the bishops and theologians of Vatican II. To say nothing of the different images of the Church we find in Luther, Zwingli and Calvin, in the theology of the Lutheran and Reformed Churches, and in the various older or more recent Free Churches and revivalist movements.

Just as the real ecclesia is constantly evolving, so the ecclesiology of the ecclesia evolves too. The possibly rather confusing and sketchy list of historical details given above, which are intended to draw in, or rather to open up, the historical perspectives of ecclesiology, may look as though they refer to a vast series of distinct and atomized images of the Church. But in reality they are all part of the history of the real Church and its theology, from the beginnings of the Church down to the present day. Does this series of events, this process, mark a progression or a retrogression, or simply a movement of ebb and flow? Is its movement that of the pendulum, is it a circle or a spiral? No historical and philosophical pattern can adequately define this series of events, which has always been progression and retrogression at one and the same time; events have not come in waves of ebb and flow, but have always been different. There has always been a dialectical pendulum movement, and at the same time a circular return to the origins of the Church and a theologically orientated advance towards a future position; there have always been changing variations on a theme, using all kinds of different modulations and counterpoint—and yet the theme has remained constant, holding everything together even at times when it has been almost unrecognizable. This is what we mean when we say that ecclesiology is essentially historical, given that the ecclesia itself is made of and for men who exist at a particular time in a particular environment, in the unrepeatable present of their constantly changing world. The "essential nature" of the Church is not to be found in some unchanging Platonic heaven of ideas, but only in the *history* of the Church. The real Church not only has a history, it exists by having a history. There is no "doctrine" of the Church in the sense of an unalterable metaphysical and ontological system, but only one which is historically conditioned, within the framework of the history of the Church, its dogmas and its theology.

While we may be able to recognize certain ecclesiological types and styles, ecclesiology is always conditioned anew by history; this is a basic fact from which there is no dispensation. It is not just that every theologian sees the Church in a different perspective, from a different personal point of view. More important, since there are such things as supra-individual contingencies, is the fact that ecclesiology belongs to the world to which the Church also belongs. This means that ecclesiology is written in various specific places at specific points in history, in a constantly changing language and a constantly changing intellectual climate, in a changing variety of historical situations affecting the world and the Church alike. Ecclesiology is a response and a call to constantly changing historical situations. This requires repeated and determined attempts to mould, form and differentiate in freedom, unless ecclesiologists give up in despair at each new situation, close their eyes to them and simply drift. The Church's doctrine of the Church, like the Church itself, is necessarily subject to continual change and must constantly be undertaken anew.

It is not easy to find the middle way between the unthinking conservation of a *dead* past, an attitude which is unconcerned about the new demands of a new present, and the careless rejection of the *living* past, an attitude which is all too concerned with the transitory novelties of the present. An ecclesiology which takes a *traditionalist* view, which sees itself as something permanent and unchanged from the beginning of time and uncritically allows itself to be enslaved by a particular age or culture now past, misunderstands what historicity is. Historicity is also misrepresented by an ecclesiology which, taking a *modernist* view, adapts itself and becomes enslaved by the present age or culture, and so abandons itself equally uncritically to the disasters of total changeability. Ecclesiology, which is the Church's expression of its self-understanding, must not be enslaved by any particular situation, be it past, present or future, any more than the Church. It must not identify itself completely with the programmes and myths, illusions and decisions, images and categories of any particular world or era.

But precisely because it is historical, ecclesiology can and must be influenced by its origin, the origin of the Church. This origin does not simply lie in an historical situation, and still less in a transcendental "principle", fabricated or interpreted philosophically, which supposedly set the history of the Church in motion. Its origin is rather "given", "appointed", "laid down" quite concretely; according to the Church's understanding of faith through the powerful historical action of God himself, acting through Jesus Christ among men and for men and so finally through men. God's salvific act in Jesus Christ is the origin of the Church; but it is more than the starting-point or the first phase of its history, it is something which at any given time determines the whole history of the Church and defines its essential nature. So the real Church can never simply leave its origins behind or ultimately distance itself from them. Those origins determine what is permanently true and constantly valid in the Church, despite all historical forms and changes and all individual contingencies. The nature of the Church is not just given to it, it is entrusted to it. Loyalty to its original nature is something the Church must preserve through all the changing history of that world for the sake of which the Church exists. But it can only do that through change (*aggiornamento*), not through immobility (*immobilismo*); it must commit itself to each new day (*giorno*) afresh, accept the changes and transformations of history and human life, and constantly be willing to reform, to renew, to rethink.

3. THE CHANGING IMAGE OF THE CHURCH IN THE NEW TESTAMENT

The Church must constantly reflect upon its real existence in the present with reference to its origins in the past, in order to assure its existence in the future. It stands or falls by its links with its origins in Jesus Christ and its message; it remains permanently dependent, for the ground of its existence, on God's saving act in Jesus Christ, which is valid for all time and so also in the present. It must never cease to reflect upon those origins. Specifically, it must meditate on the original testimony of faith, which remains a constant point of reference for the Church in any century. This original testimony is unique, incomparable and unrepeatable and as such it is actively obligatory, binding and normative for the Church in all ages. The original witness, the original message, is given to us in the writings of the Old and New Testaments. These are the writings which the community of the Church itself, in a complex process lasting several centuries, has come to recognize officially as the original, valid and true witness to God's saving activity for mankind in Christ Jesus.

(*a*) The Church has obediently professed the word which was given to it, by collecting the New Testament writings, relating them to the Old Testament and excluding fanciful speculations and exaggerations. The result is the New Testament "canon", a norm, a guideline and a boundary. The canon represents a *via media*. The Church did not, like Marcion and some present-day Protestant theologians, want to narrow down the choice by radical reduction until only the true "evangelium" was left; nor, like the gnostics and some present-day Catholic theologians, did it want to make its choice as wide as possible, including apocryphal writings and "traditions". The New Testament canon was not selected on the basis of an *a priori* principle, but pragmatically; the living faith of the Christian communities was called upon to "discern spirits".

The Church listened in faith to the word of God, as given definitively by Jesus Christ in fulfilment of the old covenant, and as repeated through the human words of these New Testament writings. The fact that these human words are the original testimony of God's word of revelation is the reason why they are incomparable and unrepeatable, uniquely binding and actively obligatory. All other testimony in the tradition of the Church, however profound or sublime, can in essence do nothing more than circle round this original testimony of God's word, interpret, commentate, explain and apply the original message according to constantly changing historical situations. Because of these constantly changing situations facing the Church in its mission, the changing questions, problems and demands of everyday life, this original message is constantly plumbed for new depths. All commentaries and interpretations, all explanations and applications must always be measured against and legitimized by the message contained in Holy Scripture with its original force, concentrated actuality, and supreme relevance. Sacred Scripture is thus the *norma normans* of the Church's tradition, and tradition must be seen as the *norma normata*.

Even the original testimonies, however, did not simply fall from heaven, are not simply supra-temporal divine documents. Nor are they—as was the hellenistic Jewish view—the writings of ecstatics filled with a divine madness which excludes all individuality and eccentricity, nor yet—as in the view of early Christian theologians—the writings of instruments, who simply transcribed, like secretaries, at the dictation of the Spirit. They are not men who are almost unreal in their persons and historical situation, but real men in all their humanity, historicity and fallibility, who bear witness to God's word in language that is often hesitant and in concepts that are often imprecise. Therefore, given that God's word can be proclaimed in human language, these testimonies are not sublime or above history, but are fundamentally historical testimonies. While Sacred Scripture is theologically normative for the believing Church, it has also, especially for the student of the Church, an historical and literary character: in this sense the Bible is the monument of a past era, a collection of ancient religious documents, which are subject to exegesis, to literary and form criticism, to the study of sources, ideas and themes, to all those disciplines which are a prerequisite of competent criticism.

For ecclesiology this means that the history of the Church, and also the history of the Church's self-understanding, began not *after* but *in* the New Testament, which itself cannot be understood without the Old Testament. The New Testament writings therefore give us more than just the antecedents and the founding of the history of the Church and of ecclesiology; they give us the first decisive phases of the by no means straightforward, indeed complex, history of the Church and its self-understanding. Different images of the Church arise not only after New Testament times, but in the New Testament itself. Indeed it is possible to say that the different emphases and perspectives, tensions and contrasts, which we can see in the ecclesiology of subsequent centuries, reflect to a very large extent the different emphases and perspectives, tensions and contrasts in the New Testament itself. This is due not simply to

326

the individuality of the different writers and the traditions they drew on, but also their different theological attitudes and those of the communities they were part of, as well as the different missionary situations for which the writings were intended. This is something of which we have only a very fragmentary knowledge, especially since many New Testament writings are occasional and conversational in character and very much conditioned by their situation. Any development takes place along several lines with different traditions, and in no sense does the last writing offer an evolved and systematically reasoned ecclesiology.

Within the New Testament there are so many different testimonies as there are witnesses and hearers of the testimonies. There are significant differences between the image of the Church which is adumbrated in Matthew and that in Luke, between the image of the Church in the gospel of St. John and that in Ephesians and Colossians, between the image of the Church in Paul's four great epistles, which with the epistles to the Thessalonians are the oldest Christian documents, and that in the pastoral epistles which are among the latest writings in the New Testament canon. There is no doubt that those images of the Church which throughout the centuries have been charismatic in character (whether of visionaries, reformers or Catholics) can appeal more to the great Pauline epistles, while those images of the Church in which office takes precedence (whether in the Catholic, Greek Orthodox, or Anglican sense) can lean more on the Acts and the Pastoral letters. Nor is there any doubt that the divergences between Pauline ecclesiology and that of the later Luke present one of the most difficult ecclesiological problems.

It is of course all too easy to play off one against the other, by contrasting the image of the Church in the two letters to the Corinthians, which are older even than the gospels we possess today, and that of the letters to Titus and Timothy, which belong to a much later stage of development, even though they claim Pauline authorship. This can be seen from the importance they give to the Spirit in the Church, to charism, to office and ordination, to preaching the word, etc. It is therefore very easy to disassociate the different images of the Church in the New

Testament by simply gathering together different ecclesiological data and hypercritically setting them down side by side where there are points of conflict, without finding in ecclesiology a deeper unity in the context of the writings as a whole. In fact all of them aim to give a positive account of Christ and his Gospel, all in their different ways and according to their different situations seek to further the cause of Christ and to preach Christ, all have their focus, their common united point of contact in the saving event brought by Christ. On the other hand it is pointless to go to the other extreme, as Catholic theology often does, whether out of uncomplicated naivety or out of the lethargy induced by systematic thinking; this way is to harmonize artificially the different New Testament images of the Church, by keeping to the apparently smooth surface of the texts instead of recognizing the contrasts that exist and probing seriously to the bottom of them. The whole art of the exegete consists in being able to make out, through the many voices of the witnesses, their unanimous testimony to Jesus Christ and his community, and to find that unanimity only through the multiplicity of the witnesses; he must be able to recognize in the many words the one Word, and the one Word only in the many words.

Only if we take the New Testament as a *whole* with *all* its writings as the positive witness of the Gospel of Jesus Christ, can we avoid the temptation to dissociate the contradictory ecclesiological statements of the New Testament, to "purify" the New Testament message and to make a selection, a *hairesis*, all of which is an attack on the unity of Scripture and of the Church. The reverse is also true. Only if we take the New Testament as a whole, with all its divergences and nuances, can we avoid the temptation to harmonize the conflicting ecclesiological statements of the New Testament, to level down its message and produce schematization and uniformity, all of which is an attack on the complexity of Scripture and of the Church. What is needed is not dissociation, but a discriminating study in depth; not harmonization but an outline which allows for variations. Ecclesiological study of the New Testament, in other words, needs, and it is no easy task, to combine catholicity, a breadth and awareness of tensions, with evangelical concentration. The

"Catholic" approach will be able, like the early Church which laid down a single canon for the Church of later ages, to hear even in the secondary testimonies of the New Testament canon the authentic Gospel of Jesus Christ; the "evangelical" approach will refuse to attach more importance to secondary New Testament testimonies than to primary ones, and will avoid making what is peripheral the centre of the Gospel, and yet will be able to interpret the secondary sources in terms of the primary ones, and peripheral matter in terms of the centre. Here we must take into account three different kinds of originality, distinguishing them and yet combining them; that of chronology (I Corinthians is earlier than Ephesians), that of authenticity (I Corinthians is genuinely Pauline, Titus probably not) and that of relevance (I Corinthians is in content nearer to the Gospel of Jesus himself than James). The use of the word "gospel" in the New Testament itself, both by the synoptics and by Paul, indicates the right approach. On the one hand the word "gospel" is not restricted to a particular doctrine (as it were, the justification of the sinner), but is fundamentally open; on the other hand, the word "gospel" in the New Testament is indissolubly linked to the saving event in Jesus Christ. It was not the New Testament writers, but Marcion who first understood the concept in a limited sense. It is certainly possible to look impartially for a "centre" in Scripture, by working exegetically from the New Testament texts rather than dogmatically from established preconceptions. It is of course easier to establish such a centre in negative terms rather than in positive terms, to establish that certain things at any rate are not the heart of Scripture, are peripheral rather than central; but this in itself can be a gain. To establish a positive centre is more difficult because of the basic diversity of the individual New Testament writings. Yet, despite the differences, a discriminating and sensitive interpretation will be able to make out the decisive common links and a fundamental inner coherence between, for example, the idea of the beginning of the eschatological reign of God in Jesus Christ, which is central to the preaching of the synoptics, and the Pauline concept of the justification of the sinner through the grace of faith alone.

(b) Modern historical-critical method provides the theologian of today with a scholarly instrument for investigating the origins of the Church which an earlier generation of theologians did not possess. Only with methodical historical thinking has it become possible to gain, to a limited extent at least, an overall view of the changes in the Church and in theology since New Testament times, of the shifts in perspective and emphasis, the improvements and deteriorations, the gains and losses. In addition, methodical historical thinking has for the first time made it possible for us to gain an insight into the extremely important changes which were taking place while the New Testament was being written (approximately between A.D. 50 and 150) and to some extent into the changes of the preceding years (from A.D. 30 to 50), to say nothing of the changes which took place during the two or three thousand years of Old Testament tradition.

Of course, the historical-critical method cannot help either the Church or individual Christians in their truly existential meditation on the word of God in Scripture, on the Gospel of Jesus Christ; at best such a method can assist and stimulate us. Our meditation must grow through God's grace from the basic roots of our Christian existence and of the Christian community, from their faith and love. But it is surely of immeasurable value for ecclesiology and thus also for the life and teaching of the Church that biblical scholarship has untiringly and painstakingly succeeded in performing, for the New Testament as well, such enormous labours, uncompleted and uncompletable though they are.

Despite the lack of original manuscripts and the fact that in many cases authentic readings were not fixed until a late date, *textual criticism* has succeeded in establishing, with the greatest possible certainty and exactitude, the original wording of biblical writings in the earliest form available to us. This has been done by external and internal forms of criticism, by taking linguistic and contextual considerations into account, and by drawing on textual history. *Literary criticism* has examined the literary integrity of the writings, elucidated differences in the legal, social and religious conditions which form the background to the writings, differences in language, chronology and in historical purpose, differences in ethical and theological conceptions. It has distinguished between oral and written traditions as sources of the writings and sorted out possible original material from later additions. It has established the age, origin, intended recipients and literary peculiarities of the writings; it has used the techniques of literary analysis to contrast them with uncanonical and contemporary Jewish and hellenistic literature, and so to determine their individuality. *Form criticism* has examined the question of their place in the lives of the community and of the individual. It has examined the genres of the writings, the framework of these small literary units, their original form, and tried to determine anew their historical reliability and the content of tradition. *Source criticism* has attempted to illuminate the pre-literary process. By analysing the oldest hymns, liturgical fragments, legal decrees, etc., and relating them to worship, preaching and catechesis, it has tried to trace the decisive origins of the Church and the first stage of its development. The vast amount of critical work which has been achieved along these lines, in the last 150 years in particular, and which has included the study of the history of ideas and themes, has always had its constructive side and its positive application. All serious biblical criticism leads automatically to hermeneutics, exegesis and biblical theology, in which the positive value of Scripture is brought out book for book, sentence for sentence, word for word, by all available means and in which great efforts are made to present these discoveries in a way comprehensible to the Church of today.

There are bound to be difficulties in all this. And it is in historical-critical research particularly—not only in exegesis, but also in the history of theology, of dogma and of the Church— that difficulties often assume such gigantic proportions, leaving us with the anxious feeling that we have lost our way in a jungle of problems, or are about to sink without trace in the changeability of everything historical. This much, however, is clear from the exciting story of modern exegesis and historical approach: what at first looks like wanton destruction will always, sooner or later, reveal its constructive potential. Wrong-headed or tendentious criticism has always been overcome by what is genuine and constructive. It is the greatest problems which have needed the greatest efforts to surmount them and have achieved the most fruitful results. Fear, and the fear of history in particular, has proved a poor counsellor in ecclesiology as elsewhere. Courage on the other hand, and particularly courage in historical thinking, has always proved of great value in the long run, even though it may have paid poor dividends at first. In ecclesiology courage means a respect for facts, and the determination to build theories on the basis of facts alone; but this honest courage must be combined with patience, a considered and thoughtful patience which recognizes that only the minutest problems can be settled in a day, and that none can be solved with a sledgehammer. We must realize that the theologian learns by his mistakes and that if he is prevented from making any, he is prevented from constructive thinking; that it takes time not only to find the truth but also for the truth to take effect in the Church generally, in the face of innumerable obstacles, of the prejudices and pretexts of an *opinio communis* which masquerades as genuine doctrine.

(c) The Christian in the Church, even if he is an historian, does not approach the Bible without preconceptions. He cannot regard the New Testament simply as the literary document of a vanished era. For him, whether it is giving doctrine, commandments or simply history, it is *kerygma*, a message with force and relevance for the present day, God's call to contemporary man. Let us examine the implications of this.

We may say that the New Testament provides "doctrine". But the Church cannot regard it simply as a theoretical textbook in which truths about God and man's salvation in Christ, which are generally valid for its doctrine, have been "deposited". As against such doctrinalist misconceptions, it is clear that for the Church the New Testament is a proclamation, a preaching of God's saving act in Christ, which calls in turn for the Church to preach the message and to realize it in faith today. We may say that the New Testament provides "commandments". But it is far from being a practical book of laws, giving the Church a detailed moral, legal and spiritual code with rigid rules and calling on men to keep these rules in order to achieve self-justification by their own efforts. As against such moralistic misconceptions, it is clear that for the Church the New Testament is God's Gospel which sets us free from the law. It promises and proffers to all who believe and who renounce their own worth before God the free gift of God: the forgiveness of sins and a new righteousness. It proclaims how man is liberated to obedience to God's will through a life of love, which is the fulfilment of the law. We may say that the New Testament provides "history". But the New Testament for the Church is not simply the history book of salvation history, in which can be found a neutral, objective, chronological account of that history, together with appropriate historical comments on its continuing development. As against all such historical misconception, it is clear that for the Church the New Testament is rather the preaching of a message, the accounts of which are always conditioned by theology. It tells of a self-revealing and merciful God who comes to meet us, who has acted once and for all in human history in Jesus Christ, and who expects from man not just an intellectual acquiescence to various historical facts but an existential decision of faith before God and for God.

In each case, then, we are concerned with the word of God. This word is testified to and made present in its full authority by human words, which themselves remain all along the line temporal and historically conditioned. The full import of what it has to say is only revealed to those who believe. It is not simply a written word which therefore belongs to the past; it is a word which always has to be preached and is therefore always actual. It is the living word of the Gospel, the saving message of God's love at work first in the Old Testament and then definitively in Jesus Christ, through his death and resurrection as the eschatological act of salvation.

From this it is very clear why, though all the changes of the times and the changes of the Church, we should reflect on the real Church of the New Testament, which was itself already in a state of change and already full of differences and variations. Not out of deference to a romantic ecclesiological love of the past, an attitude which automatically praises what is more ancient as being more perfect and sees the time of the primitive Church as the golden age of the Church. Such reflection is rather the grave duty of a theology which thinks historically and which, precisely avoiding the temptations of concentrating on any one age, even the earliest, concerns itself with the living eschatological word of God himself, the Gospel of Jesus Christ. It is this Gospel from which the Church of Jesus Christ took its origin and which in its daily life the Church continues to take its origin. This is an attitude from which no Christian theology can possibly dispense itself.

To reflect on the New Testament, therefore, does not mean that we should try unhistorically to return to the Church's origins or try to imitate the New Testament community, as the Jewish Christians of the second century or the Anabaptists of the sixteenth century tried to do. The New Testament Church is not a model which we can follow slavishly without any regard to the lapse of time and our constantly changing situation. Nor is the recitation or reproduction of Jesus' words by itself of any effect. The letter kills, it is the spirit that gives life—in ecclesiology too. If the Church wants to remain true to its nature, it cannot simply preserve its past. As an historical Church it must be prepared to change in order to fulfil its essential mission in a world which is constantly changing, which always lives in the present, not the past.

On the other hand, reflection upon the Church of the New Testament will lead us to conclude that not all the subsequent developments in the Church can be authorized by its origins; there have been errors and false developments in its history. The New Testament message, as the original testimony, is the highest court to which appeal must be made in all the changes of history. It is the essential norm against which the Church of every age has to measure itself. The New Testament Church, which, beginning with its origins in Jesus Christ, is already the Church in the fullness of its nature, is therefore the original design; we cannot copy it today, but we can and must translate it into modern terms. The Church of the New Testament alone can show us what that original design was.

Léon-Joseph Suenens
1904-

Léon Joseph Suenens was born an only child in Brussels, Belgium. His father died when Léon was four years old, and he and his mother then went to live with an uncle who was a priest. By the time he had finished high school he had decided to become a priest, and Cardinal Mercier, then Archbishop of Malines, took an interest in him, sending him to study in Rome where he obtained doctorates in theology and philosophy as well as a master's degree in canon law at the Gregorian University.

Ordained in 1927 by Cardinal Van Roey, Mercier's successor, he spent the years from 1930 to 1939 teaching philosophy at the seminary of the Archdiocese of Malines. He then became chaplain in the Belgian Army until the Nazi conquest in 1940, when he was named vice-president of the University of Louvain, a job made delicate by the Nazi occupation. In 1945 he was condemned to die along with thirty others, but Belgium was liberated a few days before the execution was to take place. Before the year was out, Cardinal Van Roey made Suenens auxiliary bishop and vicar-general of the diocese.

For the next sixteen years in this position, Suenens was much involved with the media and the laity, especially the apostolic groups Pax Christi and the Legion of Mary. His writing in the 1950s was important in broadening the under-

standing of the role of lay people in the Church beyond the "official Catholic Action" of the day.

After the death of Van Roey in 1961, Suenens became Archbishop of Malines and Primate of Belgium. Within two months he was named a cardinal by Pope John XXIII and played an important role in preparing for the opening of Vatican II in the fall of 1962. He developed a general program which was at first not adopted but which was revived toward the end of the first session, ending a deadlock over the schema on the Church. The two central themes of his plan were: 1) the Church's internal structure, and 2) its external relations. This required, as far as Suenens was concerned, "a triple dialogue: of the Church with her faithful; the ecumenical dialogue with the separated brethren; and the dialogue with the contemporary world."

Suenens became one of the most popular and effective spokesmen for progressive positions in Vatican II. He championed the restoration of lay deacons, he proposed inviting women as observers, and on the intractable question of birth control he recommended that the Church "reexamine its whole approach and not be afraid to look at its teaching on this matter to see if it is the final word." It was said that this speech received the loudest applause of any in the Council.

In 1963 Suenens was chosen to come to the United Nations in New York to explain and analyze Pope John's great encyclical, Pacem in Terris. *He returned in 1964 on a speaking tour during which, among other things, he advocated the modernization of the garb of religious women.*

The dominant theme of Vatican II, the coresponsibility of all Christians within the people of God, has had its most articulate and persistent spokesman in Cardinal Suenens. Collegiality, decentralized power, and direct dialogue at all levels, these are the great needs for a rejuvenated Church, as Suenens sees it. The selection found here is the middle chapter in his 1968 book, Coresponsibility in the Church; *it is entitled "The Demands of Our Time." Here he attempts to point out "what seem to be the great demands of the moment: the ecumenical urgency, the mission urgency, and the urgency for the church to be present to the world. We are all summoned to this threefold task, each one according to his proper function and charism, but all in close solidarity."*

CORESPONSIBILITY
IN THE CHURCH

CHAPTER II

THE DEMANDS OF OUR TIME

E very era has its vocation, every age answers to an idea and a desire of the Lord. The time in which we live is the place where we meet the "today of God." Christ has taught us to have on our lips and in our hearts the prayer, "Your will be done on earth . . ." We pray that God's will be done on this earth, our earth, the globe on which we walk, the earth of our time and generation. As we listen to what our age demands of us and place ourselves at its service, we give substance to this desire expressed by the Lord's prayer.

God is at one and the same time eternal and infinitely real; or as Peguy says, he is "both youthful and eternal."

What then is the particular vocation of our time? It seems to me that we can find it in certain words of the gospel which shed light on the whole of church history with new urgency and breadth. There is first of all the command of the Master to his disciples: "Go preach the gospel to every creature . . . and behold I am with you until the end of ages." This is a missionary mandate.

But there is one reality absolutely necessary for the fulfillment of this mission: "Father, may they be one in us, as you are in me and I am in you, so that the world may believe it was you who sent me" (Jn. 17, 21). The unity of Christians among themselves is of primary importance. It is the prelude to any acceptance of, or confidence in, the gospel message. The ecumenical summons being issued today by the Spirit of the Lord to all those who invoke his name is one of the signs of our times. We must be able to receive and be willing to understand it. Our first duty is to direct our energies toward a restoration of a visible unity whose source is the intimate unity of the Trinity. Thus the duty of ecumenical effort and that of

missionary activity are mutually related. Our inner coresponsibility is our first acceptance of the duty of coresponsibility
with all men of good will.

We are to be "one . . . so that the world may believe."
This implies, then, a presence to the world at an ever deeper
level, an insertion into this modern world, described by Pope
Paul VI as "magnificent and complex, terrible and tormented."
And thus the three great demands of our time stand out in bold
relief: the call to ecumenism, the call to be missionary, and
the call to be present to the world.

The council did not hesitate to say that the ecumenical
movement bears the obvious stamp of the Holy Spirit. The conciliar decree on ecumenism, and the directives determining its
practical application, open up possibilities that are rich with
promise.

From now on, there is a new climate of rediscovered
brotherhood. Obviously, this climate has not done away with
real doctrinal differences. There are some who seem to resign
themselves to this situation, as though it had to be permanent.
"The glaciers may melt but the Alps will remain." We cannot
share this pessimistic view. Even now men are digging into the
sides of the mountain, challenging its resistance and preparing
for tunnels.

We await the hour of full communion, and in order to
hasten it we have learned once again to pray together. We
cherish the memory of that prayer in common, presided over
by Paul VI at the end of the council, and of the meeting between Patriarch Athenagoras and Pope Paul at the end of the
synod. And now we have agreed upon a common text for
the "Our Father"; this is at once a symbol and a cause for
hope.

Then again, we have sketched some rough outlines for
concerted action. In particular, we have begun to join our
efforts in the service of the people of developing countries.
For we know that we must meet this major social problem of
our time together. An economist of world-wide reputation,
Barbara Ward, has already well described this ecumenical effort
in the service of the "third world."

This point is of immense importance. The ecumenical movement has raised such hopes and expectations that any future failure to work together, as Christians, would breed a corresponding disillusion. Yet in specifically doctrinal matters, progress is likely to be slow and the scope, though wide, possibly more limited than the more ardent spirits hope. Nor is it, in general, a matter for lay leadership.

But in the field of the kinds of social action needed to set the wealth of the West working in a new effort to mitigate world poverty—and domestic poverty, too, for that matter—the possibilities of action are very wide indeed and could become the main field of ecumenical action over the next four or five decades during which many of the crucial changes in the developing world will be taking place.

Sustained by prayer and the fraternal service of others, we cherish the desire to draw closer to one another in matters of doctrine. The many dialogues already begun contain and express this power of attraction. The search for full communion in faith is at the heart of any authentic ecumenism, and is as far removed as possible from a common pragmatism. The Lord prayed that his own consecrate themselves in truth. We must adhere first of all to this intention of the Lord, if we wish to be faithful to all he expects of us. No diplomatic compromise is possible in matters which are not at our free disposition. But there is room for long and patient efforts in order to clarify dogmatic formulas which can always be rendered more precisely, and manifest their wealth of meaning more fully.

We all know that the great obstacles that separate us from our non-Catholic brothers are the dogmas of papal primacy and infallibility. In an allocution to the members of the Secretariat for Promoting Christian Unity, Pope Paul VI recognized this obstacle himself, when he said:

We know full well that the papacy is undoubtedly the most serious obstacle on the ecumenical road. What are we to say? Should we appeal once again to the evidence that validates our mission? Should we try once again to present in precise terms what it purports to be: the necessary principle of truth, charity and unity? Should we show once again that it is a pastoral charge of direction, service and brotherhood which does not challenge the freedom or dignity of anyone who has a legitimate problem in the church of God, but which rather protects the rights of all and only claims the obedience called for among children in the same family? It is not easy for us to plead our own cause.

Here too, then, we have a new climate, which can be symbolized by two images: that of John XXIII receiving the observers at the council, and Paul VI on pilgrimage to Jerusalem and Constantinople. We begin to perceive at the level of concrete reality what a primacy of service and love can be.

After Vatican I, the papacy appeared to the non-Catholic world as an absolute monarchy, incompatible with any kind of collegiality. Men like Bismarck and Gladstone gave voice to this impression. But the very fact that John XXIII convoked a council shows quite clearly that collegiality is more than a word; and the *Constitution on the Church* has expressed its reality and significance. Theologians will have to locate the dogma of papal primacy more precisely within the context of collegiality, showing especially, as we have just said, that the primacy should be understood first of all as a service. This context of the papacy will, we hope, allow all Christians to enter more deeply into an understanding of the dogma.

But there is nothing that will free the papacy more completely from all suspicion of absolutism and authoritarianism than the application in daily life of the doctrinal principle of "primacy of service." This will be more effective than doctrinal discussion.

Michael Ramsey, primate of the Anglican church, expresses the same opinion when speaking of the famous meetings at Malines, where papers were presented attempting to define the relationships between the episcopacy and the papacy. He writes:

For a primacy should depend upon and express the organic authority of the Body; and the discovery of its precise functions will come not by discussion of the petrine claims in isolation but by the recovery everywhere of the Body's life, with its Bishops, presbyters and people. In this Body Peter will find his due place, and ultimate reunion is hastened not by the pursuit of "the Papal controversy" but by the quiet growth of the organic life of every part of Christendom.

In our opinion, theological research is indispensable, but it is in the very experience of the church that primacy must be lived out; and this is of the greatest importance. This experience will be the fruit of a coresponsibility fully accepted and lived by the bishops individually, and by the episcopal conferences, as well as by the whole Christian community. Arguments in the abstract about hypothetical conflict of power, and efforts at increasing juridical precisions, will not hasten the time of deep mutual understanding.

The council was an important landmark on the road toward doctrinal clarification. The intimate life of the church and the ecumenical dialogue itself cannot but experience the consequences of this important step.

What is true of papal primacy is also true of papal infallibility. It receives new light when placed in the context and perspective of the whole church.

In recalling that "The body of the faithful as a whole, anointed as they are by the Holy One, cannot err in matters of belief" the *Constitution on the Church* (art. 12) helps to situate better the role of episcopal inerrancy and papal infallibility in the exercise of their highest teaching office. It is the Lord who is the source of the indefectibility of his whole church. The hierarchical ministry of the gospel truth is a service to the whole community.

We hope that the time is coming when this ecclesial perspective will be more accentuated in Catholic theology, so that other Christians will be led for their part to rethink and perhaps revise their attitude toward papal infallibility.

It is undeniable that the definition of infallibility has been so stressed in Catholic ecclesiology since 1870, that the infallibility of the church itself, so obvious to all that no one thought it necessary to define it, was overshadowed and even neglected. But the inerrancy of the pope speaking *ex cathedra* was defined in reference to the infallibility of the church. The exercise of this "prerogative" is conditioned by the various limits established by the definition itself.

Before the final vote, Bishop Gasser, secretary for the Commission of the Faith at Vatican I, made this very significant declaration:

> Absolute infallibility belongs to God alone, who is the first and essential Truth, and who can never in any way be mistaken or led into error. Every other infallibility by the very fact that it is conferred for a well-defined goal has its limits and conditions. And so it is with the infallibility of the Roman pontiff.

Thus to speak of infallibility is constantly to return above all to the promise of the Lord, "I am with you until the end of ages." This divine assistance and protection is always present. The definition of Vatican I affirms that infallibility is exercised with certitude and efficacy when the Roman pontiff speaks *ex cathedra*, and only when he speaks *ex cathedra*. This is so true that in his authoritative discourse, which is of such great importance for the understanding of the definition, Bishop Gasser could say that the statement "the pope is infallible" is too imprecise. Rather, "the pope is only infallible when, in a solemn judgment, he defines for the universal church a question of faith or morals."

Already at the First Vatican Council the most enthusiastic defenders of papal infallibility refrained from proposing a "separate" infallibility. They admitted that the pope is never separated from his church, and that they too did not wish a "beheading of Peter." For, they explained, it is one thing to affirm that in certain well-defined circumstances the Roman pontiff is able personally to define a truth, and it is another thing to think that at the moment when he thus exercises his supreme dogmatic judgment the pope is actually separated from the church.

Bishop Gasser would explain later that the pope is joined to the church in many ways. He is united to it, first of all, because the head is never separated from the body, and the building cannot stand without its foundation.

He is also united by the very fact that the statements to be made in matters of doctrine arise first at a local or regional level, and only arrive at the level of the pope last of all.

A definition is justified, first of all, when there appear in some part of the church, scandals regarding the faith, disagreements, or heresies, which the leaders of the church, taken individually, or even assembled in provincial council, are not able to correct, and thus find themselves forced to refer the matter to the apostolic see.

Certainly the "first of all" in Bishop Gasser's address leaves the door open to exceptions, but nevertheless it indicates the "normal" line to be followed.

When he pronounces a definition, the Roman pontiff has the moral obligation to be informed about the truth in question. And in this regard, once again, the normal vehicle of information is the episcopacy, and at their own level, the theologians. Thus Bishop Gasser goes on to say,

We do not exclude at all the cooperation of the church; for the infallibility of the Roman pontiff is given to him, not by way of inspiration or revelation, but by way of divine assistance. That is why the pope in exercising his responsibility, according to the gravity of the problems, must use adequate means to investigate the truth as it deserves, and to state it correctly. These means are the councils and also the advice of bishops, the cardinals, the theologians, etc.

There is a question here of those instances, actually quite rare, when the pope would be obliged to pronounce a definition alone, in virtue of the promise given by Christ to Peter and his successors. And, since the pope can discover the faith of the church in other ways, one could conclude that it is not "absolutely" necessary that the pope gain his information from among the episcopacy.

Sometimes the meaning of the text of Vatican I has been overstressed and it was forgotten that what was denied there was the strict and absolute juridical necessity of consulting the bishops. Normally, it is from among the bishops first of all that the sovereign pontiff receives his information in those rare instances when he considers himself obliged to make a definition.

In fact, since there is question of a definition, the faith is at issue, and thus the ordinary teaching authority of the bishop is involved. Once again, in the words of Bishop Gasser, "The unanimous approval expressed by the actual preaching of the whole of the church's magisterium, united with its head, is also the rule of faith for pontifical definitions."

Briefly, whatever be the manner in which the pope informs himself, he must remain in perfect communion with the faith of the whole church. As Cardinal Dechamps wrote a short time after Vatican I, "Some type of consensus or actual accord in the faith is absolutely indispensable to infallibility."

It is well known that Protestants do not like the term "infallibility." Actually, this term came into theology during the 14th century; one could also use the terms "indefectibility in matters of faith," "immunity from error," or "inerrancy." In ancient times, one spoke rather of truth, as does the bible. And perhaps we should return to this manner of expressing ourselves in order to facilitate a deeper mutual understanding.

As the ecumenical dialogue continues, we are able to discern converging tendencies, movements of the Spirit, which lead toward the unity of all Christians. Truths and values which at one time seemed to cancel each other out now present themselves as complementary.

Ancient antinomies are tending to resolve themselves: tradition or scripture, hierarchy or priesthood of the faithful, papacy or collegiality. There are many examples of similar efforts to go beyond the impasse of a false dualism and to achieve harmonic unity.

Vatican II says again and again, that all hierarchy is service to the people of God, and insists upon the priestly and charismatic role of the faithful. At the same time, various studies emanating from the reform churches show that Luther was attacking the hierarchy of his time, not the hierarchical principle itself.

The council put great stress on episcopal collegiality, and upon respect for particular churches; though we perceive at the same time in many places outside of Rome a certain nostalgia for unity.

In the Protestant world we see the monks of Taizé defending the real presence in the eucharist, the relevance of monasticism, the value of celibacy for the kingdom of God, and honoring Mary under the title of Mother of the Lord. A very important Protestant work examines the Marian piety of the early reformers, and Cardinal Martin wrote the preface for the new edition of Martin Luther's commentary on the *Magnificat*.

Catholics are insisting more on the transcendent holiness of God and the complete gratuity of his gift of grace, while Protestants are tending to integrate better the concept of "good works" and the witness of faith.

Catholics are insisting on the necessity of placing sacramental rites within the context of the life of faith, while at the same time the reformers are taking another look at the question of ministry and its necessary and constitutive role within the church.

Catholics are reaffirming the importance of episcopal collegiality and its connection with the papacy, and the Orthodox and Anglicans and other "episcopal" churches are calling to mind that antiquity considered the first apostolic see, Rome, as the ultimate arbiter and center of ecclesiastical communion. We also see Protestant churches accepting the necessity for authority in the church in order that certain reforms be effected, and in so doing they are thus moving toward some kind of episcopal structure.

In brief, we see a tendency to replace opposing dilemmas by a unifying synthesis with all the enrichment that this implies for a greater realization and manifestation of true catholicity.

Not so long ago, none of these tendencies was even thought of. They witness to the fact that, over and above those things which still divide us, there is an ever growing concern for our common task. Our generation has seen effected within itself a spiritual revolution launched by the Spirit.

We once asked an Orthodox friend, who was an observer at the council, what he thought was the principal obstacle to union. He said to me, "The fact that we haven't been speaking for nine centuries." Today, dialogue has begun again, hearts are opening out to hope. The Holy Spirit will confirm and strengthen that which he has begun.

"May they be one that the world may believe." These words of the Master sound the keynote of the twofold obligation: to be ecumenical and to be missionary.

In a way exceeding any of its predecessors, Vatican II proclaimed the duty of going out to all men, even to the ends of the earth. We do not have to go too far back in history to find an age where the equation "a Christian = an apostle" was considered a paradox. It was not understood that a Christian is not truly a Christian till he is a "Christianizer"; that he has not truly received the gospel until he understands and accepts the responsibility to preach it.

As we were preparing our book *The Gospel to Every Creature*, we searched through religious literature trying to find texts which treated of the apostolic and missionary duty of every baptized Christian, but we had great difficulty in finding any. In a review of the book, we were criticized for maintaining as a fundamental text, "Go out into the whole world and proclaim the good news to all creation" (Mk. 16, 17), and for extending to every Christian an invitation, or an order, which concerned only the apostles. However, there is neither a lack of texts nor a difficulty in applying them, if we prescind from the internal distinction within the church, and raise the issue to the level of the church as a whole. The church, as such, is missionary by essence and definition. It is the church as the people of God which is entrusted, in coresponsibility, with the duty of evangelizing the world. The council said this first of all in the *Constitution on the Church*. Then, during the period between sessions, this concept matured and the council said it again with greater force and precision in the *Decree on the Church's Missionary Activity*. Let us listen to the council expressing itself in these two series of texts:

> The pilgrim church is missionary by her very nature. For it is from the mission of the Son and the

mission of the Holy Spirit that she takes her origin, in accordance with the decree of God the Father (*Decree*, art. 2).

The primary and most important task of this mission is to proclaim the good news to all men:

The church has been divinely sent to all nations that she might be "the universal sacrament of salvation" (*Constitution*, art. 48). Acting out of the innermost requirements of her own catholicity and in obedience to her Founder's mandate, she strives to proclaim the gospel to all men (*Decree*, Preface).

The church has received from the apostles this solemn mandate of Christ to proclaim the saving truth even to the ends of the earth. Hence she makes the words of the apostle her own: "Woe to me, if I do not preach the gospel," (1 Cor. 9, 16), and continues unceasingly to send heralds of the gospel until such a time as the infant churches are fully established and can themselves carry on the work of evangelizing (*Constitution*, art. 17).

Since the whole church is missionary, and the work of evangelization is a basic duty of the people of God, this sacred synod summons all to a deeper interior renewal. Thus, from a vivid awareness of their own responsibility for spreading the gospel, they will do their share in missionary work among the nations (*Decree*, art. 35).

The obligation of spreading the faith is imposed on every disciple of Christ, according to his ability (*Constitution*, art. 17).

Thus the council completely confirmed what Albert Dondeyne had written a few years earlier:

The Church is by its essence a missionary community. It continues and extends the apostolic community founded by Christ to proclaim the message. It springs from the word of God, and is at the service of that word. In its capacity as the new Israel,

it assumes and renews the mission of the chosen people in regard to the salvation of the world. The biblical
concept of election is not synonymous with lack of
concern. Election cannot be separated from the notions of mission and ministry. Divine election, while
it creates a particularly close relationship to God,
implies the notion of vocation or call, and consequently, that of responsibility before God. Through baptism
and faith, the Christian becomes a member of the
apostolic community. He enters into God's intentions
for the world. He is called to open himself out to
God's saving will for sinful humanity, and that is why
from now on his prayer will be "May your kingdom
come, may your will be done . . ." This means that
belonging to the church of Christ is at once a grace
and a responsibility: it is the duty of every Christian
to collaborate in the "building up" of the church, in
both senses of the word "edify."

There is light in this doctrine of the council, but we must
admit that the climate in the post-conciliar period is far from
corresponding to its ideals. From every side, and for the most
different reasons, the very concept of mission is under heavy
fire in the church today.

We would list as a general cause that spirit of exclusive and
horizontal humanism which, even among Christians, is leading
them to minimize the sense of God and of his transcendence,
and the sense of sin and redemption. There is such an enthusiasm
for temporal values that the work of evangelization is esteemed
but little—it seems to be a stranger to what is human, to be use-
less and too spiritual. Such an outlook is unable to understand
that true evangelization contains within itself not only a religious
dimension but a social and temporal dimension as well.

Then there are some particular reasons which militate
against the missionary concept, or at least render it a disservice.
There is first and foremost an ever growing fear of encroaching
upon liberty of conscience, a liberty accentuated by the council
itself. Then there is, too, the realization, more vivid today but
always known, that there are elements of truth, elements of the

348

gospel, scattered throughout all religions. The success realized by the concept of dialogue has served in its own way to over-shadow evangelization. It could actually appear that the more one dialogues the less one evangelizes. And in our culture, which is becoming more and more characterized by dialogue, the age of evangelization seems to have passed. But we cannot accept this kind of reasoning.

No doubt, Catholics find themselves in contact with men of more refined culture and with people more aware of the inherent value of their own religion. Thus a certain rather romantic idea of what it means to preach the gospel is rapidly disappearing. Those who wish to announce the Christian message find themselves obliged to adopt a manner of acting more in keeping with adults. But to lay aside a romantic kind of gospel preaching does not mean that we ought to abandon evangelization completely.

It is a natural instinct when one meets an adult to engage in a dialogue suitable to his person. But to dialogue is not the same as to sink the ship one stands on. It implies, of course, a certain mutual exchange, and means that the Catholic does not present himself to other believers as somebody "having it all" talking to those who have nothing. But at the same time, true dialogue demands that its participants present their own proper belief precisely and seriously, and with real foundations. Such a presentation is usually more demanding and reflective than that engaged in with someone who still has everything to learn. A Catholic has to make an effort so that his interlocutor understands Catholicism as exactly as possible. What follows, the response to this call and adherence to it, is left to the grace of the Lord. And is not this a way in which the church usually presents itself when it announces the Christian message to adults in those places where it is already established?

We say "usually." For if, in fact, our age is one characterized more and more by dialogue, and the method of ecumenical dialogue seems to be more and more called for, it is still true that in Christian countries the work of reconciliation—we used to say conversion—still remains fundamental. The *Decree on Ecumenism* makes the following observation: "It is evident that the work of preparing and reconciling those individuals who wish for full catholic communion is of its nature distinct from ecumenical action. But there is no opposition between the two, since both proceed from the wondrous providence of "God" (art. 4).

The explanation of this text is quite simple. It is possible, and even normal, that certain people are called by divine grace actually to become "Roman Catholics." Thus it is necessary that for these people the Church create or maintain structures whose goal is "to prepare" directly for reconciliation. But a manner of presentation which is possible among Christians would seem to assume a much more important role when placed in a non-Christian context. To that degree it is fitting that the church think in terms of suitable structures which can "prepare" the approach to Catholicism, thus maintaining some direct evangelical activity. Here again, one must present Catholicism in an adult or ecumenical way; and such a presentation pertains to an authentic preaching of the gospel.

There are those who tend to oversimplify things and see in the conciliar *Declaration on Religious Freedom* such a demand for respect of liberty of conscience that it would reduce all missionaries to silence. It would be the end of direct apostolic action.

Of course, the act of faith is a free act, and can tolerate no constraint. The history of the church is not without errors and deficiencies in this regard, and we must admit it. But concern to eliminate coercion is not identical with silence. Let the missionary approach the unbeliever with great respect for liberty of conscience, let him approach with tact; but let him also speak.

It is this very respect for another that urges us to speak to him. To make no effort to pass on the word of God would result in a lack of esteem for that word, and a lack of interest in those to whom it is addressed as a message of life and salvation. Vatican II in no way renders direct missionary activity out of date; it is not the patron of witnesses whom respect has rendered mute. We have to avoid this temptation to silence, and exorcise the "dumb spirits."

To be a missionary will always be a duty inspired by love for men, but first and foremost it must be inspired by love for God. The Christian mission derives its origin and its urgency from God. It is God who wishes to communicate himself, and each of us is chosen to aid in the preparation of this meeting between God and man.

God's love is a desire for free and total communion. He desires this impatiently, for this kind of impatience is inherent in any love which wishes to give itself. We say so easily that God is patient. There are many Christians who are content in the faith of this so-called patience of God, and abstain from any apostolate. God is patient because we force him to be. He is burning to give himself. So long as the chosen people made light of the covenant which he offered them, God never ceased to complain of their reluctance. Throughout all of scripture he gives free rein to his expressions of impatience, which is one aspect of his love.

We must become aware of the living relevance of our Lord's words, "I have come that they may have life and have it to the full" (Jn. 10, 10). In Christ, the Christian has an abundance that he cannot keep for himself. Of course, God's grace goes beyond the visible means of meditation, the structures and preaching of the church. But what a gift for men, to know consciously the God of our Lord Jesus Christ, the mystery of his Trinitarian life, and the greatness of a love which extends from the creation to the parousia, through all the mysteries of salvation. What greater wealth than to belong to that living communion of mystics and saints who from age to age are the glory of the living church, and the guarantee of its fidelity before God? The prodigal son's older brother stayed at home and had no idea what he owed to his father and his brethren; he found it all quite natural, while his younger brother would one day experience this reality more deeply than he. There cannot be safe and secure Christians, "older brothers," who are insensitive to the spiritual anguish of the world.

Preparatory measures are necessary in nearly every field, but it can happen that these preludes or "introductions to the matter" absorb all of one's attention. The same is true of evangelization. Today we often hear of pre-evangelization, and we readily agree to both the word and the thing, provided that the prefix does not overshadow the substantive. Pre-evangelization is justified if it results in evangelization. It is praiseworthy to honor John the Baptist; but today, as before, the precursor must give place to him for whom he did but "prepare the way."

In the name of preparation and under the pretext of taking care to make a good foundation, we run the risk of becoming absorbed in the cultural, the social, the purely human. The world is judged to be as yet unready to receive the message, and we wait, doing work which we say prepares the approach. And all this while, the light is too prudently being kept under a bushel, imprisoned in silence. At Pentecost, the world of that time was certainly not ready to receive the message; nevertheless, the apostles spoke.

The world of today is perhaps not ready to listen to us. But are we really ready to speak to it? Technical and social assistance is necessary, as is cooperation toward cultural and economic development, but this necessity can never cause us to lose sight of the need and urgency to preach the gospel by the living word of God. M. D. Chenu, commenting on the phrase used by the council, "the signs of our times," has said, "Evangelization and civilization are in different orders. To feed men is, in itself, not to save them, even when my salvation demands my feeding them. To foster culture is a far different thing than converting to the faith."

We must not chase the mirage of social messianism. The Christian message, and thus the apostolate of the church, pertains first of all to the spiritual domain: Christ has said, "My kingdom is not of this world." We must distinguish between the attitude of a church anxious to contribute its total collaboration to the solution of social problems, and the attitudes of that false messianism which makes material, or at least temporal well being, the sole object of progress.

The preaching of the gospel message to the poor cannot wait upon the improvement of their social condition. On the other hand, we must recognize that that love which is the fulfillment of the law, and which is open to what is spiritual, cannot limit itself solely to what is spirit. The Christ who once refused to turn stones into bread, declaring that man does not live by bread alone, is also the Christ who fed the multitudes in the desert. It seems to me that these two aspects of his life embody the twofold mission of the church.

We have to give man bread *and* the sacred host.

We have to teach the alphabet *and* the doctrine of Christ.

We must offer them social security *and* the providence of God.

We have to learn the value of work *and* the value of prayer.

We have to save not only souls, but *men*.

In brief, we must awaken within the church a sense of man and a sense of God. In order to answer fully the obligations of its mission in the world, the church must raise up social pioneers and saints.

There is yet another sign of our times: the summons addressed to the church to be open and render itself present to the world. This serves to put the church on guard against the temptation to turn inward, toward itself, and enclose itself in a ghetto. This warning and this summons gave birth to the *Constitution on the Church in the Modern World*, which urges Christians to enter into dialogue with the world and exercise an activity which affects their times.

The conciliar concept of renewal exceeds the limits of internal reform, indispensable as this reform may be. The church serves God when it is serving man: it is at the service of the eternal God through the service of the men of the present. The aggiornamento could deviate tragically if the church, rather than open itself out to all men of today, were to content itself with addressing its own internal problems. We must be aware of the problems of today's world, and sensitive to the problems of tomorrow. Today's problems? Those of underdevelopment, hunger and war. The problems tomorrow? The coming of the post-industrial era, of a civilization of unparalleled leisure, of a technological empire which could, unless we are on guard, enslave man instead of liberating him.

The motto of Terence, "I believe that nothing human is a stranger to me," is the motto of humanism, and it applies to the church of God. The call beyond, the intimations of the future: these can protect us, or heal us, from our narrowness of vision. The church exists for today's world, and for the world of tomorrow which will undoubtedly be quite different.

Christian eschatology does not restrict itself to announcing that final day described at the end of the Apocalypse; it also invites us to prepare for it now. It urges us to go on, carrying an authentic hope, toward the generations yet to come. Eschatology, far from being an anxious fear of some future definitive calamity, is a dynamic openness to a world in the making; a world which is groaning in the throes of childbirth, waiting for the revelation of the sons of God. It is with this vision that Vatican II wished to conclude.

In a world which is becoming more and more unified and organized on a global scale, there is no such thing as a private happening which concerns one particular group of men to the exclusion of the others. We can now apply to the great human family that which St. Paul said about the Church of Christ: "If one member suffers all the members share the sufferings, and if one member is honored, all the members share its joy" (1 Cor. 12, 26).

The ecumenical council was primarily an intra-ecclesial event, but it quickly drew the attention of the whole human family, overreaching the distinctions of nation, culture, philosophical outlook and religious persuasion.

Undoubtedly, modern techniques of information such as radio, television and the press have contributed largely to giving this intra-ecclesial event world wide publicity. They enabled millions of men scattered over five continents to be present every day at all that went on within St. Peter's Basilica. But the fact of publicity alone does not account for the ever growing interest which the world showed in the council.

It seemed rather that as the council progressed, a dialogue developed between the church and the world beyond the collective examination of conscience which was taking place there in Rome. It was as if all of humanity were questioning itself in order better to understand the human condition and to interpret "the signs of the times." As the church's aggiornamento, which was the particular goal of the council, began to take shape and actual existence, its relevance for the whole human race became clearer.

The human meaningfulness of the council could be summed up in these words: to listen, and to serve; more exactly, to listen in order to serve better.

In stating at the beginning of the *Constitution on the Church in the Modern World* that "The joys and hopes, the griefs and the anxieties of the men of this age, especially those who are poor or in any way afflicted, these too are the joys and hopes, the griefs and anxieties of the followers of Christ" (art. 4), Vatican II introduced no innovation. It did nothing but translate in more modern language the ancient commandment of Christ: "You shall love your neighbor as yourself."

Therefore, it is not the simple wish to serve humanity which constitutes the new contribution of Vatican II, but rather, the manner in which this service is understood. Vatican II goes beyond the preceding councils and shows itself to be in living union with the spirit of our time when it proclaims that to serve man means first of all to meet him and to listen to him. The council appeared within the history of the church, and of the world, as the council of dialogue.

It would be useful to consider more closely here the nature of dialogue in order to bring out its riches and promises. A dialogue has two aspects, two faces on its coin. It demands on the one hand that a person listen in order to serve better, and on the other hand that he receive in order the better to give. We will reflect a bit on these two aspects of dialogue.

To listen to the world is to open oneself to the "questions about the current trend of the world" (*Modern World*, art. 3); or as the conciliar text says elsewhere, to scrutinize "the signs of the times" (art 4). No one can deny that "Today the human race is passing through a new stage of its history. Profound and rapid changes are spreading by degrees around the whole world" (*ibid.*).

We are all involved in these changes but the important thing is that we understand them. We must take hold of them so that they do not carry us along by the force of their own momentum.

To listen, then, means also to understand, to judge, to distinguish permanent values from what is merely fleeting and of the moment, to separate the truth which brings freedom from all that can lead us into a new kind of slavery. Briefly, to listen to our age is to know it clearly and sympathetically.

Then again, we must listen carefully to what the world presents for our hearing. It is a collection of things and events that is given to us as the support of our life and the context of our action. It is also the object of our activity, the work of our hands, always to be refashioned in keeping with the changes in the human condition. The world is at once a situation conferred upon us and a task which we freely assume.

Let us first discuss the world as situation. This is nothing else than that vast ensemble of "profound and rapid changes" which result in the fact that today the human race is passing through a new stage of its history. Among these changes there are three which are principal.

There is, first of all, the prodigious advance of science and technology. This is the fundamental factor out of which flows all the rest. This advance, since it confers upon man an ever greater control of nature, has opened up a vision of inestimable possibilities and hopes for man's liberation.

There then follows as a direct consequence of this move forward in science and technology the unification of our planet, that is, the progressive abolition of those distances and mutual partitions which at one time separated individuals, people and cultures. There is the elimination of geographic distances due to the improved techniques of communication and information. There is the breaking down of economic and political barriers under the pressure of the need to internationalize the development and political life of nations. And finally, there is the reduction of ethnological and cultural distances because of the progress in education, the fight against illiteracy, and the greater knowledge of the various languages and customs of different people because of the daily meeting of various cultures in an atmosphere of respect and mutual aid.

But the evolution of modern techniques has also had another result. In effecting the unification of our planet it has made possible a heightened awareness of the people in the third world. This is the third great change in our modern world. It is the decisive event of our times, which Pope Paul VI has clearly delineated in the encyclical *Populorum Progressio*, which is, as it were, the *Rerum Novarum* of the 20th century.

The emergence of the third world is decisive because it signifies the awakening of the collective consciousness of the poor who still represent the very great majority of the human race. In this sense, it is the continuation on a global scale of that proletarian revolution which marked the history of the West during the latter half of the last century. The rise of the working masses in the industrialized countries and the rising of peoples in the developing nations are basically but two movements within the same historical process. It marks the appearance of the masses on the stage of the world; it is their entrance into history.

These three great changes: the growing power of technology, the unification of the planet, and the rise of the third world, make up one reality. They are bound to one another according to an inexorable logic and determine the direction of history. They characterize "the place and role of man in the world of today," the situation of humanity in our times.

But, as we have said, the world is also the work of man. Each new situation brings to birth new tasks. The logic within history is not of such a nature that it excludes human liberty and responsibility. This is precisely the paradox of human historical existence. It at once is within history and contributes to the making of history.

This means that the "profound and rapid changes" of which we have just spoken possess an ambivalent nature. They can turn to our good or to our ruin, depending upon our attitude toward them. Thus the liberating power of technology resides ultimately in the hands of man: everything depends upon the use he makes of it. The fact that man can use nuclear energy means that he can effect either the destruction of the human race or its progress. In the aftermath of Hiroshima, Denis de Rougemont most aptly wrote, "The bomb is not dangerous. It is but a thing . . . What is so horribly dangerous is man."

An all-powerful technocracy runs the risk of dehumanizing human society, of taking all that is sacred out of human life, of stifling what Gabriel Marcel has called "the capacity to wonder."

The same thing is true of the unification of our planet. The multiplication of contacts between peoples and cultures can mean the enriching of human life, but it also can mean its impoverishment. Humanity could destroy itself just as effectively as by the bomb, if under the pretext of unity such a movement were to suppress creative liberty and endanger the genius proper to each culture.

The awakening of the third world is the pivotal point upon which the future will turn. It is the great hope of our times because it contains the seed of the will for greater justice and a more real equality among men. But if this hope were ever to find itself with no future, its failure could bring about the very worst of disasters. Is it not significant that Père Lebret could devote a book to the subject of the awakening of the third world under the title *The Suicide or Survival of the West*? This means that the entrance into history of countries on their way to development concerns us all.

To listen to the world is, finally, to allow oneself to be affected by the anguished cry of the great throng of the poor, of all those who hunger and thirst for a more real justice. It is to put an end to our disputes, which are as ruinous as they are scandalous, and to begin to work resolutely for the building up of a more human world, a world founded, according to the famous phrase of John XXIII in *Pacem in Terris*, upon "truth, justice, love and liberty."

The building of a more human world raises numerous and difficult problems of an economic, social and political order. It is also—and let us not forget it—a spiritual and moral task. At its depths, it means the forming of a new humanity, a humanity less egoistical, more concerned for the good of all, more conscious of its solidarity within history and of its collective responsibility. In this regard, the *Constitution on the Church in the Modern World* quite appositely says, "Thus we are witnesses of a new humanism, one in which man is defined first of all by his responsibility toward his brothers and toward history" (art. 55).

"To be a man," writes Antoine de Saint-Exupéry, "is, precisely, to be responsible. It is to feel shame at the sight of what seems to be unmerited misery. It is to take pride in a victory won by one's comrades. It is to feel, when settling one's stone, that one is contributing to the building of the world."

To define man in terms of his responsibility before the bar of history is to define the man of our times, the man whom we must educate both within ourselves and around us, so that he may prove himself worthy to live within the great human family on a global scale. The development of this humanism of responsibility: this, ultimately, is the great task of our century. It is a task both spiritual and moral from which no one has the right to exempt himself, the church least of all.

Léon-Joseph Suenens

And this brings us to the other movement of dialogue. We have said that dialogue is an act of listening in order to serve better, an act of receiving in order the better to give, and so arises the question: what can the church bring to the world of today?

The formula could be reversed and we could ask: what is it that the world awaits from the church? One thing is certain and it is apparent in the growing interest of the world in the work and conclusions of the council: men of today, searching for a human world, are awaiting something from the church.

But what? Certainly not that the church take upon itself the task of directing the world and claim its part within the temporal organization of the human community. In this the expectations of the world and the desires of the church correspond perfectly.

One of the great themes of the pastoral constitution on the church is precisely that the relationship of the church to the world should be thought of in terms of the legitimate autonomy of the temporal sphere. As Paul VI pointed out in an address to the Diplomatic Corps:

> The Church stands forth as entirely disengaged from any temporal interest . . . Is this to say that the Church has abandoned the world to its own destiny, for better or worse, and has retired to the desert? Quite the contrary. She separates herself from worldly pursuits only to penetrate human society more effectively, to serve the common good, to offer her help and the means of salvation to all men. She does this in such a way today as to contrast with the attitude which has characterized certain pages of her history. This is indeed a characteristic of the council, quite often revealed in it.

What the men of today are awaiting from the church, and what the church desires to give them, is, in the famous phrase of Bergson, that the church be within the whole of this world as a sort of "soul supplement." For indeed, every "enlarged body," writes Bergson, awaits a "soul supplement." And who can doubt that the church is able to assume this role of "soul supplement"?

The church, as a living community of the disciples of Christ, is not a reality estranged from this world. As a people witnessing to Christ, itself forming part of the human family, it lives among men in a community of exchanging dialogue, in order to maintain upon this earth the living and active word of Christ.

But has not this word of Christ appeared from the very moment of its eruption in Judea and throughout all the centuries as a gospel? It is the proclamation of the good news which does not only announce good things but also makes them present and available to the degree that the message is accepted in the "obedience of faith," that is, in listening and in fidelity.

These good things are called by St. Paul the fruits of the Spirit, and he names them: "love, joy, peace, patience, kindness, goodness, fidelity, gentleness and self-control" (Gal. 5, 22-23).

As we have just heard, that which the word of Christ effects in the world through the mediation of all those who open themselves up to this word, and to the degree that they so open, is not a "flight into the desert," but rather a deep sense of who man is, a concern for men without regard to person, and a deep transformation of human relationships. It is, in effect, that very thing for which our world, searching for truth, justice and liberty, has such great need at this moment.

There is, within Christianity, a deep reverence for man, inseparable from its faith in a God who is infinitely good, and the Father of all men. For the Christian, the affirmation of God takes nothing from the greatness of man; and faith in God, when well understood, never means alienation from one's brother.

In the Christian perspective of things, respect for man, or in modern terms the recognition of man by man, has its origin ultimately in the recognition of man by God. "What is man," cries the psalmist, addressing his God in prayer, "that you remember him!"

You have made him lack but a little of God;
with glory and honour you crowned him,
gave him power over the works of your hand,
put all things under his feet" (Ps. 8, 1. 6-7).

In thus conferring upon each human person a dignity which transcends all the goods of this earth, and upon human life an infinite value, Christianity has appeared in the world as an inestimably fruitful force for humanization. It has contributed greatly to introducing and maintaining alive in the world a sacred respect for life and death, a sense of the radical equality of all human beings, and a love for truth and truthfulness ("Plain Yes or No is all you need to say," the gospel tells us). It guards an extremely and elevated notion of liberty and responsibility, delicacy and gentleness in human relations, the sense of measure and repugnance for fanaticism, fidelity in love and the sacred character of the family, and the priority of work over money. In short, it contributes to that admirable harmony of spiritual and moral values whose proper role is to save the human person from the tyranny of the anonymous forces which threaten it: an excessive mechanization of human work, a totalitarian technocracy, political dictatorship, and the anonymity of a public opinion which provides the basis for demagogy.

But there is also a Christian universalism, or if you will, a catholic dimension of Christianity. And this can aid us in resolving the difficult problem arising from the meeting of cultures in a unified world. The proper characteristic of the Christian understanding of man lies precisely in its blending together of the greatest universal comprehension with respect for the individual. Then, too, Christianity is bound to no particular culture though it is able to render all more fruitful. Christian universalism is an enriching thing. This was one of the great experiences of Vatican II, where nearly three thousand bishops coming from the most remote corners of the world worked together to update their church.

And let us say, finally, that for Christianity this sense of man is not an abstract ideology or lovely sentiment of universal sympathy lacking all contact with history. Rather, it must be the very soul and driving force of all our actions. It is the existential truth of Christianity: "If a man does not love the brother whom he has seen, it cannot be that he loves God whom he has not seen" (1 Jn. 4, 20). Or again: "But if a man has enough to live on, and yet when he sees his brother in need shuts up his heart against him, how can it be said that the divine love dwells in him? My children, love must not be a matter of words or talk; it must be genuine, and show itself in action" (1 Jn. 3, 17. 18).

And this recalls that phrase of Bernanos which so beautifully expresses the bond between love of God and the service of one's brethren: "What others are expecting of us, that is what God expects."

To love one's neighbor as oneself is thus to work for his advantage. It is, within a world which is becoming one, to assume that collective responsibility of which we have spoken and to collaborate in transforming this earth into a dwelling place worthy of man, thus making of it a home for the great human family to live in truth, justice and peace.

The creation of a social, political and economic regime which is more human and which answers to those desires for peace, justice, liberty and brotherhood which characterize our time: this is the task of the economists, jurists, social workers, men of state and international groups. And to join with all the spiritual and moral forces of our time in order to plant deeply within the hearts of men a respect for man: this is the task which the church desires to perform ever more perfectly and profoundly.

If, then, in the words of Paul VI, "The church detaches itself from the interests of this world," in keeping with the spirit of the council, it is solely in order the better to serve and to fulfill its role of *Mater et Magistra*, that is, of mother and teacher.

This, it seems to me, now that Vatican II is over, is the abiding dialogue between the church and the world for the future. The church believes itself to be the inheritor of spiritual riches which can make of this world a better place to live. It knows full well that it carries these treasures in earthen vessels, but the mission which has been confided to it far surpasses in grandeur the poverty of its messengers. It approaches the world of today as Peter once came to the man seated at the gate of the Temple. This man awaited from Peter some sign of fraternal concern. Peter simply said, "Silver or gold I have none; but what I have, I give you: in the name of Jesus Christ of Nazareth, arise and walk" (Acts 3, 6).

Without temporal power, lacking technical solutions, which are not its proper sphere, the church of Vatican II has but one ambition: to aid the world in freeing man from the bondage of ignorance, mistrust and fratricidal hatred, and to aid in the building, along with all men of good will, the humanism of tomorrow combining all the power of the forces of peace.

Karl Rahner
1904-

Karl Rahner was born in Freiburg, Germany, and received his early schooling there. In 1922 he entered the Jesuit novitiate in Feldkirch, Austria. He went to Pullach as a scholastic from 1925 to 1927. In 1929 he began his theological studies in Valkenburg, Holland, and was ordained a priest in Munich in 1932. In 1934 he was sent back to his hometown of Freiburg to take a degree in philosophy. The chair for Catholic philosophy was occupied by a mediocre scholar named Martin Honecker, under whose direction Rahner did his dissertation, but it was Martin Heidegger who was the star of Freiburg and in whom Rahner was really interested.

In 1936 he went to the University of Innsbruck where he received a doctorate in theology and was, in 1937, appointed to the faculty to teach theology. But the next year the Nazis abolished that faculty and in 1939 they also closed the Jesuit college. When the war ended in 1945 he was called to teach in Pullach and Munich. In 1948 he went back to Innsbruck, where he remained until 1963, when he was asked to return to Munich to take the chair previously occupied by Romano Guardini. In 1967 he went to the University of Muenster, but in 1972 returned to Munich.

It was while at Innsbruck that Rahner's phenomenal output of theological writing really got under way. He manifested *boundless energy and originality, contributing to major projects (e.g., he improved and enlarged Denziger's* Enchiridion Symbolorum *from its 28th through its 31st edition (1958); he played a major role in the revision of the* Lexikon für Theologie und Kirche, *a ten-volume work of more than 30,000 articles; he co-edited a series of* Quaestiones Disputatae, *and from 1954 on he gathered his own writings into volumes called* Schriften zur Theologie, *which continue to appear regularly.)*

In the decade of the 1950s Karl Rahner was looked upon by many with some suspicion. His "theological anthropology" was too novel an approach. But with the advent of Pope John XXIII it was only a matter of time until Rahner's theology began to receive signs of more favorable recognition. In 1962 he accompanied Cardinal Koenig of Vienna to Rome as theological advisor and before long Pope John named him a peritus. Pope Paul VI received him twice in private audiences in November, 1963, thanking him for his work and encouraging him to continue boldly on the path he had opened.

It would be difficult to overestimate the impact of Karl Rahner on Vatican II. His thoughtful approach to virtually every area of theology insured that he would be listened to time and time again. His familiarity with modern thought as well as the historical tradition, his pastoral commitment influencing all his speculation, and his concern to raise endlessly the crucial questions have commended him to our era. If his answers are occasionally felt to be inadequate or obscure, they at least set Christians thinking in a new and different way. He has been called the 20th-century Aquinas, to which one must reply that at least·he comes closer than anyone else on the scene, and he has also been called the "Christian Socrates," goading all to think more deeply and look more closely at the implications of their faith.

Because of the very profusion of his writings any selection on a particular theme might be replaced with another, deemed more appropriate by a given reader. What follows is a portion of his book on The Priesthood *(1973). It is based on a retreat he gave in 1961, and thus shows some of the themes on his mind right before Vatican II where he had great impact on how the church was understood.*

THE PRIESTHOOD

CHAPTER IX

THE CATHOLIC PRIESTHOOD

I. Mediating functionary of a total religious system

First of all a very secular and realistic reflection on the priest, seen from an empirical-sociological viewpoint. If the church is a visible society—and this is what the catholic church asserts, against all protestant heresies—then she has a social embodiment, and this can certainly—even though only analogically—be described in general sociological categories and terms. The same holds in a true, though provisional, sense for the priesthood. If we were to be carried away by any kind of idealism and did not see this aspect, it could lead only to disillusionment and to dangers for our priesthood.

If we consider the priest from a sociological-empirical standpoint, we might describe him as a mediating functionary of a total—but not totalitarian—religious system. The church understands herself undoubtedly as a total system, integrating and seeking to integrate (in spite of all distinctions between the natural and supernatural orders) more or less all spheres of life into itself, which exercises authority over all these spheres, at least *ratione peccati.* Hence we can certainly consider the church (particularly the catholic church with her absolute claims, which she has and must have) sociologically and phenomenonologically as a religious system and define her as a total system. Then the priest is an office-holder, a functionary, within this total religious system: as ordinary priest, as priest of the second order, a mediating functionary who in any case has superiors above him.

In the first place then, regarded from the standpoint of this world, the priest is a kind of dependent official by contrast to someone who practises a profession. Through the priesthood we enter into an hierarchical body with clearly defined ranks and a definite structure of its own. This structure is given us in advance. We have to adapt ourselves to it. In this sense therefore we are officials of a *societas perfecta*. This is an absolutely correct definition of our priestly life and existence and, even though merely external and provisional, it must not be overlooked. We belong to a larger system: while being dependent on those above us and those below, we have a particular way of life, which exists before we make our own decision; we are in this sense therefore dependent officials.

All the peculiarities, all the mental-sociological necessities and dangers of such a state of life, with which we have to come to terms, arise out of these facts. Because we are officials of such a social-religious system, we have a way of life given us in advance.

This is not self-evident: for the priest is nevertheless plainly and simply the religious man. He is and must be the one who is driven by the Spirit. He must shape and plan his life from an innermost personal centre. But—unlike a hermit or a free charismatic—he can do so only by incorporating this innermost spiritual vocation of his into this officially pre-organised system. It is obvious that this will involve tensions, problems, pain and sacrifice. In this life of a dependent official within the church as a total religious system, as distinct from that of another official belonging to a different social structure, the priest necessarily no longer has any private life. The official of a structure that is not so totally religious can put part of his time, his strength, his interest, at the disposal of this social structure and reserve the rest to himself. There is a prior agreement between the social structure and the functionary about how much of his life the latter will place at the disposal of the former.

From the very nature of the situation this cannot be the case with the functionary of a total religious system. In a sense, he is always on duty. Of course he has a private life: he sleeps, eats, has certain hobbies which offend nobody, and so on. But this is not a reserved sphere of life: it has to be justified once again by this mission, in which he devotes himself wholly and entirely to this religious structure with its absolute claims. We cannot say from the first that we would like this period for our free time, that we will not give up this hobby, that this pleasure or this comfort is undoubtedly ours, and that we shall put at the disposal of the church and our priesthood only what is then left over (even though this may be a great deal). This won't work. In the light of this sociological aspect of his life, the priest must clearly understand that he belongs body and soul, with all that he is, to this church, to her task, to her mission, her work, her destiny, and can never dissociate himself from these things. A statesman can never say that his working day is finished, that all his tasks can be left aside after office hours. He must perhaps have some recreation, perhaps do something else, but he does all this only in the light of his mission as a great statesman. The same applies *mutatis mutandis* to our priestly life.

2. The risk of institutionalising religions

If the priest, seen from the outside and sociologically, is the mediating functionary in such a total religious structure, then—since as a man of religion, as a priest, he lives in a *societas perfecta* at the service of the divine—the risk of institutionalising religion exists. The priesthood is religion given an institutional form, with definite tasks and goals. The priest does not pray simply in an outburst of enthusiasm or idealism, he has to "complete" a part of the breviary each day; it is not only when he is seized by the Spirit of God that he celebrates the eucharist, he says mass every day; he does not speak merely out of the warmth of his heart, he has to take classes, he has to talk about God even when he finds this boring.

All this belongs to the priestly life: as the life of a functionary of a *societas perfecta religiosa*, it is necessarily institutionalised religion. Anyone who felt that he could have nothing to do with this religious institutionalising could no longer be a christian. As priests we must accept the fact that we have to allow for and cope with considerably more of such institutionalising than is expected of the laity. This must not be allowed to kill the inner vitality of our religious life. We must accept the risk of such an institutionalising with trust in God and in the power of his Spirit. This Spirit has shaped his institutional, legal embodiment and guarantees constantly to cope with its limitations and rigidity.

What we accept of priestly, established institutionalism in our religious and priestly life is bearable and, if it is achieved in the right way, can even be and remain a very substantial fostering, preservation, realisation and objectification of the inner spirit of the priesthood. Of course we must see the dangers of such an institutionalising of religion, in which our priesthood is involved: the danger of over-exertion, of the unauthentic, of routine, of feeble compromise, of perversion of values, with the result that religious life then becomes a means to private life, becomes stereotyped, outwardly clericalised, the practice of a priestly life no longer in accordance with its spirit, since it is presumably deliberately over-taxed through this institutional element.

Of course it is difficult to say office every day at all meaningfully, to celebrate mass daily as participation in the last supper of Jesus Christ, as the proclamation of his death, the taking up of his cross, as the anticipated celebration of eternal life. The danger exists of exercising this ministry in a routine way, unauthentically, merely bureaucratically, in a purely external institutional fashion. We must constantly protect ourselves against this correctly and skilfully, with an intelligent psychology and by avoiding unreasonable over-exertion. God will certainly give us his grace.

3. Continuation of Christ's priesthood

We are asking what is the inner reality, what is the real meaning of such a sociological phenomenon which we must face soberly and clearly if we want to become and to be priests. It is—briefly—the continuation of the priesthood of Christ. Christ in his unity of God and man, as the grace of humanity in self-achievement and self-utterance, is plainly and simply priest; as personal agent, he is the primal sacrament fulfilled, inseparably united with the reality signified, primal sign that the infinite grace of God, which is God himself, has been bestowed on mankind eschatologically, victoriously, effectively; that is to say that Christ imparts himself through his being, through the self-achievement of his divine-human reality and through the self-utterance in which he proclaims what he is. The church and the priest must be seen from this standpoint, the priest however in the unity of the cultic and prophetic elements.

In the light of the old testament the catholic priest is a unity of cultic-levitical priesthood and the non-institutional prophetic calling. These two functions, separated in the old testament for very profound but provisional reasons, were united in Jesus Christ. The catholic priest achieves this unity of prophetical, evernew, incalculable priesthood, called to topical proclamation of the word, and the permanent, enduring cultic priesthood. At the same time, it must also be seen that the catholic priest does not continue these two functions of the eternal high priest, united in Jesus Christ, in such a way that this high priest Jesus Christ abandons his functions and disappears into the silent eternity of God, but in such a way that he is in a true sense merely the instrument of this one permanent high priest Jesus Christ. Consequently, he is only the one who can offer the sacrifice of Christ in time and space, here and now, but without multiplying it, even though the cultic celebration is multiplied; and he can speak and accomplish in his prophetic ministry only the word of Jesus Christ and no other, new word surpassing this, but can only be the ministerial actuality of this final word of Jesus Christ—which in the last resort is Christ himself.

From this standpoint we must also observe how this personally recruited prophetic priesthood of the new covenant establishes a way of life. There is a new, special mode of existence in relation to other christians and distinct from theirs, which directly sets up a state of life for the priest as prophet. By expounding his word, implementing his cultic mandate, he links this prophetic element of course with the cultic priesthood: this the catholic priest possesses in so far as he performs this expounding, proclaiming, defending, preaching, persuading function of interpreting this efficacious sacramental word in his mission, the mission which drives him out of his native, secular situation. Because he must proclaim—*opportune, importune*—the word of Christ at a point where he does not belong in virtue of his natural, secular condition, the ordained priesthood in the catholic church acquires a very special character, distinguishing it from the life of the normal christian.

Consider all these things in connection with other words of scripture which describe this essence of the christian priesthood. He is the envoy, the representative of Christ and the Father, steward of the mysteries of God (1 Cor 4:1); he is the fellow-worker of God (1 Cor 3:9). It is said of the apostles, the first priests, that they are Christ's friends (Jn 15:15), that they bear witness to Christ (Ac 1:8), that in a particularly impressive way they are the heralds, the preachers of the word of God (Rom 15:16). Always and everywhere among all nations and at all times, they preach *metanoia,* the advent of the kingdom of God. They preach the good news, by Christ's mandate, as his envoys (Eph 3:8). Their task is described as the ministry of the word. They are the dispensers of the sacraments (2 Cor 5:18); they are called teachers of the nations, fishers of men (Mt 4:19). They are described as fathers of souls, whom they beget in their supernatural life in Christ Jesus through the gospel.

4. Servants of the community

Here is something to which I would like to draw your attention. Priests—as the name suggests—are the elders, *presbyteroi,* in the community, for the community and from the community (Ac 11:30; Rom 12:8; Phil 1:1; 2 Tim 1:6). By and large, however, priests today are not of the older generation in the sense of biological age; but this relationship of service to the community is of the essence of the catholic priesthood. Although the priest's mandatory powers are given him by Christ and not given to the laity, these powers are given in a ministerial sense, since Christ loves and wills the community of the redeemed, of the justified, of those united in love. The church has an existence and structure prior to her official hierarchical constitution; and, however much the hierarchical structure belongs to her necessary being, founded by Christ, it exists in fact because this church is and must be and because Christ has redeemed and called together mankind into the community of believers, of the justified and redeemed.

We do not obtain our official powers democratically from the multitude: we have them because there is and must be the holy community of God in Jesus Christ. All these functions therefore are ministerial functions. In the last resort those in

372

the highest place are not pope and bishops, not priests, but those who believe most radically and love God most radically in Jesus Christ. First and last is and remains this inner hierarchy of holiness. All juridical, hierarchical structure has merely a ministerial and sacramental function in regard to this church of the Spirit, as Augustine in his day explained at length. We must always be aware of this in our calling. Even today we constantly hear from the faithful the reproach of clerical exclusiveness, of clerical arrogance, of clerics claiming always to know better. These attitudes are contrary to our nature as priests. We are merely ministers of reconciliation (2 Cor 5:18), "ministers of their joy" (2 Cor 1:24), those who deliver another's message and can do nothing else but—to quote Ignatius—"to unite the creature directly with its creator".

In the *Acts of the Martyrs* there is an account of the martyrdom of Bishop Felix of Thibiuca. There we read, at the end: "Bishop Felix, raising his eyes to heaven, said in a clear voice: 'God, I thank you. I have lived 56 years in this world. I have kept my virginity, I have upheld the gospels, I have preached the faith and the truth. Lord God of heaven and earth, Jesus Christ, I bend my neck as victim to you who remain for ever.' " At the close of our priestly life, by whatever kind of death it comes, we should be able to pray in these brave words.

CHAPTER X

PRIESTLY OFFICE AND PERSONAL HOLINESS

One point of the last meditation is of great importance for the correct understanding of the priesthood: it is the problem of office and person, of official mandate and personal holiness. Of course we know from what we were taught about asceticism that the priest ought to be holy and virtuous, that he ought to be a shining example to the faithful entrusted to his guidance. Nevertheless, it is a good and useful thing to consider more closely this relationship between official mandate and personal holiness: for—in spite of all exhortation to asceticism— under the influence of the idea of the *opus operatum* and official, mandatory powers, of an anti-Donatist defensive reaction, we are always tempted to see office, priesthood and its powers independently of our personal life.

At least from Augustine's time or from the time of the reformation, the catholic church has been apparently the church of objective powers, the church of the *opus operatum,* which is independent of the holiness of the ministers. We stress the fact that a person does not lose his membership of the church as a result of his own personal sinfulness, that the "objective powers" continue to be active even in the sinful priest. We train the faithful to appreciate the mass and the sacraments, even the sacramentals, without regard to the person who undertakes these sacred actions, without regard to the degree of the priest's holiness. Behind this is the objectivist, anti-Donatist feeling, which is right up to a point, but can mislead us into over-looking the firm, intrinsic unity of person and office. We need only look more closely at our moral theology in its lesser and finer ramifications to see that there are a number of problems here which have not been properly considered and that there certainly remain objectively false deviations from the right conception which combines subjective, existential religious activity on the one hand and objective accomplishment of the institutional requirements of the church on the other.

1. Love decides

Ultimately, what counts for God is simply and solely the personal, freely given love of the individual. The love which he brings about through his Holy Spirit and which cannot be brought about through anyone except the Holy Spirit of God's grace and the wholly personal unique freedom of the individual. All the rest—church, institution, sacraments, *opus operatum,* all that is regulated and institutionalised—is nothing but a means to this personal commitment, willed by God, objectively necessary and completely justified. Objective holiness of the church too in the truth of her proclamation, in the *opus operatum* of her sacraments, in the divine law which she makes her own, in her persistence to the end, is nothing but the means to this one end: that there should be believing, loving, hoping, loyal human beings, united to God.

This holds obviously for us too in so far as we are not only christians, but also priests. This does not mean at all that these two aspects are in the last resort fundamentally opposed, that we can have the one only by sacrificing the other, just as— if you like—the Donatists or Wyclif, or Hus and the protestants, thought. It remains true that there is subordination, a hierarchy of values which is important for practical questions; and in this genuine catholic hierarchy of values, love, grace, inner justification, inward commitment in freedom to God are super-ordinated to office, sacraments, institution, to any objective sum-total of obligations. This is seen still more clearly, if we reflect on the holiness of the church rightly understood.

2. Holy church

When we say that the church is the permanently holy church, we do not mean merely—as in the old covenant— that the objective institution of the church and her truth, her proclamation, is true, her sacraments are valid, her institution is permanent; but we mean also that God himself, through his predestining, efficacious grace sees to it that the church, in her members as a whole, is also always the subjectively holy church: for this is just what God wants in regard to this eschatological community of believers.

A church which was only objectively, in its institutions and its proclamation, in accordance with God's will, and in this sense holy, would not be the church of Jesus Christ, the church as eschatological reality. For it is simply and solely through Jesus Christ, because of the last days, because of the absolute, victorious power of his definitive redemption, that a church is founded which, in the power of the Holy Spirit and his grace, overtaking, not destroying, but sustaining freedom, permanently provides for the church in her members to be the subjectively holy church. But this means that the danger which both Donatists and anti-Donatists seem to fear will not arise: namely, that one day the subjectively holy church and the objectively holy church—regarded in their whole reality—might fall apart.

There cannot really be a discrepancy so great as to involve the co-existence of objectively valid sacrament, objectively valid authority, truth rightly proclaimed on the one hand, and unholy, unbelieving holder of these mandates on the other. This danger exists only for the individual as individual in the church, but not for the church as a whole. This is why, particularly after Vatican I, the church is necessarily bound to appear as the subjectively holy and—in the inexhaustible abundance of her holiness so understood—as the sign raised up to the nations, and the permanent place for the practical experience of her divine foundation.

3. Unity of existential and institutional holiness

From all this we clearly perceive that there is and must be a unity of existential and institutional holiness, necessary first of all for the church as a whole, a unity indispensable to the church, produced by God through the power of his grace. This unity of existential and institutional elements, necessary for the church, is therefore obviously required of the individual priest. Only when he realises this unity to a significiant degree is the priest the person he must be. The priesthood of the church is completely the priesthood of holy men and not of holders of office for whose meaning and importance this personal holiness is a matter of indifference. If the latter were the case it would lead to an absurd situation in which we could say that the sacraments only have to be valid in themselves, although of course they are fortunately also often fruitful.

The sacrament as such is defined in the light of its significance and of the grace it really imparts to the individual human being. It is of course easy to see the reasons why, as *opus operatum,* it can also at times be valid and yet not fruitful; but this is a sacramental situation which, from the very nature of the sacrament, ought not to exist and ought not to be allowed to exist. To this extent, the merely institutional priest of the *opus operatum,* who does not fill this with the whole force of his personality, thus sustaining what he does, preaches, ministers and so on, is not the person he ought to be.

It is not as if God in a moral ruling, for reasons more or less of edification, also requires holiness on the part of the bearer of his official, mandatory powers, because this looks better, because it is anyway more fitting; this existential holiness of the bearer of objective powers is something required by his very nature in the holy church of the eschatological situation, and absolutely required in the indestructible and also subjectively holy church. This does not mean that the office would cease to exist if this requirement were not satisfied, but it does mean that this requirement really corresponds also to the innermost nature of office in the church and is not here an additional moral requirement on Christ's part.

Some conclusions emerge now which we can think out for ourselves. I have already pointed out that Paul does not think at all simply and primarily in terms of the objective administration of the sacraments: properly speaking, his thought is dominated by the proof of the dynamism of the Spirit, by his preaching, in which his whole person is existentially involved (2 Cor 4:2, Eph 3:7) and only because of this is not indeed authorised, but becomes credible for the person who is to hear it. Here you see already how in fact it lies in the essence of priesthood to give expression in the priestly calling to this requirement of personal holiness; how understandable it is therefore when the Western priest wants and is also urged by the church to be more than a mere "massing priest", only taking care of the continuation of objective cult and objective administration of the sacraments in the church.

CHAPTER XII

THE PRIEST AND HIS SUPERIORS

The relationship of the priest to his superiors in church and order is undoubtedly a theme of great importance for the practice of the priestly life, especially for the life of a regular. We can consider the priest's relationship to ecclesiastical and to religious superiors at the same time, not only because these relationships are very similar, but because the order is itself part of the church with its constitutions and its structures approved ecclesiastically and canonically, and because religious obedience is also a part of our ecclesial-priestly obedience, particularly since his higher superiors are ordinaries for the regular as the bishop is for the secular priest.

1. Obedience as realisation of faith

First of all, we must consider obedience as an ascetic factor in the religious life as such, as a part of our spiritual life, and—within the order—as a way of achieving that inner assimilation to Christ which we want to realise as an evangelical counsel. This consideration and appreciation of obedience as an ascetic factor—independently of any practical application within the order, which has a common external aim—is undoubtedly the primary aspect under which obedience has been seen historically in the church.

Obedience in the religious life is first of all an evangelical counsel; it has been seen and lived as a way of religious renunciation. What does this mean? Every christian, as a person who is called to a supernatural end, is called to go beyond the human moral virtues of which we have direct experience in this world, in order to grasp in faith as the supreme and central value of his life a virtue which is not accessible to normal experience, but is and can be seen and grasped only in that quite unique act that we call faith: faith—that is—in the invisible, in that which has a supernatural quality. Such a faith cannot be conceived merely as a theoretical assent to a truth revealed by God which of ourselves we could not otherwise reach.

This faith must be existentially realised: the higher value and the absolute centrality of this supernatural end must be given concrete expression. This holds essentially for every christian: for every christian must be a believer, and all salutary faith is more than merely having no objections in theory to the truth of certain propositions. It is the voluntary realisation of these revealed goods of eternal life as central to us, made known and given to us only through revelation. Such an act of faith is by its nature already a kind of renunciation. The personal realisation of the higher values of the supernatural by comparison with merely human good, even moral good, can ultimately be brought about only by the voluntary sacrifice of intramundane good. This renunciation, this sacrifice, then appears as the expression of real faith in the central importance of the supernatural world, of man's destiny, transcending the present world and entering into the life of the triune God in himself.

This is an attitude that belongs to every christian life and need not consist in actively and spontaneously anticipating this renunciation. Through the darkness, the death-trend, the gloom, the pain, the finiteness and the vanity of this life, the christian is faced with the alternative either of despairing or of laying himself open, in an act of trust, faith and love, to God and his incomprehensible decrees. But the christian can deliberately approach this act of his renunciation—which belongs to the essence of christianity—by sacrificing certain positive human goods which it would be completely absurd and even unnatural to sacrifice if this world of God's supernatural self-communication did not exist.

There are circumstances in which a person might be deprived of such goods, even against his will, as a result of the situation in which life had placed him: he might be forced into poverty, he might—as Jesus said—have been born a "eunuch" (Mt 9:12). But quite freely and spontaneously to sacrifice such positive human goods, which essentially represent supreme human values, would be completely absurd, because such a sacrifice would not be at all justified, authorised or outweighed by the anticipation of a still higher value outside the natural order. That is why, incidentally, it is completely superfluous and fundamentally wrong to try to prove in terms of natural ethics—as the traditional moral philosophy did—that virginity, for instance, has a positive significance and value. This does not exclude the possibility that a particular individual in certain conditions might rightly renounce marriage, even within the natural order; but this would be justified only in a situation demanding this renunciation properly speaking against his will, not as something freely undertaken when another choice was open to him.

This is the correct theological interpretation and justification of the evangelical counsels. They are essentially acts of faith, hope and love in regard to those goods which are available only in a supernatural order, in faith, and accessible only in the grace of God. These evangelical counsels as acts of renunciation are authorised and justified only in regard to these goods, since it would be essentially absurd to sacrifice genuine human values merely for the sake of sacrifice. Renunciation of positive values never has any meaning or justification except for the sake of a higher value.

In this form, the renunciation required by the evangelical counsels does not belong simply to any christian life, but what is so realised—as renunciation, as act of faith in regard to the higher goods—is necessarily achieved once also in every other christian life, at least in death. For in death man must allow God to take all those goods which he might have offered more or less spontaneously in an act of faith inspired by the evangelical counsels: at death these goods are lost to man and, with the decline of the whole world (as man's world), the world of grace, God's life, emerges and can be grasped only in this way. Faith as total self-surrender, as loving submission of the whole person to God, is always an act of renunciation, because what is at man's disposal—whether in the field of truth or in the field of love—no longer holds that central position or provides that security which it does for someone who does not have to and does not want to believe.

The christian who undertakes obedience in a religious order of course sacrifices only up to a point positive, genuine human values. He renounces and can renounce them only in an act of faith which is a preparatory exercise of that act of faith which really involves the whole of human life and is ultimately required of every christian. We need not consider in detail the different dimensions of such (at least relatively) supreme human values as are yielded to God in the renunciation required by the three evangelical counsels. We know that obedience involves the voluntary surrender of some part of man's personal power to dispose of himself, which represents an absolutely positive value. This sort of thing has meaning for mature persons only as part of faith in God, in his love, in his supernatural grace.

Of course, independently of all this, people are always linked together in super- and subordination. But such an obedience is proved to be meaningful by the positive values which are realised through it. When we drive on the correct side of the road and thus avoid collisions, we are in fact obeying the secular authorities, but we also see the reason for it, and this voluntary limitation of our power to dispose of ourselves is rewarded, justified and shown to be good even in this world. It is therefore quite a different kind of obedience from that which is realised in the religious life, where the voluntary limitation of our power of self-disposal is not rewarded in this life. Or, if it is rewarded, it is so only up to a point. It is obvious that when men want to co-operate with each other in an order, rationally and humanly, as comrades—this too is a value that can be proved in human terms—there must be some sort of obedience. There is nothing special about this and therefore obedience of this kind ought not to be glorified by intelligent people, but should be regarded as a simple and obvious every-day fact.

This utilitarian meaning is not central to religious obe-dience and in the long run cannot justify and sustain obedience either in theory or in the practice of the religious life. It might well be reasonable if we were obedient only in this practical sense, if we were to acknowledge the necessity of co-operation for the sake of the kingdom of God and therefore the necessity of order, of leadership, of adaptation to greater teamwork. We would nevertheless at least be in danger of breaking down in our religious obedience. For there can be times when something is required of us, sacrifices are demanded, which cannot be justified in this merely rational and correct way, and then we would no longer see the point of such obedience.

No. There is an evangelical counsel, which is folly to the world, which would be meaningless apart from a radically realised faith. There is a religious obedience which requires us to sacrifice and renounce very positive values. The recom-pense of this renunciation is one that cannot be known or enjoyed in this world. Humanly speaking at least, it is possible from time to time to find obedience working out in the reli-gious life as something like stupidity, when someone has slipped into it and cannot prove the appropriateness of such obe-dience in this world. We must appreciate and stick to this sense of obedience as the christian's renunciation and as practice for a radical renunciation which is always imposed in the long run and which the christian will never be spared.

Even if it seems externally that the obedience involving a commitment of faith is not being asked of us, the fact remains that religious life as a whole, in its diffuse, general routine, without the will to this evangelical renunciation, would scarcely present a summons to a life's dedication. The whole of our life stands or falls only by the rules, by the constitutions, by the stereotyping of our life under a common denominator of renunciation, which at most overlooks the boredom, the lack of human feeling, the parsimony. But this is not an advantage and does not indicate any religious achievement: it is merely symptomatic of a deficiency in authentic, human vitality.

If however this vitality is present, then the religious life, particularly in its prosaic routine and normality, provides a challenge to obedience for someone who can bear this—especially if he is alive, humanly authentic and rich—only in a spirit of faith. If, instead of undertaking this task, he were to sink into mediocrity, to cut himself off from real life, to capitulate and compromise, and in this humanly defective state to take on the religious life, he would be like a person who had only managed a lesser calling although he had been meant for a greater; if we endure the religious life only in this way, reducing our claims and sinking into mediocrity, then we have misunderstood the meaning and purpose of obedience.

The fact that obedience is hard for us makes no difference. It would even be a bad sign either for our spirit of asceticism or for our human authenticity, vitality, and strength, if there seemed to be nothing more to obedience than regulated mediocrity, a life without sensations or excitement, a smooth, comfortable, bureaucratic existence. We would be doing our duty and receiving our food in return, we would be contented and therefore would not make any great claims on life. This is not what religious obedience really means. It is really the sacrifice of a value of central importance as an act of faith.

2. Obedience in the service of the church

Our religious obedience has of course another aspect: the ecclesial and apostolic aspect. This obedience, of a world-denying, ascetic character, as a mysterious, almost incomprehensible sacrifice of faith, is also placed at the service of ecclesial objectives. Firstly, at the service of the community life; secondly, at the service of the church's apostolate. It is as a result of these things that religious obedience and ecclesial obedience to superiors in the church acquire a new, additional meaning which has a positive value and is important for its own sake, which can sustain and justify religious obedience, not indeed as a whole, but still to a large extent.

A religious order placed at the service of the apostolate has a common task. A common work, a common external aim, needs a structuring, a unification, a general orientation of effort, and from this aspect too needs obedience. Thus ascetic obedience acquires a very practical purpose and meaning. This involves the danger of mistaking and overlooking the ultimate, religious, ascetic, even mystical aspect of faith. Obedience can retain the most essential supernaturally ascetic meaning, even when religious superiors or other authorities in the church issue orders which seem very problematic, perhaps very stupid, very wrong, very old-fashioned in relation to the apostolic purpose of obedience. It is obvious however that obedience does not cease to have meaning or justification when this apostolic objective is not attained. This of course does not mean that every order of a superior is as such always legitimate.

3. Authority and obedience

A third point that we must consider is authority and obedience in the pluralism of reality and of the christian virtues. What does this mean? We have already observed that even the radical renunciation involved in the evangelical counsels is not intended as an absolute, physical sacrifice of the values represented there (leaving aside for the time being the question of marriage and celibacy). In any case, it is possible to want to be absolutely poor in a material sense without actually being poor. Nevertheless, in this respect too, by comparison with the attitude of the lay christian, it can be a question only of a different emphasis, important quantitatively, but not of an ultimately essential difference. The layman too must renounce things which represent positive values for him, at least when God does actually take them away.

On the other hand, the religious cannot possibly live only on asceticism. A life wholly dominated by this asceticism as renunciation and sacrifice of human values would not be christian, but perhaps buddhist. If the christian wanted to turn renunciation into a single-minded attitude, monopolising all his life, he would be denying in practice, if not in theory, the reality of the human values which are not pure grace; these values would not be brought into the consummation of the kingdom of God. Both attitudes would be heretical, for ultimately the perfection of man and of the christian consists in the absolute and final salvation of christian and human realities by the supreme values of divine grace, of uncreated grace, down to the transfiguration of the body.

The attitude of the christian, also of the christian who is a religious, must imply always and everywhere the ultimate affirmation of God as God of nature and supernature in regard to all created things. That is why *a priori*, renunciation as such can never be absolute. This holds too for obedience.

Obedience cannot exist without an autonomous disposal by the individual of his freedom. Obedience and authority are very important factors in the life of the religious, which he must respect; but they could never completely guide his life. Even the religious who would leave it to his superior to approve, confirm, direct and guide the smallest details of his life, still cannot avoid putting some suggestions before the superior. Even if he declares that he will leave everything to the absolute discretion of the superior and thus allow himself to be treated "like a stick in the hand of an old man" or "like a corpse", he is by that very fact making an autonomous gesture which he could not have left to the superior to initiate.

Simply because I am free—and obedience itself is dependent on this—I must necessarily have autonomous impulses which cannot be ruled by the superior. Heaven does not first ask the superior what inspirations and impulses to bestow on the individual. The situation has changed then, even for the superior, before questions are asked. He can then always still give directions, he can choose; but he directs what has already begun, his choice has already been made by someone else. It is only as one factor in a plurality of impulses, dynamisms, that he tries to see something of what he can do about projects put before him and submitted to his authority. This does not mean merely that obedience is kept within proper and reasonable limits, which all ascetic tirades cannot set aside, but that a very considerable responsibility is imposed on us.

In other words, I can never say that everything is in the best of order because the superior has given his blessing. I have to recognise that, in spite of my obedience, I have an absolute responsibility before God which neither superiors nor obedience can take away from me. This is a truism, but you would not think so when you read the normal ascetic effusions on obedience. They overlook this fact, but they do not thereby encourage obedience: they make asceticism too cheap. For this renunciation of my freedom, of my autonomous responsibility, even with the best will in the world on the part of the most punctilious superiors and on the part of the most obliging subjects, can in fact only go part of the way. It cannot go further, since the superior cannot have merely *materia prima* to deal with in the subject, but is facing another person, someone with charisms, with the autonomous impulses of his freedom.

If authority and obedience constitute one element in a greater reality and in a pluralism of the christian virtues, obedience cannot be made to bear the whole burden of a man's spiritual life and way of life, of decisions and guidance. Superiors cannot want this, even if they sometimes behave as if they preferred subjects so completely obedient.

Here again it is clear that this pluralism is in a sense incalculable. How far I may permit myself to be influenced by the superior, how far I am active myself, when I make my own plans and when I take over what others have planned: all these things must remain within the framework of obedience. When the superior says, "Thus far and no farther", he is right and his "No" will be respected. But the possibility remains of adding larger or smaller doses of obedience and no one can deprive me of the right to make my own estimate of the dosage.

St. Ignatius does in fact say here and there that we must fulfil every wish of the superior. But he is not all that serious about it: in practice, he shows that he has no great opinion of subjects who do this. Within the framework of obedience, I must do things which are not at all to the liking of the superior. If he simply will not have this, he should have the guts and the manliness to accept his responsibility and say: "That must stop!" But in pastoral practice, in education, in scholarship, you cannot adapt yourself one hundred per cent to just any arbitrary wishes, opinions, attitudes or tastes of the superior. This would be impossible if only because you cannot in the last resort jump out of your skin, and because a superior may not always be particularly sympathetic to you.

Obviously we can assume that our superiors never order anything which they consider subjectively to be a sin. But we must certainly allow for the possibility of superiors ordering something that is objectively against the commandment of Christ and the church and of moral theology: something that is objectively impossible for the subject, but is not perceived to be such by the superior. In such a case, a person must really have the courage to appeal to his conscience and refuse to obey the commandment. This does not often occur, but its rarity may perhaps be due to the fact that we are too lax. But if anyone were to think that these simple and obvious facts justified him in grumbling, protesting, muttering about his conscience whenever something was not to his taste, he would be wrong. We cannot hope to avoid such wrong conclusions if we simply pigeon-hole the correct principles, suppressing them without openly denying them.

4. Practical conclusions

There must be a real will to obedience as an act of selflessness in faith: the will and desire to experience in this life an absolute test of faith. Why should we not want at some time to face a situation in which we are really obeying without being praised by superiors, without being recognised by men, because we seek nothing but God and because by the very fact of exercising our freedom we are surrendering ourselves to God?

Moreover, it is a part of true obedience to take the initiative and make our own decisions in the line of duty. We have not only the right, but today more than ever the duty, to take the initiative. Our apostolic situation particularly presents so many facets today, is so complicated, so far beyond the supervision of the individual superior, that a religious order would be a boring, dismal set of people unless its subjects also developed a large measure of initiative. However intelligent the superior may be, he cannot really understand something about all the modern opportunities for the apostolate. If he is intelligent and does not think he knows something about everything, he can lead his subjects only in a very formal sense; he can often in a way say no more than: "Think this over sensibly and, if you decide you must act differently, then do so. You also have my blessing for it." Thus each takes on and has to bear a large measure of responsibility.

There is also a responsibility of our own, of which no one can deprive us, even if something is quite clearly ordered; for then too we can at least be asked if we have seriously and honestly tried to discover whether sin is involved or not. This much is not only our right, but our duty. We can certainly assume that what is ordered is morally unobjectionable. But we can have no more than a presumption. We are never dispensed from the responsibility of forming our conscience in regard to what is ordered.

Real obedience includes the courage to be a troublesome subject. Not a grumbler, not one who is always complaining, who always knows better, who cannot fit in anywhere, who presumes *a priori* that whatever the superiors order is absurd and unreasonable until the contrary is proved. There are subjects like this and to some extent we have all been among them. If an unsympathetic superior orders us to do something, we are very easily inclined—and this is understandable—to look first for reasons for saying that it is absurd, instead of trying at once to understand its meaning. But all this does not alter the fact that we must have the courage to be troublesome subjects.

And, independently of the question whether a definite obligation is imposed, we should also have the will and strive constantly to be amiable, friendly, agreeable subjects, meeting our superiors too in a proper, manly and refined manner. This too belongs to the marginal, human phenomena of a religious obedience.

CHAPTER XIII

THE PRIEST AND MEN

The priest has a unique relationship with men. As the epistle to the Hebrews says (5:1), he is "appointed on behalf of men": his whole being is dedicated to the service of others. He does not exist for himself: he has a function which orientates him with his whole life, his talk, his action, his example, his sacrifice and suffering, to other human beings. He is an apostle—just that, sent to serve.

1. Love and mission

This orientation of the priest and his priesthood to other people is sustained by his christian and universal love of neighbour; it is in a true and genuine sense a fulfilment of this christian love of neighbour. Human beings, by their very nature, are always essentially related to one another. This orientation of men to one another develops and is articulated in different ways according to the diverse strata of human nature. They live in one and the same physical world; through their mutual consanguinity they belong to a special type in the biological world; they are related to one another through the exchange of objective intellectual goods and values, of truth, of goodness. They are ultimately related to each other as person to person and finally united with one another by one and the same Holy Spirit, who elevates, sanctifies and raises up into the life of God all these underlying human strata and the mutual relationships in which they are involved.

In possession of the one Holy Spirit of God and the participation in the divine life that this gives, they are united with one another and related to one another in an intimacy that cannot be surpassed, since they can make God's Holy Spirit the unitive factor between them. Thus a community is created: a community based on mutual exchange of saving, redeeming and deifying truth and on mutual benevolence which can touch the salvation—that is, the deepest core—of the other person; and a community of inexchangeable individual persons. This is and

388

remains obviously the supernatural foundation sustaining the priestly relationship to the other person.

If it is true that the priest genuinely possesses and fulfils his priestly nature only when he personally believes, hopes, loves, is justified and holy, then his relationship to the other person must as such be sustained by that infused, divine virtue of supernatural love in the Holy Spirit which justifies man and places him in an intimate relationship to God himself and his neighbour. This neighbour is really and truly loved in and with God, for God's sake and in the light of God, and can be loved deeply and intimately only through the supernatural deifying power of the Holy Spirit whom God has given to us in the supernatural life of grace. All official mandates and official equipment must be ontologically and existentially of lesser consequence than that divine self-communication which consists in justifying grace: just because it is ultimately the uncreated self-communication of God to justified man, nothing can be greater or more important than this grace. Hence it is clear that all official priestly relations to men can be based only on this supernatural love of men, no matter how important are the special mandates involved.

It follows that, whenever the priest fails to realise in his priestly calling this most radical relationship to his fellow man which exists in God himself and in his divine life, he will also fail to come up to the requirements of his work as a priest. It follows likewise that all inner vitality, closeness, personal esteem for the other person must be included in the "heart to heart" of christian love of neighbour. Face the fact that you are properly a priest only if you truly love your neighbour as God in his Holy Spirit gives men power to love.

This priestly relationship to our neighbour should be sustained by supernatural love and, up to a point, represents a quite specific fulfilment of this love. The priest in his mission formally and explicitly wills his neighbour's salvation, his supernatural union with God, and thus expresses and makes official the inner core of love of neighbour, which is to love him in as much as he is loved by God. From this standpoint too we see how the merely authoritative, official, institutional factor not only does not define and cannot constitute by itself the relationship of the priest to men, but that this real, warm, vital, selfless, genuine love for the other person as such belongs to the priestly relationship to men.

2. Humble authority

Of course, the priest's relationship—in as much as he is a priest to the other person, even if it is not something higher than other relationships—is certainly something special. For there is an important, if perhaps supplementary factor underlying this relationship ontologically, supernaturally, ethically, which constitutes in the priesthood a special mission and thus a specific relationship to our neighbour. "We are ambassadors for Christ", says St Paul (2 Cor 5:20).

We are apostles, commissioned, sent on an official, authoritative mission to men. This gives a specific character to our universal christian love in which we really want the salvation of the other person. This ministering function is an authoritative function: the priest acts in the name of God. He is present as God's envoy. He proclaims God's word, not his own; it is God's grace he administers, not men's.

When we thus rightly claim God's authority before the people to whom we are sent, we must never forget that this authority is to be realised only in faith on both sides; otherwise it cannot be really present at all. For that reason, it is not to be compared with other authorities known to men, personal or otherwise; and it is just this that must also be seen in the way in which the claim to priestly authority in regard to men is asserted. People must see that this messenger himself is committed and sent in a conscience enlightened by faith and does not come to men as one wielding power and full of his own importance. The person who feels this authoritative function of the priest as directed at himself must be able to observe how this assertion of authority humbles the priest, makes him more unassuming, and seems to him more of a burden than anything else, since he perceives his own inadequacy as a bearer of this divine mandate.

It is a question of an authority over men different from any other that we know. The identity between the claim to authority and the holder of this authority is not the same in the priest as it is in the learned person in regard to the unlearned, the father in regard to the infant, political authority in regard to its subjects. This must be made clear in our behaviour towards other men. There must be no more of what is regarded as clerical arrogance, clerical self-confidence, clerical lust for power, which still exists even today. But today priestly authority can no longer be linked with greater learning as in the middle ages or with the colour of our skin as missionaries to savages. In former times this sort of thing was perhaps inevitable. The medieval priest simply could not avoid making the distinction that he could read and write while Charlemagne could not. Vestiges of this way of thinking continue to influence us even today, but it is just this odd sort of mix-up that we must avoid. We are not more clever, better educated, not necessarily more mature, nor does the very fact of being priests make us more holy, but we have to invoke an authority which humbles us in regard to other men.

3. An important, but not the sole function

This priestly function in regard to other men is one particular function and relationship within the totality of human functions, dimensions and relationships. At some point every man is tempted to assert his own self-confidence—which in a sense is necessary for his existence—by claiming an absolute importance for himself and his task, at least in the circle which at all interests him. This tendency exists also among the clergy. This is always a danger for ourselves, and in fact in two ways: either we exaggerate our importance and minimise that of all other men or we become uncertain of the value of our priestly life: we feel that we are out-manoeuvred and not really taken seriously. Both attitudes are wrong.

We must quite calmly recognise that the priest too is a player, an important player, in the great drama that God produces in world history and in which he himself takes part in his eternal Word, the Word made man. But this is not to say that he is unique, just because from one particular aspect he plays a decisive role; it does not mean that all others are insignificant, that all other functions depend on us. We must strive to gain the humility, the courage, the inner self-assurance, to feel that we are God's envoys and to allow other people to live in a different way.

The priest must see things without prejudice: he is sent by God; he must fulfil his function within the totality of human life and human history. He need not feel threatened in his self-consciousness, self-confidence and self-respect, if there are things in science which he does not understand, if he is not up to date in matters of art, if he is not just the right person in other human relationships and dimensions.

This priestly function—and this is precisely what constitutes its closest relationship to christian love of neighbour—is ultimately one which is related to the individual as such. In the last resort, priests don't exist for the church, but for men's salvation. But this salvation of men must always be established through the freedom of the individual person. Of course the priest has ecclesiastical functions, which are related to the church as community, but these too are themselves directed to the salvation of the individual. He has to bear witness to christianity and the grace of God, and thus clearly show that priesthood, church and so on have nothing to do with a power-complex in society.

The conception of the priestly function as one of ministry to the individual human being in his individual salvation is more than ever necessary today. It is of course also a function which, even though sustained by christian love of neighbour, is not always for that reason accepted joyously and gratefully. There is really the "in season and out of season" (2 Tim 4:2) in the priest's relationship to his neighbour. The priest must also bear witness to his neighbour of God's truth, which can be painful, and of God's law, which can be hard. He must also stand up for the rights of God, even though these rights of God, which he claims, are ultimately nothing more than the right of love in which God wills to give himself as infinite bliss to men and claims no other right but to love man and with this love of his to be accepted by man. But for someone who is still immature as a human being and a christian, this right of God, which a priest must defend, may seem hard. Even then the priest has to exercise this function.

Karl Rahner

4. The priest and particular classes of men

Every priest has a certain affinity to particular types of men. He should easily make contact with these, but as priest he must also be accessible to men generally. Every priest therefore should meet men quite boldly, but at the same time without putting on airs. Take a look at the particular classes of men whom you will meet as a priest and ask yourself: How far am I succeeding in establishing an inner relationship with very young children, schoolchildren and students, with narrow-minded, pious people who are also and must be allowed in the kingdom of God, with university people, with the proletariat, with dubious characters, with those on the fringe of the church, with artists, with the sick and the dying? If we look at our practical behaviour as priests, we shall certainly see that our personal affinity for certain classes of men means that we have little time left over for the rest. We then tend to avoid other priestly tasks. And perhaps we over-estimate the work that we do as a result of our inner affinity for one group of people. We may perhaps be unfair to priests who have a special pastoral relationship with other people.

5. The priest and woman

After speaking of the priest's relationship with different classes of people, this would seem to be the place to consider expressly the priest's relationship to woman. You are old enough to know the importance, the difficulty, the burden, the arduousness of celibacy. In the Latin church you took on this obligation of celibacy as subdeacons. There is scope for a good deal of thought on the question of celibacy in the light of the principles of pastoral theology and also on its suitability in one respect or another. Why should we expect to be able to realise all our human possibilities in any one form of life, just because it is good and holy? A doctor cannot realise in his life just that fullness of life which a musician realises. He seizes on *one* value and—in this finite life, in this finite time, with finite resources, with finite human possibilities—necessarily renounces others. This holds too if we reach out for the value, for the evangelical way of life, represented by celibacy. This we must calmly and clearly affirm, in order then to live in absolute fidelity in accordance with our acceptance of this way of life.

There is of course very much more that could be said on this subject. Celibacy should not be made the centre of the priestly life, as if it were the most important thing in our life. It is not the easiest or the most obvious thing. It is a great and important task, a hard task, even though not the most central in our life, genuinely and completely to make this renunciation, to make it in such a way that nothing will be destroyed or left uncultivated which is not compensated by the spiritual power, the divine love, resulting from this way of life. Even if, strictly in terms of moral theology, celibacy is achieved without sin, it creates genuinely human dangers which can and must be avoided. There is the danger of becoming desiccated; of lapsing— as Clement of Alexandria said long ago—in a sublime, but only too real way into misanthropy through celibacy; of not escaping altogether unscathed as a result of attaching too much impor- tance to comfort, repose, an easy conscience. These dangers must be avoided.

Ultimately, this is possible only if we keep alive the positive ideals of our calling, if we have intellectual interests, if we work hard, if we have a healthy ambition and a healthy desire to achieve something, if we cultivate a life of prayer and enter as closely as possible into a personal union with God. Finally there must be a firm will to renunciation, and pedagogic and psychological prudence in regard to ourselves, so that all these things are not made more difficult than they really are: in other words, to live intelligently the life we have chosen and to shoulder the burden freely and gladly accepted out of love for Jesus Christ and for souls, in such a way that it absorbs no more strength than is necessary for coming to terms with this task. If we have no more spiritual force left over, because we are sitting—so to speak—on the powder barrel of our sexuality and have to use all our force on preventing an explosion, then we have certainly misunderstood and realised in the wrong way the celibacy that God offered us as his true grace.

The priest has to deal with human beings and when he really loves these human beings in a priestly spirit, in labour and sacrifice, he has really fulfilled his christianity and his own proper destiny. For it is true that the law is summed up in the one commandment of love of neighbour (Mt 22:39) and the person who selflessly finds his neighbour has also found God.

Richard Peter McBrien
1936-

Richard P. McBrien was born in Hartford, Connecticut, in 1936. He was ordained a priest from St. John Seminary in Brighton, Massachusetts in 1962 and served as assistant pastor in a parish in West Haven, Connecticut, as well as Newman chaplain at Southern Connecticut State College for the following year. He then went to Rome where he completed his doctorate in theology at the Gregorian University in 1965. From that time until 1974 he was on the faculty of the Pope John XXIII National Seminary in Weston, Massachusetts, and in 1970 he also joined the theology faculty of Boston College, where he continues to teach.

From his first publication, McBrien's central concern has been the meaning of the Church. In 1966 he published The Church in the Thought of Bishop John Robinson; Do We Need the Church? *followed in 1969, and in the next year came* Church: The Continuing Quest. *The selection that follows is taken from his 1973 book,* The Remaking of the Church: An Agenda for Reform. *The year it appeared he was president of the Catholic Theological Society of America. Cardinal Suenens wrote a preface for the book.*

McBrien's basic thesis is that the contemporary church is facing a crisis that is "the product of a theory-and-practice gap." His thirteen-point agenda is presented not as any kind of iron-

clad solution but as a "catalyst," meant to offer the type of concrete steps that might result in the resolution of the present crisis. He presents his analysis in terms of competing theories and practices, contending that there are three such pairs discernible, which he simply designates A, B, and C.

Theory A and Practices A characterized the life of the Church before Vatican II. Theory B and Practices B are those of Vatican II, while Theory C and Practices C are post-Vatican II. As McBrien sees it, proper remaking of the Church must include bringing "organizational operations of the Church into conformity with . . . the historic goals or mission of that Church," and the general membership must be motivated to "accept and pursue" those goals. Such an analysis allows one to put present polarization between groups in the Church into a more intelligible framework. While differences in practice, such as in liturgical rites, provoke immediate reactions because of their high visibility, too seldom is attention called to the differences in theory that lead to acceptance or rejection of the practices.

As Cardinal Suenens observes, one need not agree with all thirteen points of McBrien to benefit from his work. He has provided the service of expressing in readily understandable language a program for completing the changes begun by Vatican II so as to bring the Church closer to the kind of community intended by Christ. The fact that some of the proposals would call for energetic readjustment of outlooks and attitudes throughout the Church is a measure of how serious the author is about Church renewal.

THE REMAKING
OF THE CHURCH

CHAPTER III

AN AGENDA FOR REFORM

I f the present crisis within the Catholic Church is the product of a theory-and-practice gap, as described in the preceding chapter, then one can legitimately conclude that a constructive resolution of the crisis depends in very large measure on the closing of this gap. Practices, both institutional and personal, will have to be brought into conformity with the best theory; and alternate theories will have to be modified to correspond with the practical reality. If such a convergence of theory and practice does not in fact take place, then it is difficult to see how the Church can change its present course toward increasing institutional dissolution. Societies and communities cannot tolerate long-term intellectual and practical schizophrenia, and remain viable and healthy, any more than individuals can.

This view, of course, is shared by many others outside the formal discipline of theology. A canonical colloquium sponsored by the School of Canon Law at the Catholic University of America in May 1972 declared:

On the one hand, through Vatican II and the theological developments following it, the whole community is gradually appropriating a new vision of the Church and of its life, including priestly life and ministry. On the other hand, the present legal system of the Western Church dates back more than sixty years and originated in a significantly different understanding of the life of the Christian community. This growing discrepancy between vision and law gives rise to increasing tension. It creates a need for greater flexibility and instruments of harmony, since a community cannot long remain strong with a new understanding of its goals and an old set of norms to realize them.

I have been arguing throughout this book that differing attitudes on practical matters are only symptomatic of differing attitudes on theoretical questions. Catholics reject proposals for widening the process for selecting bishops, for example, not because they think the present system produces better leaders, but because they think that no other system can be reconciled with the divine plan. The Church is a monarchical institution by the will of Christ. Who becomes a bishop is a matter of such importance (since it involves adding yet another link in the chain of apostolic succession) that it must be reserved to the Church's absolute monarch, the Pope. Similarly, Catholics reject proposals for expanding the conditions under which Catholics and Protestants can participate in a common Eucharist, not because they dislike Protestants or regard them as inferior people, but because they perceive intercommunion of any kind, under any circumstances, as a compromise of the fundamental principle that the Catholic Church is the "one, true Church of Christ" and that all other Christian communities can be nothing more than ecclesiastical pretenders, without valid ministries or sacraments. Finally, Catholics reject the idea of deliberative parish councils (and their equivalents at other levels of ecclesiastical life), not because they distrust the judgment of nonordained Christians or because they entertain the naive notion that priests are invested with the fullness of wisdom and sound judgment, but because they perceive the Church as a hierarchically structured, visible society, founded and organized from the top down, according to a pyramid model. Decision-making must be unilateral; the Church, after all, is not a democracy. And so the process goes.

The judgment set forth in the preceding paragraph is empirically substantiated, in part at least, by the recent sociological investigation of the American Catholic priesthood, conducted by the National Opinion Research Center, University of Chicago, under the direction of the Reverend Andrew M. Greeley. In one of the most striking conclusions of the report, the authors cite the following as the first of eight "serious problems" facing the priesthood:

Richard Peter McBrien

Large numbers of priests are dissatisfied with the way the ecclesiastical structure is shaped and the way decision-making power is distributed; but the leadership of the Church does not share this dissatisfaction. Furthermore, it would appear that differences between younger and older priests on the distribution of power and authority are rooted in ideological differences about the nature of the Church and religion.

I shall offer in this chapter some specific proposals which, in my judgment and in the judgment of various formal groups and professional societies in the contemporary Catholic Church, belong on any agenda of serious ecclesiastical reform. In each instance, I shall identify the ecclesiological assumptions which inform the usual objections to these proposals, and I shall also recall and underline the relevant theological principles which can legitimate these reform measures. There are thirteen proposals in all. They are reducible to two principal goals: (1) to bring the organizational operations of the Church into conformity with, and place them at the service of, the historic goals, or mission, of that Church; and (2) to draw upon the resources of the whole Church in the fulfillment of this mission, by motivating the general membership to accept and pursue the Church's goals. This can happen only if the membership is allowed and encouraged to participate actively in the various processes through which these goals are identified and achieved. Our abiding concern, therefore, is with the quality and exercise of leadership. It is the leadership of an organization which clarifies organizational goals and which motivates people to accept and pursue those goals. The leadership also exercises major control over the institutional processes by which these goals are pursued. In the absence of a coup d'état of one kind or another, institutional change comes only after those in positions of official leadership are persuaded, gradually or suddenly by force of events outside their immediate control, to channel their power toward institutional transformation. Furthermore, the rank-and-file of any organization—and the Church is no exception—will not apply themselves to the pursuit of that organization's goals if they do not perceive those goals as inseparable from their own personal goals. The task of demonstrating the connection

401

between organizational objectives and personal objectives is a function of leadership. Leadership, in other words, is responsible for identifying and clarifying goals, on the one hand, and for motivating people to accept and pursue those goals, on the other hand.

The Problem of Institutional Response

There is no such thing as a perfect organization or a perfect society, certain claims to that effect notwithstanding. But the theoretical plan of such an ideal organization serves a useful purpose in helping us to evaluate the nature, and to study the direction, of actual organizations. We can measure organizational responses against hypothetical norms of perfection.

An inevitable organizational pathology is its tendency to maintain institutional equilibrium. Organizations, even radical, left-wing, revolutionary societies, are institutionally conservative. It is the rare organization indeed that votes itself out of existence once it recognizes that its original purposes have already been fulfilled.

However, the environment in which an organization finds itself will not permit it to remain at rest. The environment constantly stimulates the organization and impinges upon it, ultimately forcing it, over the long run, and sometimes even suddenly over the short run, to make changes or perish. It is this interaction between the conservative tendency toward equilibrium (maintaining the status quo), on the one hand, and the external disturbances, on the other hand, which cause various changes in the organization. The organization's response to this tension can go in four directions, one of which we can set aside at once; namely, its complete destruction. The other three directions have been designated in different ways, e.g., the way of tenacity, the way of elasticity, and the way of self-determination. How the organization responds to its environment and to the pressure for change depends on its particular structure.

The three options can be illustrated by the elements in the following example: a rock (the way of tenacity), some kelp (the way of elasticity), and a porpoise (the way of self-determination), with the ocean serving as the common environment (see Glossary, p. 168). The rock neither gives nor interacts with the

402

ocean any more than can be helped. Water wears it away and it does nothing to rebuild itself, relying instead on its integrality to continue its existence. The kelp, on the other hand, has some of the resistant features of the rock and is also, to some extent at least, self-determinative, but generally it relies on its elasticity to preserve its integrality. It allows itself to give and to yield to the conformations imposed upon it by the tides, the currents, etc., but it still manages to interact with the ocean in such a manner as to preserve itself. Finally, there is the porpoise which, unlike the rock and the kelp, can control to a great degree its interactions with its watery environment. It can go after food or not; it can swim against the tide and currents; its time and energy are not totally taken up with maintaining itself in existence.

The ways of tenacity and elasticity seem to be at least as good as that of self-determination, if mere survival alone is at issue. Indeed, they may even be better. But in terms of the perfect organization, they have settled the problem of integrality at too low a level. They have compromised too soon, having closed off any chance of real growth toward perfection. Self-determination, on the other hand, is a way which alone offers the possibility of continual improvement, and self-determination alone gives the opportunity for working toward the ideal. However, there is a price to be paid. The organization must be prepared to sacrifice a large amount of its integrality, i.e., it cannot act as if it were a completely closed, totally self-sufficient system (*societas perfecta!*). It must continually invest itself, taking the essential risks inherent in the investment process. The organization cannot stand pat.

While the Church is a mystery, it is also a human institution. Monophysitism is no less heretical for ecclesiology than it is for Christology. As a human institution, it follows, to a greater or lesser degree, the laws of organizational behavior. As a mystery, i.e., as the sacrament of Christ and of God, it is forever called to perfection. Organizational theory, however, insists that the perfect organization neither exists nor can exist in this world order. Such theory is validated by theology, and specifically by eschatology. On this side of the Parousia nothing can be identified completely with the Kingdom of God. Everything, including the Church, labors under some measure of imperfection. The Church is always on the way, but not yet there. In the meantime, everything is to be judged by the final goal. All reality is subordinated to, and measured against, the promised future, the fully realized Kingdom. Just as it is proper to hold aloft the Kingdom of God as the transcendent goal and norm of our present moral strivings, so it is proper to hold aloft the ideal of the perfect organization as the ultimate goal and norm of our present institutional strivings.

Every organization's fundamental tendency is toward self-preservation. If institutions could remain completely at rest, they would do so, but then, of course, they would die. That which does not change at all is dead. Every organization, however, finds itself in a given environment which will not allow the organization to remain at rest. The environment constantly stimulates and impinges upon the organization, forcing it to change or to perish. There is in every organization, including the Church as well, a tension created by this dialectical interaction between the organization's conservative tendency to maintain equilibrium and the various external disturbances ("signs of the times"?).

The Church's institutional response can follow four paths. The first we rule out; namely, the way of complete destruction. Adopting that response, the Church would sadly decide that the interaction is not worth the energy and so would simply stop functioning: a kind of self-administered euthanasia. This may be a response of sorts, but it is one that is hardly viable. Indeed, there would be no point at all to this book if I were to judge it so.

This leaves the Church with three other choices. Each of these choices, I should strenuously argue, is based upon three separate theologies of the Church. Theory and practice are inextricably linked. The first choice—the way of tenacity—is based on the assumption that the Church is so thoroughly divine in nature that its human character is really insignificant. The human side of the Church is but the mindlessly pliant instrument of the divine, a relationship conceived in much the same way as some nineteenth-century Catholic theologians assumed that the human writer of Sacred Scripture functioned at a level no more self-determinative than that of a guitar pick in a musician's fingers. Thus, since the Church is, for all practical purposes, totally divine, it cannot endure or tolerate substantial institutional change. The institutions, after all, are the external expression of the divine presence. To tamper with ecclesiastical structures is to tamper with the reality of God. Accordingly, the Church may be in the world, but it is surely not of the world. The world is somehow separate from the Church. The Church is over against the world, existing there as a ghetto in a city, or a diplomatic sanctuary in a battle zone, or a cyst in an organism: taking what it can, but giving nothing in return. To give in return would constitute interaction, and interaction would end its status as a wholly separate, totally self-contained organization.

But like the rock, this kind of Church cannot completely avoid the effects of its environment. Something of its institutional self is bound to be worn away gradually, as we see it happening today, although not so gradually. And yet, by the force of its own rigid theology, that Church can do nothing to rebuild itself. The Lord may give, and the Lord may take away, but man can do nothing. The Theory A Catholic, who prefers the way of tenacity as a matter of theological principle, perceives as well as anyone else the attrition process now at work in the Church. He has an explanation, and he has a response. The explanation is that God is testing his people, summoning them to heroic steadfastness and fidelity in a time of material reversal; the response is to hold the line, to stand firm, and to do whatever one can to restore the institutional elements of the status quo ante. Such a Church, of course, is no longer on the road to perfection. Improvement is rendered impossible. Furthermore, this view of the Church cannot be reconciled with the Church's own official self-understanding. The Theory A Catholic, who proudly asserts his loyalty to church doctrine, finds himself strangely and uncomfortably out of step with some significant elements of that doctrine. The Church is not over against the world; it is *in* the world. Indeed, the Church is that part of the world which alone confesses and celebrates the Lordship of Jesus Christ. But its mission is to the world, for the sake of the Kingdom. The Church must discern the redemptive presence of God and respond creatively and courageously to that presence, facilitating the divine entrance, enabling it to break through and renew the face of the earth. The Catholic Church has officially eschewed the way of tenacity. It has chosen some other institutional response. It has done so because —the truth must be stated bluntly and boldly—the Catholic Church no longer accepts Theory A as an expression of its official self-understanding.

The second choice—the way of elasticity—is based on the assumption that the Church is so human and so relative an organization that its abiding, spiritual elements are really insignificant. The Church must be, first and foremost, a spearhead for social reform or a locus for interpersonal encounter. Whether it preserves the historic Eucharist, whether it remains faithful to the doctrinal tradition of earlier ecumenical councils, whether it retains an ordained ministry—these concerns are entirely secondary. If, on the one hand, the Church is where the action is, or, on the other hand, the Church makes personal growth possible, then nothing else is finally important. In a time of change, the Church's only reasonable response can be to move with the times, to test the waters, to put its ear to the ground. Any structures will do, so long as these purposes are promoted.

But like the kelp, this kind of Church can interact with its environment only to the point where it can preserve itself in existence. If it loses its "relevance," it is dead. It is a Church, therefore, ever in pursuit of the new, the popular, the trendy— and ever at their mercy. The terms are set exclusively by the environment. The Church, in this view, is an organization without initiative, without anything distinctive to contribute, without any special resources of its own. To the Theory A Catholic, all institutional reform is an expression of mindless elasticity. He is right in challenging the way of elasticity as a viable means of achieving ecclesiastical renewal, but he is wrong in concluding that every effort toward institutional reform is an exercise in compromise and retreat. The way of elasticity, to be sure, is wrong because it devalues those elements of the Church which make the Christian community historically distinctive. The Church is set apart from all other communities, societies, and institutions by reason of its corporate conviction, rooted in its New Testament origins, that Jesus of Nazareth is "the key, the focal point, and the goal of all human history." Jesus alone is the Lord and Christ of history. The company of his disciples must be obedient to the Lord's will by breaking the bread of his body and sharing the cup of his blood, until he comes (Acts 2:42). It is a community called upon to embody his presence beyond his own time, and to make straight the paths to the Kingdom of God at the end. Its mission must indeed include social action (*diakonia*) and the Church must be for its members and all others a place where human growth occurs through the experience of community (*koinonia*). But it remains nonetheless the one community wherein the Lordship of Jesus and the power of his Spirit is proclaimed and celebrated, or else it is no longer the Church at all.

The ways of tenacity and elasticity can ensure a temporary, even long-term, survival of sorts, but the Church is called to a higher purpose than mere institutional survival. It is a living organism, the Body of Christ, a Spirit-filled community. Where the Spirit is, there must be life. If it is Christ's Body, then it must be a living body. The Risen Lord lives! A ghetto Church, holding the line against the winds of change, but losing the war inch by inch, bears no resemblance to the eschatological community of the New Testament, utterly committed to the coming reign of God, a community open to the future, a Church of supreme hope. Neither does a flaccid Church, with a wet thumb in every breeze, and losing its soul in the process, bear any resemblance to the tiny company of disciples who embraced the crown of martyrdom rather than deny their Lord and God. The Church of the New Testament was a community holding fast to the teachings it had been given, faithfully celebrating the Lord's Supper until the day of final redemption.

The third choice, the way of self-determination, is based on the assumption that the Church is a mystery: a visible, human sign of the invisible presence of the transcendent God in the midst of the world. The Church's own transcendent character forecloses the way of elasticity; its fully human, institutional character forecloses the way of tenacity. The way of self-determination alone offers the possibility of continual improvement. The door to perfection is not prematurely shut. The ideal remains the norm and the goal. But there is a price to be paid.

The Church must give as well as take, let go as well as hold fast. It must continually invest its resources and accept the risks that accompany such investment.

Like the porpoise, the Church controls to a great degree its interactions with the changing environment. Such a Church can still take initiatives. No longer preoccupied with survival, while living along the margin of social existence, the Church can move here and there as it discerns the presence of the Spirit of God. If God is not bound to sacred precincts, neither can that community be bound which calls itself his People.

The Problem of Motivation

Institutional reform is impossible unless the people whom the institution embraces become willing, and indeed enthusiastic, participants in the process of reform. This raises the question of motivation.

In any organization there are differences in performance among people doing the same kind of work. These differences reflect not only differences in ability but also differences in motivation. At any given point in time people vary in the extent to which they are willing to direct their energies toward the attainment of an organization's objectives.

The problem of motivating employees in a business or in any corporate enterprise is as old as organized activity itself, but it is only within the last fifty years that the scientific method has been brought to bear on its solution. There are at least three major approaches to the problem of personal motivation within organizations: the way of paternalism, the way of scientific management, and the way of participative management (see Glossary, p. 168).

The paternalistic method assumes that people who are satisfied with their job will more likely be effective at that job. The more one rewards the worker, the harder he works. His motivation is essentially one of gratitude and loyalty. The essence of this approach is to make an organization a source of important rewards—rewards for which the only qualification is membership in the organization (e.g., pension plans, group insurance, subsidized education, recreation programs, comfortable working conditions, accross-the-board wage increases, job security, and predictable promotion patterns).

But there is little evidence that any of these policies has had a direct effect on worker productivity or performance. The relevant distinction here is between a person's satisfaction with the job and his motivation to perform effectively in that job. It was once assumed, incorrectly, that these two things went hand in hand, that a person who was satisfied with his job would necessarily be effective at it. During the last twenty years or so there have been large numbers of research studies conducted to test the accuracy of this assumption, and these studies have shown no consistent or meaningful relationship between job satisfaction and effective performance. Effective performers were as likely to be dissatisfied with their jobs as they were to be satisfied, and vice versa. It might be concluded, therefore, that the paternalistic approach has not been a very effective strategy for resolving the problem of motivation.

The scientific management method assumes, on the other hand, that a person will be motivated to work if rewards and penalties are attached directly to his performance. Thus, rewards are conditional, not unconditional. They are contingent upon effective performance (e.g., wage incentives, promotion on the basis of merit, recognizing and rewarding special accomplishment). Penalties are meted out for failure (e.g., warnings, reprimands, even dismissals). This second method depends on an external control system and is based on the principle of reinforcement, i.e., if a person undertakes an action and this action is followed by a reward, the probability that the action will be repeated is increased, and vice versa.

This method, too, has severe limitations. There are an exceedingly large number of outcomes which are potentially gratifying or aversive to human beings and only a small number of these outcomes are under direct managerial control. It is particularly difficult for the external control system to encompass the higher order of needs for esteem and self-actualization, as detailed by Abraham Maslow. Indeed, certain rewards and penalties relevant to social needs are under the control of the informal organization, and these sanctions may work against the formal control system. A second limitation to the external control system is its reliance on some reasonably objective method of measuring or assessing performance. As the organization's complexity increases, the variables increase with it. Meanwhile, the possibility of total control decreases proportionately.

The participative management method assumes that individuals can derive satisfaction from doing an effective job per se. They can become personally involved in their work, taking pride in the evidence that they are effectively promoting the objectives of the organization. One of the basic elements of the different theories of participative management is the integration of the planning and the doing. The person is given broad goals or objectives and is enabled and encouraged to determine for himself how they are to be achieved. This makes the job more of a challenge than if the person were simply told what to do and when to do it. A second common element in these theories is the reduction in the use of authority as a means of control. The supervisor or manager plays a helping role rather than an authoritative one. Finally, there is much more reliance on the use of work groups as problem-solving and decision-making units. Where decisions affect a whole unit, the supervisor meets with all those affected by the potential decision and encourages them to participate in the process of finding a solution. The opportunity to participate in the decision-making process creates a sense of involvement and commitment on the part of the affected individuals and enhances identification of their personal goals with the corporate goals and objectives of the organization.

The applicability of the preceding discussion to the problem of ecclesiastical reform should be clear. Those who perceive the Church according to Theory A will generally opt for the paternalistic method of organizational management. Membership in the Church automatically confers benefits available to all on an equal basis. One is already within the Kingdom of God. All are given the gifts of faith, hope, and charity. All have the right to receive the sacraments. And when we move from the general to the particular (e.g., to the ordained ministry of the Church), the paternalistic method is even more apparent. Priests are related to their bishop as sons to father. By the very fact of ordination the priest is guaranteed a lifetime occupation, with group insurance, retirement plans, subsidized education, comfortable working conditions, wage increases based on years of ordination, job security, and predictable promotion patterns based on seniority. But there is no evidence that materially comfortable working conditions make priests more effective or give them a greater sense of identification with the mission of the whole Church. On the contrary, large numbers of priests are dissatisfied with the way the ecclesiastical structure is shaped and the way decision-making power is distributed. Significantly, the leadership does not share this dissatisfaction.

The scientific management method is perhaps lodged somewhere between Theory A and Theory B. It retains some of the values of Theory A insofar as it employs an external control system; and it moves closer to Theory B insofar as it cherishes competence and has high regard for professional standards. But there is a limit to what professionalization can accomplish. Catholics, and priests in particular (to continue with our earlier example), need more than hierarchical approval or the incentive of recognition and promotion based on merit. They have certain needs which the organization alone cannot fulfill.

Those who understand the Church as the whole People of God, wherein all—laity, religious, and clergy alike—are responsible for the mission of the Church, are drawn to the participative management approach. The most important question for the Church is not how it is to be governed or how it is to be structured, but what it is to do. The membership of the Church must know, first of all, what their purpose is, what their goals are; and then they must be encouraged and motivated to pursue those goals, not as something extrinsic to themselves but as something identifiable with their own personal goals. Since all are responsible for the mission in the first instance, all must be involved somehow in the process by which that responsibility is determined and exercised.

Furthermore, the Theory C Catholic understands that the Church is a collegial, not a monarchical, organization. Authority is not dominative, but diaconal. The bishop and pastor stand in the midst of the community as those who serve. Problems that affect a particular group must be solved, whenever possible, at the level of that particular group. In the Catholic social encyclicals this was known as the principle of subsidiarity. The opportunity to participate in the decision-making process creates a sense of involvement and commitment on the part of the affected church members and helps them to perceive, if such is indeed the case, that the corporate goals of the Church are not at cross-purposes with their own goals; on the contrary, that the Church's goals and their own are fundamentally the same. To further the mission of the Church is to further the good of oneself and of one's loved ones.

Maslow has suggested that the principles of participative management are most useful in managing persons with strong needs for self-actualization. The Christian is called to put on Christ, to grow up in him, to become a new creature (2 Cor. 5:17)—it is a rhetoric not of stagnation but of growth, development, and actualization. Just as the ways of tenacity and elasticity work against the possibility of the Church's growth toward perfection, so the ways of paternalism and scientific management (reinforcement) work against the possibility of the individual Christian's growth toward perfection. The two areas, of institutional response and of motivation, thereby converge. Institutional reform requires the way of self-determination; motivation for mission requires the way of participative management. Autocratic leadership and unilateral decision-making, although sanctioned by Theory A, will inevitably frustrate—and have frustrated—the very purpose for which such leadership is consciously exercised: the Church's growth in holiness, its advance toward perfection, its movement toward the final Kingdom of God. In the final analysis, we find that good organizational and motivational theory corresponds with good canonical and theological principles.

NEXUS

The remainder of this chapter is an exercise in practical ecclesiology. It is an attempt to apply a contemporary theology of the Church (Theory C) in institutional, structural ways; first, by identifying the ineffective and sometimes harmful structures; second, by proposing constructive alternatives; and, third, by identifying the relevant theological principles which are at issue in the debate, both pro and con.

Richard Peter McBrien

An Agenda for Reform—Problems and Proposals

1. PRINCIPLES OF CONSTITUTIONALISM

The present ecclesiastical system reflects only one phase in the total institutional history of the Church; namely, its feudalistic and monarchical experience. The system does not reflect at all the alternate experience of constitutionalism which the Church itself was, in large part, responsible for initiating in the Western world. The present system exemplifies numerous qualities of monarchical absolutism: Pope and bishops remain for all practical purposes the exclusive rulers in the Church, combining the legislative, executive, and judicial powers in one hand. Despite the recent creation of councils, authority is still exercised in many places without being subject to effective accountability.

Accordingly, the Church must move from a system of monarchical absolutism to some form of constitutionalism which, Brian Tierney has reminded us, "is not something foreign to the tradition of the Catholic Church. If we chose to adopt constitutional forms in the structure of the modern church, we should not be borrowing from an alien system. Rather we should be reclaiming a rich part of our own inheritance."

Constitutionalism involves three basic elements: the limitation of power, accountability, and openness to correction. The limitation of power is achieved by *(a)* a division of power between central and regional governing bodies; *(b)* the separation of legislative, executive, and judicial power; and *(c)* guarantee of individual rights, including due process of law. Accountability is ensured by *(a)* the electoral process; *(b)* freedom of information, whereby the exercise of official power is a matter of public record; and *(c)* freedom of discussion and debate regarding the policy and performance of office holders as well as the ultimate assumptions of the community itself. And, finally, openness to correction is ensured by *(a)* regular meetings of legislative bodies; *(b)* reinterpretation of law by tribunals; and *(c)* permanent commissions charged with the responsibility of proposing legal reforms.

2. DECENTRALIZATION OF POWER

Because power remains concentrated at the top and decisions are formulated there in secret, the rank-and-file among the laity, religious, and clergy have become largely indifferent to the operations of the Church (except in those relatively few instances where the membership have become angry and hostile). The principle of participative management is inoperative. When the decisions of the monarchical leadership are not received with evident enthusiasm, indeed when these decisions are frequently ignored, the officeholder appeals to his divinely given authority and reminds the membership of their duty to obey it. But the motivation remains extrinsic: accept what has been decreed (even in the case of Vatican II directives), not because of its intrinsic merit, but because it bears the stamp of official approval.

Accordingly, the Church must put into practice at once its own time-honored principle of subsidiarity that a higher agency or group should never do for a lower agency or group what that lower agency or group can do for itself. There must be a decentralization of power which restores to particular churches their ancient freedom to adapt the discipline of the Christian life and ministry to their own distinctive needs and situation. Parish councils, diocesan pastoral councils, and national pastoral councils must become more than rubber-stamp agencies. (The denial of a local church's right to establish such councils is theologically outrageous. And yet, for all practical purposes, that is what the Vatican did when, in early 1973, it forbade the Church in Holland to convene its national pastoral council.) Such councils must have deliberative as well as consultative power. They should be, in other words, the policy-making bodies for their own communities. At all levels these fundamental conditions must be fulfilled: *(a)* the body should meet regularly according to its own rules; *(b)* the body should choose its own officers and determine its own rules of procedure and agenda; *(c)* the deliberations of the body should be open and should be publicized; *(d)* the body should have its own secretariat, with full access to relevant information and with the assistance of experts.

3. PLANNING AND RESEARCH

The Catholic Church has at present no institution dedicated to research and planning. There is perhaps no other large organization in the modern world which has less idea of what it is doing, how much it is accomplishing, or where it is going, than does the Catholic Church. Social research is identified with the gathering of statistics to provide *ad hoc* answers to specific questions. Information-gathering proceeds according to uneven and often unreliable methods, and policy planning, which comparable organizations regard as absolutely essential, has hardly existed at all. Of course, if one insists that the Church's response to its environment must be the way of tenacity, then the need for research and planning is minimal or nonexistent. If, on the other hand, one regards the path of self-determination as the only theologically and pastorally viable response on the part of the ecclesiastical institution, then planning and research become as essential to the Church as they clearly are to any similarly complex organization.

Accordingly, *(a)* offices devoted to research and planning for the long-range development of the Church are necessary at the central, national, diocesan, and parish levels; so, too, *(b)* an office of financial management; *(c)* permanent means of assessing public opinion in the Church; and *(d)* a public relations department whose function would be to provide information to church members and the public at large on policies, procedures, and related matters.

4. PRINCIPLES OF ACCOUNTABILITY

Neither does the Church have any agency committed to supervising the collective operations of the whole ecclesiastical machinery. Decisions affecting large numbers of people and large amounts of money are made day after day, at international, national, and diocesan levels. These really important decisions are made in secret, but even after they have become public, the rank-and-file membership of the Church have no institutionalized recourse against those decisions. They are forced to use the power of publicity in the hopes of embarrassing the leadership and forcing it to reconsider its initial judgment.

Accordingly, the Church needs a public adversary system which will provide a check and balance in this area. The explicit responsibility of such a system would be the development and presentation of an effective adversary position on each project or activity funded by the leadership, to assess them for fidelity to the interests of the whole Church and to its mission. The duties of the adversary agency would include effective investigation into sloppy management procedures, hidden expenditures, and performance. The adversary system would also be charged with questioning the need for every program, developing alternate ideas and approaches, and establishing machinery for the constructive, ongoing evaluation of the pros and cons of each issue. To avoid the development of its own internal bureaucracy and the establishment of an unhealthy symbiotic relationship between itself and its assigned agency or agencies within the Church, each adversary project should be terminated and its functions wholly abolished after a period of three years. A different project team and apparatus would then be formed to assess and criticize the project for the next three-year period. Funding for this adversary system could be based on this formula: 1 percent of the total amount appropriated for any given project would finance the adversary process.

5. SELECTION OF BISHOPS

Bishops are still chosen in the Catholic Church according to the criterion of conformity. Any one of the hundreds of Catholic pastors, teachers, educators, administrators, theologians, catechists, journalists, sociologists, psychologists, and so forth, who associated himself with the public dissent against *Humanae Vitae* is automatically disqualified, under present standards, for advancement to this office of pastoral leadership. And yet 70 percent of the American Catholic priests surveyed in the National Opinion Research Center (NORC) study supported the election of bishops by the clergy of the diocese, a position which is entirely in accord not only with the ancient canonical principle that "he who governs all should be elected by all," but also with the ancient and long-standing practice of the election of bishops by the clergy and laity.

Accordingly, the Church must return at once to its adherence to both the principle and the practice. It is essential that the process include all the major elements within a given local community, selected by the diocesan pastoral council from its own members: diocesan priests, religious men and women, laywomen and laymen. The committee for the selection of bishops should have a limited term of office, although for the sake of continuity the terms of the individual members ought not to terminate all at the same time. It is also essential that this selection committee be fully informed of the needs of the diocese and have access to every kind of information it may require to make responsible judgments about the various candidates. It is equally imperative that the committee consult as widely as possible and encourage public discussion. Existing recommendations for reform in this area are inadequate because they leave unchallenged the power of outside bishops, papal delegates, and the Pope himself in the final selection process. A bishop should be the choice principally of the community he is to serve. An agreed-upon nominee who meets opposition from external sources should not thereby be rejected, except after public discussion involving the full disclosure of reasons for such opposition. In the end, the Pope accepts rather than approves the decision of the local church.

If one grants a central argument of this book, that the present crisis in the Catholic Church involves a crisis of confidence in its leadership, then this kind of change has more immediate pastoral import than most of the other recommendations included herein.

6. PAPAL POWER

One of the major elements in the Theory A ecclesiology was its italicization of the papacy in the life and mission of the Church. Even the cautious scholar Yves Congar has acknowledged that the power and importance of the Pope have been exaggerated since the First Vatican Council and particularly during the pontificate of Pius XII. Many Catholics still have the idea that all of the Pope's judgments, at whatever level they are expressed (encyclicals, decrees, sermons, comments to pilgrims, reported comments in *L'Osservatore Romano*, etc.), are to be accepted as true. For all practical purposes, the Pope is never wrong; to criticize him, however, is always wrong. There has been such an identification of the Pope with Christ (*Vicarius Christi*) that one is led even to the conclusion that to differ with the Pope is to differ with the Lord himself. Canonically, of course, the authority of the Pope is supreme and unchallengeable. His decisions are final, and no other major decisions are final until they have received his approval: whether the issue is priestly celibacy, the appointment of bishops, the admission of women to the priesthood, or the substitution of vegetable oil for olive oil in the administration of the sacrament of the sick.

Accordingly, the Church must willingly, and perhaps painfully, demythologize its understanding of the papacy, bringing its perceptions into greater conformity with New Testament and historical scholarship and contemporary theological reflection. While he remains the symbol of faith and unity for all the churches of the world, and while his office retains, in principle, the greatest authority for moral and doctrinal utterance, the Pope himself can no longer function as an absolute monarch, embodying in his single person all executive, legislative, and judicial power—without limitation, without accountability, without the possibility of correction.

General policy decisions affecting the universal Church should be reserved, not to the Pope alone, but to the Pope and the International Synod of Bishops. The function of the Curia is to assist in the execution of these decisions. In the course of such execution, the Curia may issue administrative directives concerned with interdiocesan or supranational questions, but it should have no administrative authority in purely local matters. Problems which are national, not international, in character should be within the competence of the national conference of bishops rather than the Pope, and the same would be true of problems at regional and diocesan levels, in keeping with the Church's fundamental principle of subsidiarity. The election of the Pope by the International Synod of Bishops rather than by the College of Cardinals and some limitation of tenure (e.g., ten years, renewable) would serve to modify the present absolutely monarchical pattern.

Richard Peter McBrien

What has been said of the papal office is true, in a slightly different sense, of the episcopal office. Many bishops continue to perceive themselves as responsible directly to the Pope alone, as if they were his delegates or vicars within a given administrative subdivision of the one Church. They do not think of the people within their diocese as the constituency to whom they are constantly responsible and accountable. They exercise their authority, not according to the method of participative management, but according to the method of paternalism. And they wonder why their priests, religious, and laity are not universally motivated to collaborate with them in the pursuit of the Church's mission.

Accordingly, the Church must also willingly demythologize its understanding of the episcopal office, bringing its perceptions into greater conformity with New Testament and historical scholarship and contemporary theological reflections. While the bishop shall remain the symbol of faith and unity within the local church, and while his office retains, in principle, great authority for moral and doctrinal utterance, the bishop personally can no longer function within his diocese as its absolute monarch, embodying in himself all executive, legislative, and judicial power, limited only by his personal and canonical loyalties to the Pope.

The diocesan community is to be governed by its pastoral council, and decisions should be reached on the basis of a consensus of the bishop and the council. The bishop, too, should be selected by the people he is to serve and for a term of office that is limited. Furthermore, the still current practice of a bishop's moving from one diocese to another, as if up a career ladder, should be ended immediately. Finally, the bishop should perceive himself and his diocese as part of a community of bishops and dioceses. By episcopal ordination he is a member of the whole episcopal college, and of its various national and regional segments. He cannot forbid in his community what is legitimately permitted in others. He cannot demand of his people, and especially of his priests and religious, what is not demanded of others in similar circumstances. The highly inequitable treat-

419

ment of dissenters against *Humanae Vitae* from diocese to diocese is an example of this pastoral discrepancy. Finally, he—and his brother bishops—must recognize that there are other successions besides the succession of their own pastoral office; namely, the successions of prophets and of teachers. Bishops must simply stop identifying the teaching charism with their own offices, as if it did not belong also to the whole Church and particularly to that group in the Church who were known, from New Testament times, as the *didaskaloi* (today's translation: "theologians"). If the Church is to be truly reformed, its prophets and theologians will have to assert their independence, not from the Church in whose service they always remain, but from the bishops who are perennially tempted to co-opt and/or control them. The question usually asked after a brief dissertation on the need for complete theological freedom is: "Who, then, will control the theologians?" That question is as theologically intelligible as the questions: "Who, then, will control the bishops?" and "Who will control the Pope?" It is the Spirit alone who guarantees the unity of the Church.

8. A BILL OF RIGHTS

Legal reforms begin with protests within a society against the established government. The protests are specific and concrete; they are centered on individuals and on the punishments imposed on them. The protests engender discussions and debates that soon rise to the level of general principles. There have been many controversies in recent years over violations of the rights of individuals, groups, and institutions. The inadequacy of existing procedures for dealing with such controversies was dramatically illustrated, again, by the events following the publication of *Humanae Vitae*. Many Catholic laity, religious, and clergy are still vulnerable to arbitrary administrative action against their own interests. Where they are spared such unpleasantness, it is more a matter of benign paternalism rather than of legal protection. In the meantime, freedom is demanded for the Church outside, but it is not always granted inside.

Accordingly, a bill of rights ought to be formulated and promulgated throughout the Church, in accordance with an open, collegial process already suggested above, specifying those

Richard Peter McBrien

areas where the protection of Christian freedom is of absolute necessity:

— The right to freedom in the search for truth, without fear of administrative sanctions.

— The right to freedom in expressing personal beliefs and opinions as they appear to the individual, including freedom of communication and publication.

— The right of individuals to access to objective information, in particular about the internal and external operations of the Church (information such as an adversary agency might require).

— The right to develop the unique potentialities and personality traits proper to the individual without fear of repression by the Christian community or church authorities.

— The right of the Christian to work out his salvation in response to the unique challenges offered by the age and society in which he lives.

— The rights of persons employed by, or engaged in the service of, the Church to conditions of work consonant with human dignity as well as the right to professional practices comparable to those in the society at large.

— The right to freedom of assembly and of association (such as the formation of an association of priests, even alongside the established senate of priests in a given diocese).

— The right to participate according to our gifts from the Spirit, in the teaching, government, and sanctification of the Church.

— All the rights and freedoms of Christians without discrimination on the basis of race, color, sex, birth, language, political opinion, or national or social origin.

— The right to effective remedies for the redress of grievances and the vindication of their rights.

— In all proceedings in which one of the parties may suffer substantial disadvantage, the procedure must be fair and impartial, with an opportunity for submission to boards of mediation and arbitration. (Due process has already been accepted in principle by the American Catholic bishops, but it has not yet been adopted in most of the dioceses.)

— In all procedures, administrative or judicial, in which penalties may be imposed, the accused shall not be deprived of any right, office, or communion with the Church except by due process of law; said due process shall include, but not be limited to, the right not to be a witness against oneself; the right to a speedy and public trial; the right to be informed in advance of the specific charge against him; the right to confront the witnesses against him; the right to have the assistance of experts and of counsel for his defense; and a right of appeal.

9. ECCLESIASTICAL COURTS

The numbers and spiritual situation of Catholics who remarry after divorce have created a grave pastoral issue within the Church in the United States, and this situation has been seriously aggravated by procedural jurisprudence and personal weaknesses which leave many cases unsolved or insoluble in the external forum. In the meantime, longstanding efforts to resolve such cases in the internal forum have been suspended summarily by a private communication from the Vatican. Most Catholics ignore their Church's marriage tribunals when they find themselves outside the canonical limits by reason of divorce and remarriage. Either they accept their outlaw status and remain away from the sacraments (and perhaps from church entirely) or they decide in the privacy of their own consciences that they are innocent before God and therefore still eligible to receive the sacraments. But there is a tiny minority who do indeed take the Catholic Church's intricate matrimonial procedures to heart. They bring their cases before the Church's courts, expecting a swift and fair hearing. In too many instances, however, their cases have been shunted aside for two and three years, long beyond the time when a decision might retain meaning and purpose. Often they are faced with judges who represent the most extreme right-of-center views on the ecclesiastical spectrum: men of inflexible, rigid, authoritarian, Theory A views.

Accordingly, some substantial revision of the Church's official matrimonial procedures and of its court system is mandatory. Regional courts should be developed under the aegis of the episcopal conferences. Parties should be fully apprised during the proceedings of the evidence upon which the decisions of formal courts will be based, and the parties should be given full opportunity to argue all the issues in dispute. The procedure of these courts should aim at simplicity and speed, for justice delayed is justice denied. Courts should always give reasons for their decisions and should afford opportunity for the expression of judicial dissents. The only criterion for personnel in the courts should be professional competence. No one should be disqualified on grounds of sex or lack of clerical status. Insofar as possible, formal courts should be staffed by fulltime and professionally trained personnel. Judges should be appointed for a term of years. In the interest of their independence, they should not be removable by executive order. The binding interpretation of the laws of the Church, including those pertaining to marriage, should be reserved to the courts; executive offices or commissions should not have the right to make such interpretations. The procedure in marriage cases should be as simple, flexible, and expeditious as possible because: *(a)* the subject matter of the case is theological, i.e., the existence of a sacrament; *(b)* the most intimate rights of the parties are concerned; *(c)* the proceeding is not truly adversary; *(d)* the relevant evidence can often be collected from the parties themselves; and *(e)* delay can cause irreparable injustice to the parties and to their children.

Internal forum solutions (as, for example, the allowing of divorced-and-remarried Catholics to receive the sacraments), reached in accordance with sound principles of moral theology, should be respected and not be distorted by excessive administrative regulations such as questionnaires, processes, decrees, records, etc. Episcopal guidelines should take into account the need for instruction of the Catholic community so that all its members will have Christian compassion for those whose marriages have ended in divorce, will appreciate more deeply the holiness and indissolubility of Christian marriage, and respect the need to resolve such cases in the external forum, if possible, whether by the present procedure or by another procedure in which the judgment of the community of believers be expressed. No more should be required of Catholics than what is certainly required by divine institution, as seen in the light of the full Christian tradition of the East as well as the West, and no one should be excluded from ecclesiastical and sacramental Communion unless this is proved to be an absolute demand of divine law.

But perhaps even more thoroughgoing reform is required in marriage tribunal procedure. The responsibility of diocesan tribunals and the regional courts recommended above should be carefully limited, and the judgmental process shifted, for most cases, to the local parish community, in accordance with the principle of subsidiarity. Such a local tribunal would be staffed by the pastor and a board of laypeople. Occasionally, of course, someone might request that his or her marriage actually be declared null, and such petitions could still be handled by the diocesan or regional tribunal. In all tribunal deliberations the traditional *favor juris* granted to the marriage bond should be reversible. Thus, a first marriage would enjoy the benefit of the law so long as there remained some chance of saving it; but the right of a person to enter into a second marriage should enjoy the benefit of the law when it is obvious that the first marriage is beyond repair. No one should be obliged to life-long celibacy on the mere ground of a slight possibility that the previous marriage may have been valid. According to Bernard Häring, there should be no absolute tutiorism militating against the basic human right to marry. When a parish board, therefore, judges that a person is disposed to enter a second marriage "in the Lord," then the marriage would be permitted in the Church. But where it is judged otherwise and the person went through a ceremony anyway, outside the Church, then a second judgment would have to be made regarding the worthiness of that person to receive the Eucharist. All of these judgments would be pastoral in character. The judges would truly be "ministers of reconciliation."

10. WOMEN IN THE CHURCH

It is being said that the Church, and particularly the Catholic Church, is the last major institution in the Western world still dominated by the philosophy and spirit of male chauvinism. Women are positively and completely excluded from every position of official ecclesiastical leadership. It is still widely assumed within the Church that, before God, women are inherently inferior to men.

Accordingly, this radical inequity must be abolished in a way that is at once decisive and pedagogically direct: by admitting women to ordination to the diaconate, the priesthood, and the episcopacy. Such a course would simply reflect the growing consensus among theologians of Catholic and Protestant traditions alike that there is no insurmountable biblical or dogmatic obstacle to the ordination of women and that ordination of women must come to be part of the Church's life. Thus, qualified women should be given full and equal participation in policy- and decision-making, and voice in places of power, in the churches on local, regional, national, and international levels. Seminary education in all the churches should be opened to qualified women, and such women should, of course, be admitted to ordination. In the meantime, the pertinent ecclesiastical agencies (e.g., North American Area Council, World Alliance of Reformed Churches, and the Bishops' Committee on Ecumenical and Interreligious Affairs) should establish and fund an Ecumenical Commission on Women, inviting all churches to join with them on an equal basis in responsibility and funding for this commission and in sharing the fruits of its labors. In the end, it is of the utmost importance that once women are admitted to ordination they not be forced into patterns of ministry that have been developed with a view to an exclusively male clergy.

11. RENEWAL OF RELIGIOUS COMMUNITIES

Religious orders are institutions within an institution. All the problems that beset the Church as a whole affect each of these particular groups in much the same way. Therefore, what has been recommended to the whole Church is to be recommended to these specialized groups within the Church. There is another dimension to religious orders, however, beyond their reality as churches within the Church. In their original inception, these communities functioned as prophetic agents within, but also over against, the rest of the Church. They came into being in response to missionary needs that were no longer being fulfilled properly. Their apostolates not only met those needs, but exercised a prophetic judgment upon the rest of the Church in the process. Today, however, many of these religious communities have become defenders of the old order rather than harbingers of the new. Instead of summoning the whole Church along the path of self-determination and thereby toward continued growth in Christ, these groups often tend to fortify and stiffen the Church in its penchant for the way of tenacity. At the other extreme, smaller groups within some of the orders, in a frenetic reaction against the establishment's tenacity, may have confused elasticity with self-determination.

Accordingly, particular religious communities (some of which may remain attached to orders) must become once again prophetic agents within the Church Universal. They should serve as models of what we have called self-determination and participative management.

Within the religious communities themselves, the members must be provided with all those modern benefits which enlightened social progress sees as basic for one's well-being, but, even more importantly, they must have the opportunity of participating in those decisions which are determinative of their own lives. The communities should reemphasize their solidarity with the poor of the world. There should be a renewed sense of accountability for the resources of the community. Fraternal support and encouragement must be given to those members of the community engaged in the apostolates for peace and justice.

Within the institutions which many of these communities direct, there should be just wages, adequate working conditions, adequate social security benefits to all employees, irrespective of race, creed, color, or sex. There should be full cooperation with such programs as Project Equality and particular concern for the rights of women at every level. Finally, in the many educational institutions staffed by religious groups, the students must be challenged repeatedly to be outstanding in their commitment to justice, and the schools themselves must be credible signs of this commitment.

Within the Church, these communities must become a public voice, calling the Church to practice justice unstintingly. They must call for austerity in the life-style of the whole Church. They must urge the fullest possible participation by the membership of the Church in decision-making, including the selection of leadership. They should urge a renewed sense of accountability of the resources of the Church. And they should work for full equality in the exercise of the rights of women.

Within the larger human community, religious communities must speak out on issues of peace and justice and involve themselves in movements to correct injustices. They should press for a foreign policy which shifts a government's priorities away from concern for military dominance. They should try to develop a coherent religious voice to heighten the consciousness of the nation in terms of its real impact on the world and to call attention to the gap between that impact and Christian responsibility.

12. THE MINISTRY OF THE ORDAINED

The crisis in the Catholic priesthood is already well known. There is widespread dissatisfaction among the clergy with the exercise of ecclesiastical authority and with the rigid enforcement of traditional life-styles. The thousands of priests who have resigned, and continue to resign, from the active ministry over the last several years is evidence enough of the depth and extent of this dissatisfaction, but the sharp decline of candidates for the ministry and the clergy's indifference to vocational recruitment are even more ominous indications of what is happening.

Accordingly, the Church must recognize the need for a pluriformity of ministerial life-styles and for drawing these ministers more fully into the decision-making process. There are three basic principles that must be translated into practice: the collegial character of the Christian priesthood; the principle of subsidiarity; and the fact that priests have the same personal rights as any other member of the Church.

In the United States today the principal source of conflict and dissatisfaction among Catholic priests is the manner by which authority is exercised within the Church. Unilateral decisions, emanating from a monarchical understanding of the Church, must yield to truly consultative and even deliberative decision-making. Such consultation is not based on any concession or privilege. It is derived, as we have seen earlier, from the nature of the Church itself and from the conviction that the gifts of the Spirit are available to all. Consultation, however, is not achieved when the process is secret to the extent that each person expresses his opinion in isolation from others. Furthermore, there is nothing in the law of the Church to prevent bishops from changing the consultative character of the votes of councils into deliberative or decisive votes. On the contrary, a recent statement of the Vatican's Congregation for the Clergy allowed that priests' councils could not function as deliberative bodies "unless the universal law of the Church provides otherwise or the bishop in individual cases judges it opportune to attribute a deliberative vote to the council." There should be care, however, that the priests' senate does not become a competitive agency alongside or over against the diocesan pastoral council. Conflicts should be resolved by dialogue and by the joint consideration of questions. Disharmony might be avoided if these two councils were made in effect a bicameral consultative or deliberative organ. It would be preferable, however, that the diocesan pastoral council should function as the diocesan policy-making body, and that priests themselves have some representation on that council. Meanwhile, the priests' senates could serve as a forum for the expression of concerns of special interest to the clergy, and its deliberations might, in turn, be submitted to the diocesan pastoral council for consideration. However that issue is to be resolved, it is essential that priests, and others in the diocese, have some meaningful role in the selection of ecclesiastical leadership.

Priests who wish to leave their diocese and engage in the ministry elsewhere should be free to do so. The bishop should not deny permission without a showing of grave necessity in his own diocese. As a corollary of this principle, bishops should not refuse permission to priests or deacons for service in their dioceses without just cause, such as a showing of grave unworthiness, incompetence, or a lack of real need in that diocese. Canon 144 provides clearly that an ordained minister should not be recalled to his diocese without just cause and that the requirements of natural equity should always be observed. Bishops may not arbitrarily recall their priests from other dioceses, but they should welcome their voluntary return to the service of the diocese of their incardination. At present, violations of these rights can be remedied only by recourse to the Vatican. Priests and deacons must be given the opportunity of recourse to regional or national administrative tribunals for speedy redress of wrongs.

In principle it should be agreed that the ordained minister has the same rights and freedoms as the other members of the Church, except as these may be extended or limited by the legitimate needs of the ministry he exercises. The ordained minister should have the right to resign from the exercise of the ministry formally acknowledged in ecclesiastical law. Nothing further, beyond a resignation submitted to the bishop, should be demanded of him. Employment by a church or church-related organization should not be denied those who have resigned from the active ministry.

With regard to pastoral ministries, the Vatican II decree on the pastoral office of bishops in the Church and the apostolic letter implementing it provide a broad base for experimentation, adaptation, and creative innovation in parish structures. The bishop is clearly empowered to innovate, without restriction, for the good of souls. This would include the establishment of "team ministries," "floating parishes," student communities, professional or occupational groupings, etc. The only necessary elements for a parish are an identifiable community and a stable pastoral office; determined buildings or defined territory are of secondary importance and nonconstitutive.

The principal criterion for continuation in the ministerial office should be effective performance, reviewed at regular intervals. Among the criteria to be employed are: competence in liturgical celebration, effective preaching, genuine social concern, ability to lead (to clarify the goals of the Church and to motivate people to pursue them), ecumenical sensitivity, and skill in pastoral counseling. Continuing education of the clergy remains a matter of highest importance. Why is it, Richard Dillon asks, that "suddenly, in the laicization process, the church adopts a policy of stern scrutiny such as was never enforced in the priest's recruitment and formation! The high ideals of priestly formation set forth in the encyclicals and curial instructions stand in ludicrous contrast to the practice of most seminaries, where a shortage of numbers dictates the collapse of standards and an uneducated, undisciplined clergy emerges to minister to an increasingly impatient laity."

Vatican II acknowledged that the obligation of clerical celibacy derives from a law of the Church, not from a law of God. The council also affirmed that the right to marry is "universal and inviolable." Consequently, sacred orders should no longer be regarded as a diriment impediment to marriage. The right to marry, as an inviolable and universal right, must always remain in the disposition of the person. Since this change will eventually come about, the leadership should begin now to prepare the general membership of the whole Church so that they will easily, and for the right reasons, accept a married clergy.

13. ECUMENICAL RELATIONSHIPS

The ecumenical movement has faltered so noticeably in recent years that articles have begun to appear asking if we are now in a postecumenical era or whether we have simply reached an impasse in the quest for Christian unity. On the Protestant side, resistance and especially apathy have stalled the forward thrust of the Consultation on Church Union (COCU); on the Catholic side, there has been a tightening of regulations governing intercommunion and a stubbornly silent rejection of proposals for some mutual recognition of ministries. The desire to maintain institutional integrity (the way of tenacity) accounts for much of the resistance on the Protestant side; and devotion to a particular notion of apostolic succession accounts for much of the resistance on the Catholic side, particularly among the leadership.

Accordingly, the Catholic Church will have to accept the implications of its own conciliar teaching that the Body of Christ embraces non-Catholic Christians as well as Catholics, the varying degrees of incorporation into the Church notwithstanding. This will require an official endorsement of intercommunion on some limited basis and also a public acceptance of the validity of some non-Catholic ordained ministries. Meanwhile, the results of the various bilateral conversations that have been taking place in the United States since 1965 must be disseminated more widely and more effectively than heretofore. The primary responsibility for publicity should probably be assigned to the ecumenical officers and commissions of the individual denominations and eventually to an ecumenical board which would oversee and coordinate the consultations in the United States with one another, with consultations in other nations, and with the international dialogues. This agency might also sponsor on occasion trilateral and multilateral conversations as was done, for example, in the case of the National Council of Churches (NCC) consultation on the Eucharist in 1970. Such an ecumenical board might be placed under the aegis of the Faith and Order Commission of the NCC, provided that such a step would not be unacceptable to those communions which are not now members of Faith and Order. Beyond what such an ecumenical board might accomplish by way of coordination and publicity, the responsible agencies of the various churches should take steps to ensure that the clergy and laity are kept informed of the theological developments taking place in the consultations. The dialogues could profitably be presented for study in episcopal seminars (which might well be ecumenical in composition), diocesan clergy conferences (to which clergy of other denominations might appropriately be invited), adult education programs, and popular literature.

Furthermore, these consultation reports must be followed up with appropriate formal action by the churches involved. The normal practice thus far in the Catholic Church has been for the National Conference of Catholic Bishops to receive the reports and forward them to the Papal Secretariat for the Promotion of Christian Unity. Beyond this, the bishops should sponsor further studies, publicize the areas of doctrinal agreement, and give appropriate pastoral directives. In the absence of some implementation of the principles accepted by the bilateral groups, the gap between theological discussion and pastoral practice will widen to the point where the value of further discussion will inevitably be challenged on all sides.

The consultations themselves might be elevated in quality by a better selection process for their members. Professional societies within the Church (e.g., the Catholic Theological Society of America, the Canon Law Society of America, or the Catholic Biblical Association) might be requested formally to make recommendations of qualified theologians and of those whose academic disciplines are of immediate concern to theology. No qualified scholar, even though he be someone who has resigned from the active ministry, should be excluded from these dialogue groups.

In the last several years the Catholic Church has joined many metropolitan and state councils of churches and has become a member of the Faith and Order Commission on both the national and the world level. The possibility of Catholic membership in the National Council of Churches and the World Council of Churches is being actively considered. Such steps are already long overdue, even though they will not necessarily produce dramatic results in themselves.

The most serious practical problem with the ecumenical movement today is that it remains essentially the concern of specialists. Until the rank-and-file membership perceives the importance and relevance of ecumenism to their own Christian lives, it will tend to remain stalled in its own tracks. True motivation for mission, as I have argued earlier in the chapter, requires that the individual members of the Church be able to identify the organizational objectives with their own personal objectives.

A number of theological arguments and counterarguments related to each of these 13 items are then briefly reviewed, after which McBrien summarizes his case as follows:

—Ed.

Summary

The present crisis of excessive conflict and polarization in the Catholic Church is theologically explicable in terms of a theory-and-practice gap. Catholics, and other Christians, hold fundamentally different views about the nature and mission of the Church. They endorse or resist proposed changes in the institutional operations of the Church on the basis of those differing views. On the other hand, the Church's official magisterium, i.e., at Vatican II particularly, has articulated and disseminated an understanding of the Church which is not the same as the ecclesiology taught and accepted in the decades preceding the council. And yet most of the present structures of the Church—its laws, disciplinary regulations, customs, administrative procedures, etc.—were created at a time when a different vision of the Church prevailed. Thus, the Church has officially moved beyond its previous self-understanding without, however, allowing its new vision to permeate and transform the given institutional apparatus. This discrepancy between theory and practice, unfortunately, is not without serious pastoral consequences. It gives rise to growing tensions, frustrations, and even schismatic tendencies. The Church cannot long sustain this kind of excessive internal conflict. Indeed, the persistence of this conflict is at the root of the present malaise of Catholic life and practice. It is a matter of utmost pastoral urgency, therefore, that the Church brings its institutional expressions into conformity with its theological perceptions. The various proposals offered in this chapter, by way of an agenda for reform, are designed for the reconciliation of theory and practice and, ultimately, for the remaking of the Church in our time.

Avery Dulles

1918-

Avery, son of John Foster Dulles, was born in Auburn, New York, in 1918. He graduated from Harvard University in 1940, the same year that he became a Roman Catholic. He stayed on for a year of postgraduate work in law, then served in the U.S. Naval Reserve from 1942 to 1946, achieving the rank of lieutenant and being decorated with the Croix de Guerre. In 1946 he entered the Jesuits and published an account of his conversion, entitled A Testimonial to Grace.

After studying philosophy and theology at Woodstock College, he was ordained a priest in 1956. He did his doctoral work at the Gregorian University in Rome, completing the degree in 1960. He then joined the Woodstock faculty. When that institution was moved to Manhattan in 1969, Dulles was also named to the Fordham faculty. Then in 1974 he was named to the faculty of the Catholic University in Washincton, D.C. In 1970 he received the Cardinal Spellman award for distinguished achievement in theology.

In the years after Vatican II, Dulles established himself as clearly the most competent ecclesiologist in the country. This first became clear in 1967 with the publication of The Dimensions of the Church. Revelation Theology followed in 1969, and then The Survival of Dogma in 1971, which won a Christopher award in 1972. The work from which the following *selection is taken,* Models of the Church, *appeared in 1974, and was followed in 1977 by* The Resilient Church.

Models of the Church *consists of twelve chapters, of which the first and last are given here. The book is dedicated to Gustave Weigel, whose work in ecclesiology Dulles acknowledges building upon.*

The book is itself a model of clarity and organization. The first chapter introduces the approach and its significance, then the next five chapters present five basic models of the Church. Then in turn these models are applied to five basic areas of theology to see what each of them brings out: eschatology, notes of the Church, ecumenism, ministry, and revelation.

This book is a marvelous example of what has happened in post-Vatican II Catholic theology. Following the lead of thinkers like Karl Rahner and Bernard Lonergan, Dulles here demonstrates a method that puts one on a higher level, able to view the strengths and weaknesses of earlier efforts that worked entirely within a single model. The possibilities for deeper understanding that are thereby opened can readily be appreciated. This is undoubtedly Dulles at his best, and the book has all the earmarks of a classic.

MODELS OF THE CHURCH

I

THE USE OF MODELS IN ECCLESIOLOGY

In May 1972 the New York *Times* carried a typical exchange of views about what is happening in the Catholic Church in the United States. It reported the assessment of an Italian theologian, Battista Mondin, to the effect that the Church in America is falling apart. Two days later the *Times* published a letter to the editor in which the writer conceded, "[Mondin] is right that the traditional Church is near collapse," but then added: "The disasters he mentions are only such to those churchmen who are so stuck in conservatism and authority that they cannot see the Gospel of Christ for the Code of Canon Law. . . . My feeling, as a member of an adapting religious community, is that these are the best days of the church."

Disputes of this type are going on everywhere these days. Christians cannot agree about the measure of progress or decline because they have radically different visions of the Church. They are not agreed about what the Church really is.

When we ask what something is we are normally seeking a definition. The classical way to define a thing is to put it into a category of familiar objects and then to list the distinguishing characteristics that differentiate it from other members of the same category. Thus we say that a snail is a slow-moving gastropod mollusk, or that a chair is a piece of furniture designed for people to sit on. In definitions such as these we are dealing with external realities that we can see and touch, and we are able to pin them down fairly well in terms of familiar categories.

It used to be thought, at least by many, that the Church and other realities of faith could be defined by a similar process. Thus the Church, according to Robert Bellarmine, is a specific type of human community (*coetus hominum*). "The one and true Church," he wrote in a celebrated passage, "is the community of men brought together by the profession of the same Christian faith and conjoined in the communion of the same sacraments, under the government of the legitimate pastors and especially the one vicar of Christ on earth, the Roman pontiff." This definition, as contemporary commentators have noted, comprises three elements: profession of the true faith, communion in the sacraments, and submission to the legitimate pastors. By applying these criteria, Bellarmine is able to exclude all persons who in his opinion do not belong to the true Church. The first criterion rules out pagans, Moslems, Jews, heretics, and apostates; the second rules out catechumens and excommunicated persons; the third rules out schismatics. Thus only Roman Catholics remain.

It is significant that Bellarmine's definition is entirely in terms of visible elements. He even goes so far as to maintain that, whereas *profession* of the true faith is essential, actual belief, being an internal and unverifiable factor, is not. A man who professes to believe but does not believe in his heart would be on this definition a member of the Church, whereas a man who believed without professing to believe would not be. Bellarmine's concern against the Reformers (especially Calvin) is to show that the true Church is a fully visible society—as visible, he says, as the Kingdom of France or the Republic of Venice. No doubt this concern reflects something of the spirit of the seventeenth century. The baroque mentality wanted the supernatural to be as manifest as possible, and the theology of the period tried to reduce everything to clear and distinct ideas.

This clarity, however, was bought at a price. It tended to lower the Church to the same plane as other human communities (since it was put in the same general category as they) and to neglect the most important thing about the Church: the presence in it of the God who calls the members to himself, sustains them by his grace, and works through them as they carry out the mission of the Church. There is something of a consensus today that the innermost reality of the Church—the most important constituent of its being—is the divine self-gift. The Church is a union or communion of men with one another through the grace of Christ. Although this communion manifests itself in sacramental and juridical structures, at the heart of the Church one finds mystery.

The term "mystery" has been used in many ways in the biblical and nonbiblical religions. For present purposes, the usage of the Pauline epistles (1 Cor., Eph., and Col.) would be of central importance. The mystery par excellence is not so much God in his essential nature, or the counsels of the divine mind, but rather God's plan of salvation as it comes to concrete realization in the person of Christ Jesus. In Christ are "unsearchable riches" (Eph. 3:8); in him dwells the whole fullness of God (Col. 3:9); and this fullness is disclosed to those whose hearts are open to the Spirit which is from God (1 Cor. 2:12).

Vatican Council II, after rejecting an initial schema on the Church in which the first chapter was entitled "The Nature of the Church Militant," adopted as the title of its first chapter, "The Mystery of the Church," and this change of titles is symptomatic of the whole ecclesiology of the Council.

The term mystery, applied to the Church, signifies many things. It implies that the Church is not fully intelligible to the finite mind of man, and that the reason for this lack of intelligibility is not the poverty but the richness of the Church itself. Like other supernatural mysteries, the Church is known by a kind of connaturality (as Thomas Aquinas and the classical theologians called it). We cannot fully objectify the Church because we are involved in it; we know it through a kind of intersubjectivity. Furthermore, the Church pertains to the mystery of Christ; Christ is carrying out in the Church his plan of redemption. He is dynamically at work in the Church through his Spirit.

When the New Testament tells us that marriage is "a great mystery in reference to Christ in the Church" (Eph. 5:32), it is implied that the union of the human with the divine, begun in Christ, goes on in the Church; otherwise marriage would not be a figure of the Church. In a word, the mystery is "Christ in you, your hope of glory" (Col. 1:2).

This general conception of mystery as applied to the Church was set forth by Paul VI in his opening address at the second session of the Council. He declared: "The Church is a mystery. It is a reality imbued with the hidden presence of God.

It lies, therefore, within the very nature of the Church to be always open to new and ever greater exploration."

The mysterious character of the Church has important implications for methodology. It rules out the possibility of proceeding from clear and univocal concepts, or from definitions in the usual sense of the word. The concepts abstracted from the realities we observe in the objective world about us are not applicable, at least directly, to the mystery of man's communion with God. Some would therefore conclude that ecclesiology must be apophatic; that we can have only a *theologia negativa* of the Church, affirming not what is but only what it is not. In a certain sense this may be conceded. In some respects we shall in the end have to accept a reverent silence about the Church, or for that matter about any theological reality. But we should not fall into the negative phase prematurely, until we have exhausted the possibilities of the positive.

Among the positive tools that have been used to illuminate the mysteries of faith we must consider, in the first place, images. This consideration will lead us into some discussion of cognate realities, such as symbols, models, and paradigms—tools that have a long theological history, and are returning to their former prominence in the theology of our day.

Referring to the debate on the schema *De Ecclesia* at the first session of Vatican II, Gustave Weigel, a council *peritus*, observed, in the last article published before his death:

> The most significant result of the debate was the profound realization that the Church has been described, in its two thousand years, not so much by verbal definitions as in the light of images. Most of the images are, of course, strictly biblical. The theological value of the images has been stoutly affirmed by the Council. The notion that you must begin with an Aristotelian definition was simply bypassed. In its place, a biblical analysis of the significance of the images was proposed.

As Paul VI noted in the address already quoted, the Church has continually sought to further its self-understanding by meditation on the "revealing images" of Scripture: "the building raised up by Christ, the house of God, the temple and tabernacle of God, his people, his flock, his vine, his field, his city, the pillar of truth, and finally, the Bride of Christ, his Mystical Body." These are approximately the same images used in the Vatican II Constitution on the Church, *Lumen gentium*, in its first chapter.

The Bible, when it seeks to illuminate the nature of the Church, speaks almost entirely through images, most of them, including many of those just mentioned, evidently metaphorical. Paul Minear, in his book, *Images of the Church in the New Testament*, lists some ninety-six such images. Even if we rule out a few of these as not being really figures of the *Church*, we shall agree that the New Testament is extremely luxuriant in its ecclesiological imagery.

Ecclesiology down through the centuries has continued to meditate upon the biblical images. Following in the footsteps of Church Fathers such as Origen, the Venerable Bede (eighth century) finds the Church in Eve and Mary, in Abraham and Sarah, in Tamar, Rahab, Mary Magdalene, in the woman with the flux of blood, in the valiant woman of Proverbs, in Zacchaeus, the Canaanite woman, the ark of Noah, the Temple, the vine, Paradise, the moon, etc. Thus there is nothing new in the fact that images play a prominent role in contemporary ecclesiology.

In these images it is difficult to draw the line between proper and metaphorical usage. For the most part, we are dealing with metaphors, but we must reckon with the fact that human language itself becomes bent by theological usage so that figures that were originally metaphorical can be properly though still analogously predicated. For example, terms such as "People of God" and "Body of Christ" are often considered, in their ecclesiastical application, something more than mere metaphors.

The psychology of images is exceedingly subtle and complex. In the religious sphere, images function as symbols. That is to say, they speak to man existentially and find an echo in the inarticulate depths of his psyche. Such images communicate through their evocative power. They convey a latent meaning that is apprehended in a nonconceptual, even a subliminal, way. Symbols transform the horizons of man's life, integrate his perception of reality, alter his scale of values, reorient his loyalties, attachments, and aspirations in a manner far exceeding the powers of abstract conceptual thought. Religious images, as used in the Bible and Christian preaching, focus our experience in a new way. They have an aesthetic appeal, and are apprehended not simply by the mind but by the imagination, the heart, or, more properly, the whole man.

Any large and continuing society that depends on the loyalty and commitment of its members requires symbolism to hold it together. In secular life, we are familiar with the bald eagle, the black panther, the *fleur-de-lis*. These images respectively arouse courage, militancy, and purity. The biblical images of the Church as the flock of Christ, the Bride, the Temple, or whatever, operate in a similar manner. They suggest attitudes and courses of action; they intensify confidence and devotion. To some extent they are self-fulfilling; they make the Church become what they suggest the Church is.

Religious imagery is both functional and cognitive. In order to win acceptance, the images must resonate with the experience of the faithful. If they do so resonate, this is proof that there is some isomorphism between what the image depicts and the spiritual reality with which the faithful are in existential contact. Religious experience, then, provides a vital key for the evaluation and interpretation of symbols.

With regard to the Church Paul Minear has rightly said:

> Its self-understanding, its inner cohesion, its *esprit de corps*, derive from a dominant image of itself, even though that image remains inarticulately imbedded in subconscious strata. If an unauthentic image dominates its consciousness, there will first be subtle signs of malaise, followed by more overt tokens of communal deterioration. If an authentic image is recognized at the verbal level but denied in practice, there will also follow sure disintegration of the ligaments of corporate life.

To be fully effective, images must be deeply rooted in the corporate experience of the faithful. In times of rapid cultural change, such as our own, a crisis of images is to be expected. Many traditional images lose their former hold on people, while the new images have not yet had time to gain their full power. The contemporary crisis of faith is, I believe, in very large part a crisis of images. City dwellers in a twentieth-century democracy feel ill at ease with many of the biblical images, since these are drawn from the life of a pastoral and patriarchal people of the ancient Near East. Many of us know very little from direct experience about lambs, wolves, sheep, vines, and grapes, or even about kings and patriarchs as they were in biblical times. There is need therefore to supplement these images with others that speak more directly to our contemporaries. The manufacturing of supplementary images goes on wherever the faith is vital. Today we experience some difficulty, however, since our experience of the world has become, in so many respects, secular and utilitarian. Our day-to-day life provides very few objects having numinous overtones that would make them obvious sources of new religious imagery—though there are some brilliant suggestions for new imagery in the writings of theologians such as Paul Tillich, Teilhard de Chardin, and Dietrich Bonhoeffer.

For an image to catch on in a religious community conditions have to be ripe psychologically. As Tillich used to say, images are not created or destroyed by deliberate human effort. They are born or they die. They acquire or lose power by a mysterious process that seems beyond man's control and even beyond his comprehension.

Images are immensely important for the life of the Church—for its preaching, its liturgy, and its general *esprit de corps*. We live by myth and symbol—by connotations as much as by denotations. In religious education a constant effort must be made to find images that faithfully communicate the Christian experience of God. Theology itself depends heavily on images. For theology, however, the unanalyzed image is of very limited value. The theologian is not primarily concerned, as the preacher is, with the question whether a given image is readily available and meaningful to the ordinary Christian in the pews. By using historical scholarship and empathetic imagination, the theologian can work with images that have lost their power and relevance for the majority of men today.

When the theologian uses images he does so for the purpose of gaining a better understanding of the mysteries of faith, or in the matter that interests us here, of the Church. He knows that images are useful up to a point, and that beyond that point they can become deceptive. Thus he employs images in a reflective, discriminative way. When he hears the Church called the flock of Christ, he is aware that certain things follow and others do not. It may follow, for instance, that the sheep (i.e., the faithful) hear the voice of their master (Christ), but it does not follow that the members of the Church grow wool. As a theoretician the theologian has to ask himself what are the critical principles leading to an accurate discrimination between the valid and invalid application of images.

When an image is employed reflectively and critically to deepen one's theoretical understanding of a reality it becomes what is today called a "model." Some models are of a more abstract nature, and are not precisely images. In the former class one might put temple, vine, and flock; in the latter, institution, society, community.

The term "model" has for some time been in use in the physical and social sciences. I. T. Ramsey, among others, has shown its fruitfulness for theology. When a physicist is investigating something that lies beyond his direct experience, he ordinarily uses as a crutch some more familiar object sufficiently similar to provide him with reference points. Billiard balls, for example, may serve as models for probing the phenomena of light. Some models, such as those used in architecture, are scale reproductions of the reality under consideration, but others, more schematic in nature, are not intended to be replicas. They are realities having a sufficient functional correspondence with the object under study so that they provide conceptual tools and vocabulary; they hold together facts that would otherwise seem unrelated, and they suggest consequences that may subsequently be verified by experiment. As I. T. Ramsey has said, "In any scientific understanding a model is better the more prolific it is in generating deductions which are then open to experimental verification and falsification."

As Ramsey's analysis shows, the term "model," as employed in modern physics, is practically synonymous with analogy, if this latter term is shorn of some of the metaphysical implications it has in neo-Scholastic theology.

Having seen a little of the use of models in the physical sciences, let us reflect on the transfer of the method of models to theology. Ewert Cousins has written lucidly of the similarities and differences between the two fields:

> Theology is concerned with the ultimate level of religious mystery, which is even less accessible than the mystery of the physical universe. Hence our religious language and symbols should be looked upon as models because, even more than the concepts of science, they only approximate the object they are reflecting. . . .
>
> To use the concept of model in theology, then, breaks the illusion that we are actually encompassing the infinite within our finite structures of language. It prevents concepts and symbols from becoming idols and opens theology to variety and development just as the model method has done for science. Yet there is a danger that it will not go far enough, for it may not take sufficiently into account the level of religious experience. The theologian may copy the sciences too closely. He may take the scientific method as a normative model. . . . In so doing the theologian may not take into account the subjective element at the core of religion. The religious experience has a depth that has no correlate in our experience of the physical universe. The religious experience touches the innermost part of the person. . . .

Taking these remarks into consideration, one may perhaps divide the uses of models in theology into two types, the one explanatory, the other exploratory.

On the explanatory level, models serve to synthesize what we already know or at least are inclined to believe. A model is accepted if it accounts for a large number of biblical and traditional data and accords with what history and experience tells us about the Christian life. The gospel parables of growth, such as those of the wheat and the tares, the mustard seed, and the leaven, have been valued because they give intelligibility to phenomena encountered in the Christian community since its origins, for example, its capacity for rapid expansion, the opposition it encounters from within and without, the presence of evil even in the midst of the community of grace, and so forth. These images suggest how it is possible for the Church to change its shape and size without losing its individuality. They point to a mysterious life principle within the Church and thus harmonize with the biblical and traditional doctrine of the indwelling of the Holy Spirit. These botanical models, however, have obvious limits, since they evidently fail to account for the distinctively interpersonal and historical phenomena characteristic of the Church as a human community that perdures through the generations. Thus societal models, such as that of God's People on pilgrimage, are used to supplement the organic metaphors.

The more applications a given model has, the more it suggests a real isomorphism between the Church and the reality being used as the analogue. The analogy will never be perfect because the Church, as a mystery of grace, has properties not paralleled by anything knowable outside of faith.

By the exploratory, or heuristic, use of models, I mean their capacity to lead to new theological insights. This role is harder to identify, because theology is not an experimental science in the same way that physics, for example, is. Theology has an abiding objective norm in the past—that is, in the revelation that was given once and for all in Jesus Christ. There can be no "other gospel" (cf. Gal. 1:8). In some fashion every discovery is ultimately validated in terms of what was already given in Scripture and tradition. But even the past would not be revelation to us unless God were still alive and giving himself to mankind in Jesus Christ. Thus the present experience of grace enters intrinsically into the method of theology. Thanks to the ongoing experience of the Christian community, theology can discover aspects of the gospel of which Christians were not previously conscious.

For example, we shall be considering in a later chapter the Servant model of the Church. This is a relatively new model, based on the biblical image of Israel, and later of Christ, as Servant of God. The recent application of this model to the

Church has made us conscious in our time, as our forbears were not conscious, of the Church's responsibility to assist the welfare of man on earth and hence to contribute to social and cultural life.

With respect to the heuristic function of images, there is a particular problem of verification in theology. Because the Church is mystery, there can be no question of deductive or crudely empirical tests. Deduction is ruled out because we have no clear abstract concepts of the Church that could furnish terms for a syllogism. Empirical tests are inadequate because visible results and statistics will never by themselves tell us whether a given decision was right or wrong.

In my own view, theological verification depends upon a kind of corporate discernment of spirits. John Powell, S.J., shows that this type of spiritual perception is closely connected with the "connaturality" to which we have already referred. Thanks to the interior presence of the Holy Spirit, the whole Church and its members have a new life in Christ.

> As this life of Christ is deepened in us by the Holy Spirit, there is created in the Christian a "sense of Christ," a taste and instinctual judgment for the things of God, a deeper perception of God's truth, an increased understanding of God's dispositions and love toward us. This is what Christians must strive to attain individually and corporately; theologians call it Christian *connaturality*. It is like a natural instinct or intuition, but it is not natural, since it results from the supernatural realities of the Divine Indwelling and the impulses of grace. No account of dialectical or analytical facility, which is purely human, can provide this connatural instinct. It is increased only by the continual nourishment of the life of God that vivifies the Christian.

Thanks to this grace-given dynamism toward the things of God, the faithful, insofar as they are docile to the Spirit, tend to accept whatever in their religious experience leads to an intensification of faith, hope, and charity, or to an increase of what Paul in the fifth chapter of Galatians calls the fruits of the Holy

Spirit—love, joy, peace, patience, kindness, and the like (cf. Gal. 5:22-25). Where the result is inner turbulence, anger, discord, disgust, distraction, and the like, the Church can judge that the Spirit of Christ is not at work. We assess models and theories, therefore, by living out the consequences to which they point.

Paul VI points this out in his first encyclical, *Ecclesiam suam*: "The mystery of the Church is not a mere object of theological knowledge; it is something to be lived, something that the faithful soul can have a kind of connatural experience of, even before arriving at a clear notion of it." In our present context one might say: Because the mystery of the Church is at work in the hearts of committed Christians, as something in which they vitally participate, they can assess the adequacy and limits of various models by consulting their own experience. A recognition of the inner and supernatural dimension of theological epistemology is one of the major breakthroughs of our time. In this type of knowledge, theory and practice are inseparably united. The Church exists only as a dynamic reality achieving itself in history, and only through some kind of sharing in the Church's life can one understand at all sufficiently what the Church is. A person lacking this inner familiarity given by faith could not be a competent judge of the value of the models.

An example might clarify the method of discernment I have in mind. In the Middle Ages, the notion of vicarious satisfaction took on great importance in the theology of penance. With the increased acceptance of juridical models of the Church in that period, there resulted an elaborate theology of indulgences. The theory was applied to practice, giving rise to a vigorous spiritual traffic. Financially the theory succeeded: The empty coffers of the Holy See were replenished. But was this success a confirmation of the theory? Only the evangelically sensitive Christian could judge whether the effects on the spiritual lives of Christians were those intended by Christ for his Church. Martin Luther carried many of the faithful with him in his protest, which was, at least in part, based on deep evangelical concerns. Since the sixteenth century the Church, I think, has come to recognize that there was much justice in Luther's complaints regarding indulgences. This recognition calls for a theological response that has not yet been fully worked out in

Roman Catholic theology. A model that leads to practical abuses is, even from a theoretical standpoint, a bad model.

As already stated, the models used in theology are not scale reproductions. They are what Max Black calls "analogue models" or what Ian Ramsey calls "disclosure models." Because their correspondence with the mystery of the Church is only partial and functional, models are necessarily inadequate. They illumine certain phenomena but not others. Each of them exhibits what can be seen by comparison with some particular reality given in our human experience of the world—e.g., the relationship of a vine to its branches, of a head to a body, or of a bride to a husband. Pursued alone, any single model will lead to distortions. It will misplace the accent, and thus entail consequences that are not valid. For example, the analogy of the head and body would suggest that the members of the Church have no personal freedom and autonomy in relationship to Christ and his Spirit. In order to offset the defects of individual models, the theologian, like the physicist, employs a combination of irreducibly distinct models. Phenomena not intelligible in terms of one model may be readily explicable when another model is used.

Admitting the inevitability of such a pluralism of models, theology usually seeks to reduce this pluralism to a minimum. The human mind, in its quest for explanations, necessarily seeks unity. A unified field theory in theology would be able to account for all the data of Scripture and tradition, and all the experience of the faithful by reference to some one model. At various times in the history of the Church it has seemed possible to construct a total theology, or at least a total ecclesiology, on the basis of a single model. Such a dominant model is, in the terminology of this book, a paradigm. A model rises to the status of a paradigm when it has proved successful in solving a great variety of problems and is expected to be an appropriate tool for unraveling anomalies as yet unsolved. I am here employing the term "paradigm" in approximately the meaning given to it by Thomas S. Kuhn. He speaks of paradigms as "concrete puzzle-solutions which, employed as models or examples, can replace explicit rules as a basis for the solution of the remaining puzzles of normal science."

As a model succeeds in dealing with a number of different problems, it becomes an object of confidence, sometimes to such an extent that theologians almost cease to question its appropriateness for almost any problem that may arise. In the Scholasticism of the Counter Reformation period, the Church was so exclusively presented on the analogy of the secular state that this model became, for practical purposes, the only one in Roman Catholic theological currency. Even today, many middle-aged Catholics are acutely uncomfortable with any other paradigm of the Church than the *societas perfecta*. But actually this societal model has been displaced from the center of Catholic theology since about 1940.

In 1943 Pius XII gave quasicanonical status to the image of the Mystical Body. "If we would define and describe this true Church of Jesus Christ—which is the One, Holy, Catholic, Apostolic, Roman Church—we shall find no expression more noble, more sublime, or more divine than the phrase which calls it 'the Mystical Body of Jesus Christ.' " The Mystical Body analogy reached its highest peak of popularity between 1940 and 1950. In the late forties theologians became conscious of certain deficiencies in the model and attempted to meet these by appealing to other models, such as People of God and Sacrament of Christ.

Vatican Council II in its Constitution on the Church made ample use of the models of the Body of Christ and the Sacrament, but its dominant model was rather that of the People of God. This paradigm focused attention on the Church as a network of interpersonal relationships, on the Church as community. This is still the dominant model for many Roman Catholics who consider themselves progressives and invoke the teaching of Vatican II as their authority.

In the postconciliar period still another model of the Church has begun to struggle for supremacy: that of the Church as Servant or Healer. This model is already suggested in some of the later documents of Vatican II, notably the Constitution on the Church in the Modern World (*Gaudium et spes*). This model, with its outgoing thrust, has increased the Catholic Christian's sense of solidarity with the whole human race in its struggles for peace, justice, and prosperity.

As we contemplate the theological history of the Catholic Church over the past thirty years, we cannot but be impressed by the rapidity with which, after a period of long stability, new paradigms have begun to succeed one another. From 1600 to 1940 the juridical or societal model was in peaceful possession, but it was then displaced by that of the Mystical Body, which has been subsequently dislodged by three other models in rapid succession: those of People of God, Sacrament, and Servant. These paradigm shifts closely resemble what Thomas Kuhn has described as "scientific revolutions." But the revolutions he describes have occurred in the pursuit of purely scientific goals. The new scientific paradigms have been accepted because, without sacrificing the good results attained by previous paradigms, they were able in addition to solve problems that had proved intractable by means of the earlier models.

With regard to the ecclesiological revolutions we have mentioned, it seems clear that the new paradigms have in fact cleared up certain problems not easily solved under the predecessors. To a great extent, however, the motives for the shift have been practical and pastoral rather than primarily speculative. Changes have been accepted because they help the Church to find its identity in a changing world, or because they motivate men to the kind of loyalty, commitment, and generosity that the Church seeks to elicit. The People of God image, for example, was adopted in part because it harmonized with the general trend toward democratization in Western society since the eighteenth century. Since Vatican II the Servant Model has become popular because it satisfies a certain hunger for involvement in the making of a better world—a hunger that, although specifically Christian in motivation, establishes solidarity between the Church and the whole human family.

Whatever may be said of the relative merits of the various paradigms, one must recognize that the transition from one to another is fraught with difficulties. Each paradigm brings with it its own favorite set of images, its own rhetoric, its own values, certitudes, commitments, and priorities. It even brings with it a particular set of preferred problems. When paradigms shift, people suddenly find the ground cut out from under their feet. They cannot begin to speak the new language without already committing themselves to a whole new set of values that may not be to their taste. Thus they find themselves gravely threatened in their spiritual security. Theologians, who ought to be able to shift their thinking from one key to another, often resist new paradigms because these eliminate problems on which they have built up a considerable expertise, and introduce other problems with regard to which they have no special competence.

It should not be surprising, therefore, that in the contemporary Church, rocked by paradigm shifts, we should find phenomena such as polarization, mutual incomprehension, inability to communicate, frustration, and discouragement. Since the situation is simply a fact of our times, we must learn to live with it. It will greatly help, however, if people can learn to practice tolerance and to accept pluralism. We must recognize that our own favorite paradigms, however excellent, do not solve all questions. Much harm is done by imperialistically seeking to impose some one model as the definitive one.

Because images are derived from the finite realities of experience, they are never adequate to represent the mystery of grace. Each model of the Church has its weaknesses; no one should be canonized as the measure of all the rest. Instead of searching for some absolutely best image, it would be advisable to recognize that the manifold images given to us by the Scripture and Tradition are mutually complementary. They should be made to interpenetrate and mutually qualify one another. None, therefore, should be interpreted in an exclusivistic sense, so as to negate what the other approved models have to teach us. The New Testament, for example, combines the images of Temple and Body of Christ in logically incoherent but theologi cally opposite ways. In 1 Pet. 2:5 we are told that Christians are a Temple built of living stones, whereas Paul in Eph. 4:16 says that the Body of Christ is still under construction. This "profuse mixing of metaphors," Paul Minear reminds us, "reflects not logical confusion but theological vitality."

In the following chapters an effort will be made to illumine the mystery of the Church through certain dominant models that have become paradigmatic in modern theology. Without attempting to be all-inclusive, I shall concentrate on five such models. In this way I think it will be possible to characterize the leading ecclesiological schools, to identify the most common positions, and to appreciate the internal consistency of various styles of theology. Such a method will present in a clearer light the options that face the theologian, and will show that if he adopts a given model or combination of models, he commits himself in advance to a whole series of positions regarding particular problems.

In the next five chapters the five basic models will be presented with some assessment of their respective strengths and weaknesses. Then in five additional chapters we shall consider how the models lead to diverse positions regarding certain acute problems in contemporary theology. Finally, in a reflective overview, an attempt will be made to summarize the values and limitations of the various models. Although all the models have their merits, they are not of equal worth, and some presentations of some models must positively be rejected.

XII

THE EVALUATION OF MODELS

In all the previous chapters we have been engaged in what Bernard Lonergan might call dialectic as distinct from doctrinal theology. We have been exploring the basic models of the Church that have arisen in history as a result of the differing points of view or horizons of believers and theologians of different ages and cultures. Each of the models, self-evidently, has its own uses and limitations. We must now face the problem, to what extent are the models compatible or incompatible? Are the differences of horizon mutually exclusive or mutually complementary? Are all the models equally good, or are some superior to others? Are they an opaque screen that shuts off the reality of the Church, or a transparent screen that permits us to grasp the Church as it really is? If the latter, what really is the Church? What is the best model?

The critique and choice of models depends, or should depend, on criteria. But here lies the rub. On reflection it becomes apparent that most of the criteria presuppose or imply a

choice of values. The values, in turn, presuppose a certain understanding of the realities of faith. If one stands committed to a
given model it is relatively easy to establish criteria by which
that model is to be preferred to others. Each theologian's criteria
therefore tend to buttress his own preferred models. Communication is impeded by the fact that the arguments in favor of
one's own preferred model are generally circular: They presuppose the very point at issue.

Some examples will make this clearer. Persons drawn to
the institutional model will show a particularly high regard
for values such as conceptual clarity, respect for constituted
authority, law and order. They reject other models, and perhaps
especially the second, as being too vague, mystical, and subjective. Partisans of the communion model, on the other hand,
find the institutional outlook too rationalistic, ecclesiocentric,
and rigid. They label it triumphalist, juridicist, and clericalist.
An analogous dispute arises between champions of the third
and fourth models. Adherents of the sacramental ecclesiology,
appealing to the principle of incarnation, find the kerygmatic
theologies too exclusively centered on the word; whereas kerygmatic theologians find the sacramental model too complacent
and insufficiently prophetic. Promoters of the servant model, in
turn, denounce the other four as being too introspective and
churchy.

In passing one may note that the tensions here referred to
are similar to those long recognized in comparative ecclesiology
under rubrics such as priestly vs. prophetic, catholic vs. protestant, sacred vs. secular. But these dichotomies are too crude
to do justice to the full spectrum of positions.

In any effort at evaluation we must beware of the tendency
of each contestant to polemicize from a standpoint within his
own preferred position. To make any real progress we must seek
criteria that are acceptable to adherents of a number of different
models. Seven such criteria (not all of them equally appealing to
all members of all theological schools) come to mind:

1. *Basis in Scripture.* Nearly all Christians feel more comfortable if they can find a secure biblical basis for a doctrine
they wish to defend—the clearer and more explicit the better.

2. *Basis in Christian tradition*. Not all Christians set the same value on tradition, but nearly all would agree that the testimony of Christian believers in the past in favor of a given doctrine is evidence in its favor. The more universal and constant the tradition the more convincing it is.

3. *Capacity to give Church members a sense of their corporate identity and mission*. Christian believers generally are convinced that they do have a special calling as Christians, and they turn to theology to clarify this. Theology has a practical function of supporting the Church in its faith and mission.

4. *Tendency to foster the virtues and values generally admired by Christians*. By their total upbringing Christians are inclined to prize faith, hope, disinterested love of God, sacrificial love of fellow men, honesty, humility, sorrow for sin, and the like. If they find that a doctrine or theological system sustains these values, they will be favorably inclined toward it; if it negates these values they will suspect that the idea is erroneous.

5. *Correspondence with the religious experience of men today*. In recent years there has been a revolt against making either the Bible or tradition a decisive norm apart from the experience of believers themselves. Granted the tremendous cultural shifts that have been taking place, it is to be expected that men today will approach the Christian message from a new point of view. Some models, much honored in the past, may prove to be excessively bound up with the concerns and dominant images of a culture not our own.

6. *Theological fruitfulness*. As noted in our first chapter, theological revolutions, like scientific revolutions, occur when the paradigms previously in use are found to be inadequate for the solution of present problems, and when better paradigms come into view. One criterion for the selection of new paradigms is their ability to solve problems that proved intractable by appeal to the older models, or to synthesize doctrines that previously appeared to be unrelated.

7. *Fruitfulness in enabling Church members to relate successfully to those outside their own group*—for example, to Christians of other traditions, to adherents of non-Christian religions, and to dedicated secular humanists.

To measure each of our five basic models by all seven of these criteria would at this point be wearisome. The indications already given in earlier chapters may be sufficient. In a summary way, it may be proposed that the first criterion gives good support to the community and kerygmatic models; the second criterion, to the community model (though modern Roman Catholic tradition favors the institutional as well); the third criterion, to the institutional and kerygmatic models; the fourth criterion, to the sacramental and servant models; the fifth criterion, to the community and servant models; the sixth criterion, to the sacramental model, and the seventh criterion, to the community and servant models.

This variety of results makes it apparent that certain types of persons will be spontaneously drawn to certain models. Church officials have a tendency to prefer the institutional model; ecumenists, the community model; speculative theologians, the sacramental model; preachers and biblical scholars, the kerygmatic model; and secular activists, the servant model.

Are we then to conclude with an agreement to disagree—with a sterile repetition of the maxim, "*chaqu'un à son gout*"? This author's total life-experience prompts him to reject any such conclusion. He is convinced that to immure oneself behind a fixed theological position is humanly and spiritually disastrous. It is important at all costs to keep open the lines of communication between different theological schools and traditions.

Two general working principles may be invoked to support a reconciling approach. Neither of these principles is strictly demonstrable, but both of them seem to be favored by the accumulated experience of many good and wise persons. The first is that what any large group of Christian believers have confidently held over a considerable period of time should be accepted unless one has serious reasons for questioning it. Even if one comes to the conclusion that the tenet was false, one should at least make the effort to unveil the positive reason that made people accept error and thus to disclose the truth at the heart of the heresy.

The second working principle is the view of John Stuart Mill, which commended itself to F. D. Maurice and H. Richard Niebuhr, to the effect that men are more apt to be correct in what they affirm than in what they deny. "What we deny is generally something that lies outside our experience, and about which we can therefore say nothing."

On the basis of these two principles, we must presume that the basic assertions implied in each of our five ecclesiological types are valid. Each of them in my opinion brings out certain important and necessary points. The institutional model makes it clear that the Church must be a structured community and that it must remain the kind of community Christ instituted. Such a community would have to include a pastoral office equipped with authority to preside over the worship of the community as such, to prescribe the limits of tolerable dissent, and to represent the community in an official way. The community model makes it evident that the Church must be united to God by grace, and that in the strength of that grace its members must be lovingly united to one another. The sacramental model brings home the idea that the Church must in its visible aspects—especially in its community prayer and worship—be a sign of the continuing vitality of the grace of Christ and of hope for the redemption that he promises. The kerygmatic model accentuates the necessity for the Church to continue to herald the gospel and to move men to put their faith in Jesus as Lord and Savior. The diaconal model points up the urgency of making the Church contribute to the transformation of the secular life of man, and of impregnating human society as a whole with the values of the Kingdom of God.

On the other hand, it must be recognized that we cannot without qualification accept all five models, for they to some extent come into conflict with each other. They suggest different priorities and even lead to mutually antithetical assertions. Taken in isolation, each of the ecclesiological types could lead to serious imbalances and distortions. The institutional model, by itself, tends to become rigid, doctrinaire, and conformist; it could easily substitute the official Church for God, and this would be a form of idolatry. As a remedy, the structures of the Church must be seen as subordinate to its communal life and mission.

The second model, that of mystical communion, can arouse an unhealthy spirit of enthusiasm; in its search for religious experiences or warm, familial relationships, it could lead to false expectations and impossible demands, considering the vastness of the Church, the many goals for which it must labor, and its remoteness from its eschatological goal. As a remedy, one must call for patience, faith, and a concern for the greater and more universal good.

The third model, the sacramental, could lead to a sterile aestheticism and to an almost narcissistic self-contemplation. As a remedy, attention must be called to the values of structures, community, and mission brought out in the other models.

The fourth model, the kerygmatic, runs the risk of falling into the exaggerations of biblicist and fundamentalistic sects. It tends to oversimplify the process of salvation, to advertise "cheap grace," to be satisfied with words and professions rather than to insist on deeds, especially in the social and public arena. As a remedy, one must stress the necessity of incarnating one's faith in life and action.

The fifth model, the diaconal, could easily give the impression that man's final salvation is to be found within history, and could lure the Church into an uncritical acceptance of secular values, thus muting its distinctive witness to Christ and to its own heritage. As an antidote, one must insist on the provisional character of any good or evil experienced within history, and on the importance of looking always to Christ and to his Kingdom.

Granting the distinctive values of each of the five models and the undesirability of accepting any one model to the exclusion of the others, the question arises whether we ought not to look for some supermodel that combines the virtues of each of the five without suffering their limitations. Without asserting that the five models studied in this book are the only possible ones, I would be skeptical of the possibility of finding any one model that would be truly adequate; for the Church, as we have seen in Chapter I, is essentially a mystery. We are therefore condemned to work with models that are inadequate to the reality to which they point.

Our method must therefore be to harmonize the models in such a way that their differences become complementary rather than mutually repugnant. In order to do so, we shall have to criticize each of the models in the light of all the others. We must refrain from so affirming any one of the models as to deny, even implicitly, what the others affirm. In this way it may be possible to gain an understanding of the Church that transcends the limitations of any given model. We shall be able to qualify each of the models intrinsically in such a way as to introduce into it the values more expressly taught by the others. The models, as I understand them, are sufficiently flexible to be mutually open and compenetrable.

This being so, there is nothing to prevent a given theologian from building his own personal theology on one or another of the paradigms in the tradition. If one begins, for example, with the model of the Church as servant, one may then work backward and integrate into this model the values of the other four. One may say, for instance, that the Church serves mankind precisely by looking to Jesus, the Servant Lord, and by subjecting itself to the word of the gospel. Only by acknowledging the sovereignty of God's word can the Church avoid an uncritical and unhealthy complacency. The idea of the Church as servant of the gospel, moreover, may be said to imply that of the Church as sacrament, for it is precisely in serving that the Church most perfectly images forth the Son of man, who came to serve and offer his life as a ransom for the many. A servant Church can effectively herald the gospel as a triumphal Church could not. Only in becoming a faithful servant of the Servant Lord can the Church effectively proclaim the good news of the Christian revelation. Thus the three models of servant, herald, and sacrament in many respects merge to make up a composite picture.

The coalescence, moreover, does not stop at this point. It is precisely this servant Church that can best claim to be the Body of Christ—the same Body that in Jesus himself has been bruised for our sakes and made whole again by God. It is this servant Church, and no other, that can dare to claim that the Spirit of Christ really dwells in it. With its divine Lord this Church can say, "The Spirit of the Lord is upon me, because he has anointed me to preach good news to the poor. He has sent me to proclaim release to the captives and recovering of sight to the blind, to set at liberty those who are oppressed, to proclaim the acceptable year of the Lord" (Lk. 4:18-19). In this body the mutual hostilities of men are brought to an end and the members are united into a holy Temple in the Lord.

Within this servant Body, anointed by the Spirit of the Lord, there will be diversities of charism and service. There will be some who will be chosen by the Spirit and approved by the communities for offices of leadership. The flock of Christ will not be without pastors, committed to a life of dedicated service. There will be order and discipline, humility and obedience. In other words, there will be Church polity. Ecclesiastical office must seek to preserve the true spirit of the gospel and at the same time to adjust the Church to the needs of the times. There will be doctrine too, for the faith of the Church will be constantly nourished by the better formulation of that to which all are committed in Christ. The organization of the Church need not be pitted against its spirit and its life. According to the logic of the incarnation, the Church will seek always to strengthen its life by appropriate visible structures. The Church will not be an invisible "Kingdom of the Spirit," but a human institution, similar in many respects to other societies.

For blending the values in the various models, the sacramental type of ecclesiology in my opinion has special merit. It preserves the value of the institutional elements because the official structures of the Church give it clear and visible outlines, so that it can be a vivid sign. It preserves the community value, for if the Church were not a communion of love it could not be an authentic sign of Christ. It preserves the dimension of proclamation, because only by reliance on Christ and by bearing witness to him, whether the message is welcomed or rejected, can the Church effectively point to Christ as the bearer of God's redemptive grace. This model, finally, preserves the dimension of worldly service, because without this the Church would not be a sign of Christ the servant.

One of the five models, I believe, cannot properly be taken as primary—and this is the institutional model. Of their very nature, I believe, institutions are subordinate to persons, structures are subordinate to life. "The sabbath was made for man, not man for the sabbath" (Mk. 2:27). Without calling into question the value and importance of institutions, one may feel that this value does not properly appear unless it can be seen that the structure effectively helps to make the Church a community of grace, a sacrament of Christ, a herald of salvation, and a servant of mankind.

In harmonizing the models, we should not behave as if we were trying to fit together the pieces of a difficult jigsaw puzzle. In a puzzle, one has no other data than the objective elements that have to be combined. In the field of theology the models must be seen against the horizon of the mysterious, nonobjective experience of grace from which they arose and by which they must, in turn, be revitalized. As we say in our first chapter, only the grace experience, or, in other terminology, the inner enlightenment of the Holy Spirit, supplies man with the necessary tact and discretion so that he can see the values and limits of different models.

One final caution may be in order. Theologians often tend to assume that the essence of the Church somehow exists, like a dark continent, ready-made and awaiting only to be mapped. The Church, as a sociological entity, may be more correctly viewed as a "social construct." In terms of sociological theory, one may say that the form of the Church is being constantly modified by the way in which the members of the Church externalize their own experience and in so doing transform the Church to which they already belong. Within the myriad possibilities left open by Scripture and tradition, the Church in every generation has to exercise options. It becomes what its leaders and its people choose to make of it. The fact that the Church of a certain century may have been primarily an institution does not prevent the Church in another generation from being more conspicuously a community of grace, a herald, a sacrament, or a servant.

The future forms of the Church lie beyond our power to foresee, except that we may be sure that they will be different from the forms of yesterday and today. The Church will not necessarily mirror the secular society of tomorrow, for it must avoid the kind of conformity with the world condemned by the Apostle (Rom. 12:2). On the other hand, the Church will have to make adjustments in order to survive in the society of the future and to confront the members of that society with the challenge of the gospel.

In view of the long-range changes going on in secular society and the impact they have been having on the Church in recent decades, it seems prudent to predict that the following five trends, already observable in recent Church history, will continue:

1. *Modernization of structures.* The current structures of the Church, especially in Roman Catholicism, bear a very strong imprint of the past social structures of Western European society. In particular, the idea of an "unequal" society, in which certain members are set on a higher plane and made invulnerable to criticism and pressure from below, savors too much of earlier oligarchic regimes to be at home in the contemporary world. In its stead, modern society is adopting a more functional approach to authority. The task of Christianity will be to harmonize the right kind of functionalism and accountability with the evangelical idea of pastoral office as a representation of Christ's own authority. Here the Church, in my opinion, has an important contribution to make to the modern world. The traditional Christian conception of authority as an exigent service remains valid and potentially fruitful.

2. *Ecumenical interplay.* The present denominational divisions among the Churches, in great part, no longer correspond with the real issues that respectively unite and divide Christians of our day. The debates that separated the churches in 1054 and 1520, while they may be revived in contemporary controversy, are no longer the really burning issues. Some method must be found to overcome these inherited divisions so that committed Christians in different denominational traditions may find each other once again in the same community of faith, dialogue, and worship. Short of full reunion there may be many possibilities of mutual recognition, doctrinal accord, joint worship, and practical cooperation.

3. *Internal pluralism.* Pluralism is already very great, perhaps too great, in some of the Protestant churches, but it has been shown to assert itself in Roman Catholicism. The strong centralization in modern Catholicism is due to historical accidents. It has been shaped in part by the homogeneous culture of medieval Europe and by the dominance of Rome, with its rich heritage of classical culture and legal organization.

In the Counter Reformation this uniformity was increased by an almost military posture of resistance to the inroads of alien systems of thought such as Protestantism and deistic rationalism. The decentralization of the future will involve a certain measure of de-Romanization. There is little reason today why Roman law, the Roman language, Roman conceptual schemes, and Roman liturgical forms should continue to be normative for the worldwide Church. With increasing decentralization, the Catholic Church in various regions will be able to enter more vitally into the life of different peoples and to relate itself more positively to the traditions of other Christian denominations.

4. *Provisionality*. In a world of increasing "rapidation" and "future shock" the Church must continue to provide a zone of relative stability and to enable the faithful to relate meaningfully to their religious past. But the Church must not allow itself to become a mere relic or museum piece. It must prove capable of responding creatively to the demands of new situations and to the needs of generations yet to come. Church decisions will increasingly take on the form not of immutable decrees but of tentative measures taken in view of passing needs and temporary opportunities.

5. *Voluntariness*. In the "post-Constantinian" or "diaspora" situation of our day, the Church will not be able to rely to the same extent as formerly on canonical penalties and sociological pressures in order to keep its members in line. Anyone at any time will be able to opt out of the Church without fearing legal or social sanctions. Furthermore, the internal pluralism of the Church itself will be such that directives from on high will be variously applied in different regions, so that the top officers will not be able to control in detail what goes on at the local level.

In this situation the Church will have to rule more by persuasion and less by force. The officers will have to obtain a good measure of consensus behind their decisions, and this in turn will require increased dialogue. To some extent this development may seem a humiliation for the Church, but in another sense it may appear as progress. The Church will be better able to appear as a home of freedom and as "a sign and a safeguard of the transcendence of the human person."

All these predictions seem to be solidly based on the major social trends of recent centuries. If the Church is to carry out its mission effectively, it must take cognizance of these social movements. But will it in fact enter vigorously into dialogue with the new world that is being born before our eyes, or will it on the contrary become more than ever a vestige of the past? In principle it would be possible for the Church to refuse to adapt itself as the times require, and thus to become an ossified remnant of its former self. Such a Church would no doubt continue to exist thanks to the richness of its heritage, but it would no longer be the home of living faith and prophetic commitment.

Because the Church carries with it so large a heritage from the past, there is a constant temptation for its members to cling to the ways of their ancestors and to resist the call to confront the world of today. In the wake of Vatican II, with its large promises of renewal and reform, we are presently witnessing a new surge of legalism and reaction. The staying power of the conservatives, and their determination to adhere to ancient forms, have surpassed the expectations of starry-eyed reformers who expected to have an easy time of it after the last Council. Will static traditionalism have the last word? Or will churchmen of prophetic vision arise to lead the People of God resolutely into the future?

What the Church is to become depends to a great degree on the responsiveness of men, but even more importantly, it depends on the free initiatives of the Holy Spirit. If man is free and dynamic, the Spirit of God is even more so. To carry out their mission in the Church, Christians must therefore open their ears and hear "what the Spirit says to the churches" (Apoc. 2:17). It is not enough for them to listen to the Church unless the Church, through its responsible leaders, is listening to the Spirit. The Spirit alone can give the necessary judgment and discretion. "The spiritual man judges all things, but is himself judged by no one" (1 Cor. 2:15).

Like the Israelites of old, many Christians today are saying, "Our bones are dried up, our hope is lost; we are clean cut off" (Ezek. 37:11). The Lord must say to us, as he did to Ezekiel, "Behold, I will open your graves, and raise you from your graves, O my people" (v. 13). If life is to be breathed into those dead bones of doctrinal, ritual, and hierarchical organization that, in the eyes of many viewers, now constitute the Church, the Spirit of the Lord must send prophets to his people. The charismatic movement of the past few years gives signs, not wholly unambiguous, that the Holy Spirit may be answering the longings of men's hearts.

Under the leading of the Holy Spirit the images and forms of Christian life will continue to change, as they have in previous centuries. In a healthy community of faith the production of new myths and symbols goes on apace. The ecclesiologists of the future will no doubt devise new models for thinking about the Church. But what is new in Christianity always grows out of the past and has its roots in Scripture and tradition. On the basis of the relative continuity of the past two thousand years it seems safe to predict that the analogues and paradigms discussed in this book will retain their significance for ecclesiology through many generations yet to come.